Hana-Kimi

For You in Full Blossom

story and art by
HISAYA NAKAJO

HANA-KIMI
For You in Full Blossom
VOLUME 7
STORY & ART BY HISAYA NAKAJO

Translation/David Ury
English Adaptation/Gerard Jones
Touch-Up Art & Lettering/Gabe Crate
Design/Izumi Evers
Editor/Jason Thompson

Managing Editor/Megan Bates
Editorial Director/Elizabeth Kawasaki
Editor in Chief/Alvin Lu
Sr. Director of Acquisitions/Rika Inouye
Sr. VP of Marketing/Liza Coppola
Exec. VP of Sales & Marketing/John Easum
Publisher/Hyoe Narita

Printed in the U.S.A.

Published by VIZ Media, LLC, P.O. Box 77010, San Francisco, CA 94107

Shôjo Edition
10 9 8 7 6 5 4 3 2

First printing, July 2005
Second printing, November 2006

VIZ
MEDIA

www.viz.com
store.viz.com

CONTENTS

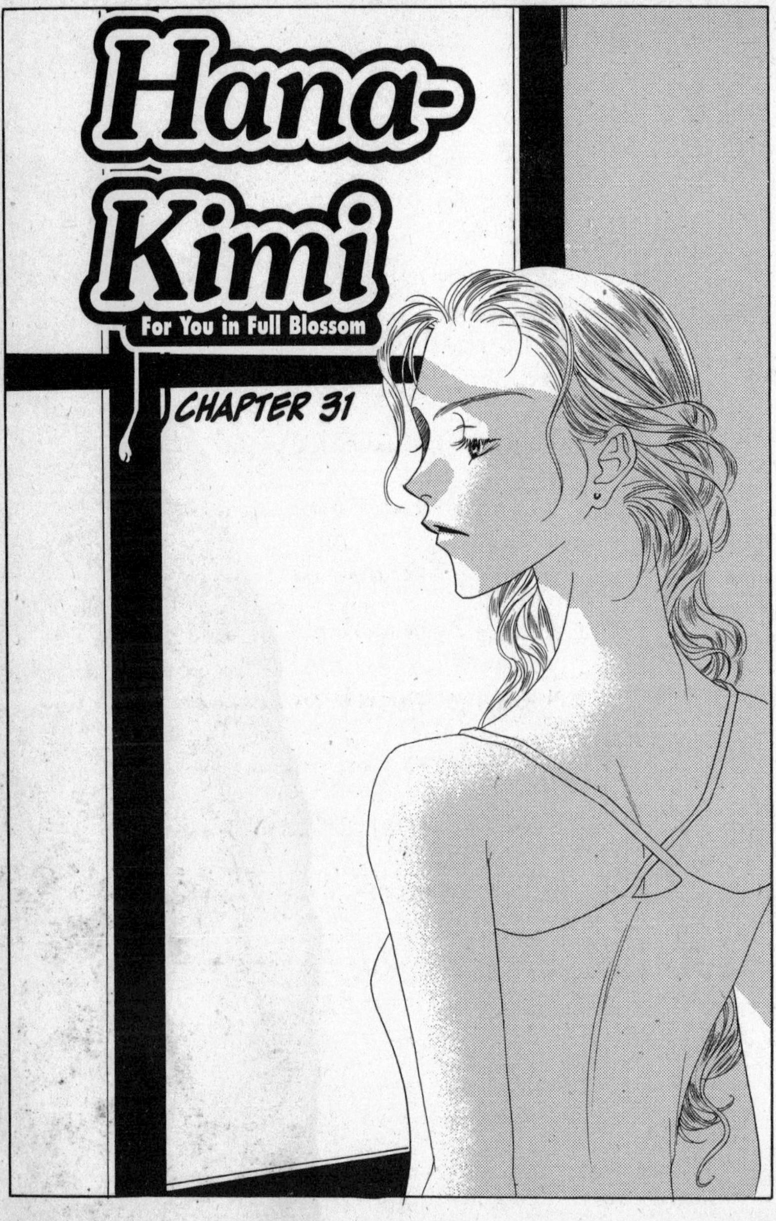
Hana-Kimi
For You in Full Blossom
CHAPTER 31

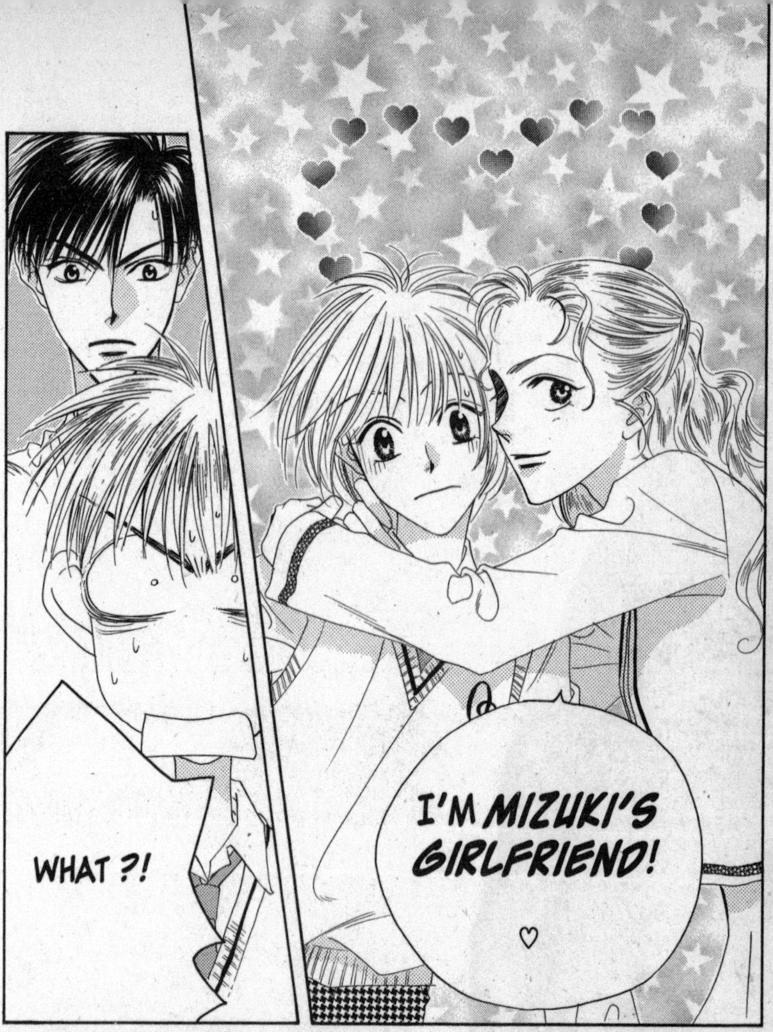
I'M MIZUKI'S GIRLFRIEND!
WHAT?!

FOREIGN DRAMAS

STAR TREK

AS A SELF PROCLAIMED TREKKIE (HEH) I CAN'T GET ENOUGH OF THIS SHOW! I ACTUALLY PREFER "THE NEXT GENERATION" WITH CAPTAIN PICARD TO THE OLD SERIES WITH CAPTAIN KIRK. I ESPECIALLY LIKE THE ANDROID, LT. COMMANDER DATA. "VOYAGER" AND "DEEP SPACE NINE" ARE OKAY TOO, BUT I LIKE THIS ONE THE BEST.

As for the movies, I like "First Contact" best.

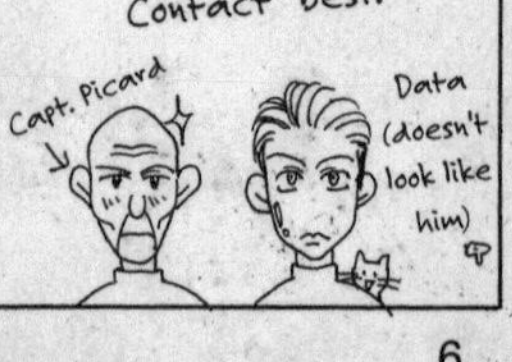
Capt. Picard
Data
(doesn't
look like
him)

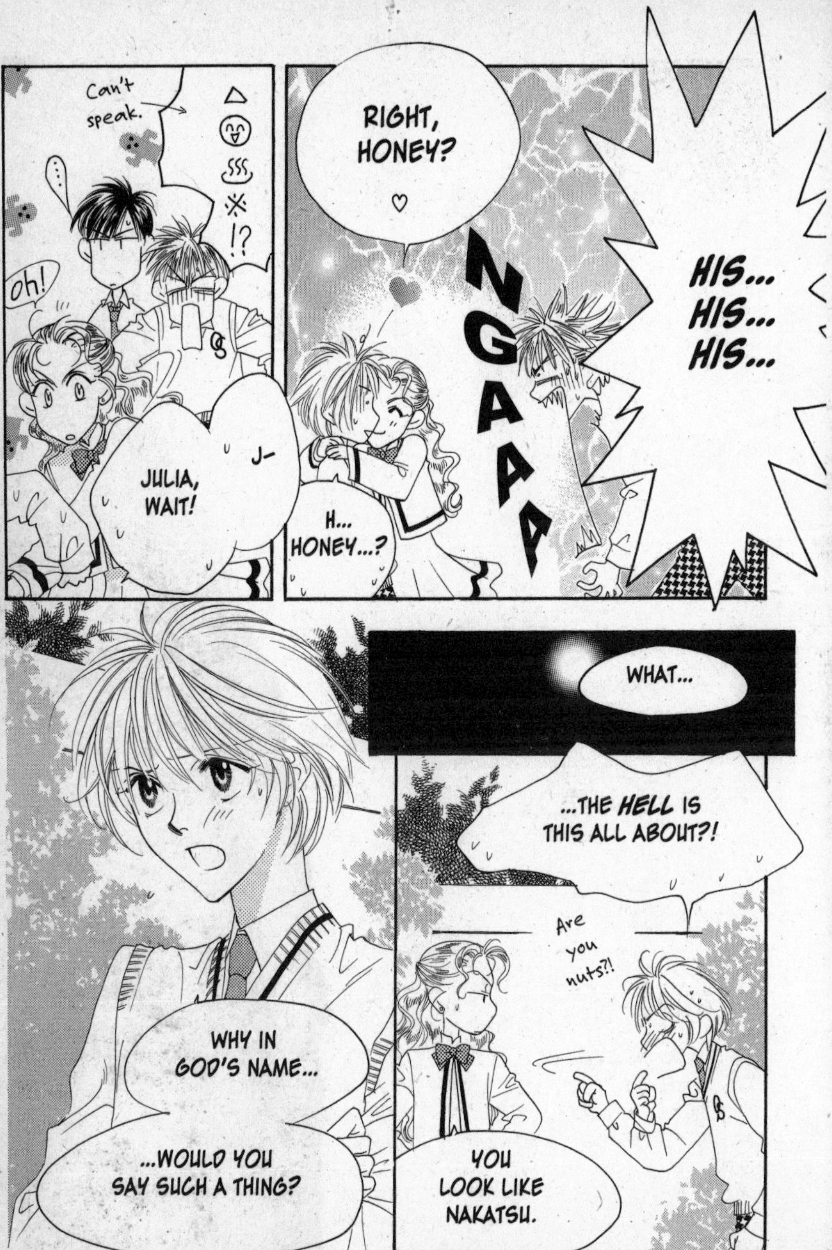
HIS... HIS... HIS...
RIGHT, HONEY? ♡
NGAAA
H... HONEY...?
!?
Can't speak.
...
oh!
J—
JULIA, WAIT!
WHAT...
...THE *HELL* IS THIS ALL ABOUT?!
Are you nuts?!
YOU LOOK LIKE NAKATSU.
WHY IN GOD'S NAME...
...WOULD YOU SAY SUCH A THING?

NOTE: SIDEWAYS BALLOONS MEANS THEY'RE SPEAKING ENGLISH.

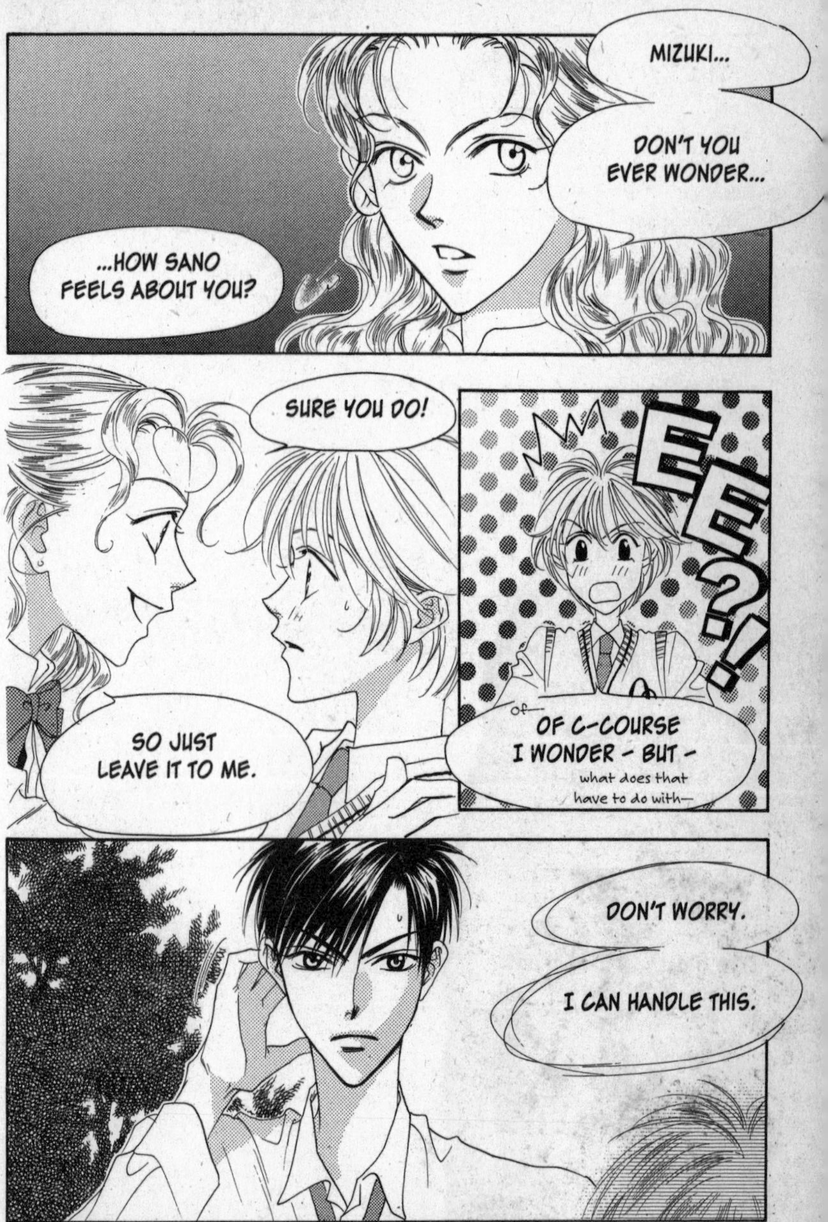
MIZUKI...
DON'T YOU EVER WONDER...
...HOW SANO FEELS ABOUT YOU?
EE?!
of—
OF C-COURSE I WONDER - BUT -
what does that have to do with—
SURE YOU DO!
SO JUST LEAVE IT TO ME.
DON'T WORRY.
I CAN HANDLE THIS.

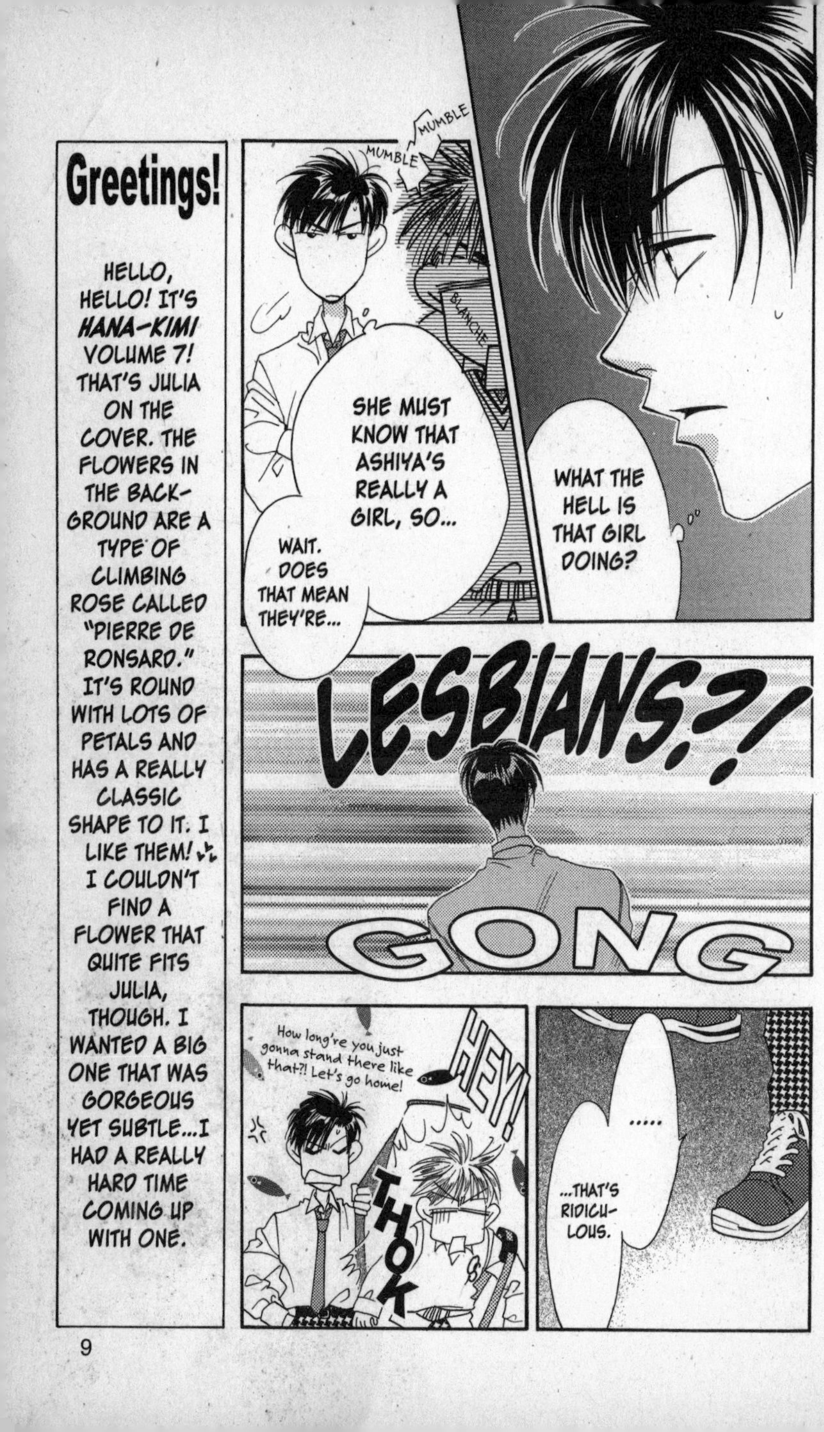
WHAT THE HELL IS THAT GIRL DOING?
MUMBLE MUMBLE
BLANCHE
SHE MUST KNOW THAT ASHIYA'S REALLY A GIRL, SO...
WAIT. DOES THAT MEAN THEY'RE...
LESBIANS?!
GONG
.....
...THAT'S RIDICU-LOUS.
HEY!
How long're you just gonna stand there like that?! Let's go home!
THOK

Greetings!

HELLO, HELLO! IT'S *HANA-KIMI* VOLUME 7! THAT'S JULIA ON THE COVER. THE FLOWERS IN THE BACK-GROUND ARE A TYPE OF CLIMBING ROSE CALLED "PIERRE DE RONSARD." IT'S ROUND WITH LOTS OF PETALS AND HAS A REALLY CLASSIC SHAPE TO IT. I LIKE THEM! I COULDN'T FIND A FLOWER THAT QUITE FITS JULIA, THOUGH. I WANTED A BIG ONE THAT WAS GORGEOUS YET SUBTLE...I HAD A REALLY HARD TIME COMING UP WITH ONE.

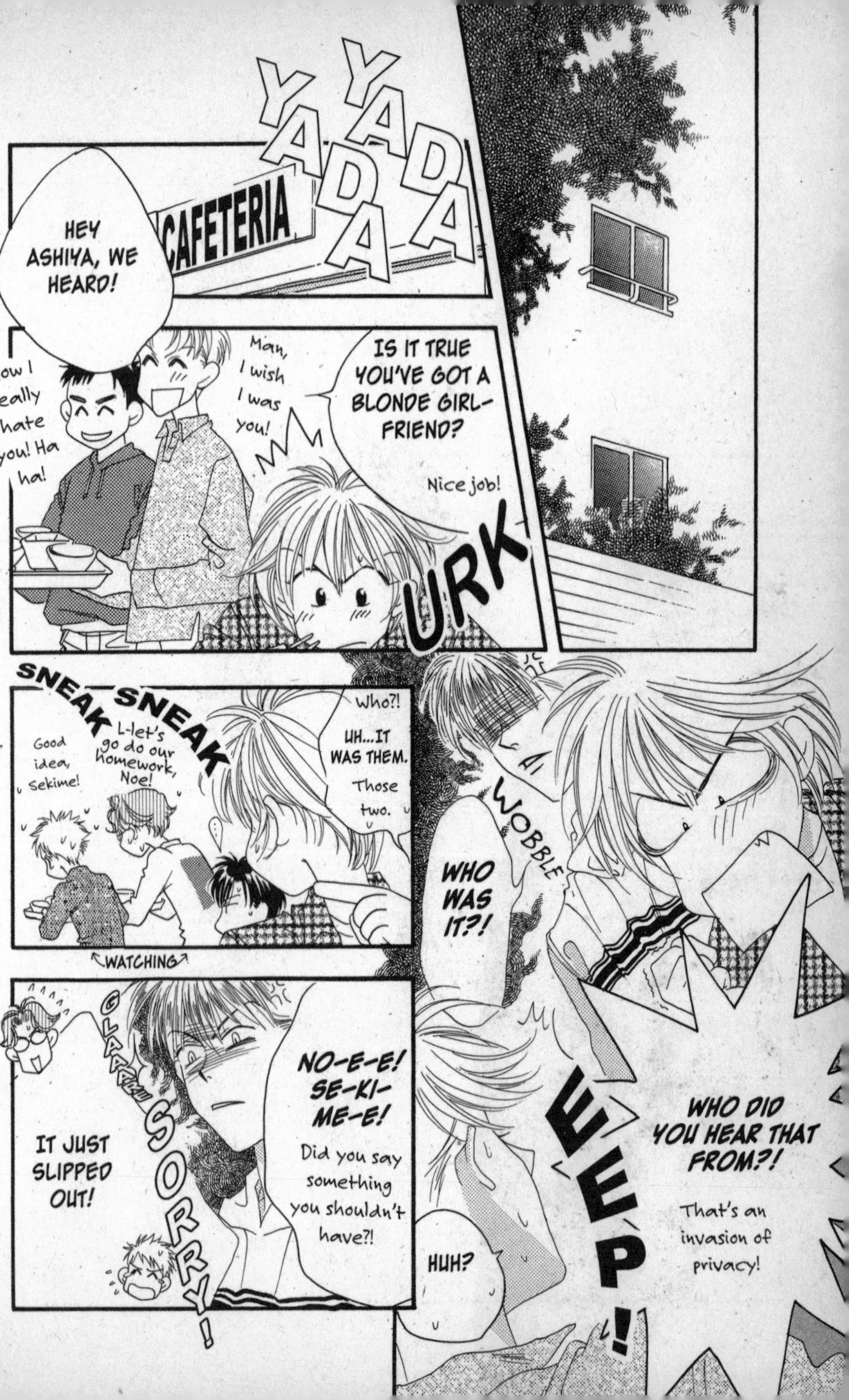
YADA YADA
CAFETERIA
HEY ASHIYA, WE HEARD!
IS IT TRUE YOU'VE GOT A BLONDE GIRL-FRIEND?
Nice job!
Man, I wish I was you!
Now I really hate you! Ha ha!
URK
WOBBLE
WHO WAS IT?!
WHO DID YOU HEAR THAT FROM?!
That's an invasion of privacy!
EEP!
HUH?
Who?!
UH...IT WAS THEM.
Those two.
SNEAK SNEAK
L-let's go do our homework, Noe!
Good idea, Sekime!
WATCHING
NO-E-E! SE-KI-ME-E!
Did you say something you shouldn't have?!
GLAAARE
SORRY!
IT JUST SLIPPED OUT!

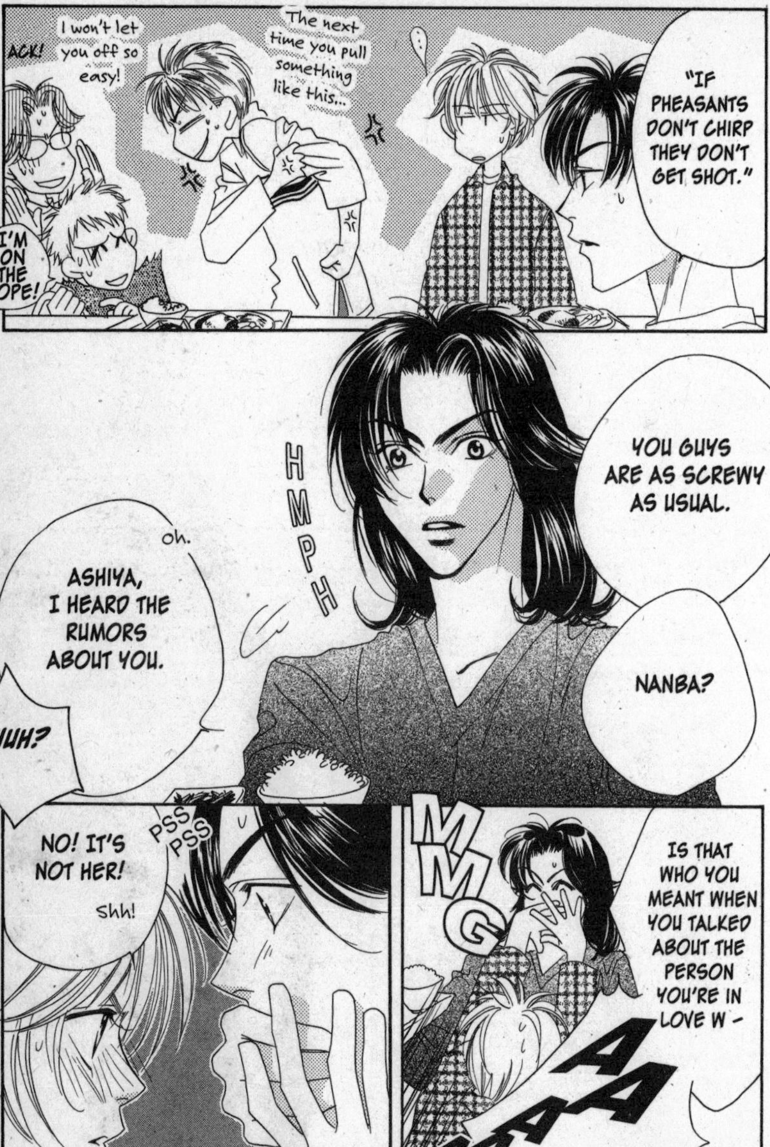
"IF PHEASANTS DON'T CHIRP THEY DON'T GET SHOT."
The next time you pull something like this...
I won't let you off so easy!
ACK!
I'M ON THE ROPE!
YOU GUYS ARE AS SCREWY AS USUAL.
HMPH
NANBA?
oh.
ASHIYA, I HEARD THE RUMORS ABOUT YOU.
HUH?
IS THAT WHO YOU MEANT WHEN YOU TALKED ABOUT THE PERSON YOU'RE IN LOVE W-
MMG
AAAAAAA!
NO! IT'S NOT HER!
PSS PSS
Shh!

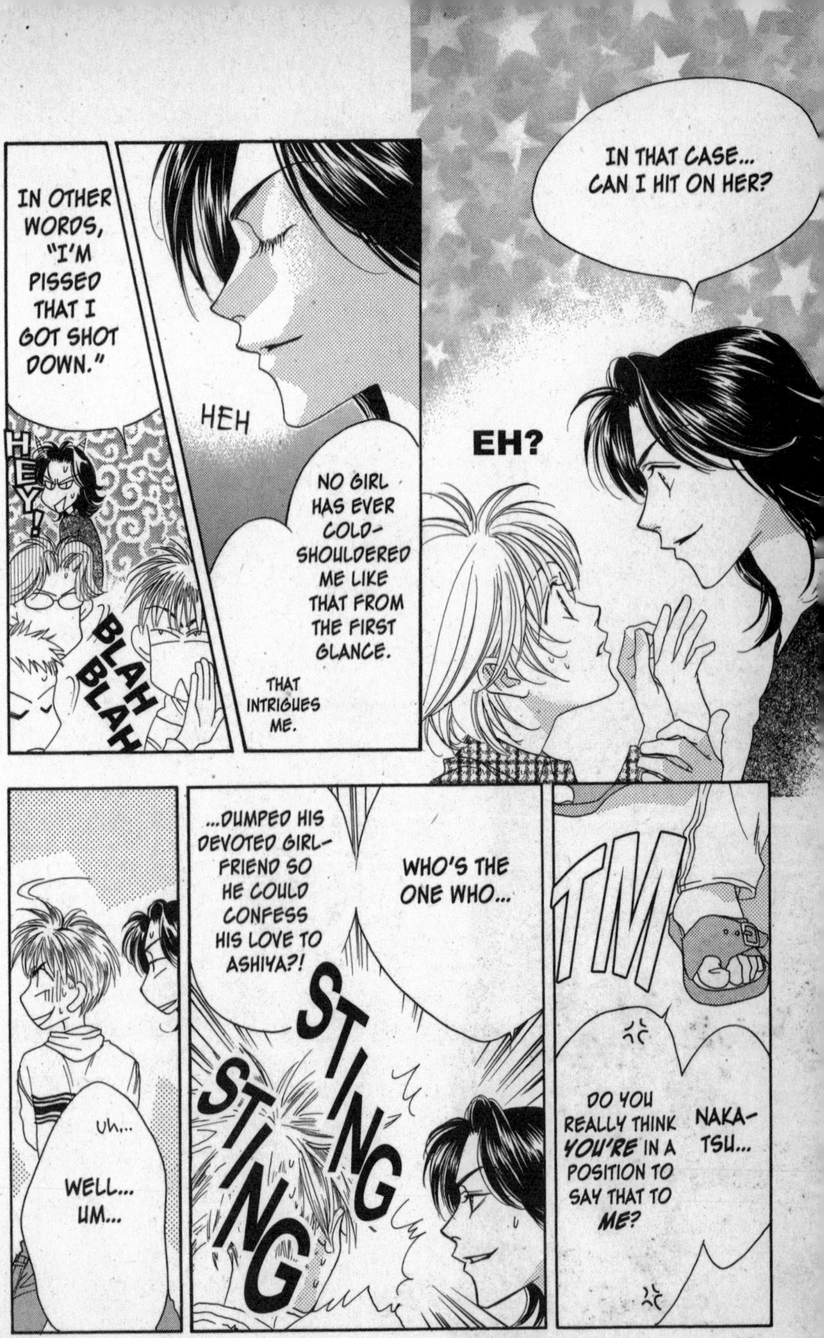
IN THAT CASE... CAN I HIT ON HER?
EH?
HEH
NO GIRL HAS EVER COLD-SHOULDERED ME LIKE THAT FROM THE FIRST GLANCE.
THAT INTRIGUES ME.
IN OTHER WORDS, "I'M PISSED THAT I GOT SHOT DOWN."
HEY!
BLAH BLAH
TM
NAKA-TSU...
DO YOU REALLY THINK *YOU'RE* IN A POSITION TO SAY THAT TO *ME*?
WHO'S THE ONE WHO...
...DUMPED HIS DEVOTED GIRL-FRIEND SO HE COULD CONFESS HIS LOVE TO ASHIYA?!
STING
STING
uh...
WELL... UM...

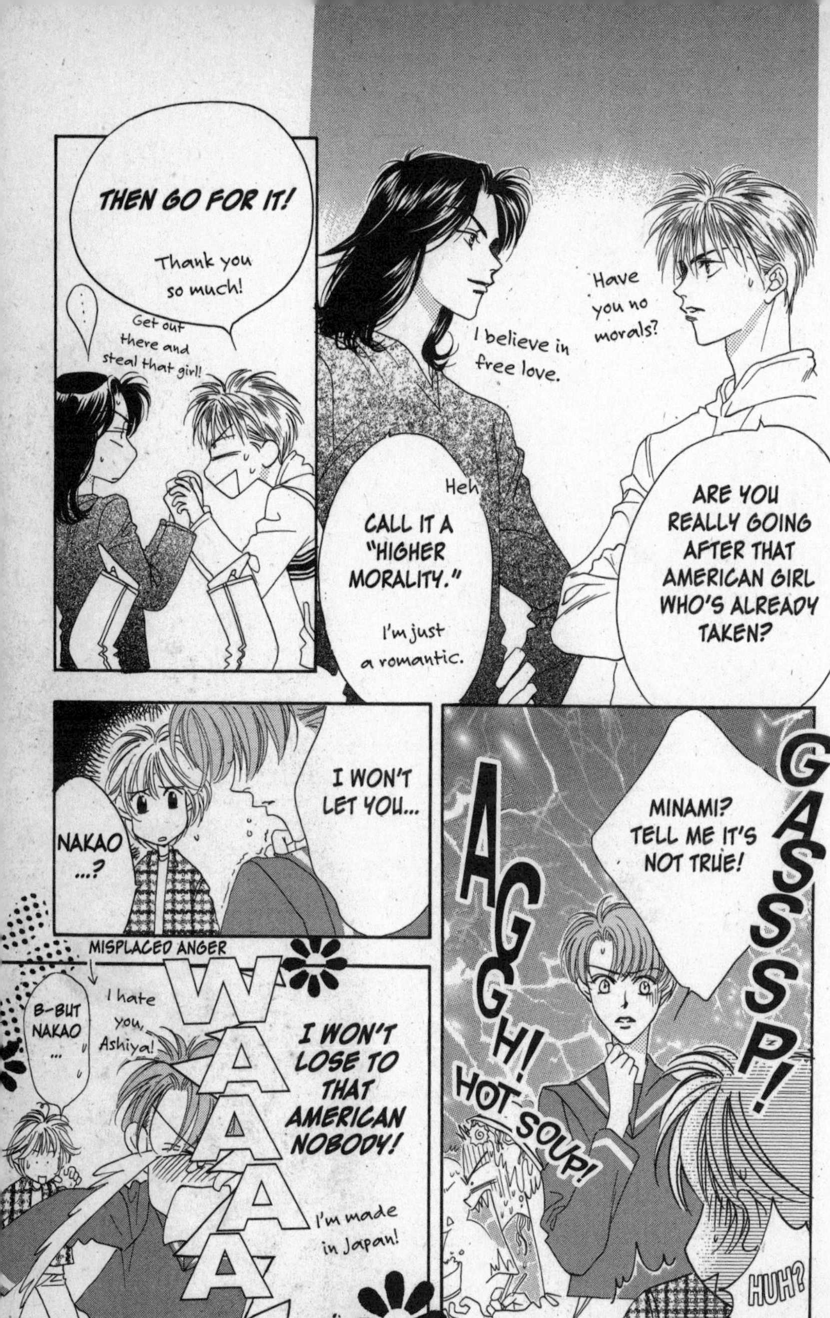

Have you no morals?
I believe in free love.
ARE YOU REALLY GOING AFTER THAT AMERICAN GIRL WHO'S ALREADY TAKEN?
Heh
CALL IT A "HIGHER MORALITY."
I'm just a romantic.
THEN GO FOR IT!
Thank you so much!
...
Get out there and steal that girl!
MINAMI? TELL ME IT'S NOT TRUE!
GASSSP!
AGGH!
HOT SOUP!
HUH?
I WON'T LET YOU...
NAKAO ...?
MISPLACED ANGER
WAAAAA
I WON'T LOSE TO THAT AMERICAN NOBODY!
I'm made in Japan!
I hate you, Ashiya!
B-BUT NAKAO ...

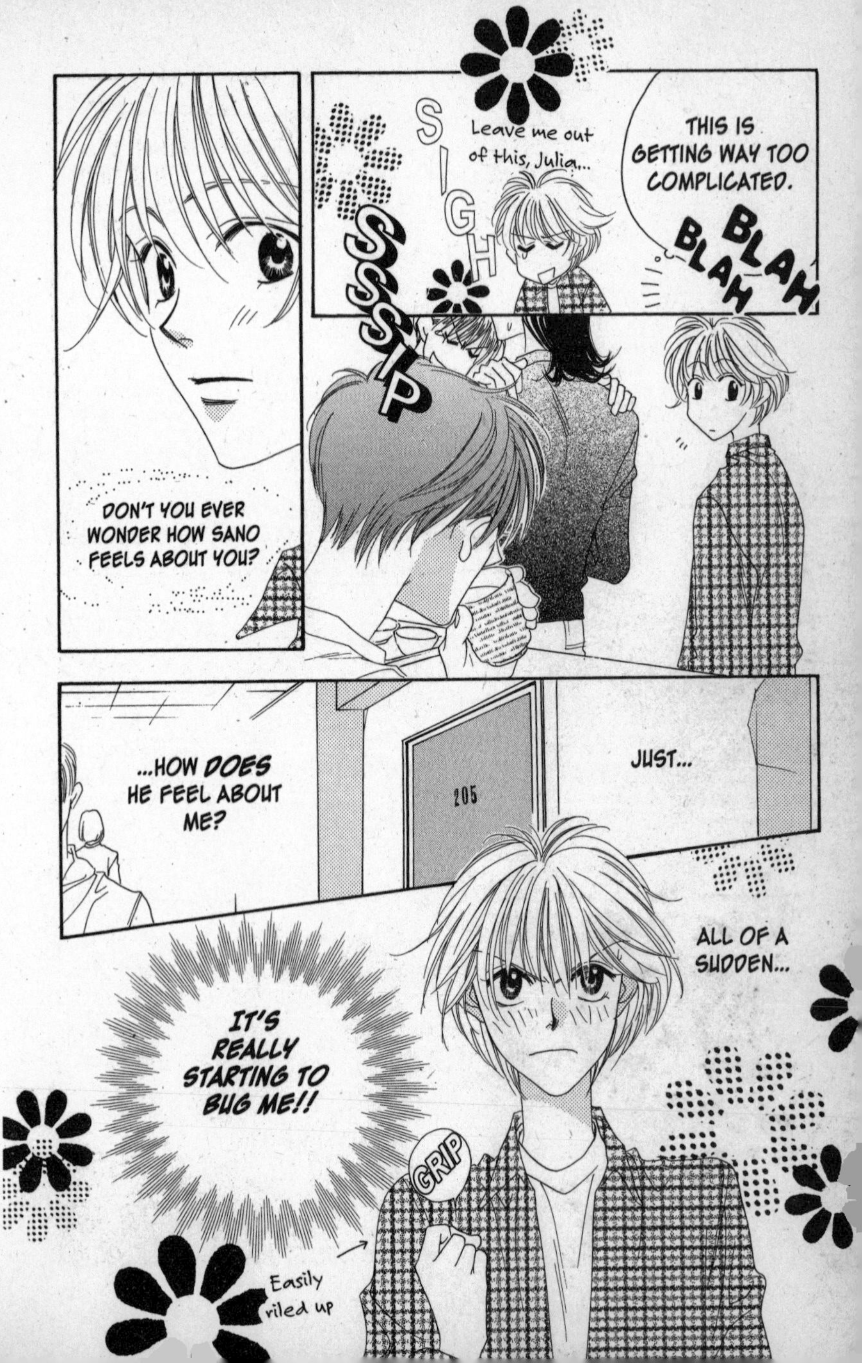
THIS IS GETTING WAY TOO COMPLICATED.
BLAH BLAH
SIGH
Leave me out of this, Julia...
SSSIP
DON'T YOU EVER WONDER HOW SANO FEELS ABOUT YOU?
JUST...
...HOW DOES HE FEEL ABOUT ME?
205
ALL OF A SUDDEN...
IT'S REALLY STARTING TO BUG ME!!
GRIP
Easily riled up

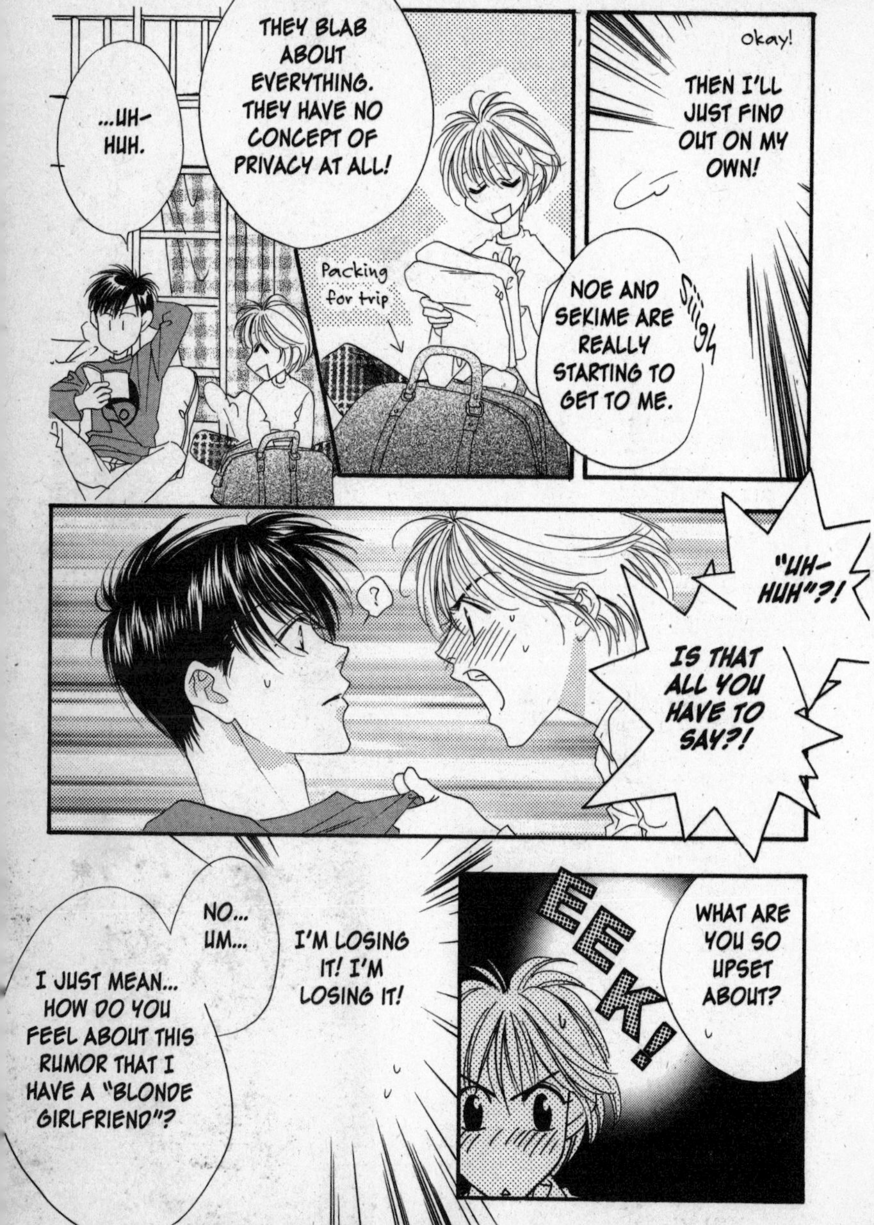
Okay!
THEN I'LL JUST FIND OUT ON MY OWN!
Siiigh
NOE AND SEKIME ARE REALLY STARTING TO GET TO ME.
THEY BLAB ABOUT EVERYTHING. THEY HAVE NO CONCEPT OF PRIVACY AT ALL!
Packing for trip
...UH-HUH.
"UH-HUH"?!
IS THAT ALL YOU HAVE TO SAY?!
?
WHAT ARE YOU SO UPSET ABOUT?
EEK!
I'M LOSING IT! I'M LOSING IT!
NO... UM...
I JUST MEAN... HOW DO YOU FEEL ABOUT THIS RUMOR THAT I HAVE A "BLONDE GIRLFRIEND"?

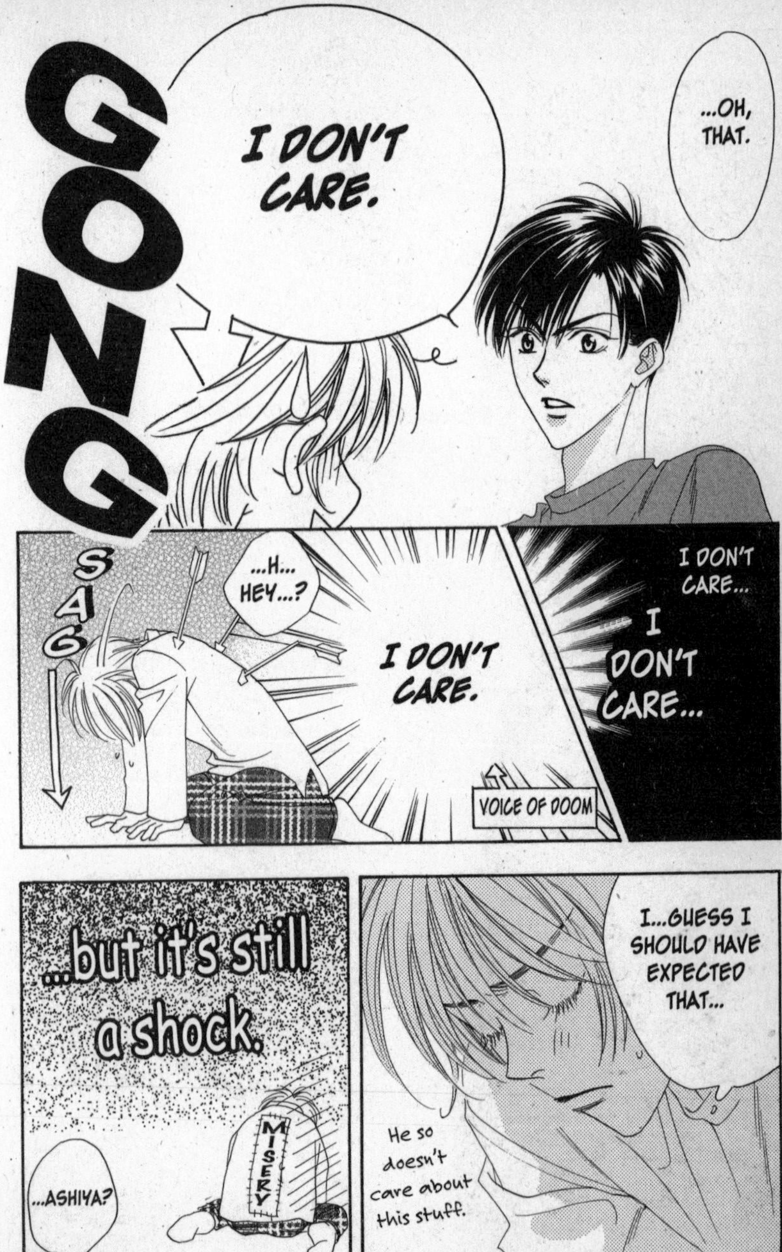
...OH, THAT.
I DON'T CARE.
GONG
I DON'T CARE...
I DON'T CARE...
...H... HEY...?
I DON'T CARE.
VOICE OF DOOM
SAG
I...GUESS I SHOULD HAVE EXPECTED THAT...
He so doesn't care about this stuff.
...but it's still a shock.
MISERY
...ASHIYA?

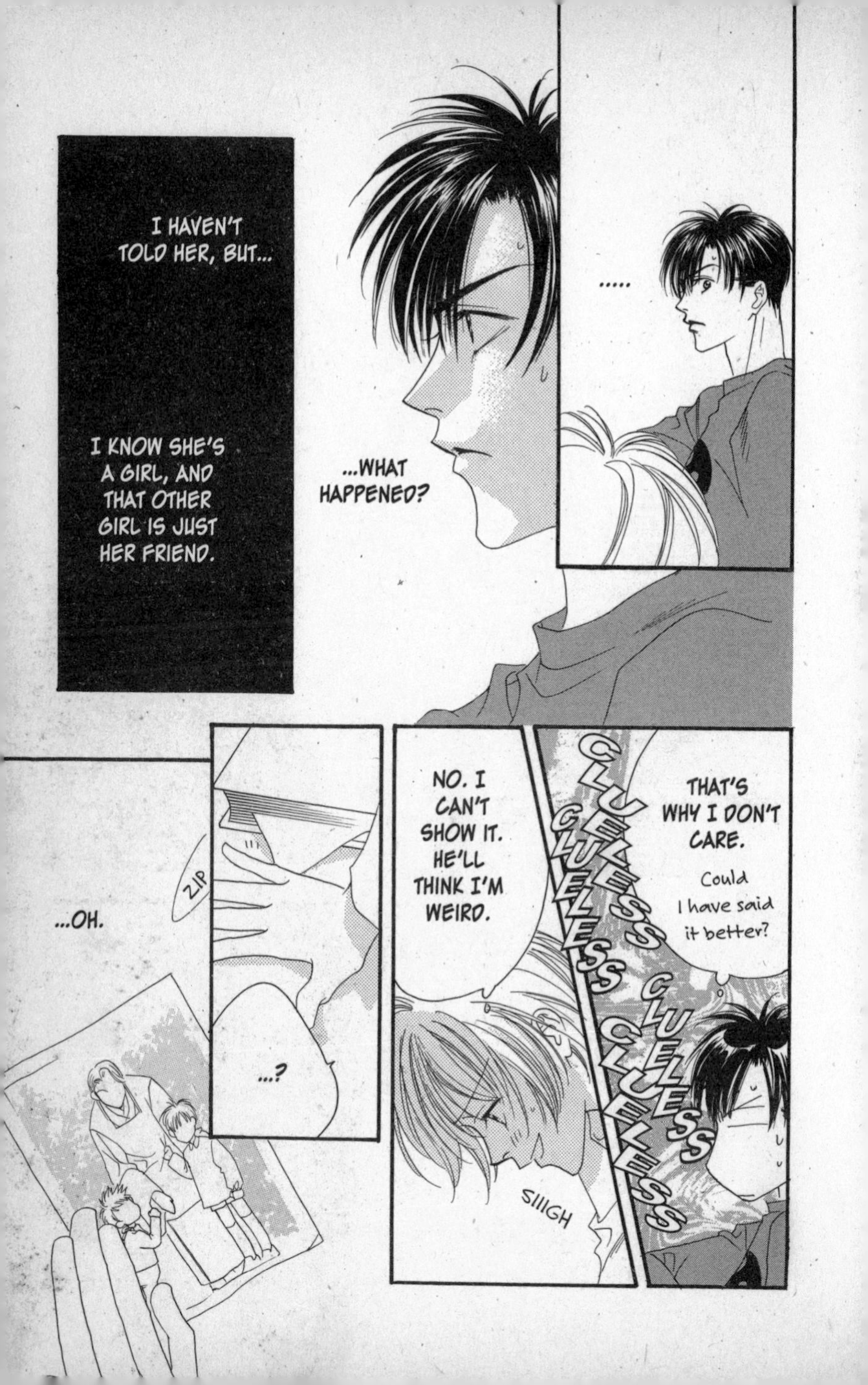
.....
...WHAT HAPPENED?
I HAVEN'T TOLD HER, BUT...
I KNOW SHE'S A GIRL, AND THAT OTHER GIRL IS JUST HER FRIEND.
THAT'S WHY I DON'T CARE.
Could I have said it better?
CLUELESS CLUELESS
CLUELESS CLUELESS
NO. I CAN'T SHOW IT. HE'LL THINK I'M WEIRD.
SIIIGH
ZIP
...?
...OH.

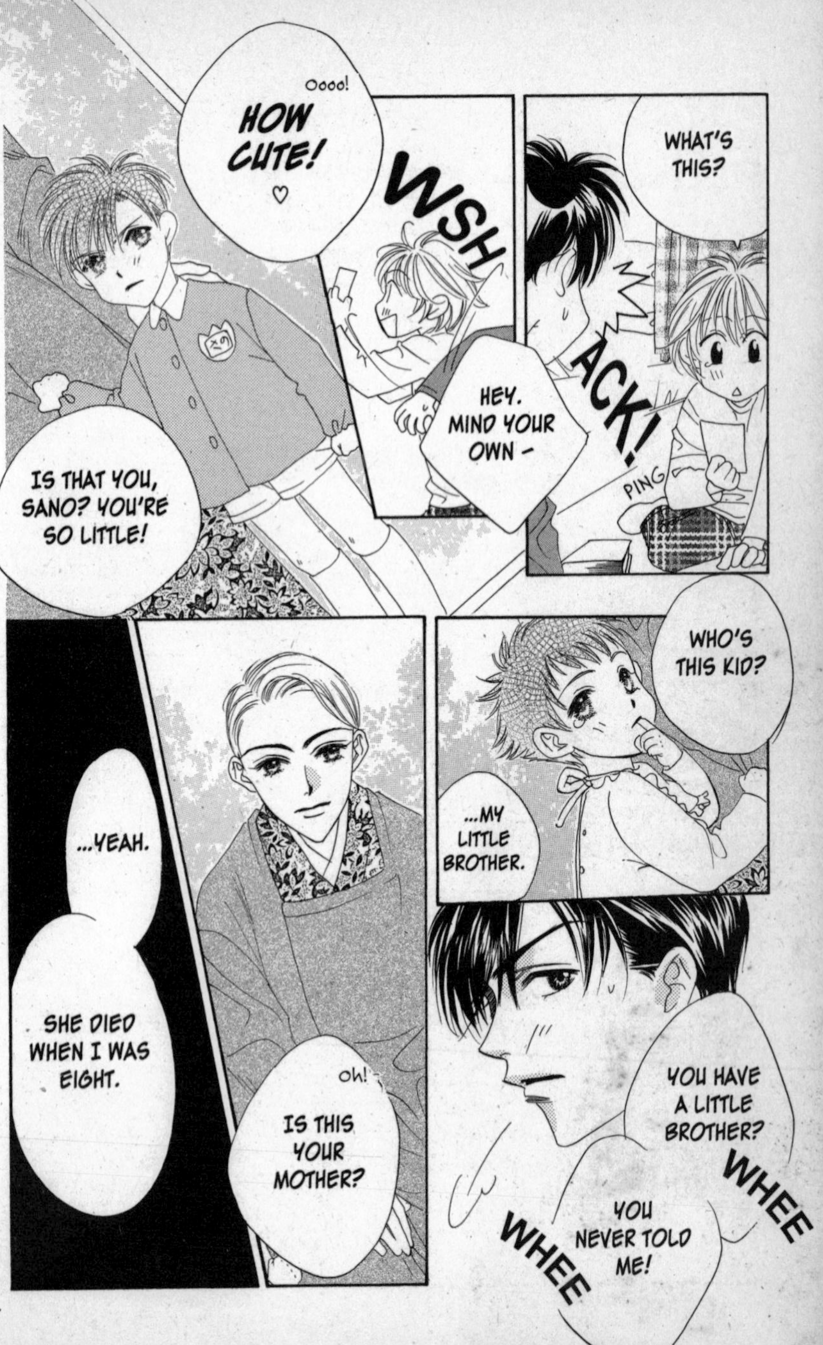
WHAT'S THIS?
ACK!
PING
HEY. MIND YOUR OWN -
WSH
Oooo!
HOW CUTE! ♥
IS THAT YOU, SANO? YOU'RE SO LITTLE!
WHO'S THIS KID?
...MY LITTLE BROTHER.
YOU HAVE A LITTLE BROTHER?
WHEE
WHEE
YOU NEVER TOLD ME!
Oh!
IS THIS YOUR MOTHER?
...YEAH.
SHE DIED WHEN I WAS EIGHT.

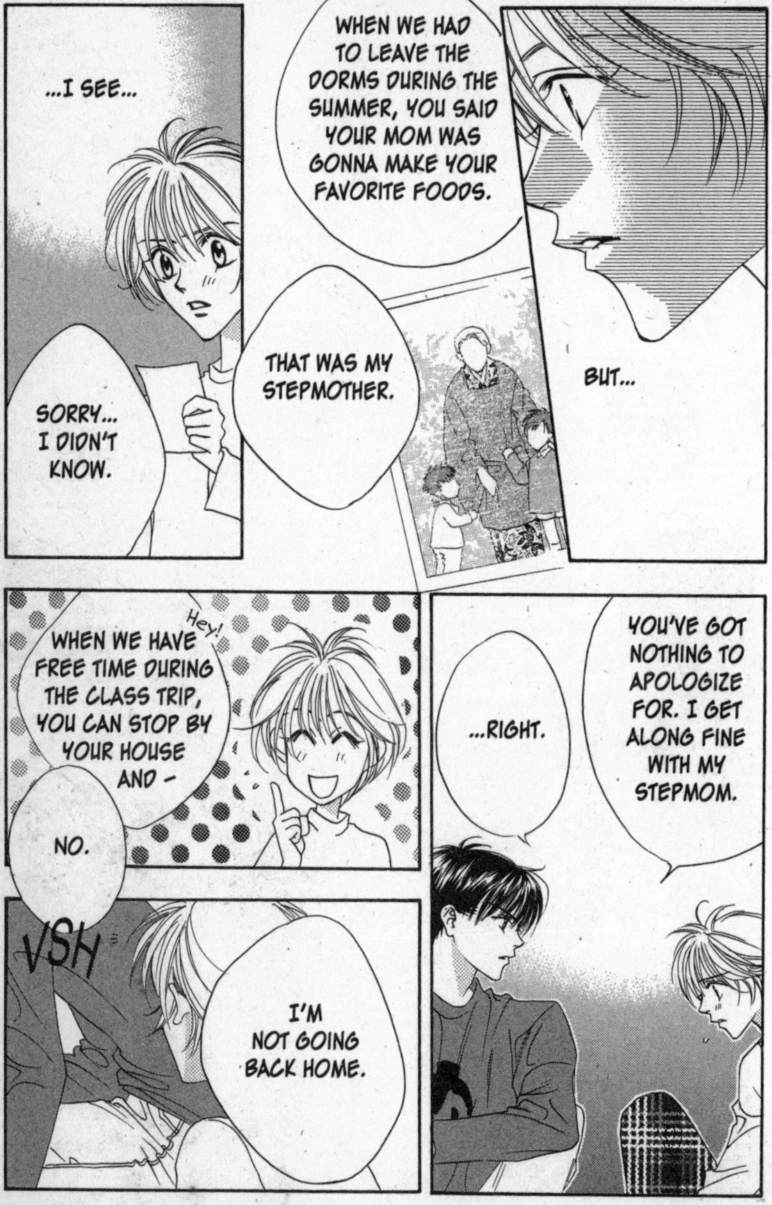
WHEN WE HAD TO LEAVE THE DORMS DURING THE SUMMER, YOU SAID YOUR MOM WAS GONNA MAKE YOUR FAVORITE FOODS.
BUT...
THAT WAS MY STEPMOTHER.
...I SEE...
SORRY... I DIDN'T KNOW.
YOU'VE GOT NOTHING TO APOLOGIZE FOR. I GET ALONG FINE WITH MY STEPMOM.
...RIGHT.
Hey!
WHEN WE HAVE FREE TIME DURING THE CLASS TRIP, YOU CAN STOP BY YOUR HOUSE AND -
NO.
VSH
I'M NOT GOING BACK HOME.

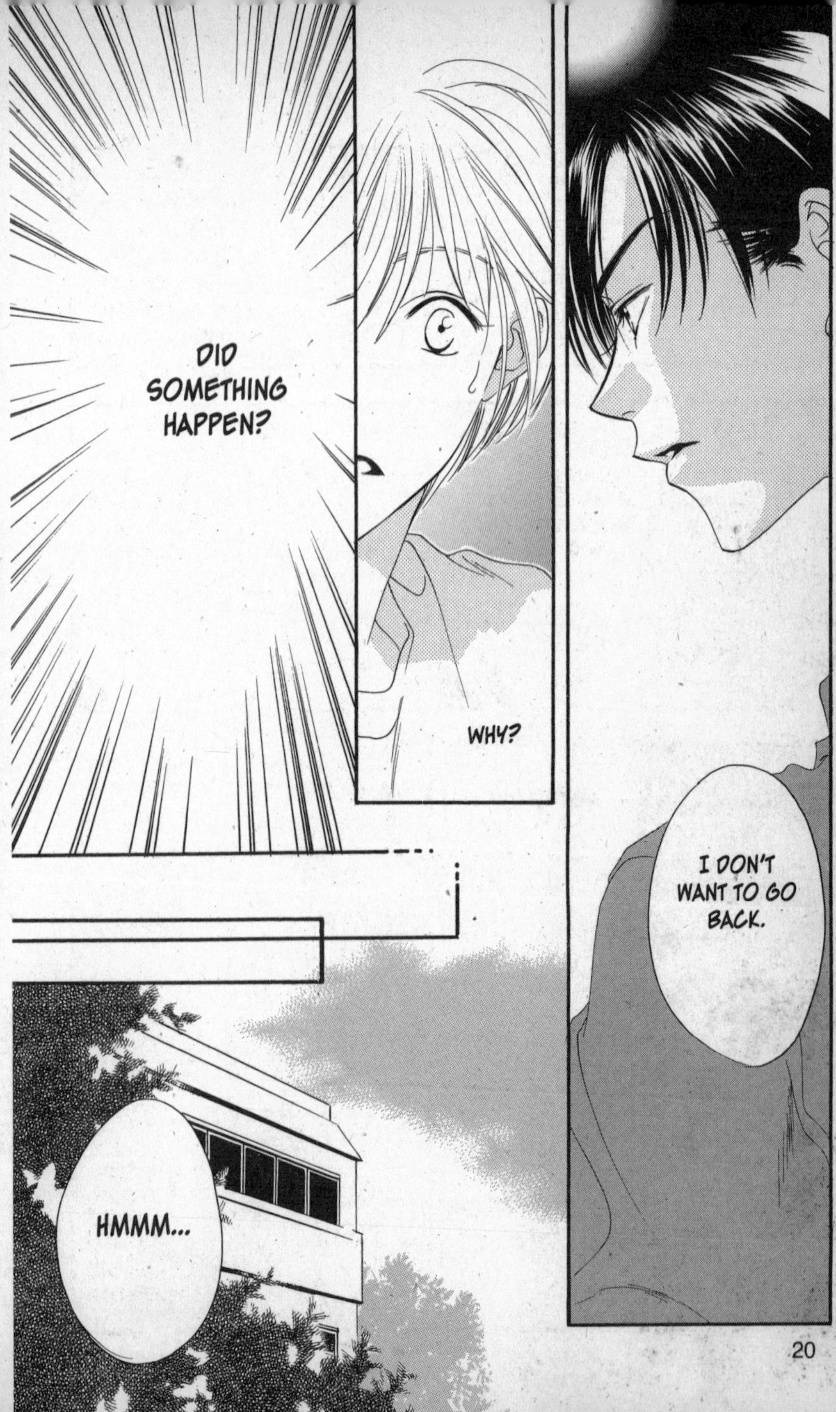
I DON'T WANT TO GO BACK.
WHY?
DID SOMETHING HAPPEN?
HMMM...

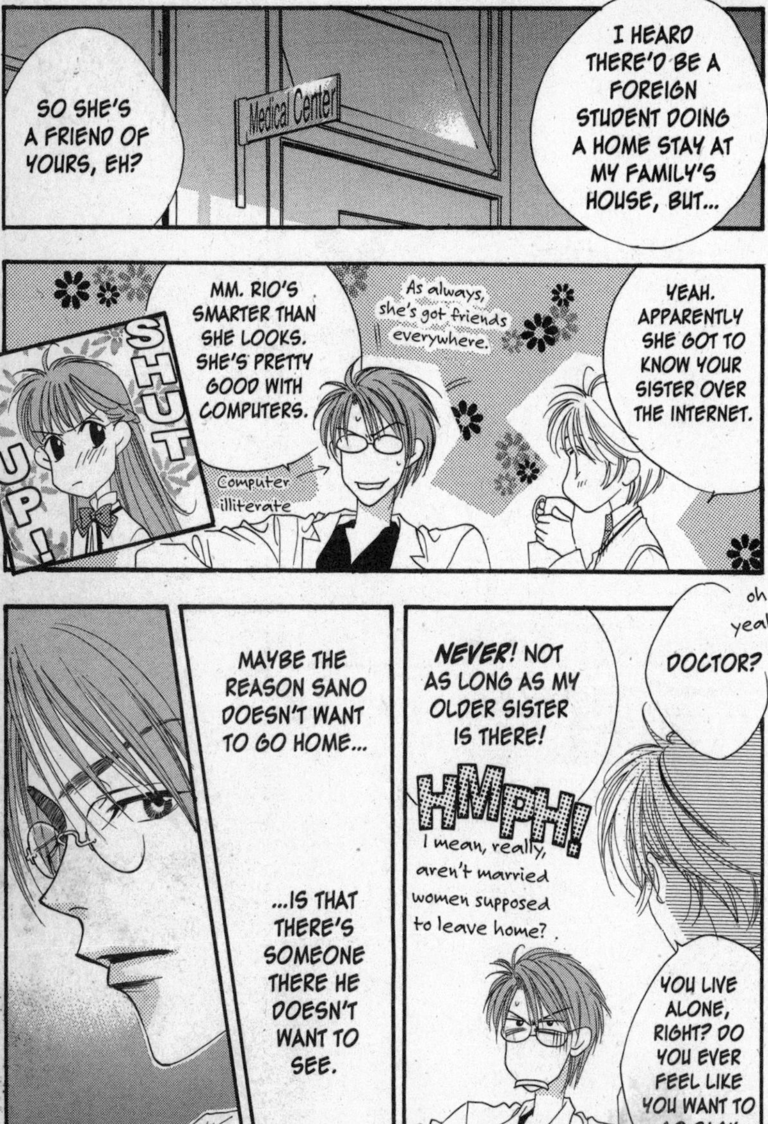
I HEARD THERE'D BE A FOREIGN STUDENT DOING A HOME STAY AT MY FAMILY'S HOUSE, BUT...
Medical Center
SO SHE'S A FRIEND OF YOURS, EH?
YEAH. APPARENTLY SHE GOT TO KNOW YOUR SISTER OVER THE INTERNET.
As always, she's got friends everywhere.
MM. RIO'S SMARTER THAN SHE LOOKS. SHE'S PRETTY GOOD WITH COMPUTERS.
Computer illiterate
SHUT UP!
oh yeah~
DOCTOR?
YOU LIVE ALONE, RIGHT? DO YOU EVER FEEL LIKE YOU WANT TO GO BACK HOME?
NEVER! NOT AS LONG AS MY OLDER SISTER IS THERE!
HMPH!
I mean, really, aren't married women supposed to leave home?
MAYBE THE REASON SANO DOESN'T WANT TO GO HOME...
...IS THAT THERE'S SOMEONE THERE HE DOESN'T WANT TO SEE.

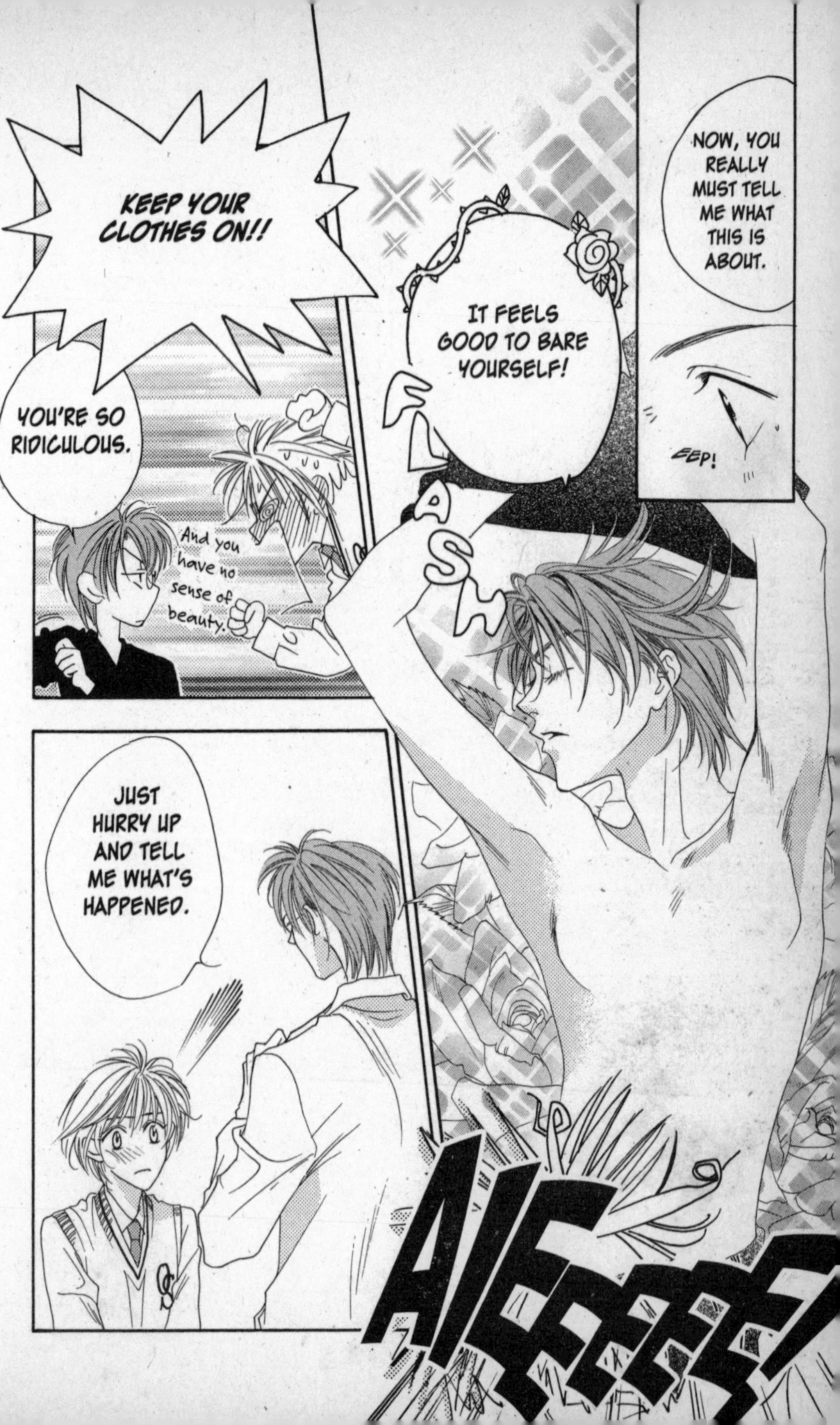
NOW, YOU REALLY MUST TELL ME WHAT THIS IS ABOUT.
EEP!
IT FEELS GOOD TO BARE YOURSELF!
FLASH
AIEEEEE!
KEEP YOUR CLOTHES ON!!
YOU'RE SO RIDICULOUS.
And you have no sense of beauty.
JUST HURRY UP AND TELL ME WHAT'S HAPPENED.

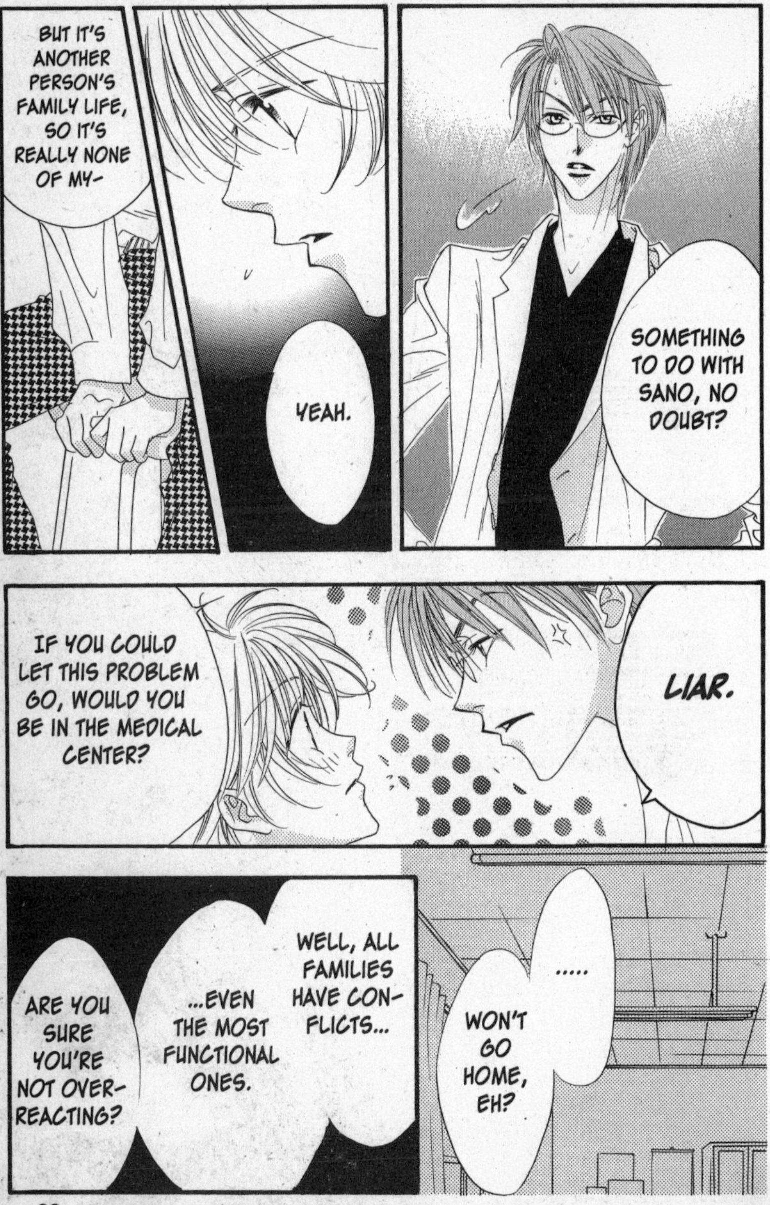
SOMETHING TO DO WITH SANO, NO DOUBT?
YEAH.
BUT IT'S ANOTHER PERSON'S FAMILY LIFE, SO IT'S REALLY NONE OF MY-
LIAR.
IF YOU COULD LET THIS PROBLEM GO, WOULD YOU BE IN THE MEDICAL CENTER?
.....
WON'T GO HOME, EH?
WELL, ALL FAMILIES HAVE CONFLICTS...
...EVEN THE MOST FUNCTIONAL ONES.
ARE YOU SURE YOU'RE NOT OVER-REACTING?

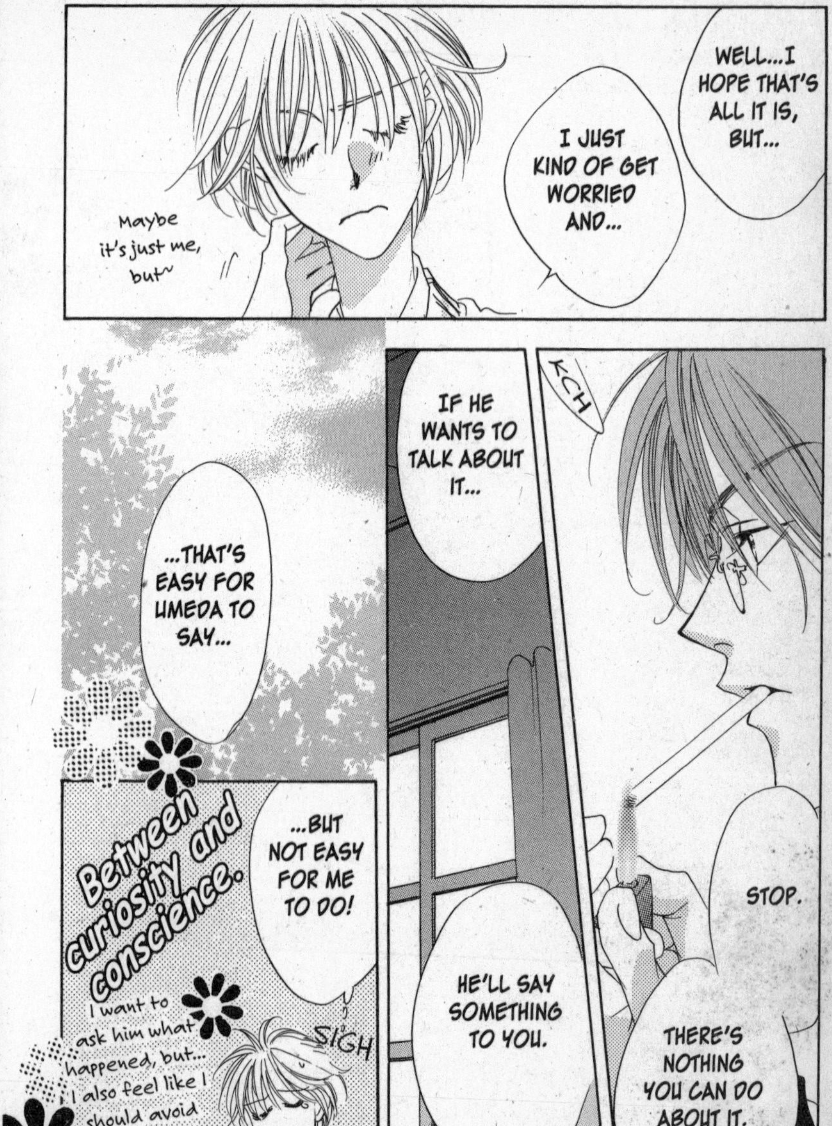
WELL...I HOPE THAT'S ALL IT IS, BUT...
I JUST KIND OF GET WORRIED AND...
Maybe it's just me, but~
KCH
STOP.
THERE'S NOTHING YOU CAN DO ABOUT IT.
IF HE WANTS TO TALK ABOUT IT...
HE'LL SAY SOMETHING TO YOU.
...THAT'S EASY FOR UMEDA TO SAY...
...BUT NOT EASY FOR ME TO DO!
SIGH
Between curiosity and conscience.
I want to ask him what happened, but... I also feel like I should avoid the subject.

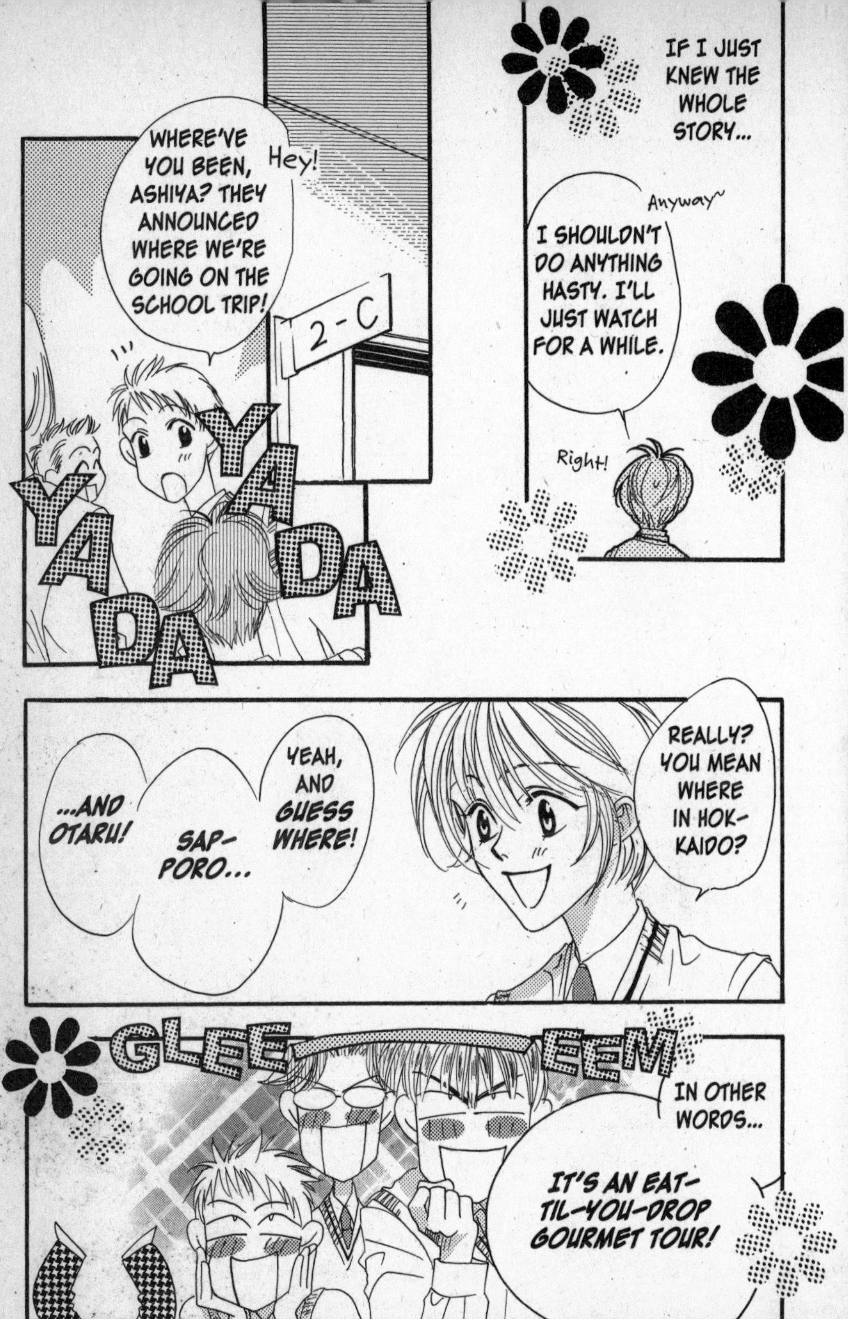
IF I JUST KNEW THE WHOLE STORY...
Anyway~
I SHOULDN'T DO ANYTHING HASTY. I'LL JUST WATCH FOR A WHILE.
Right!
Hey!
WHERE'VE YOU BEEN, ASHIYA? THEY ANNOUNCED WHERE WE'RE GOING ON THE SCHOOL TRIP!
2-C
YA DA YA DA
REALLY? YOU MEAN WHERE IN HOK-KAIDO?
YEAH, AND GUESS WHERE!
SAP-PORO...
...AND OTARU!
GLEEEEM
IN OTHER WORDS...
IT'S AN EAT-TIL-YOU-DROP GOURMET TOUR!

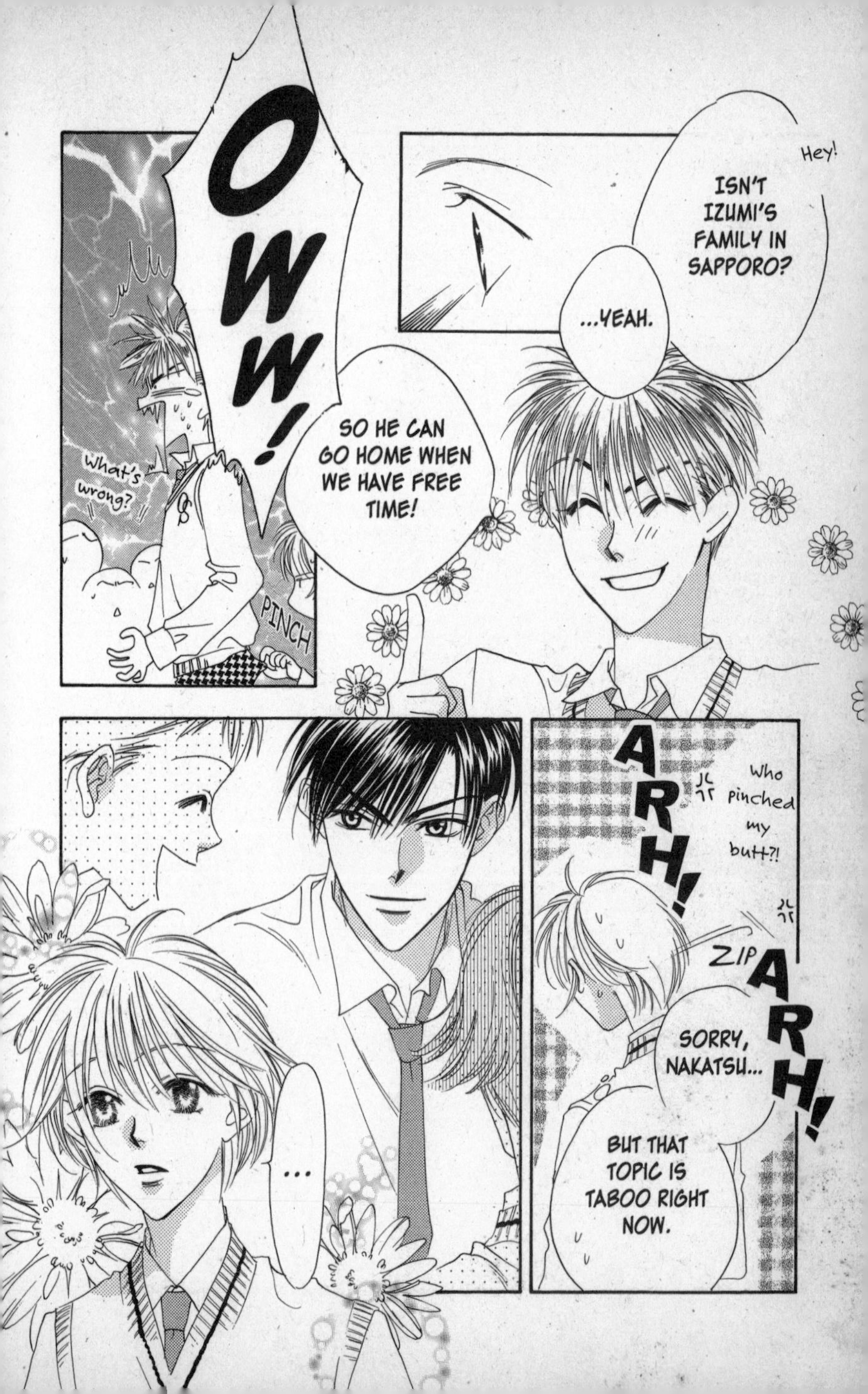
Hey!
ISN'T IZUMI'S FAMILY IN SAPPORO?
...YEAH.
SO HE CAN GO HOME WHEN WE HAVE FREE TIME!
OWW!
What's wrong?
PINCH
ARH!
Who pinched my butt?!
ZIP
ARH!
SORRY, NAKATSU...
BUT THAT TOPIC IS TABOO RIGHT NOW.
...

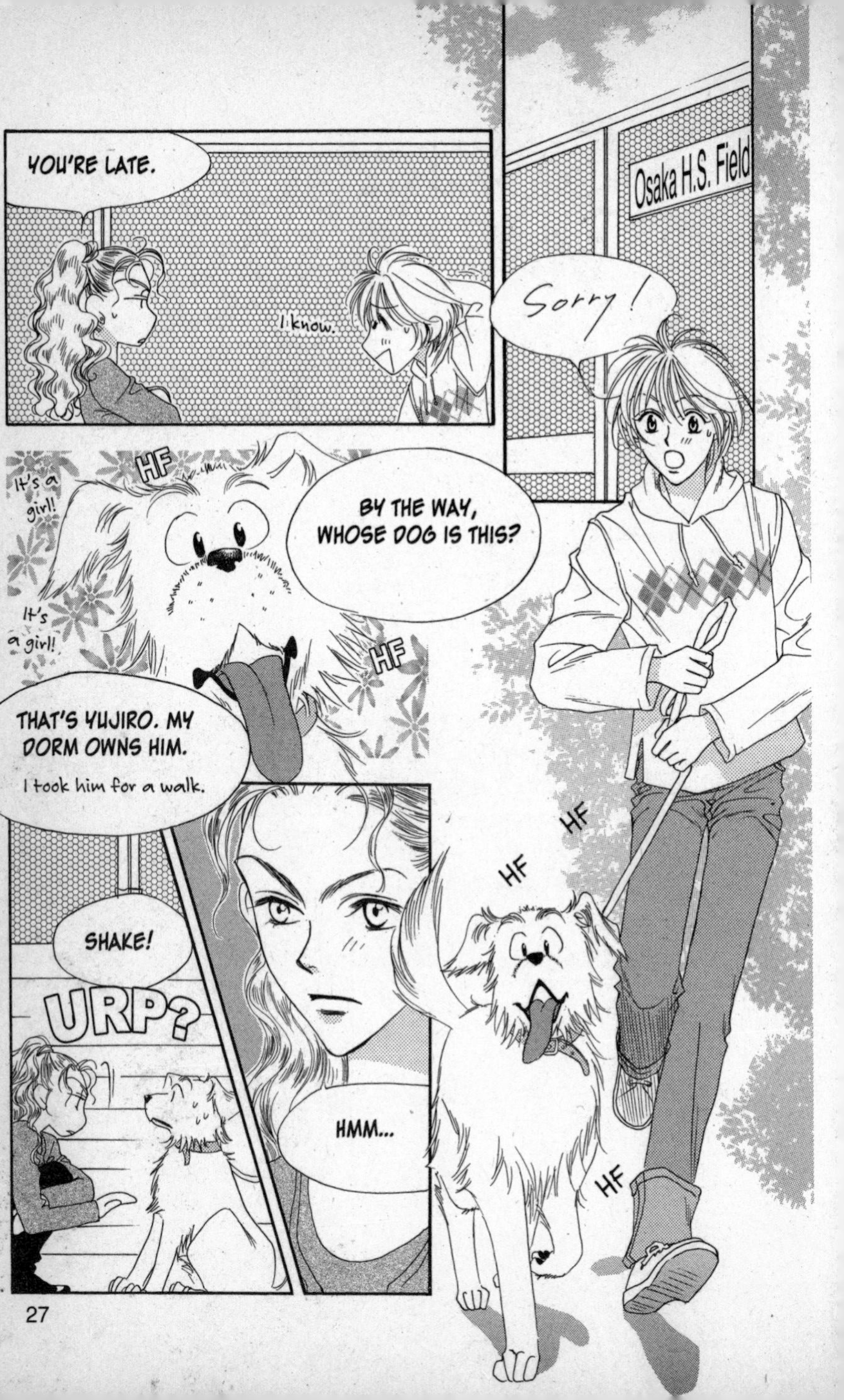
Osaka H.S. Field
Sorry!
HF
HF
HF
YOU'RE LATE.
I know.
BY THE WAY, WHOSE DOG IS THIS?
HF
HF
It's a girl!
It's a girl!
THAT'S YUJIRO. MY DORM OWNS HIM.
I took him for a walk.
HMM...
SHAKE!
URP?

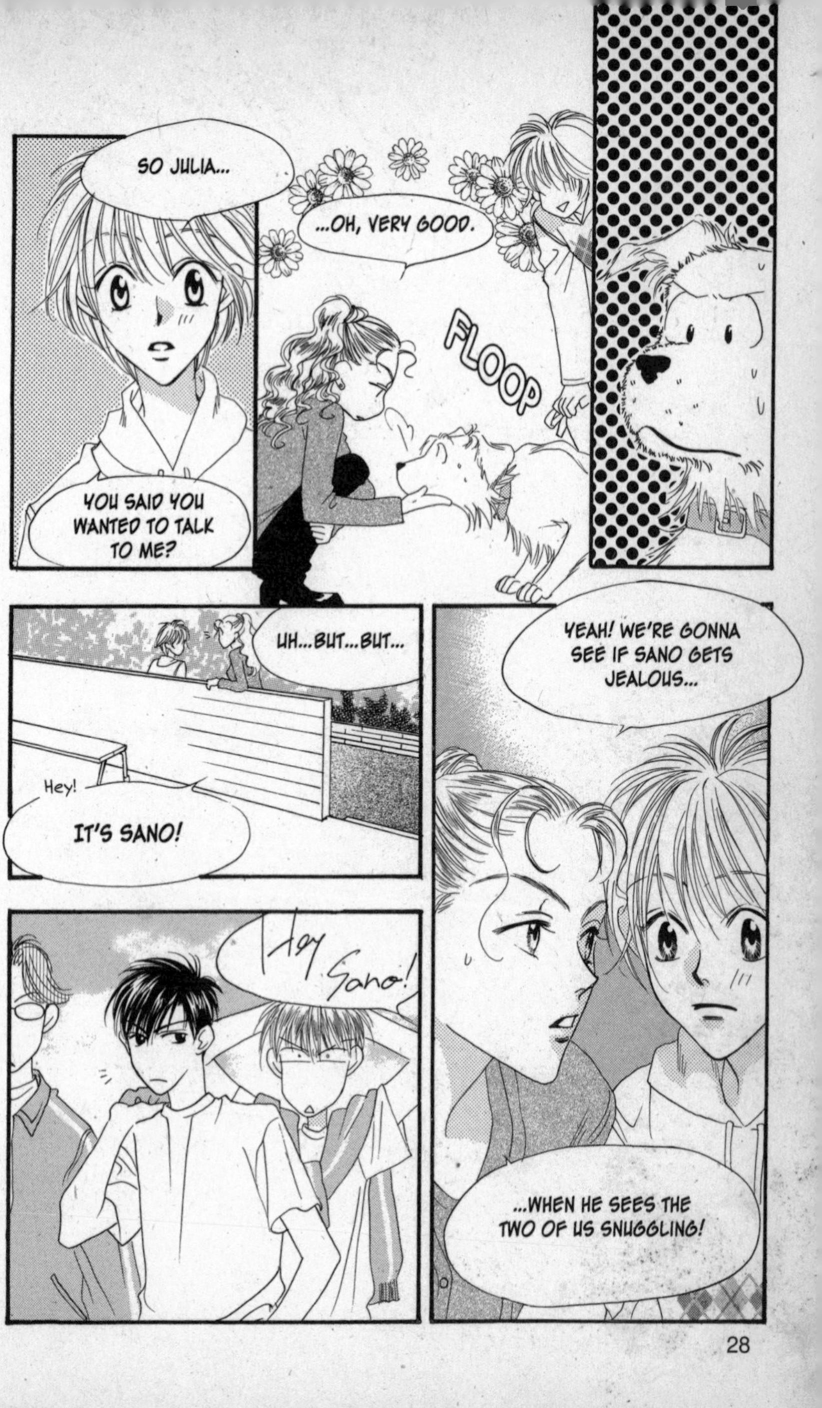
...OH, VERY GOOD.
FLOOP
SO JULIA...
YOU SAID YOU WANTED TO TALK TO ME?
YEAH! WE'RE GONNA SEE IF SANO GETS JEALOUS...
...WHEN HE SEES THE TWO OF US SNUGGLING!
UH...BUT...BUT...
Hey!
IT'S SANO!
Hey Sano!

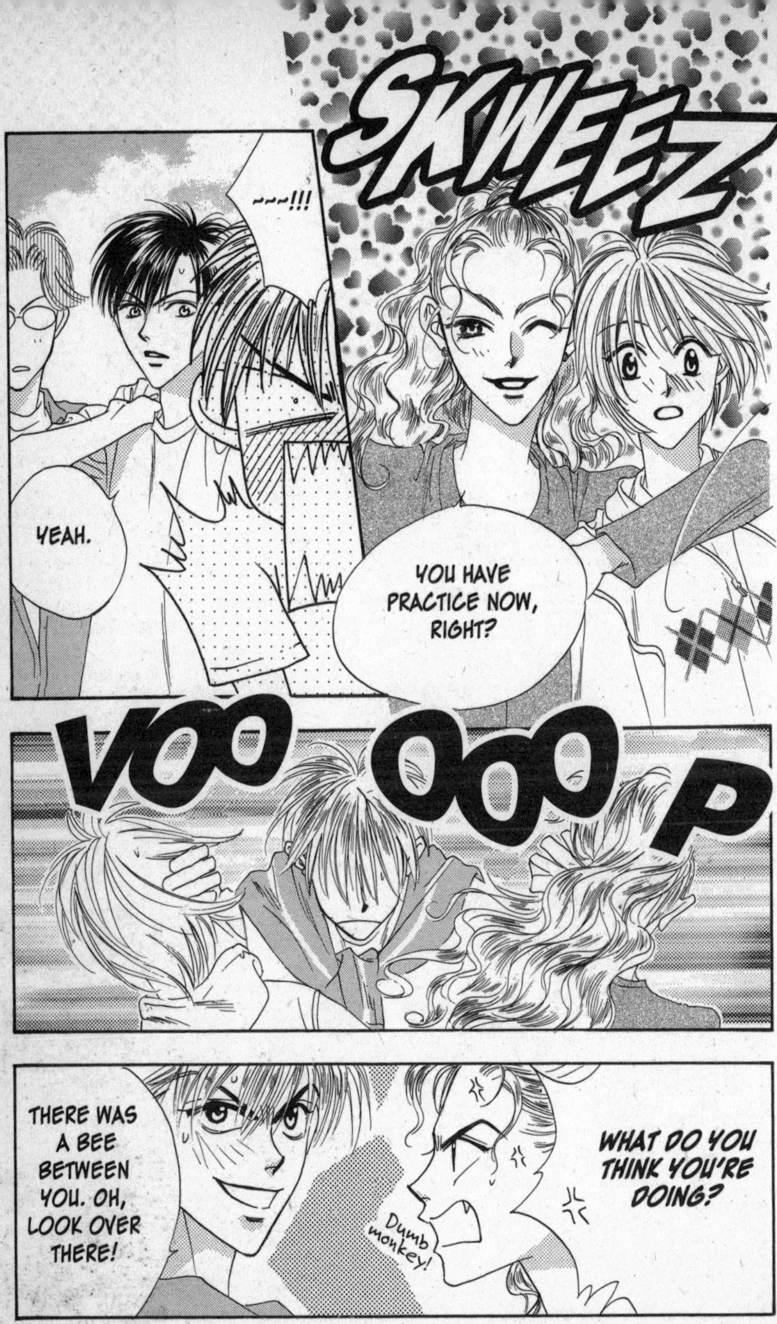
SKWEEZ
YOU HAVE PRACTICE NOW, RIGHT?
~~~!!!
YEAH.
VOO OOO P
WHAT DO YOU THINK YOU'RE DOING?
Dumb monkey!
THERE WAS A BEE BETWEEN YOU. OH, LOOK OVER THERE!
~~~

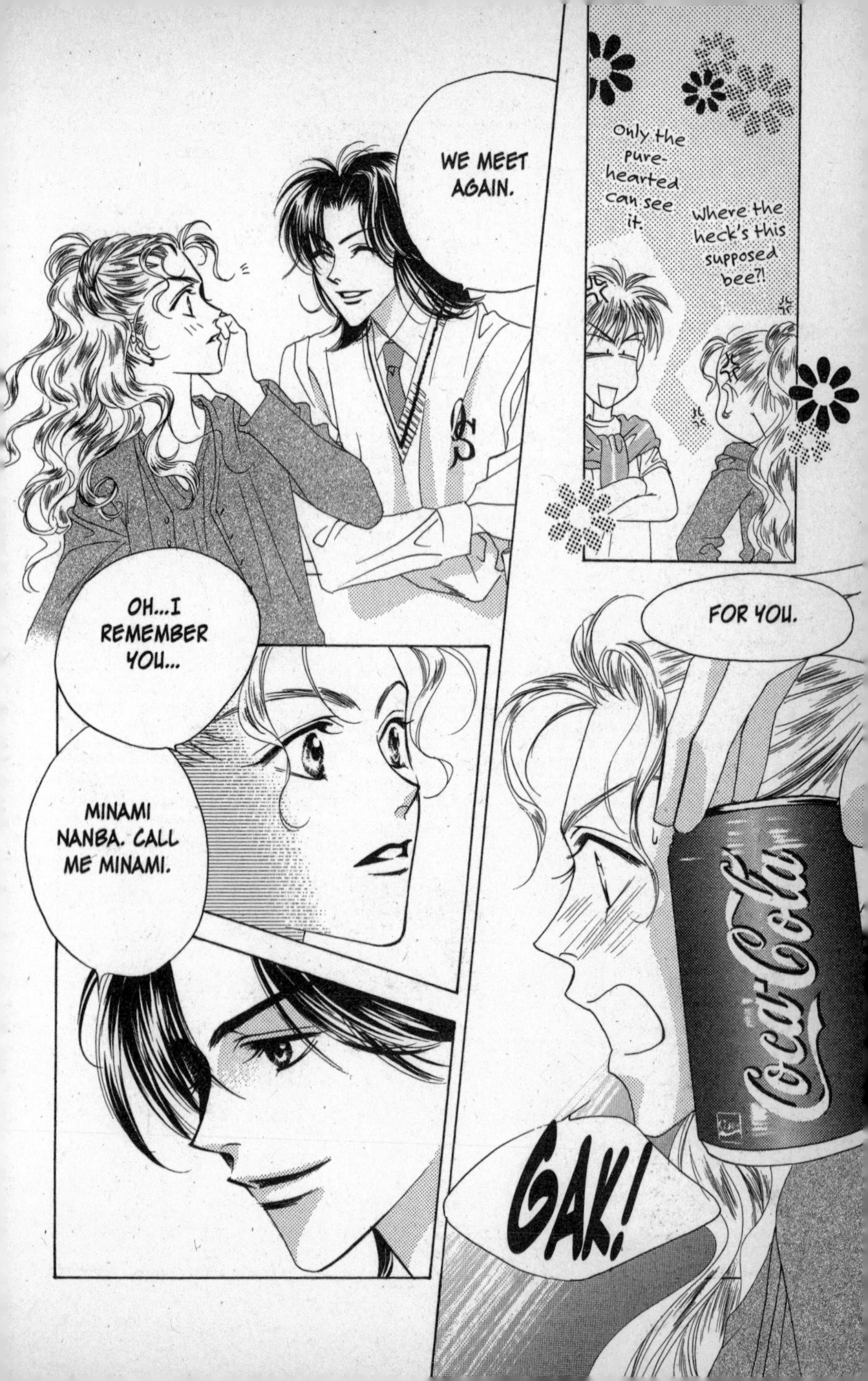
Only the pure-hearted can see it.
Where the heck's this supposed bee?!
WE MEET AGAIN.
OH...I REMEMBER YOU...
FOR YOU.
GAK!
MINAMI NANBA. CALL ME MINAMI.
Coca-Cola

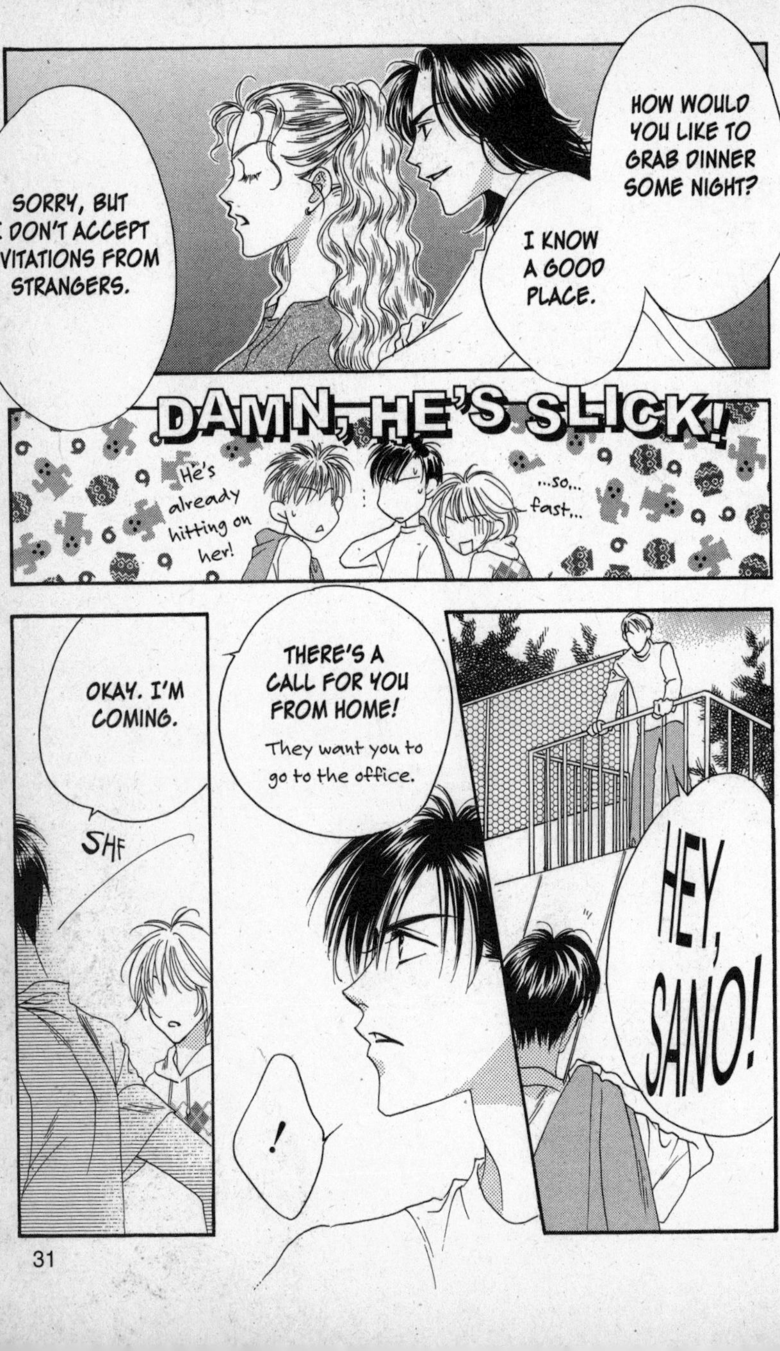
HOW WOULD YOU LIKE TO GRAB DINNER SOME NIGHT?
I KNOW A GOOD PLACE.
SORRY, BUT I DON'T ACCEPT INVITATIONS FROM STRANGERS.
DAMN, HE'S SLICK!
...so... fast...
He's already hitting on her!
HEY, SANO!
!
THERE'S A CALL FOR YOU FROM HOME!
They want you to go to the office.
OKAY. I'M COMING.
SHF

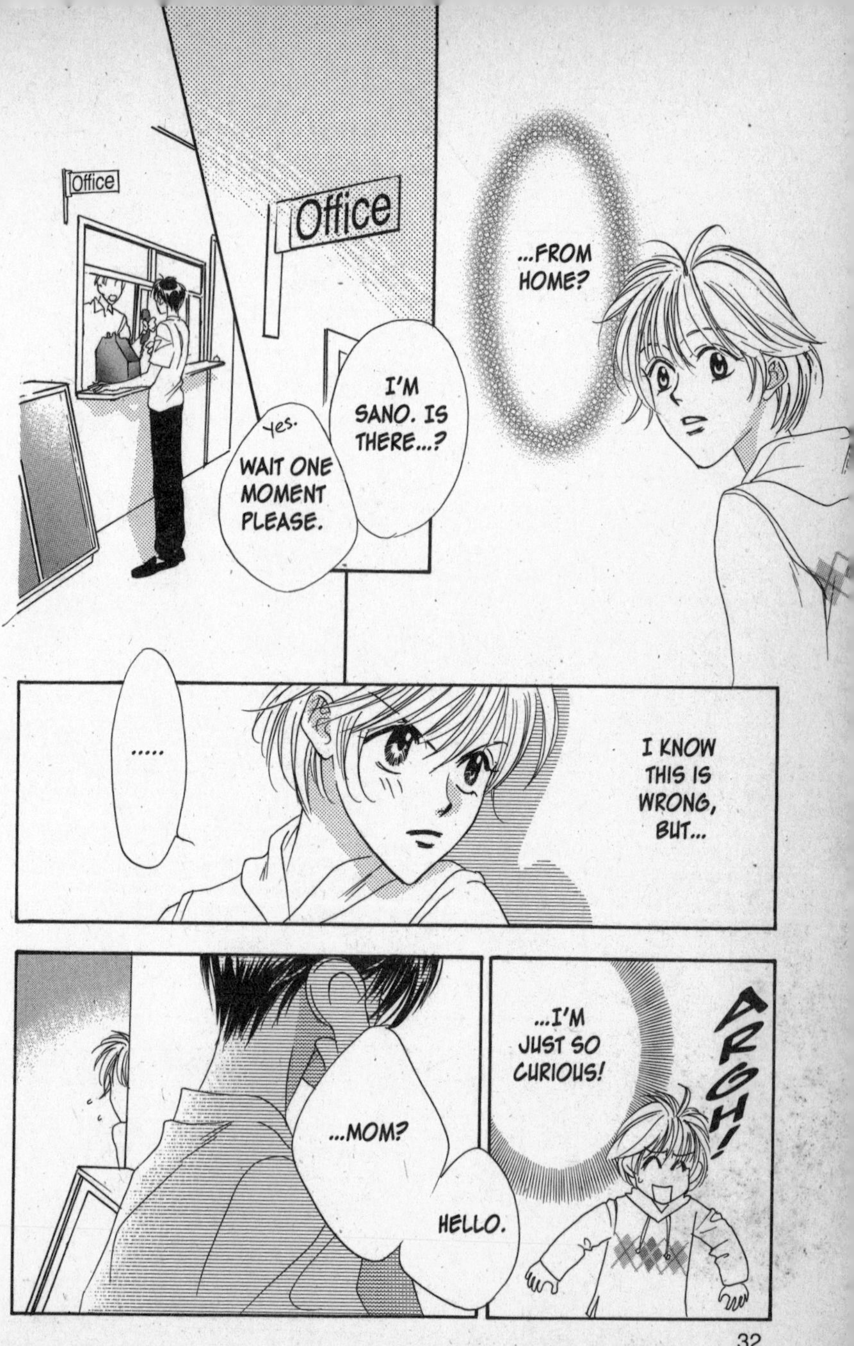
...FROM HOME?
Office
Office
I'M SANO. IS THERE...?
Yes.
WAIT ONE MOMENT PLEASE.
I KNOW THIS IS WRONG, BUT...
.....
...I'M JUST SO CURIOUS!
ARGH!
...MOM?
HELLO.

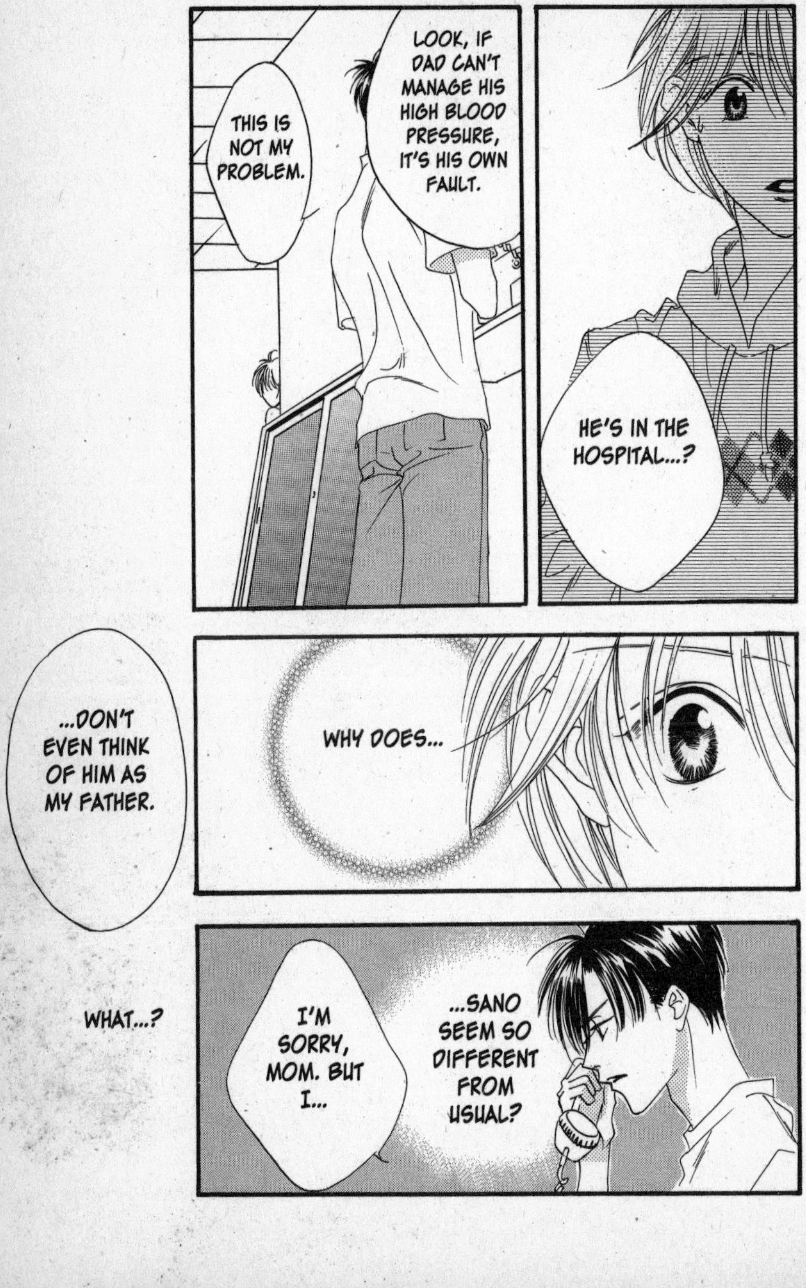
HE'S IN THE HOSPITAL...?
LOOK, IF DAD CAN'T MANAGE HIS HIGH BLOOD PRESSURE, IT'S HIS OWN FAULT.
THIS IS NOT MY PROBLEM.
WHY DOES...
...SANO SEEM SO DIFFERENT FROM USUAL?
I'M SORRY, MOM. BUT I...
...DON'T EVEN THINK OF HIM AS MY FATHER.
WHAT...?

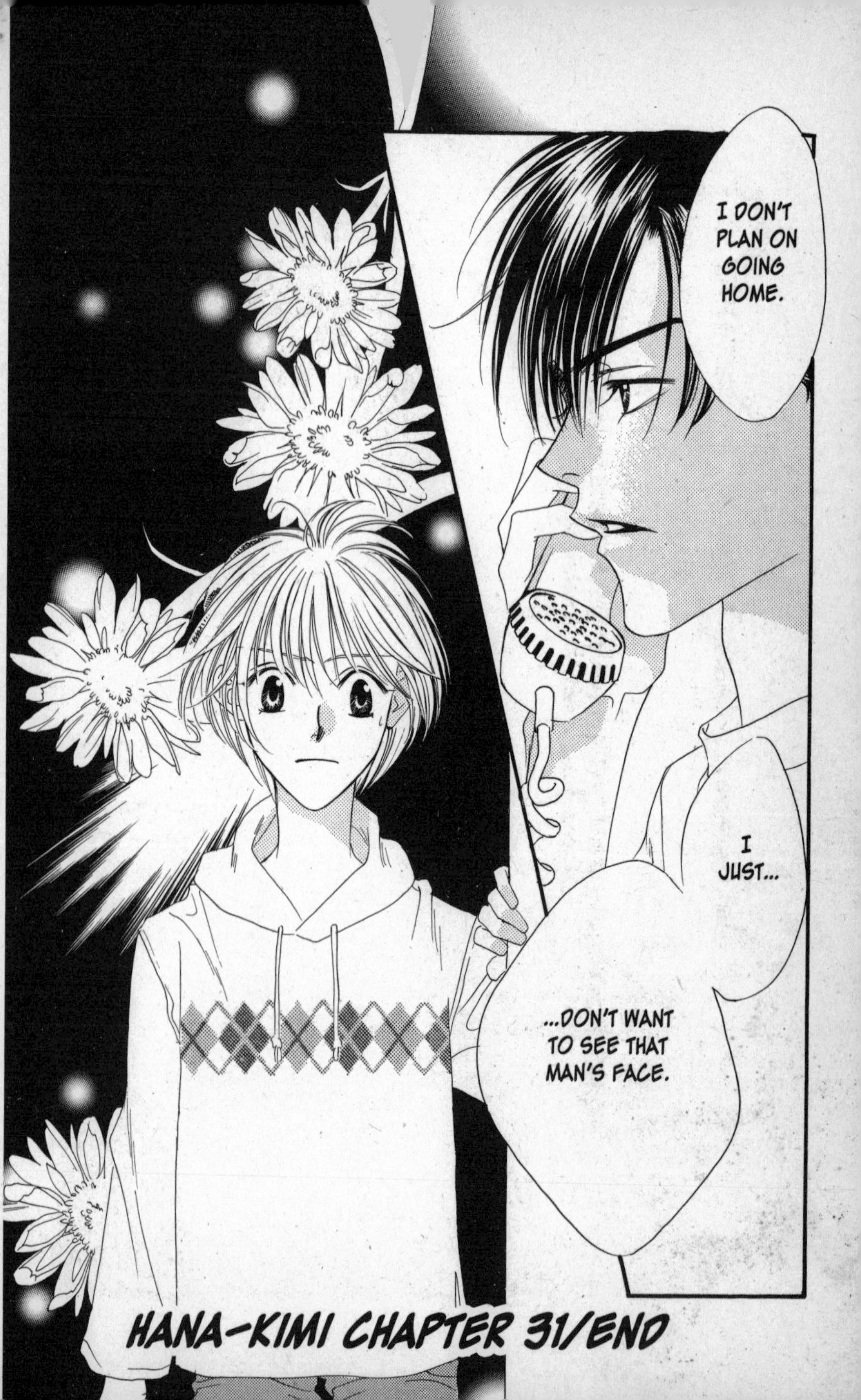
I DON'T PLAN ON GOING HOME.
I JUST...
...DON'T WANT TO SEE THAT MAN'S FACE.
HANA-KIMI CHAPTER 31/END

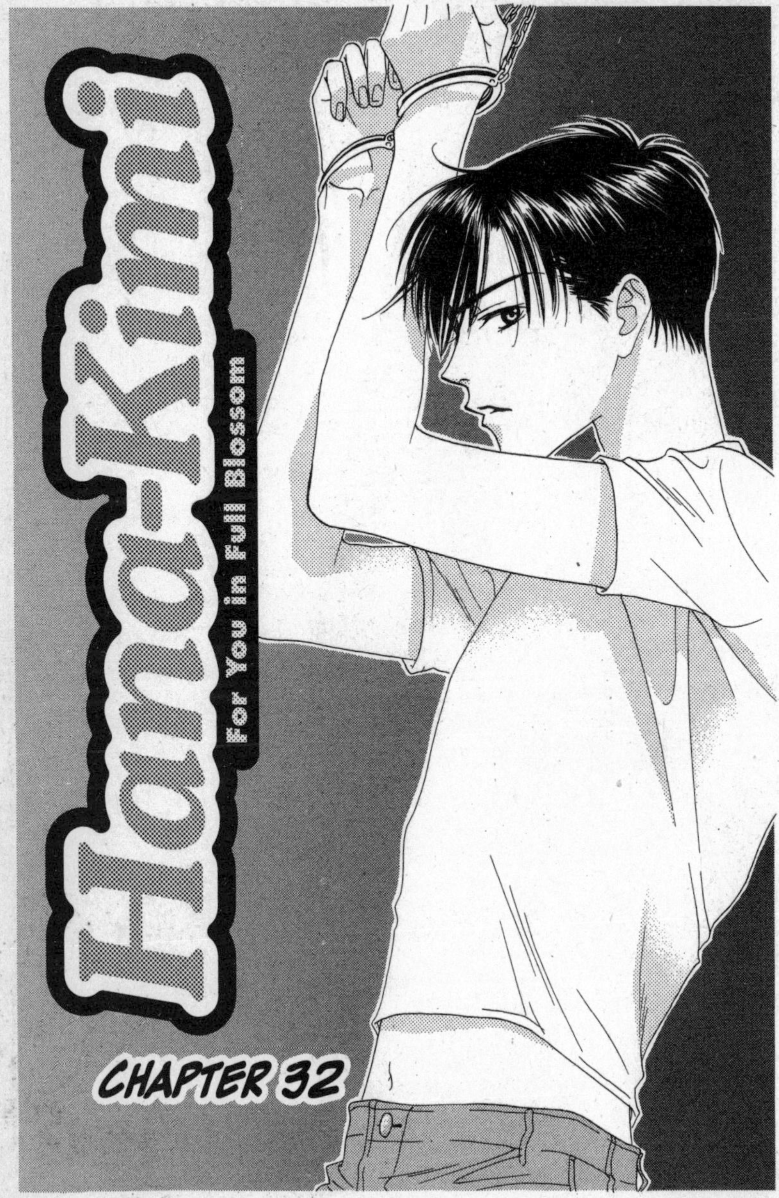
Hana-Kimi
For You in Full Blossom
CHAPTER 32

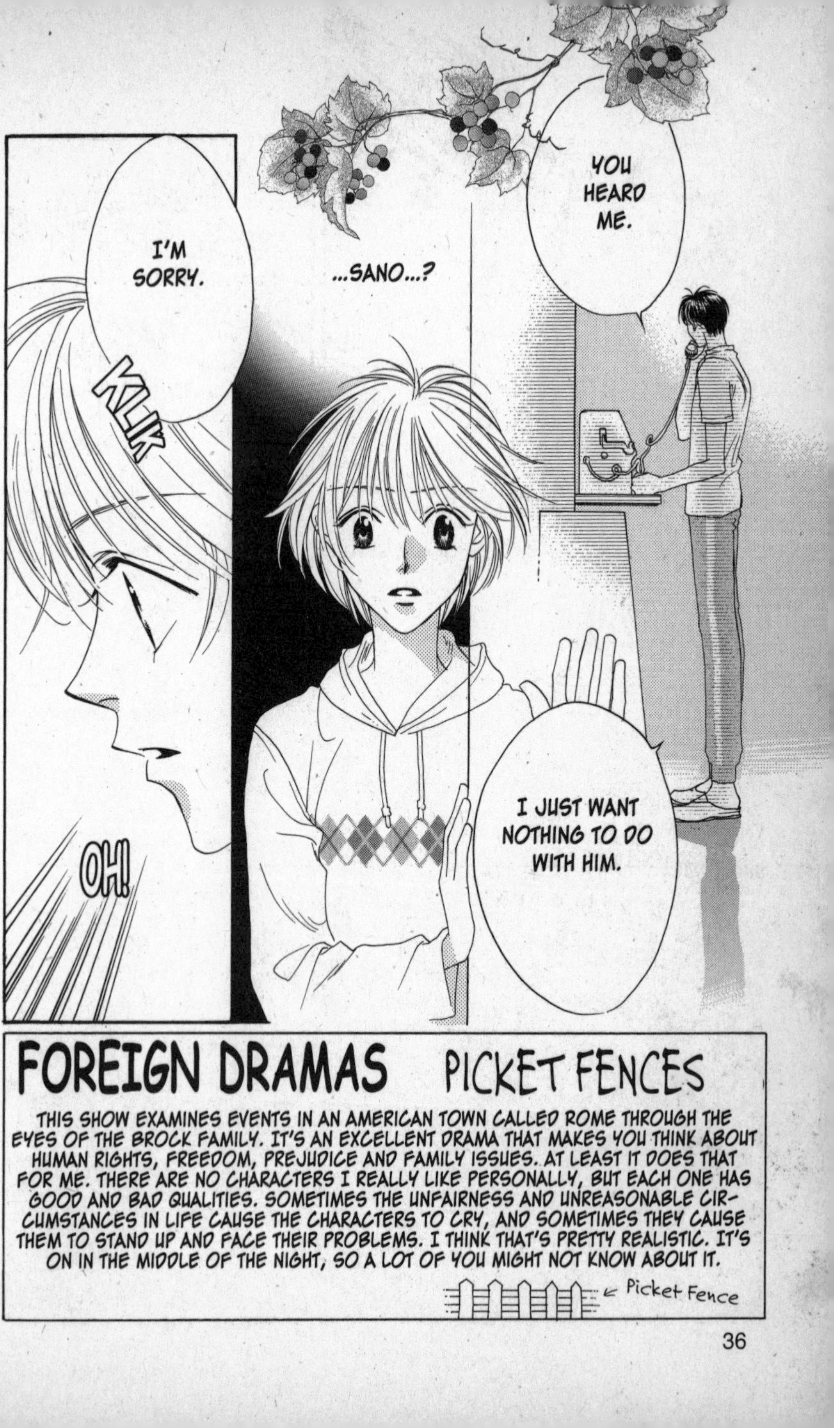
YOU HEARD ME.
...SANO...?
I JUST WANT NOTHING TO DO WITH HIM.
I'M SORRY.
KLIK
OH!

FOREIGN DRAMAS PICKET FENCES

THIS SHOW EXAMINES EVENTS IN AN AMERICAN TOWN CALLED ROME THROUGH THE EYES OF THE BROCK FAMILY. IT'S AN EXCELLENT DRAMA THAT MAKES YOU THINK ABOUT HUMAN RIGHTS, FREEDOM, PREJUDICE AND FAMILY ISSUES. AT LEAST IT DOES THAT FOR ME. THERE ARE NO CHARACTERS I REALLY LIKE PERSONALLY, BUT EACH ONE HAS GOOD AND BAD QUALITIES. SOMETIMES THE UNFAIRNESS AND UNREASONABLE CIRCUMSTANCES IN LIFE CAUSE THE CHARACTERS TO CRY, AND SOMETIMES THEY CAUSE THEM TO STAND UP AND FACE THEIR PROBLEMS. I THINK THAT'S PRETTY REALISTIC. IT'S ON IN THE MIDDLE OF THE NIGHT, SO A LOT OF YOU MIGHT NOT KNOW ABOUT IT.

← Picket Fence

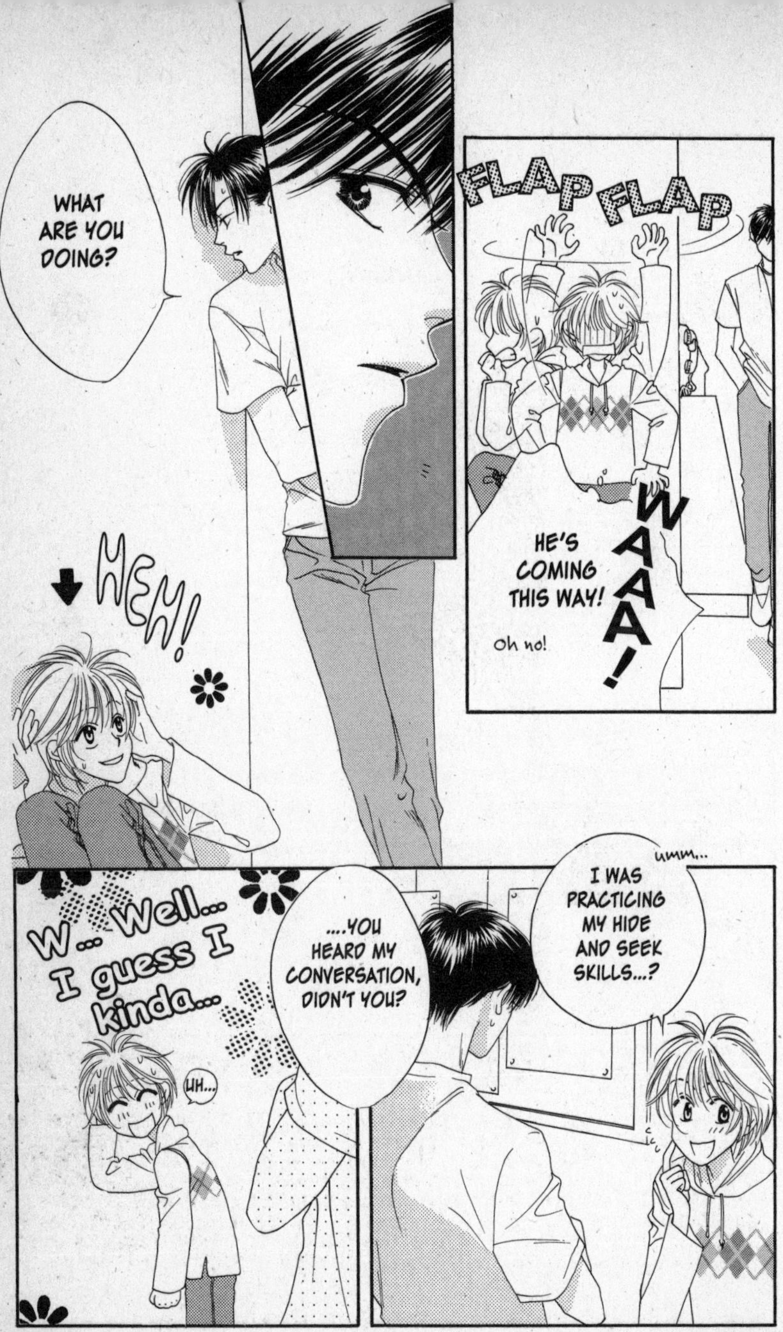
FLAP FLAP
HE'S COMING THIS WAY!
WAAA!
Oh no!
WHAT ARE YOU DOING?
HEH!
umm...
I WAS PRACTICING MY HIDE AND SEEK SKILLS...?
....YOU HEARD MY CONVERSATION, DIDN'T YOU?
W... Well... I guess I kinda...
UH...

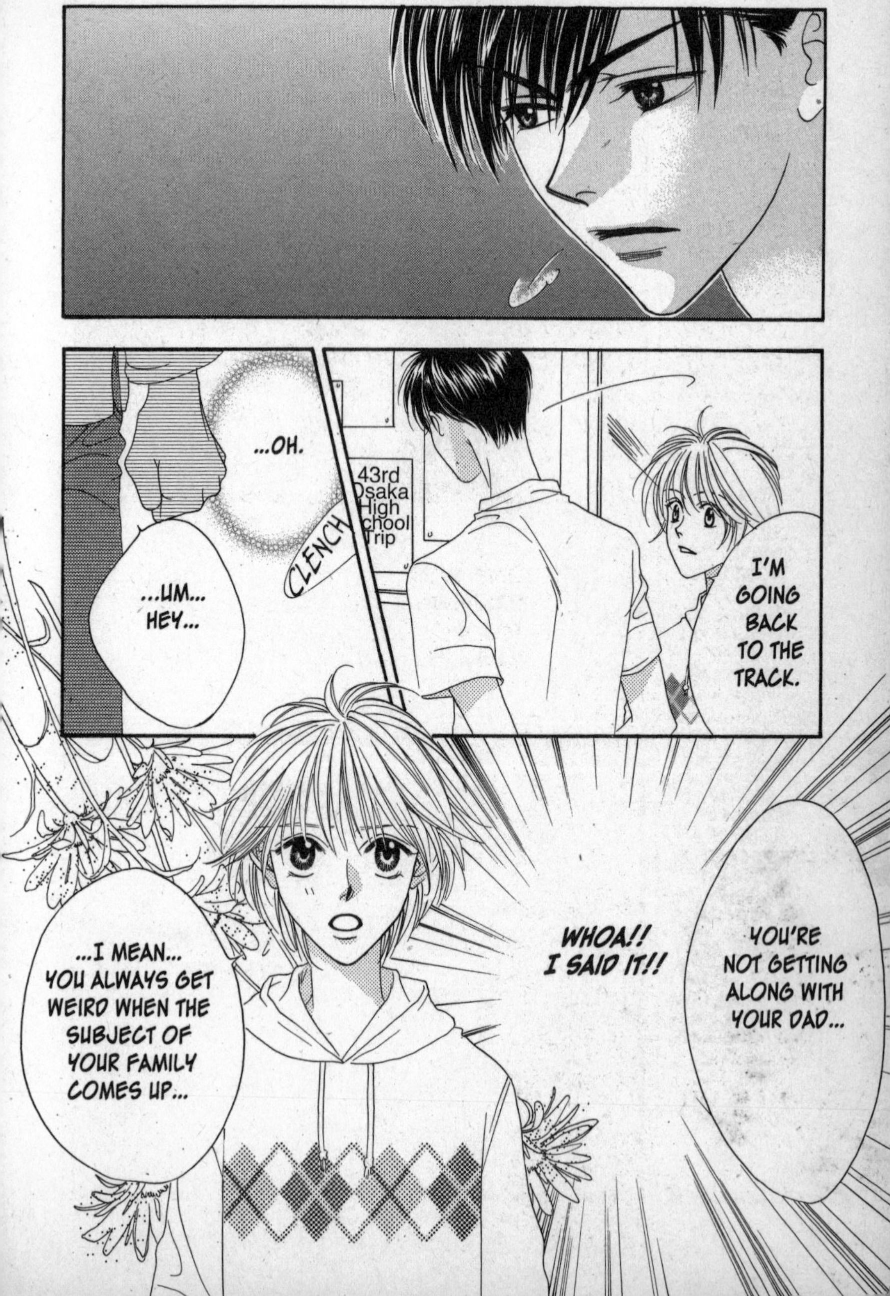
I'M GOING BACK TO THE TRACK.
CLENCH
...OH.
...UM... HEY...
YOU'RE NOT GETTING ALONG WITH YOUR DAD...
WHOA!! I SAID IT!!
...I MEAN... YOU ALWAYS GET WEIRD WHEN THE SUBJECT OF YOUR FAMILY COMES UP...

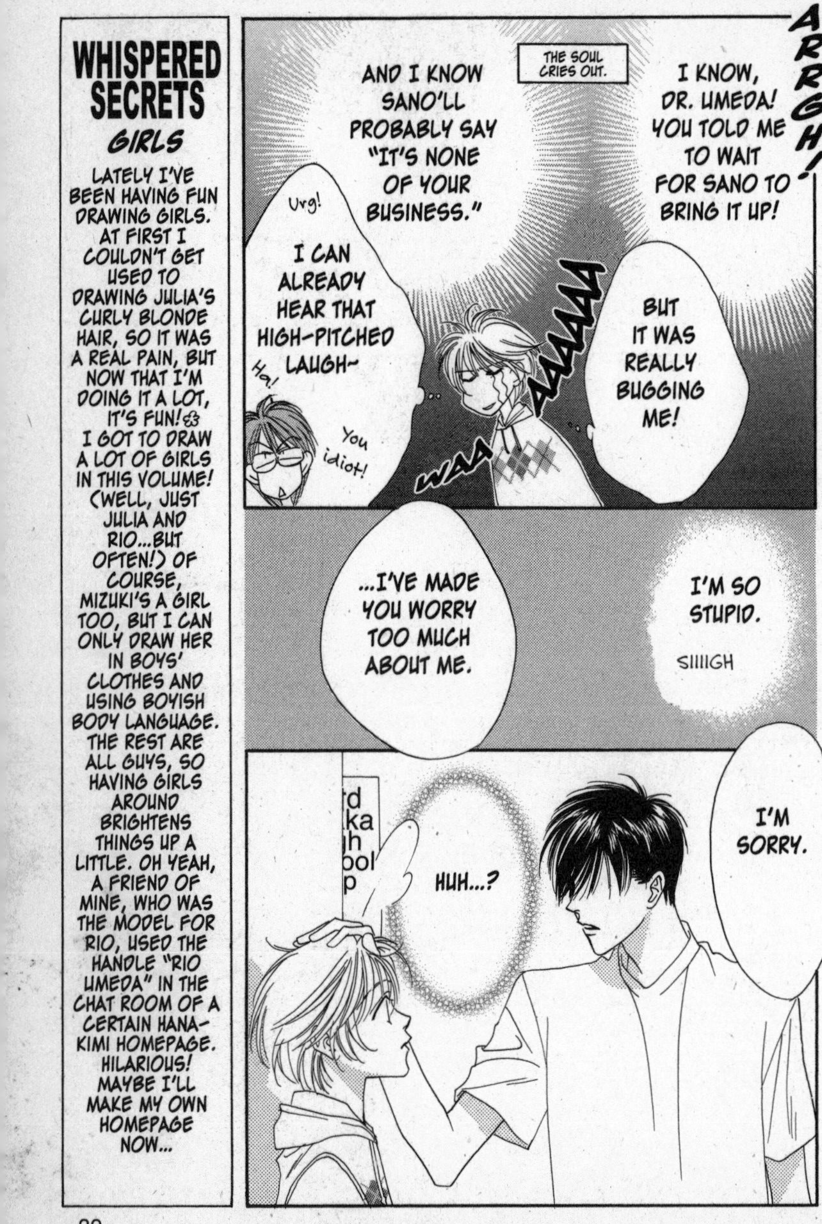
ARRGH!
I KNOW, DR. UMEDA! YOU TOLD ME TO WAIT FOR SANO TO BRING IT UP!
THE SOUL CRIES OUT.
AND I KNOW SANO'LL PROBABLY SAY "IT'S NONE OF YOUR BUSINESS."
BUT IT WAS REALLY BUGGING ME!
WAA AAAAAA
I CAN ALREADY HEAR THAT HIGH-PITCHED LAUGH~
Urg!
Ha!
You idiot!
I'M SO STUPID.
SIIIGH
...I'VE MADE YOU WORRY TOO MUCH ABOUT ME.
I'M SORRY.
HUH...?

WHISPERED SECRETS

GIRLS

LATELY I'VE BEEN HAVING FUN DRAWING GIRLS. AT FIRST I COULDN'T GET USED TO DRAWING JULIA'S CURLY BLONDE HAIR, SO IT WAS A REAL PAIN, BUT NOW THAT I'M DOING IT A LOT, IT'S FUN! ✿ I GOT TO DRAW A LOT OF GIRLS IN THIS VOLUME! (WELL, JUST JULIA AND RIO...BUT OFTEN!) OF COURSE, MIZUKI'S A GIRL TOO, BUT I CAN ONLY DRAW HER IN BOYS' CLOTHES AND USING BOYISH BODY LANGUAGE. THE REST ARE ALL GUYS, SO HAVING GIRLS AROUND BRIGHTENS THINGS UP A LITTLE. OH YEAH, A FRIEND OF MINE, WHO WAS THE MODEL FOR RIO, USED THE HANDLE "RIO UMEDA" IN THE CHAT ROOM OF A CERTAIN HANA-KIMI HOMEPAGE. HILARIOUS! MAYBE I'LL MAKE MY OWN HOMEPAGE NOW...

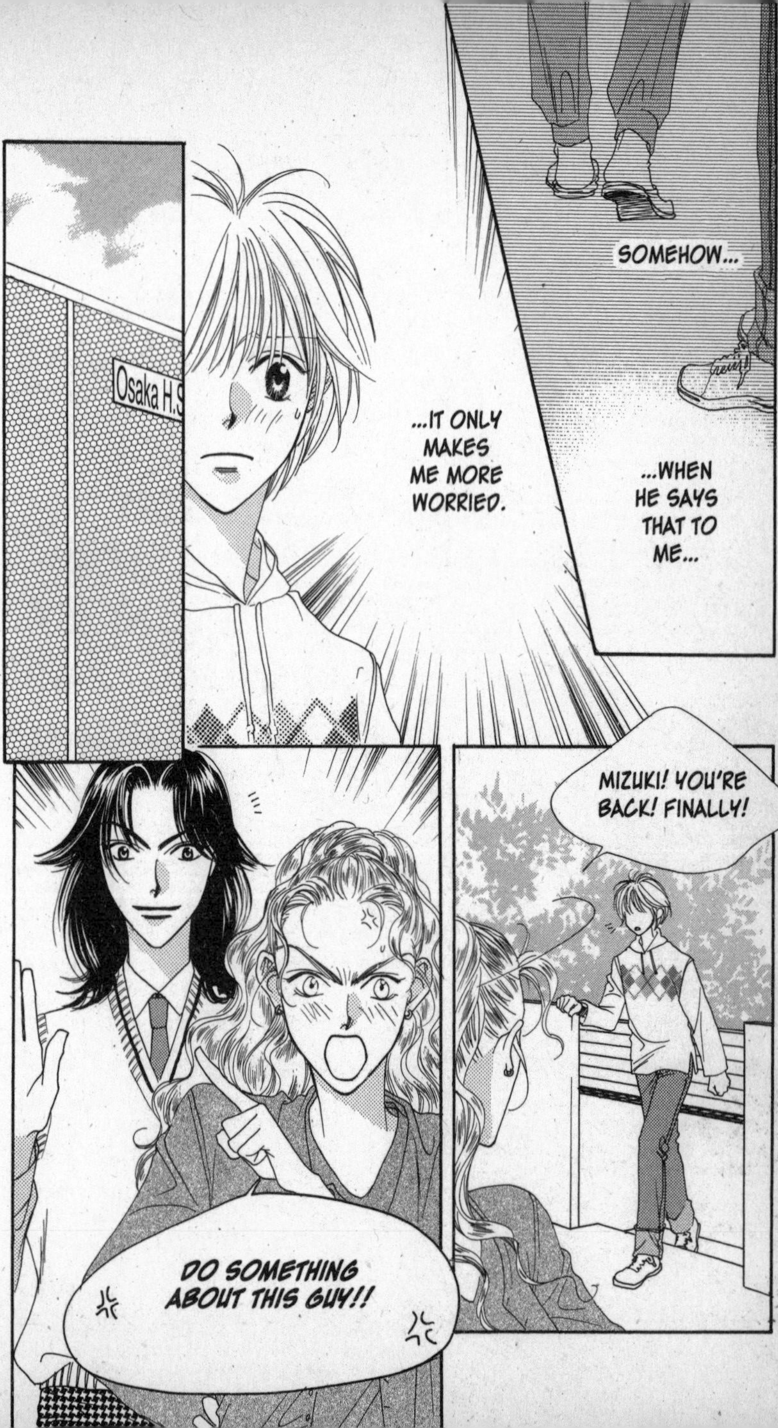
SOMEHOW...
...WHEN HE SAYS THAT TO ME...
Osaka H.S
...IT ONLY MAKES ME MORE WORRIED.
MIZUKI! YOU'RE BACK! FINALLY!
DO SOMETHING ABOUT THIS GUY!!

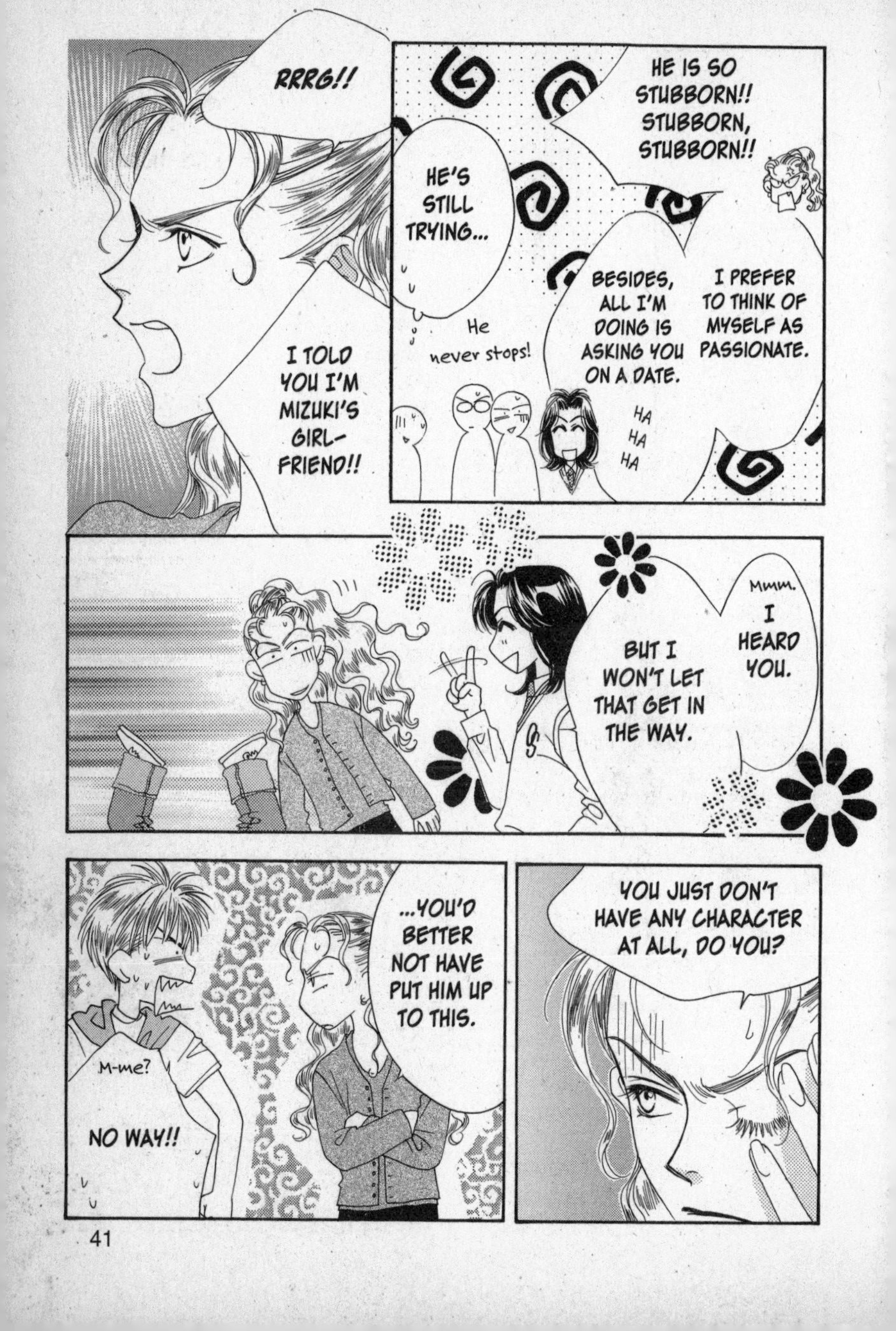
HE IS SO STUBBORN!! STUBBORN, STUBBORN!!
I PREFER TO THINK OF MYSELF AS PASSIONATE.
BESIDES, ALL I'M DOING IS ASKING YOU ON A DATE.
HA HA HA
HE'S STILL TRYING...
He never stops!
RRRG!!
I TOLD YOU I'M MIZUKI'S GIRL-FRIEND!!
Mmm. I HEARD YOU.
BUT I WON'T LET THAT GET IN THE WAY.
YOU JUST DON'T HAVE ANY CHARACTER AT ALL, DO YOU?
...YOU'D BETTER NOT HAVE PUT HIM UP TO THIS.
M-me?
NO WAY!!

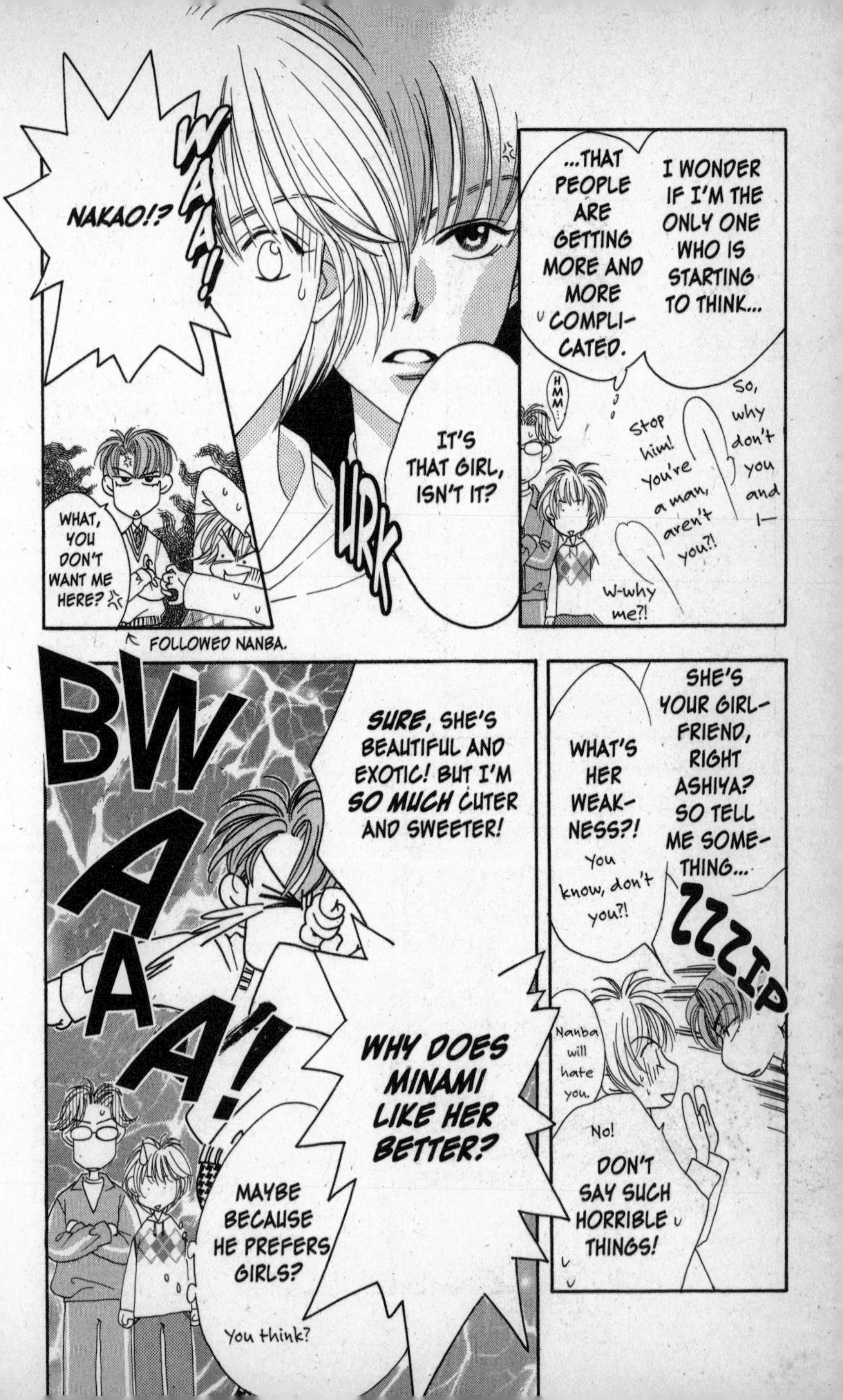

I WONDER IF I'M THE ONLY ONE WHO IS STARTING TO THINK...
...THAT PEOPLE ARE GETTING MORE AND MORE COMPLICATED.
HMM...
So, why don't you and I—
Stop him! You're a man, aren't you?!
W-why me?!
IT'S THAT GIRL, ISN'T IT?
URK
WAAA!
NAKAO!?
WHAT, YOU DON'T WANT ME HERE?
FOLLOWED NANBA.
SHE'S YOUR GIRLFRIEND, RIGHT ASHIYA? SO TELL ME SOMETHING...
WHAT'S HER WEAKNESS?!
You know, don't you?!
ZZZIP
Nanba will hate you.
No!
DON'T SAY SUCH HORRIBLE THINGS!
SURE, SHE'S BEAUTIFUL AND EXOTIC! BUT I'M SO MUCH CUTER AND SWEETER!
BWAAA!
WHY DOES MINAMI LIKE HER BETTER?
MAYBE BECAUSE HE PREFERS GIRLS?
You think?

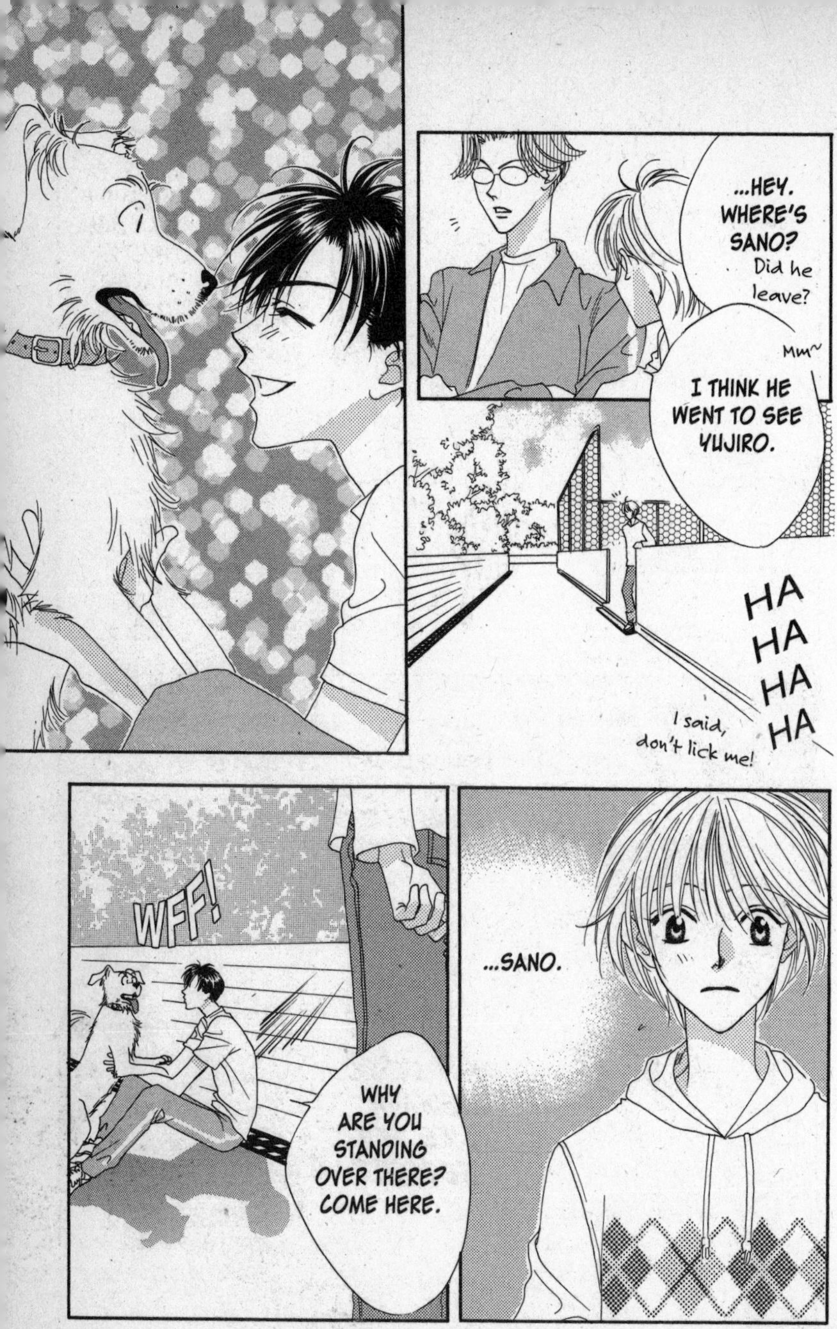
...HEY. WHERE'S SANO?
Did he leave?
Mm~
I THINK HE WENT TO SEE YUJIRO.
HA HA HA HA
I said, don't lick me!
...SANO.
WFF!
WHY ARE YOU STANDING OVER THERE? COME HERE.

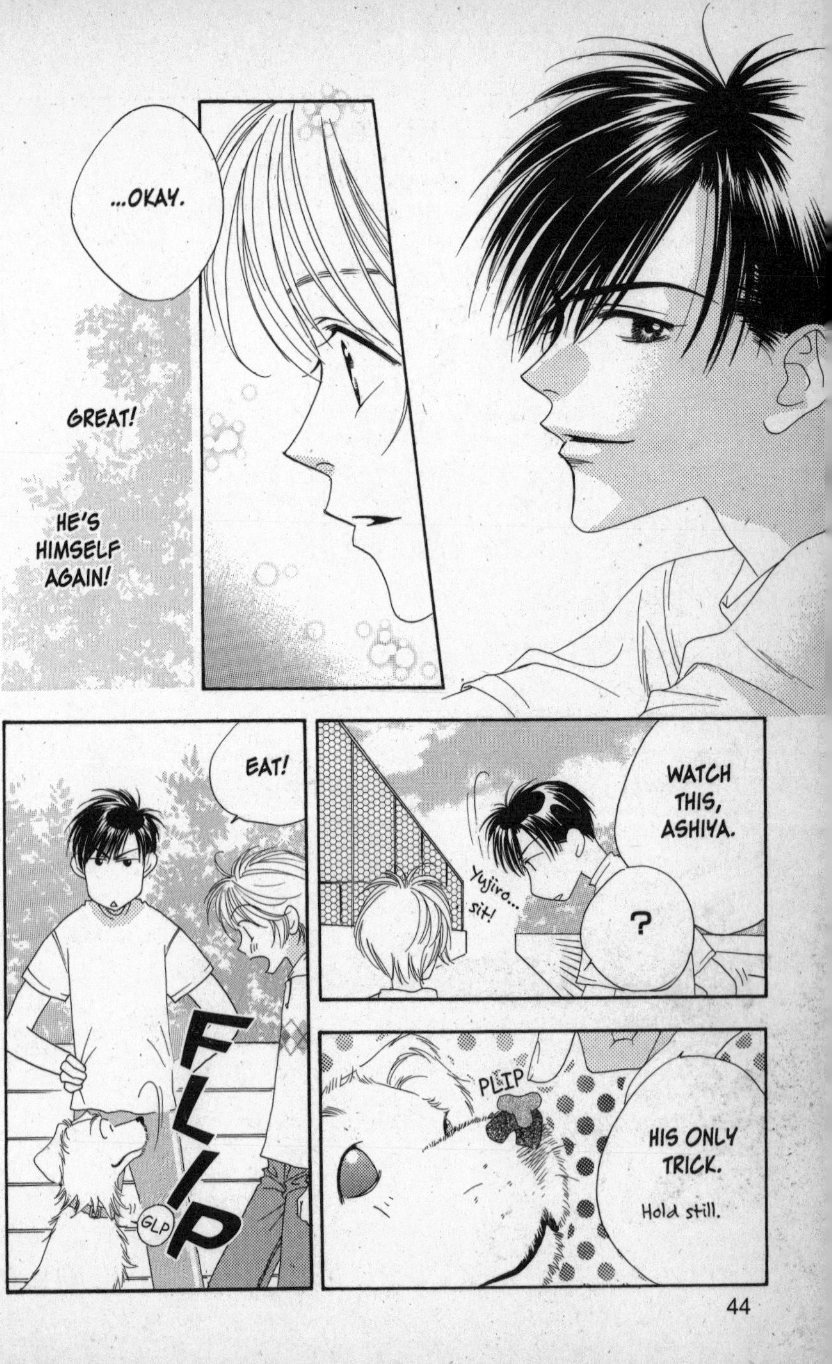
...OKAY.
GREAT!
HE'S HIMSELF AGAIN!
WATCH THIS, ASHIYA.
Yujiro... sit!
?
PLIP
HIS ONLY TRICK.
Hold still.
EAT!
FLIP
GLP

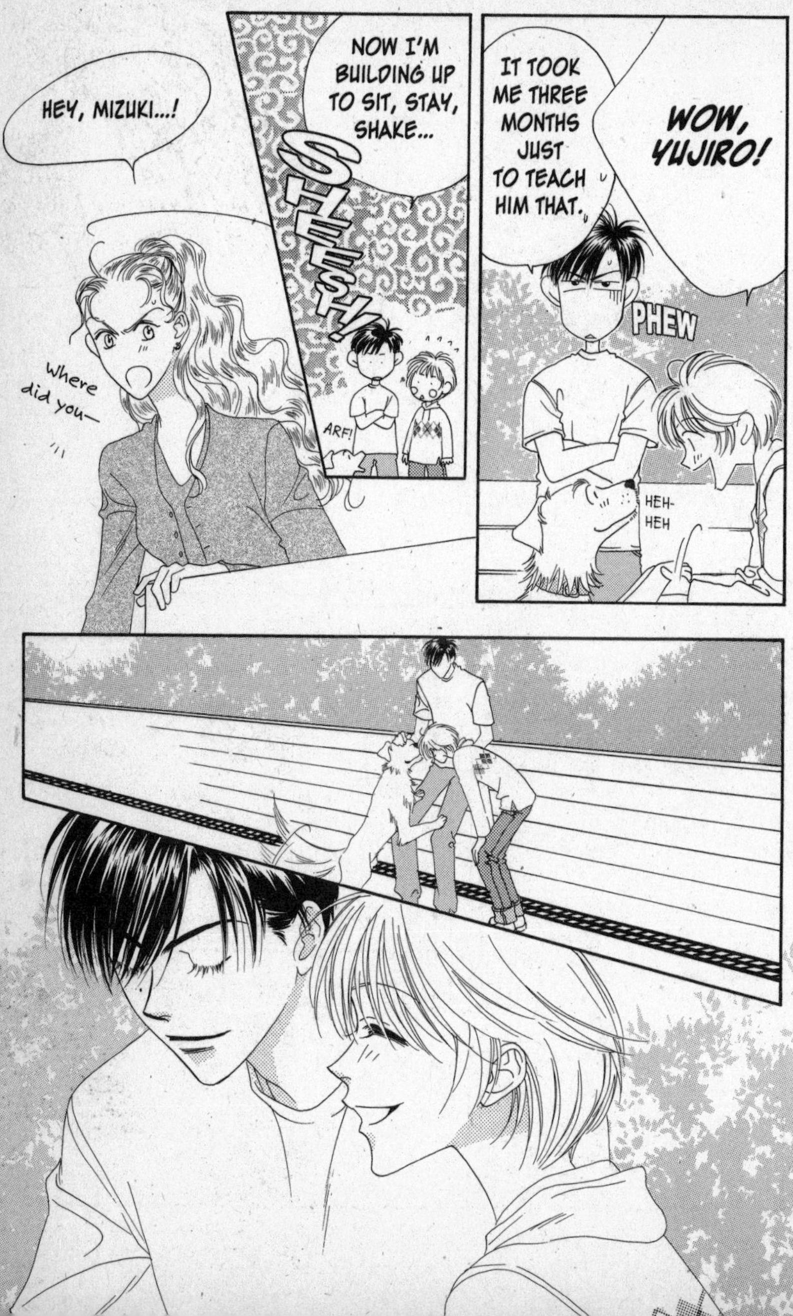
WOW, YUJIRO!
IT TOOK ME THREE MONTHS JUST TO TEACH HIM THAT.
PHEW
HEH-HEH
NOW I'M BUILDING UP TO SIT, STAY, SHAKE...
SHEESH!
ARF!
HEY, MIZUKI...!
Where did you—

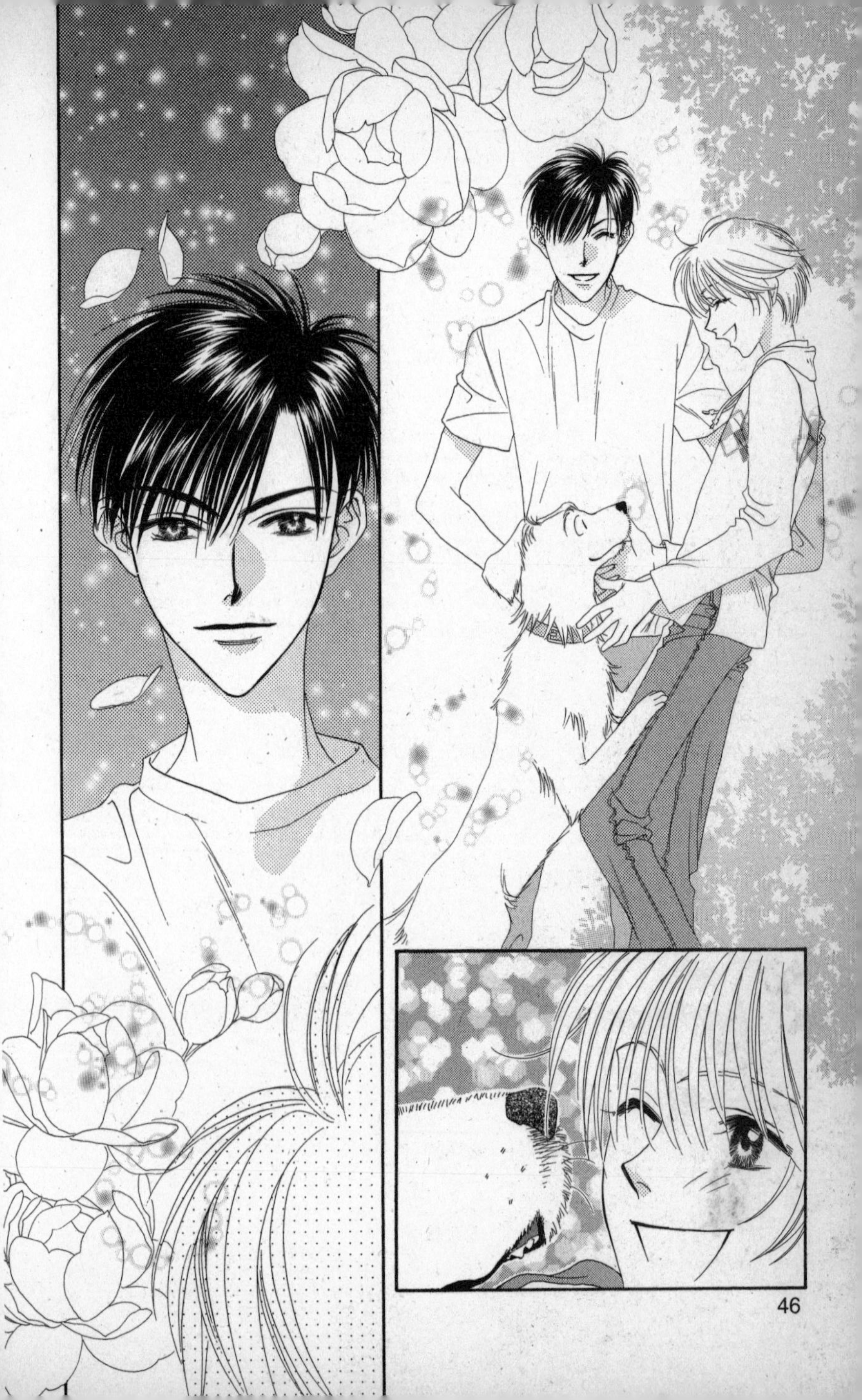

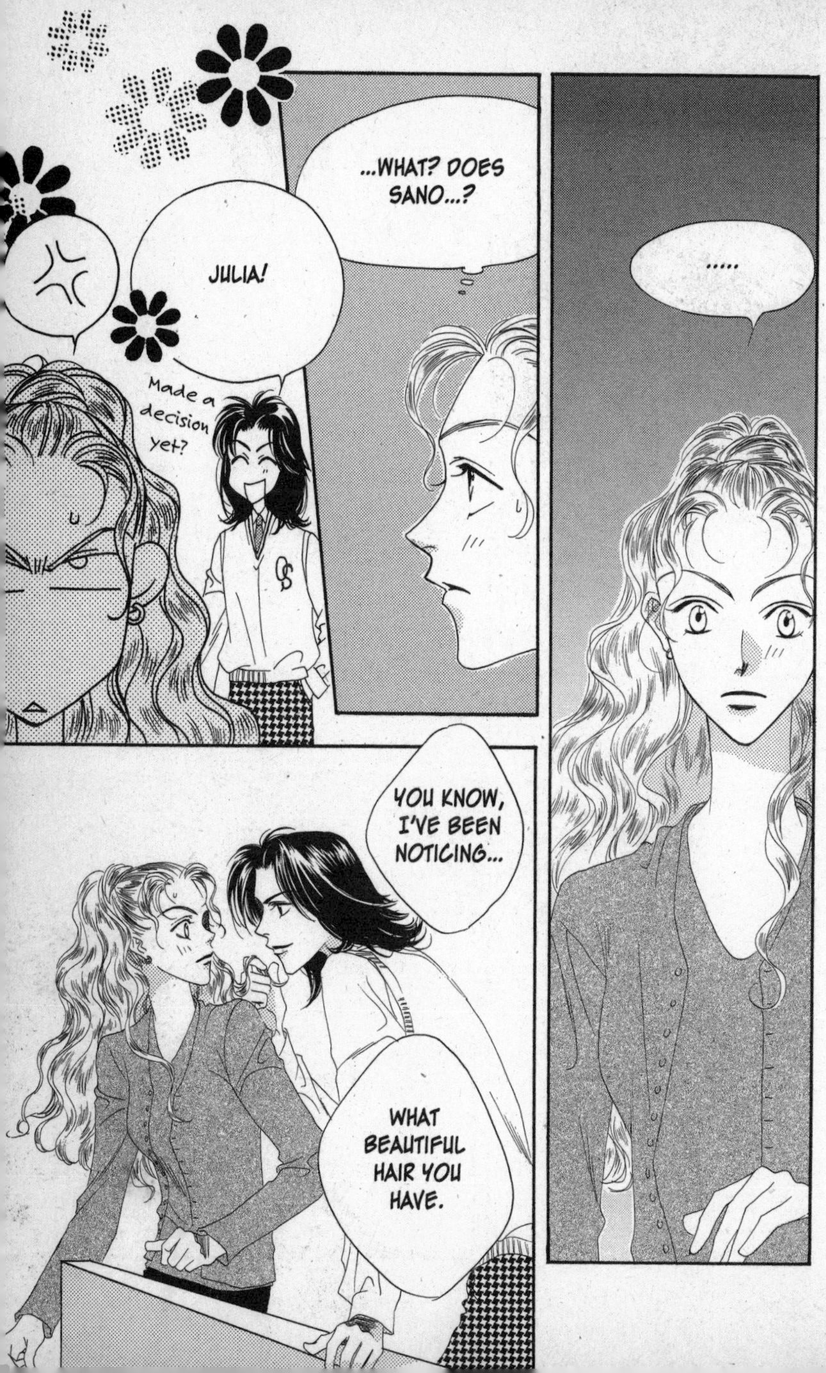
.....
...WHAT? DOES SANO...?
JULIA!
Made a decision yet?
YOU KNOW, I'VE BEEN NOTICING...
WHAT BEAUTIFUL HAIR YOU HAVE.

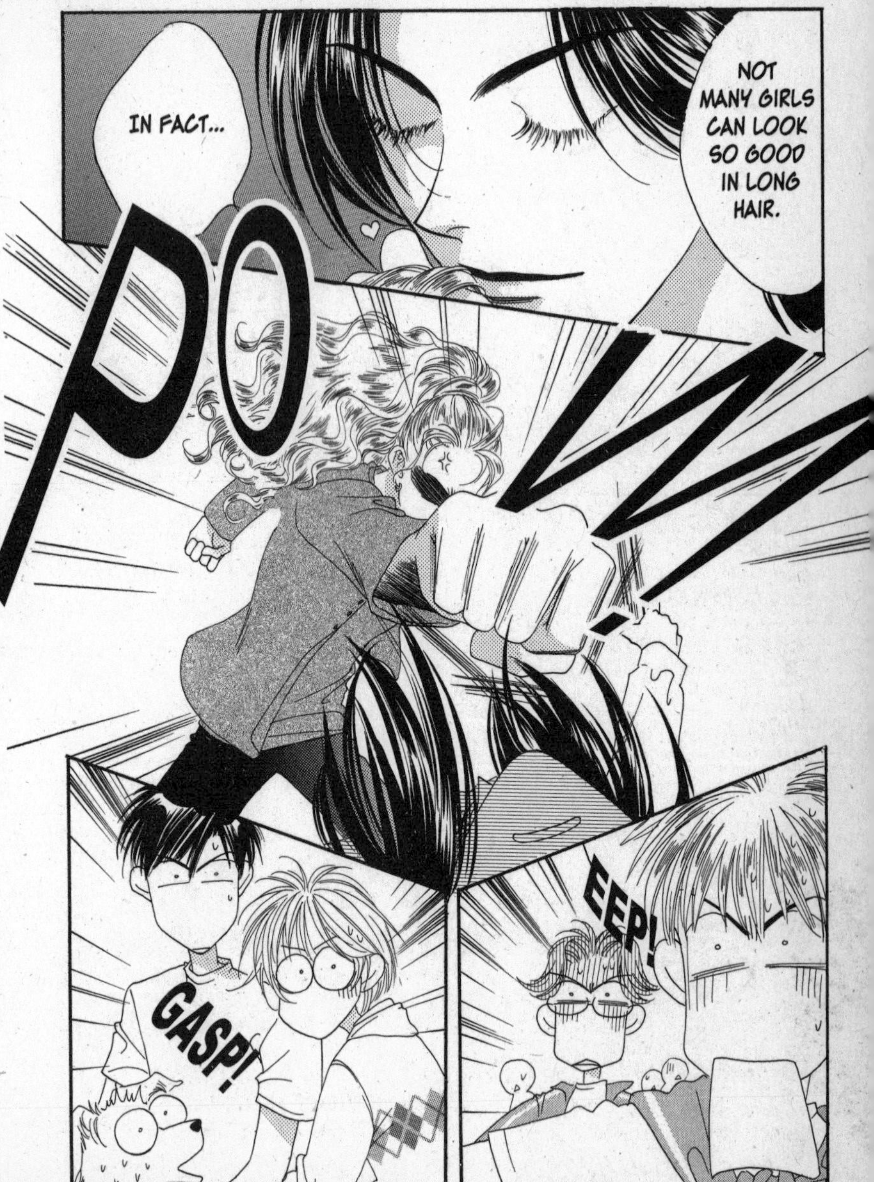
NOT MANY GIRLS CAN LOOK SO GOOD IN LONG HAIR.
IN FACT...
POW
EEP!
GASP!

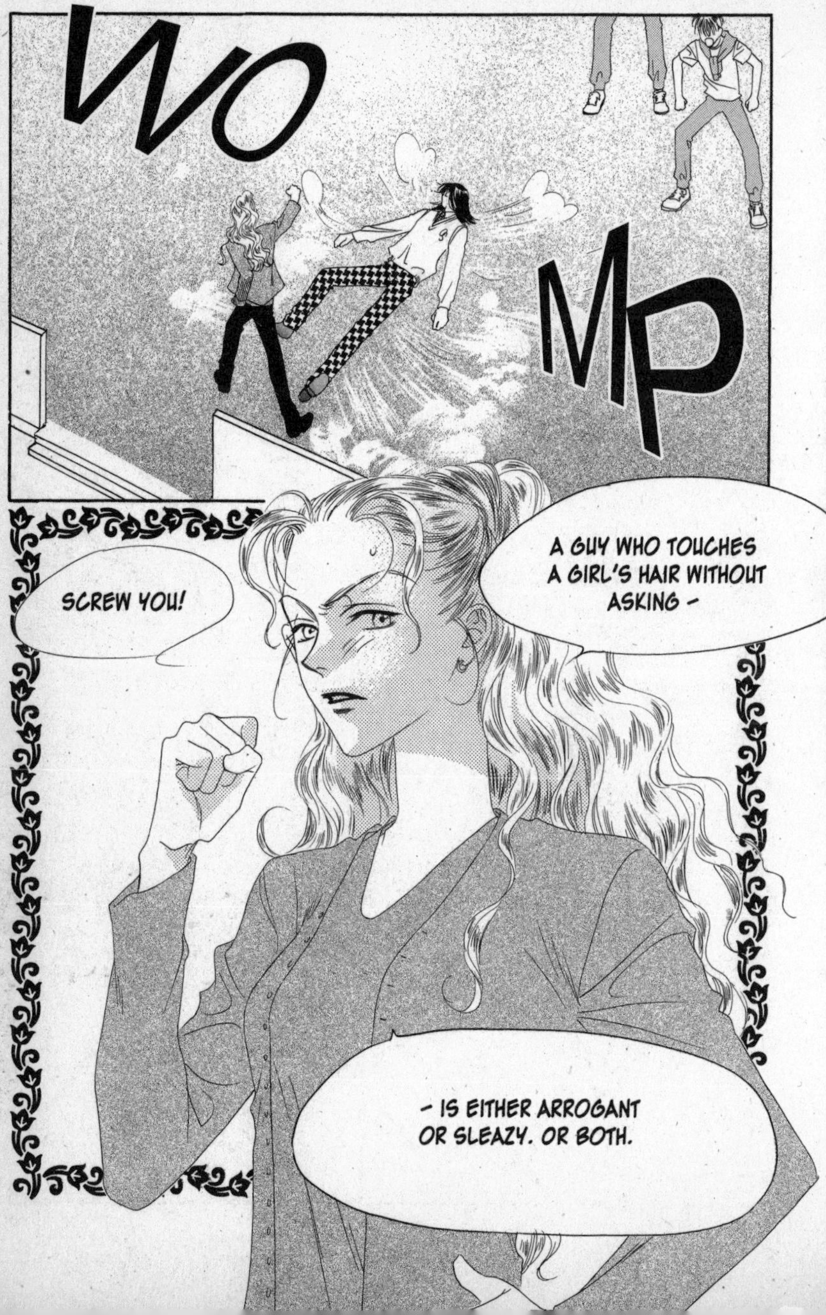
WOMP
A GUY WHO TOUCHES A GIRL'S HAIR WITHOUT ASKING -
SCREW YOU!
- IS EITHER ARROGANT OR SLEAZY. OR BOTH.

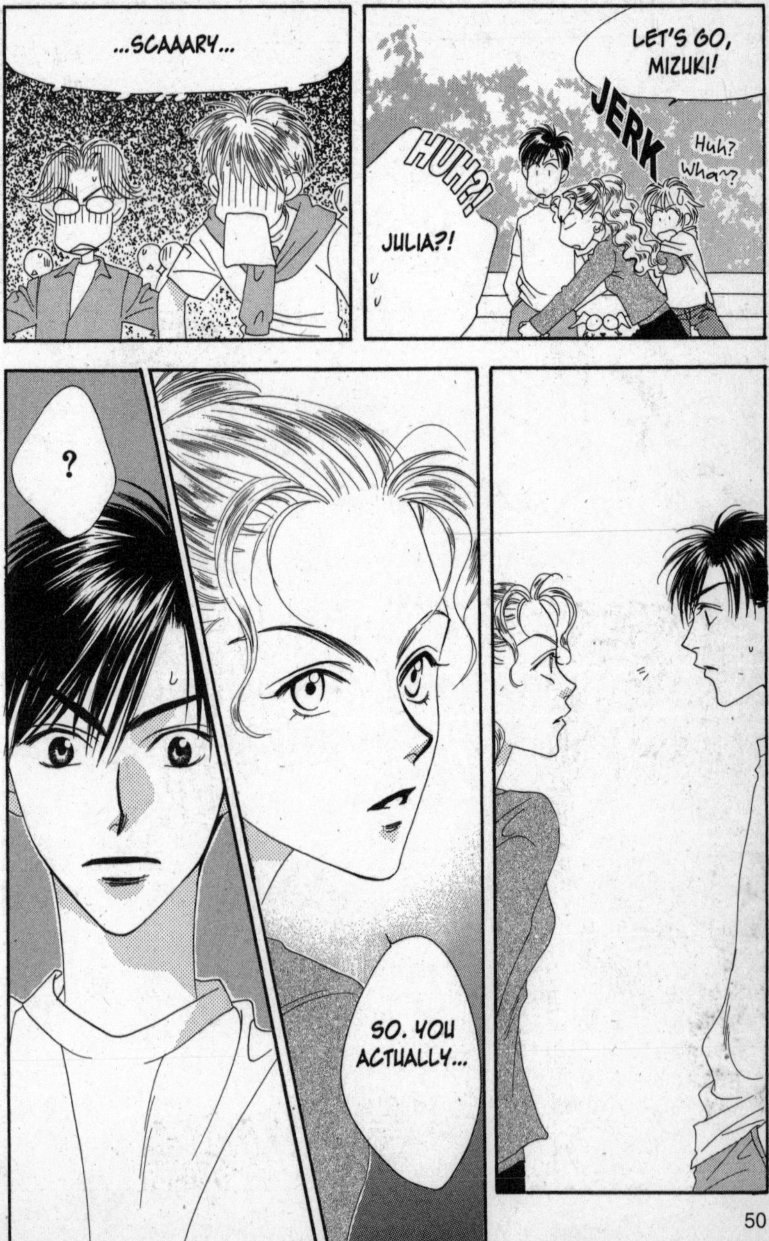
LET'S GO, MIZUKI!
JERK
Huh? Wha~?
HUH?!
JULIA?!
...SCAAARY...
?
SO. YOU ACTUALLY...

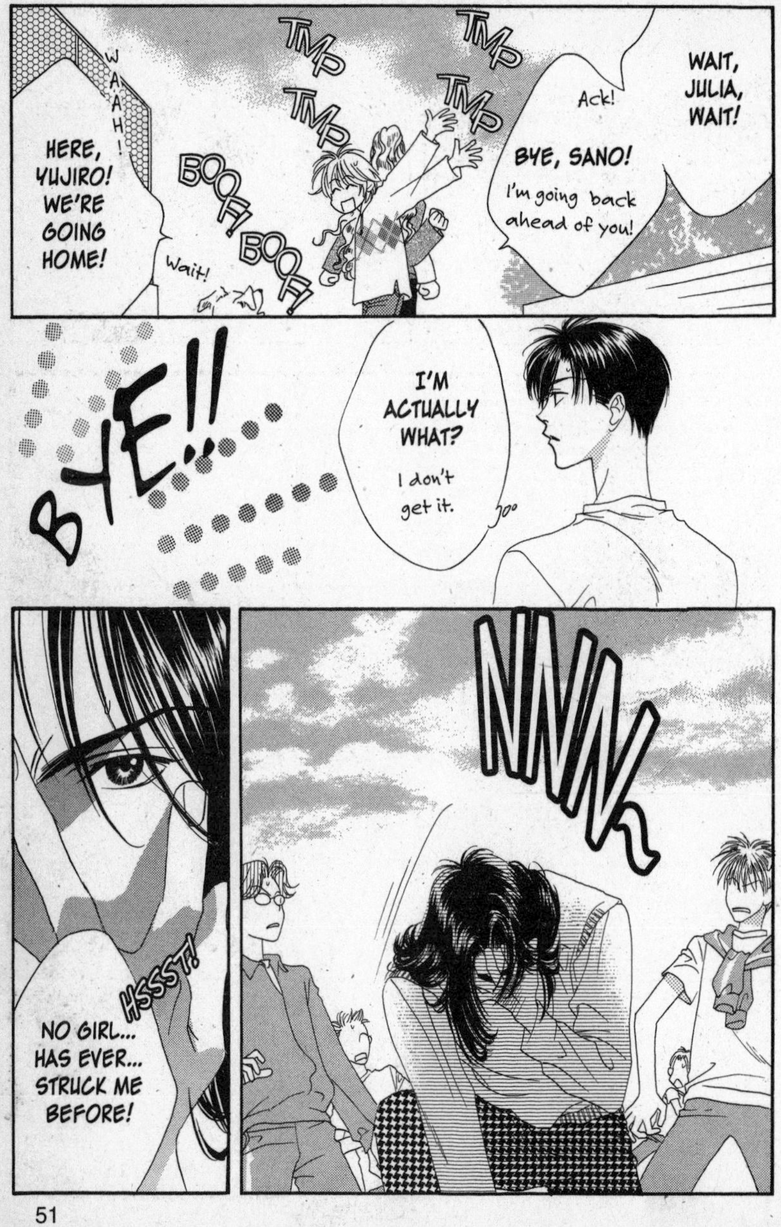
WAIT, JULIA, WAIT!
Ack!
BYE, SANO!
I'm going back ahead of you!
TMP
TMP
TMP
TMP
BOOF! BOOF!
Wait!
HERE, YUJIRO! WE'RE GOING HOME!
WAAAH!
I'M ACTUALLY WHAT?
I don't get it.
BYE!!
NNN
HSSST!
NO GIRL... HAS EVER... STRUCK ME BEFORE!

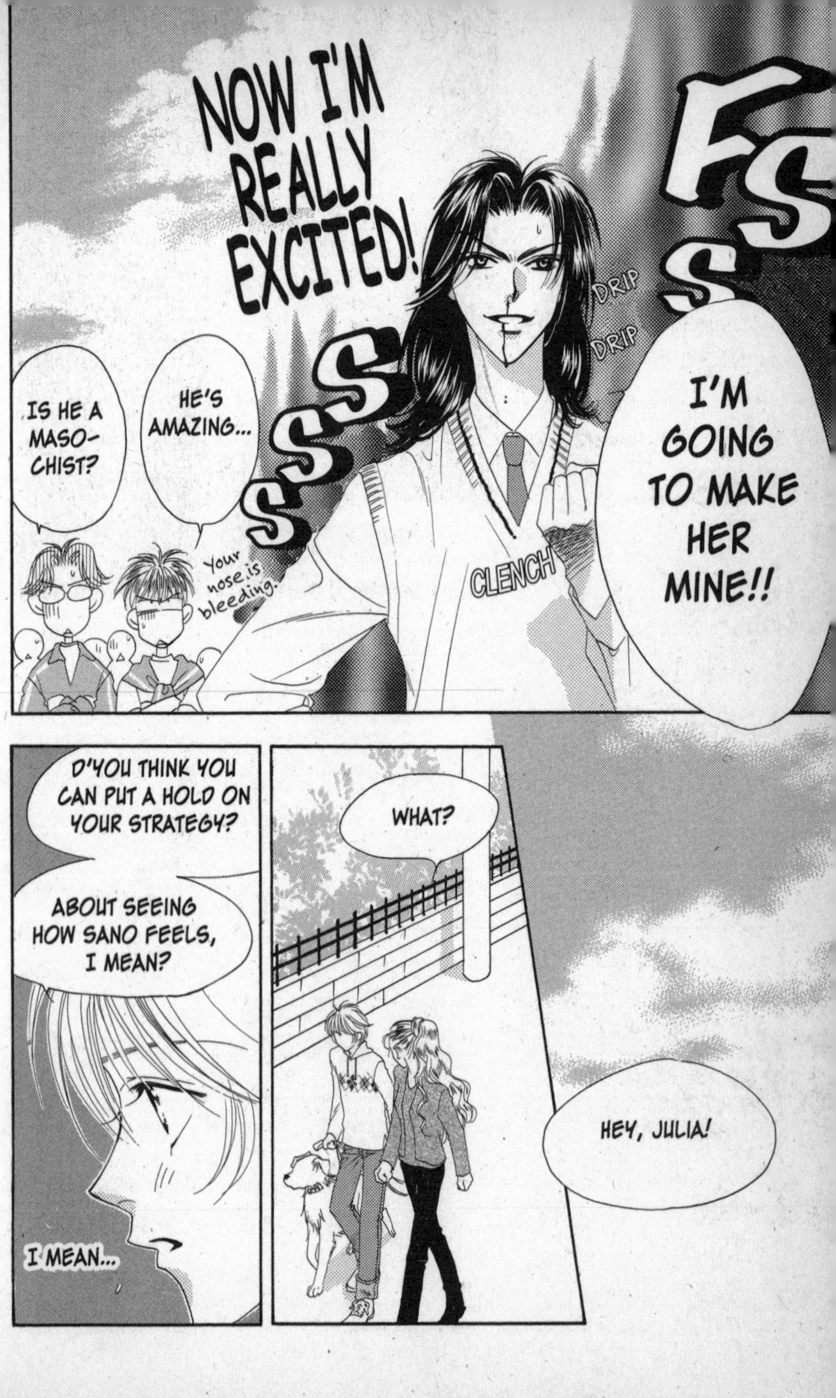
FSSS
NOW I'M REALLY EXCITED!
DRIP
DRIP
I'M GOING TO MAKE HER MINE!!
CLENCH
SSSS
HE'S AMAZING...
IS HE A MASO-CHIST?
Your nose is bleeding.
HEY, JULIA!
WHAT?
D'YOU THINK YOU CAN PUT A HOLD ON YOUR STRATEGY?
ABOUT SEEING HOW SANO FEELS, I MEAN?
I MEAN...

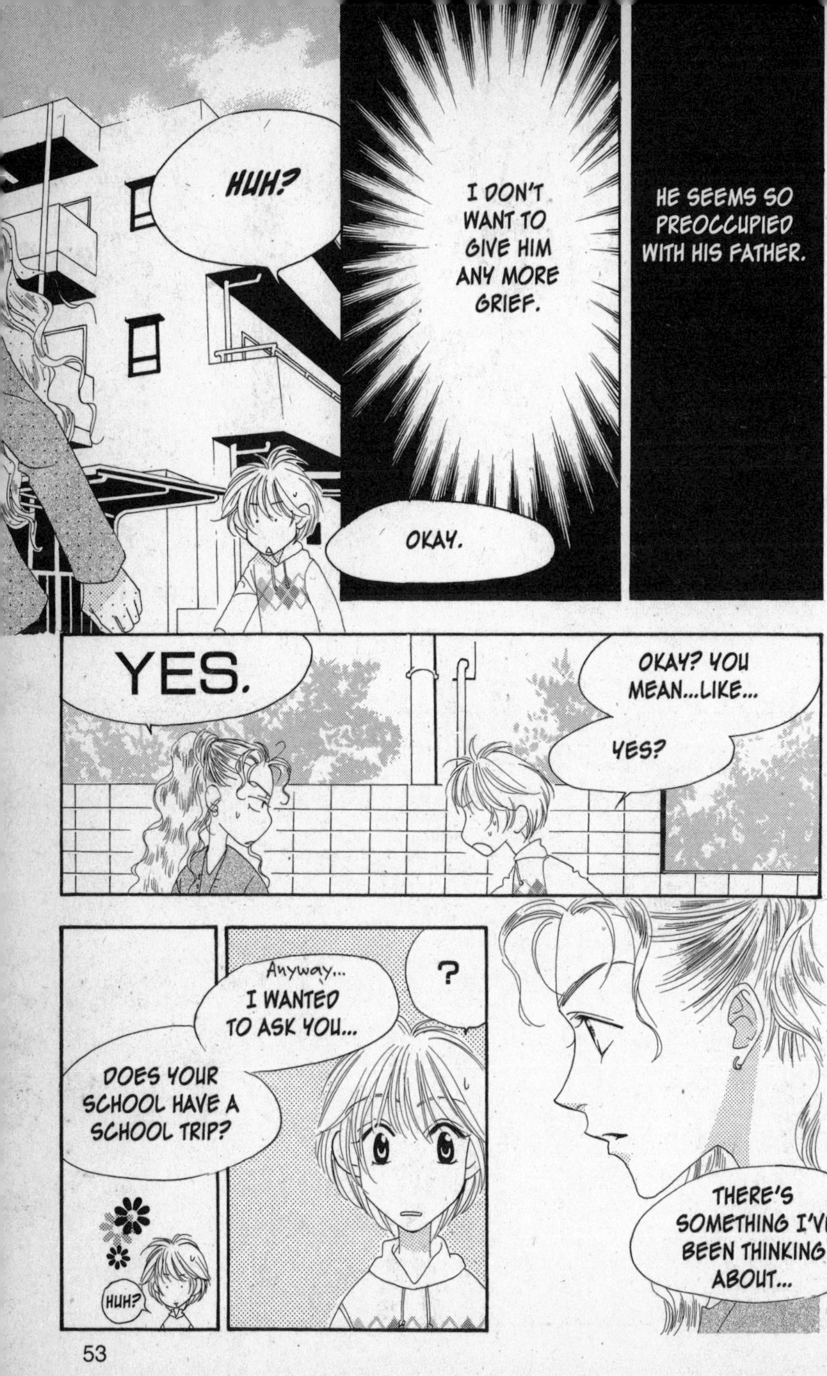
HE SEEMS SO PREOCCUPIED WITH HIS FATHER.
I DON'T WANT TO GIVE HIM ANY MORE GRIEF.
OKAY.
HUH?
OKAY? YOU MEAN...LIKE...
YES?
YES.
THERE'S SOMETHING I'VE BEEN THINKING ABOUT...
?
Anyway... I WANTED TO ASK YOU...
DOES YOUR SCHOOL HAVE A SCHOOL TRIP?
HUH?

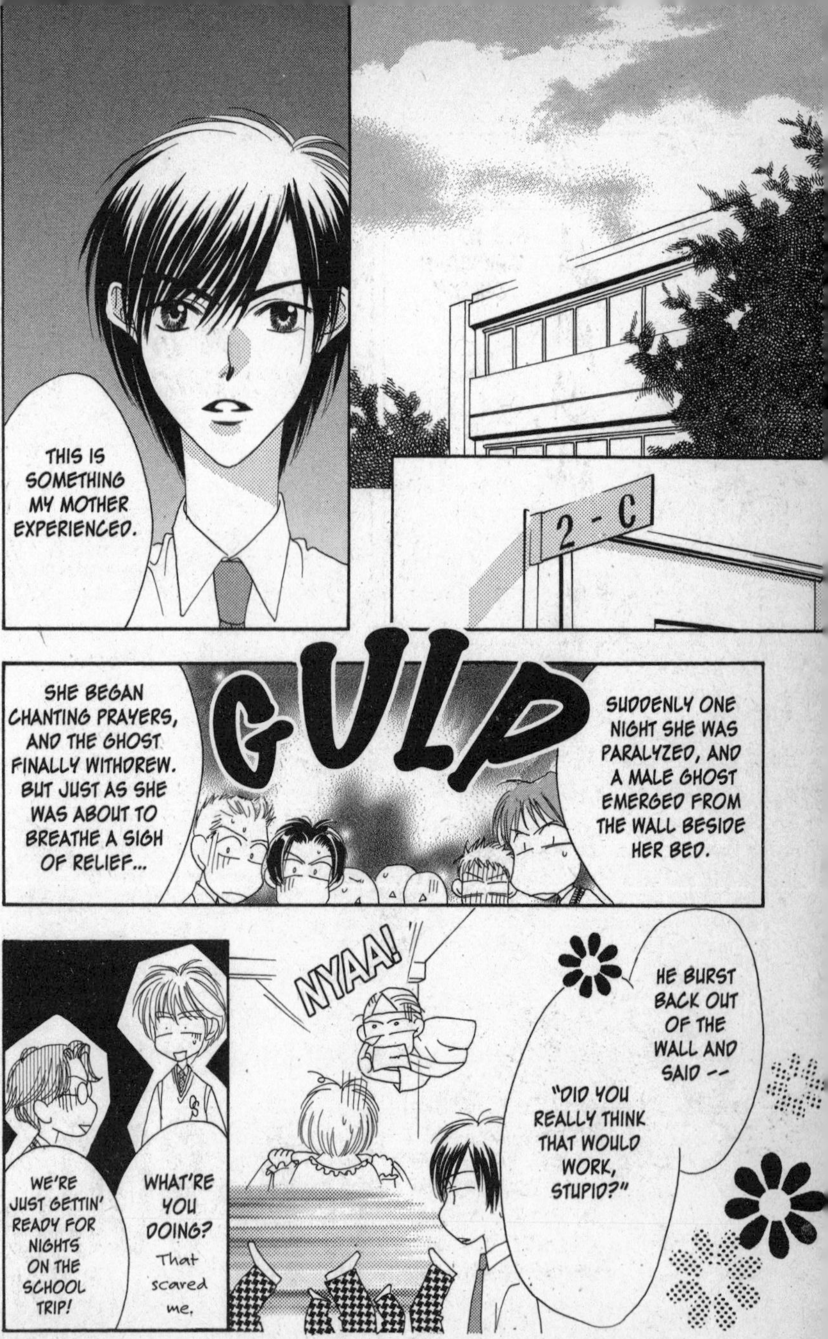
2-C
THIS IS SOMETHING MY MOTHER EXPERIENCED.
SUDDENLY ONE NIGHT SHE WAS PARALYZED, AND A MALE GHOST EMERGED FROM THE WALL BESIDE HER BED.
GULP
SHE BEGAN CHANTING PRAYERS, AND THE GHOST FINALLY WITHDREW. BUT JUST AS SHE WAS ABOUT TO BREATHE A SIGH OF RELIEF...
HE BURST BACK OUT OF THE WALL AND SAID --
"DID YOU REALLY THINK THAT WOULD WORK, STUPID?"
NYAA!
WHAT'RE YOU DOING? That scared me.
WE'RE JUST GETTIN' READY FOR NIGHTS ON THE SCHOOL TRIP!

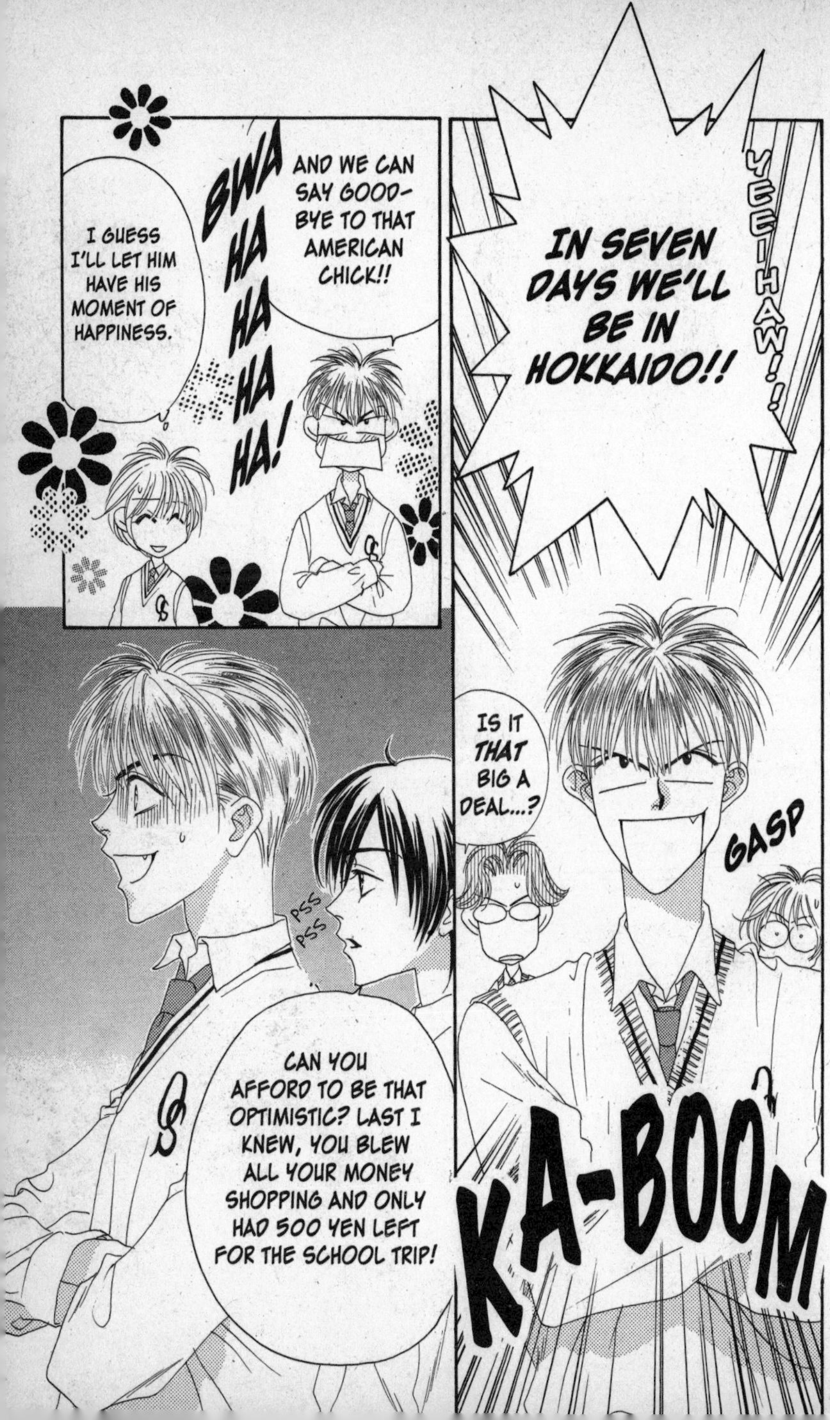
IN SEVEN DAYS WE'LL BE IN HOKKAIDO!!
YEEHAW!!
IS IT THAT BIG A DEAL...?
GASP
KA-BOOM
AND WE CAN SAY GOOD-BYE TO THAT AMERICAN CHICK!!
BWAHAHAHAHAHA!
I GUESS I'LL LET HIM HAVE HIS MOMENT OF HAPPINESS.
PSS PSS
CAN YOU AFFORD TO BE THAT OPTIMISTIC? LAST I KNEW, YOU BLEW ALL YOUR MONEY SHOPPING AND ONLY HAD 500 YEN LEFT FOR THE SCHOOL TRIP!

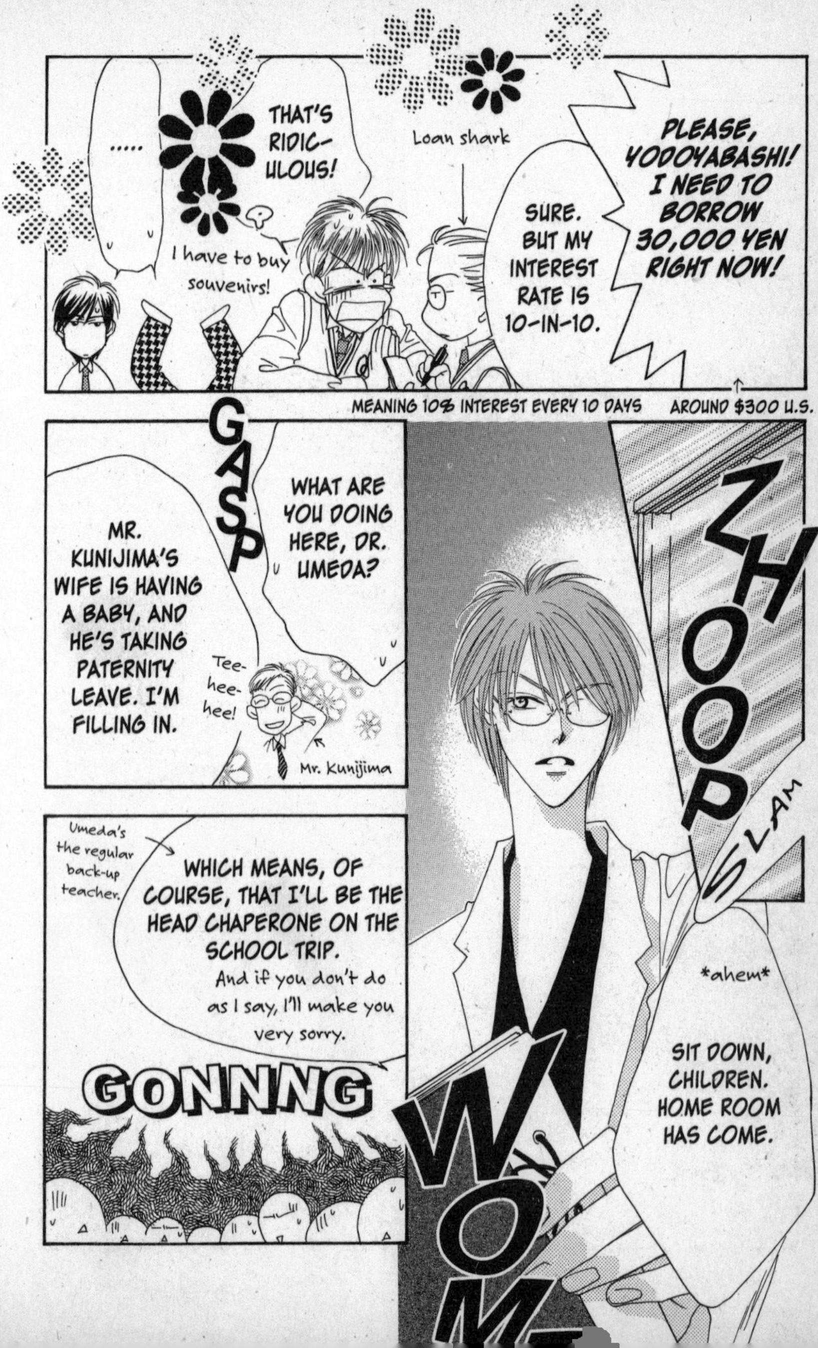
PLEASE, YODOYABASHI! I NEED TO BORROW 30,000 YEN RIGHT NOW!
SURE. BUT MY INTEREST RATE IS 10-IN-10.
Loan shark
THAT'S RIDICULOUS!
I have to buy souvenirs!
.....
AROUND $300 U.S.
MEANING 10% INTEREST EVERY 10 DAYS
ZHOOP
SLAM
ahem
SIT DOWN, CHILDREN. HOME ROOM HAS COME.
WOMP
GASP
WHAT ARE YOU DOING HERE, DR. UMEDA?
MR. KUNIJIMA'S WIFE IS HAVING A BABY, AND HE'S TAKING PATERNITY LEAVE. I'M FILLING IN.
Tee-hee-hee!
Mr. Kunijima
WHICH MEANS, OF COURSE, THAT I'LL BE THE HEAD CHAPERONE ON THE SCHOOL TRIP.
And if you don't do as I say, I'll make you very sorry.
Umeda's the regular back-up teacher.
GONNNG

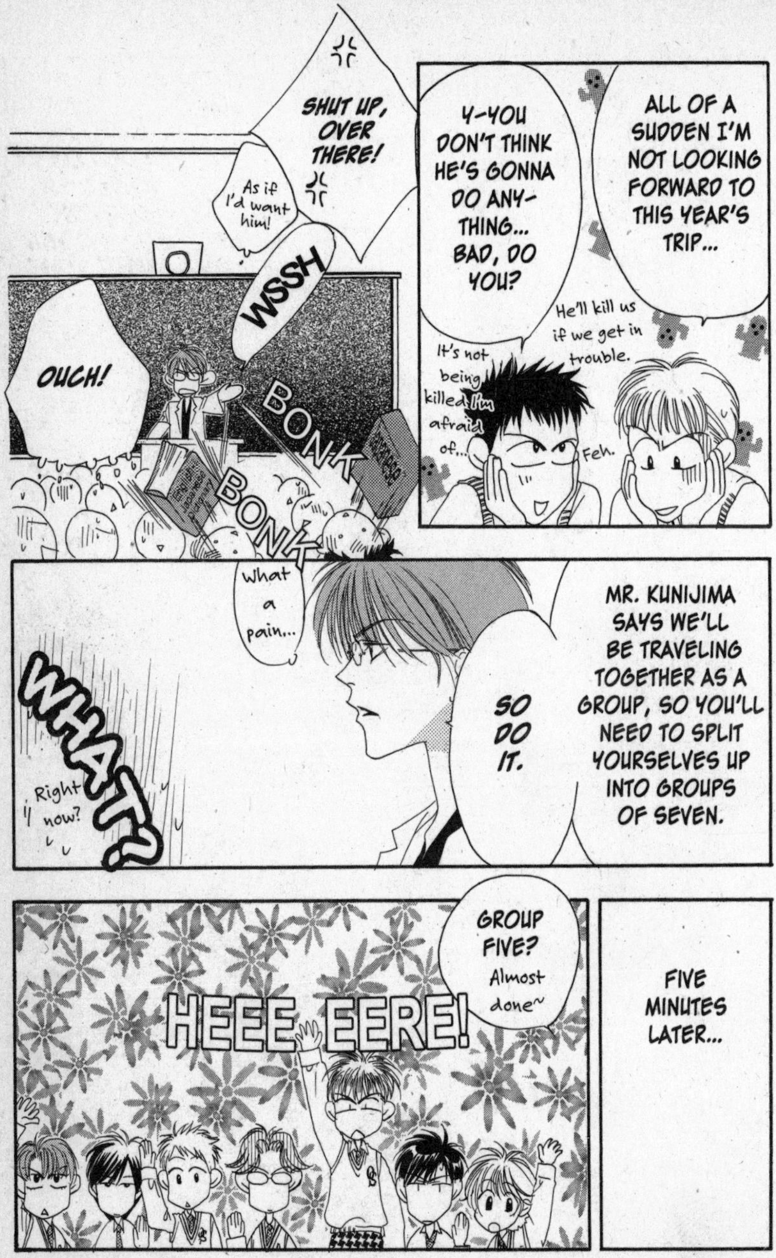
ALL OF A SUDDEN I'M NOT LOOKING FORWARD TO THIS YEAR'S TRIP...
Y-YOU DON'T THINK HE'S GONNA DO ANYTHING... BAD, DO YOU?
He'll kill us if we get in trouble.
Feh.
It's not being killed I'm afraid of...
SHUT UP, OVER THERE!
As if I'd want him!
WSSH
BONK
BONK
OUCH!
MR. KUNIJIMA SAYS WE'LL BE TRAVELING TOGETHER AS A GROUP, SO YOU'LL NEED TO SPLIT YOURSELVES UP INTO GROUPS OF SEVEN.
SO DO IT.
What a pain...
WHAT?
Right now?
FIVE MINUTES LATER...
GROUP FIVE? Almost done~
HEEE EERE!

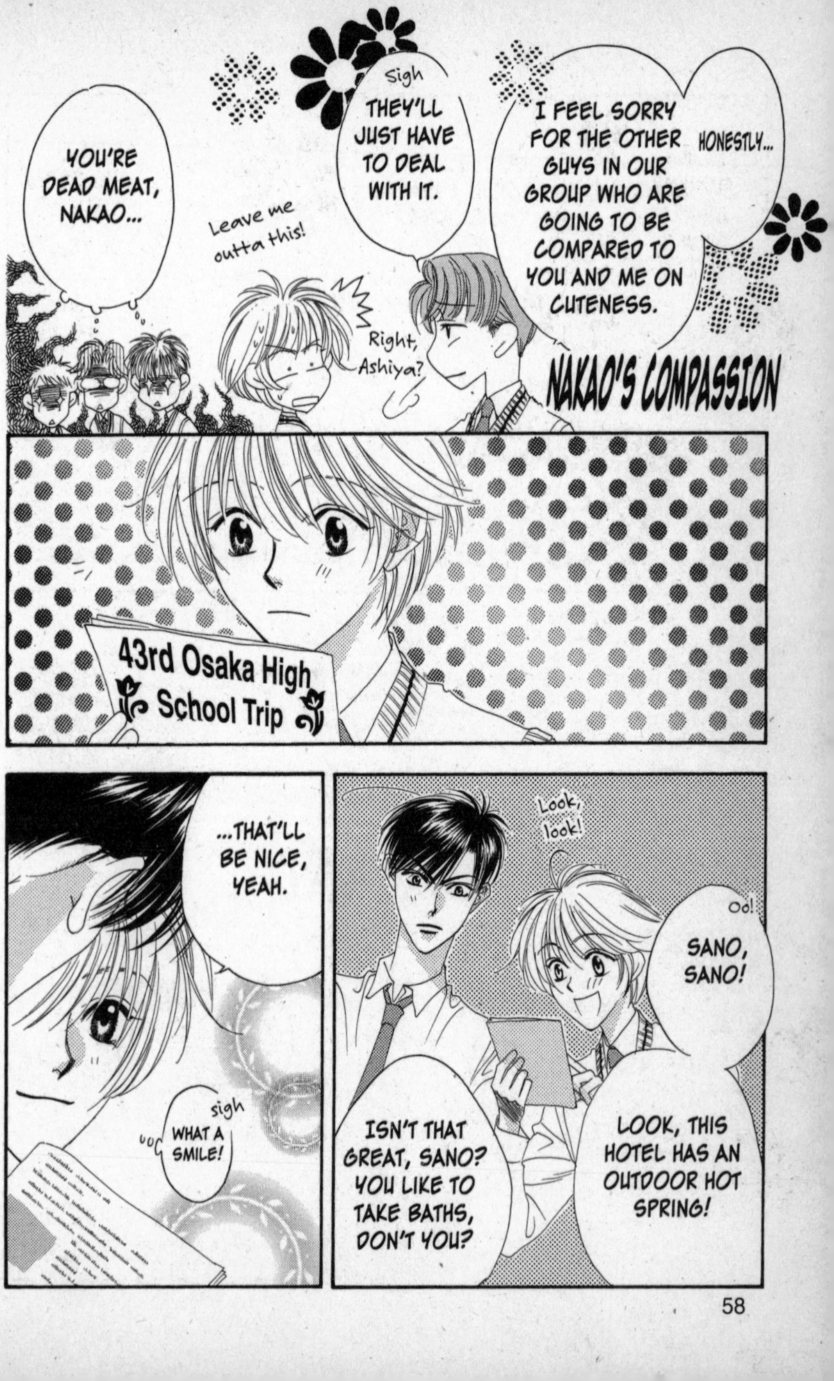
HONESTLY...
I FEEL SORRY FOR THE OTHER GUYS IN OUR GROUP WHO ARE GOING TO BE COMPARED TO YOU AND ME ON CUTENESS.
Sigh
THEY'LL JUST HAVE TO DEAL WITH IT.
Right, Ashiya?
Leave me outta this!
YOU'RE DEAD MEAT, NAKAO...
NAKAO'S COMPASSION
43rd Osaka High School Trip
Look, look!
Oo!
SANO, SANO!
LOOK, THIS HOTEL HAS AN OUTDOOR HOT SPRING!
ISN'T THAT GREAT, SANO? YOU LIKE TO TAKE BATHS, DON'T YOU?
...THAT'LL BE NICE, YEAH.
sigh
WHAT A SMILE!

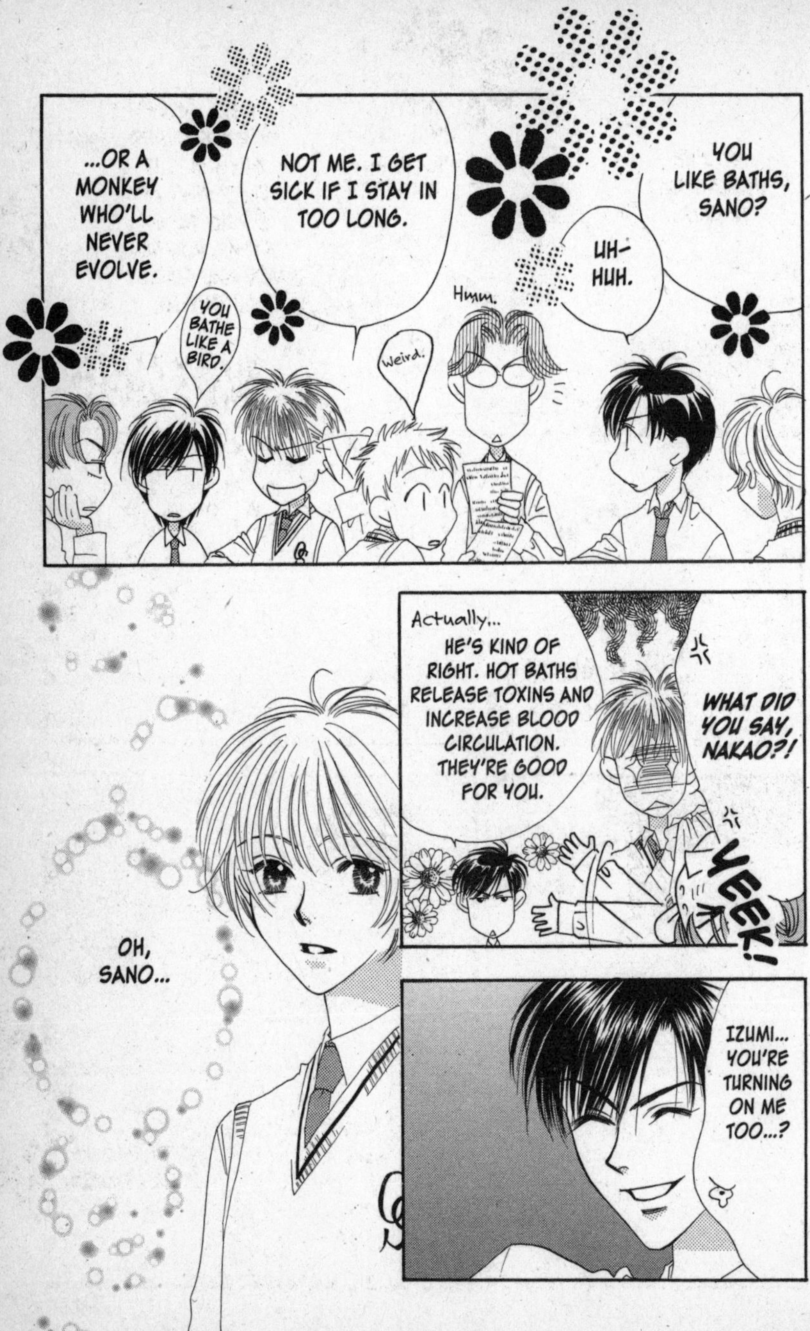
YOU LIKE BATHS, SANO?
UH-HUH.
Hmm.
Weird.
NOT ME. I GET SICK IF I STAY IN TOO LONG.
YOU BATHE LIKE A BIRD.
...OR A MONKEY WHO'LL NEVER EVOLVE.
Actually...
HE'S KIND OF RIGHT. HOT BATHS RELEASE TOXINS AND INCREASE BLOOD CIRCULATION. THEY'RE GOOD FOR YOU.
WHAT DID YOU SAY, NAKAO?!
YEEK!
IZUMI... YOU'RE TURNING ON ME TOO...?
OH, SANO...

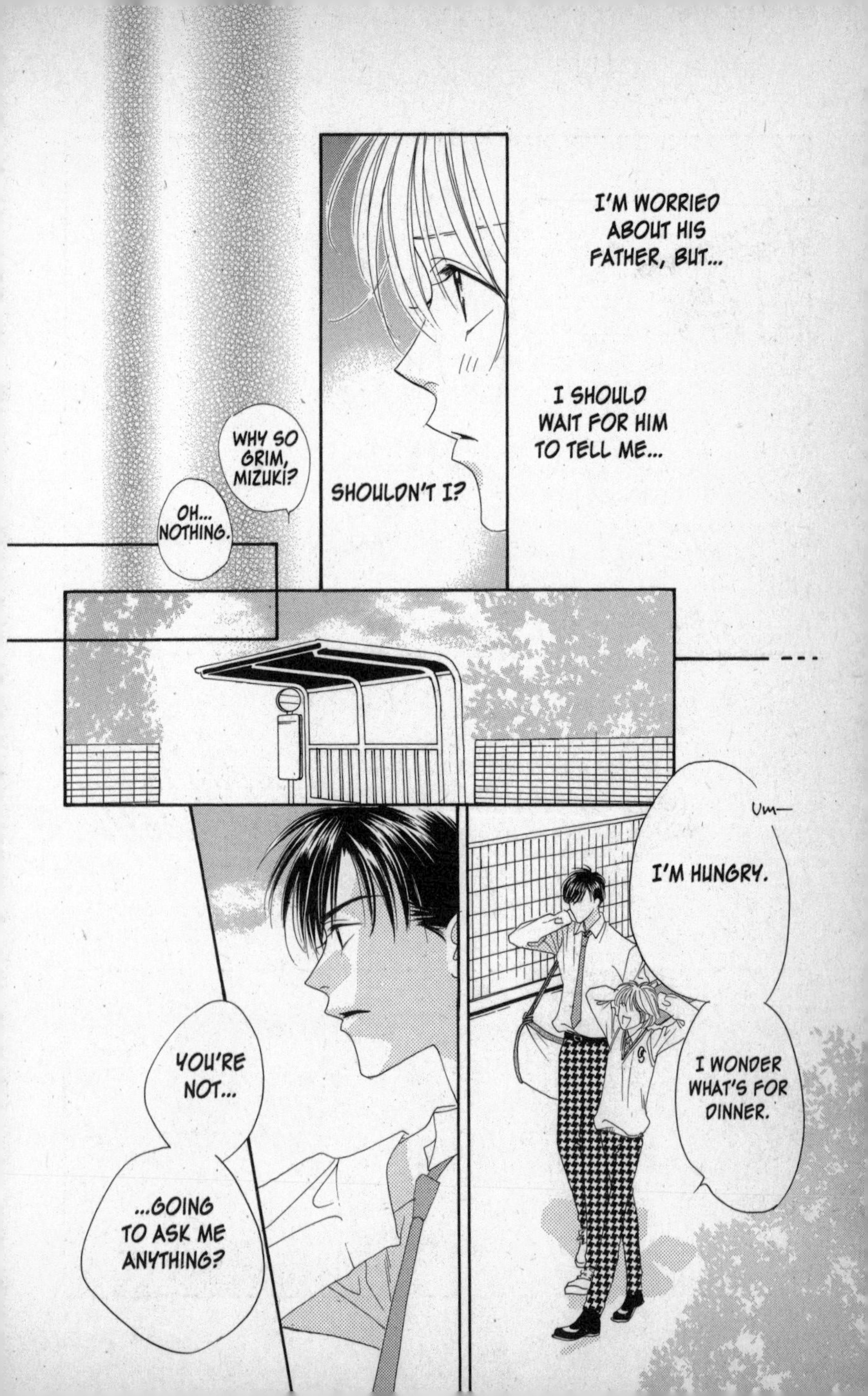
I'M WORRIED ABOUT HIS FATHER, BUT...
I SHOULD WAIT FOR HIM TO TELL ME...
SHOULDN'T I?
WHY SO GRIM, MIZUKI?
OH... NOTHING.
Um—
I'M HUNGRY.
I WONDER WHAT'S FOR DINNER.
YOU'RE NOT...
...GOING TO ASK ME ANYTHING?

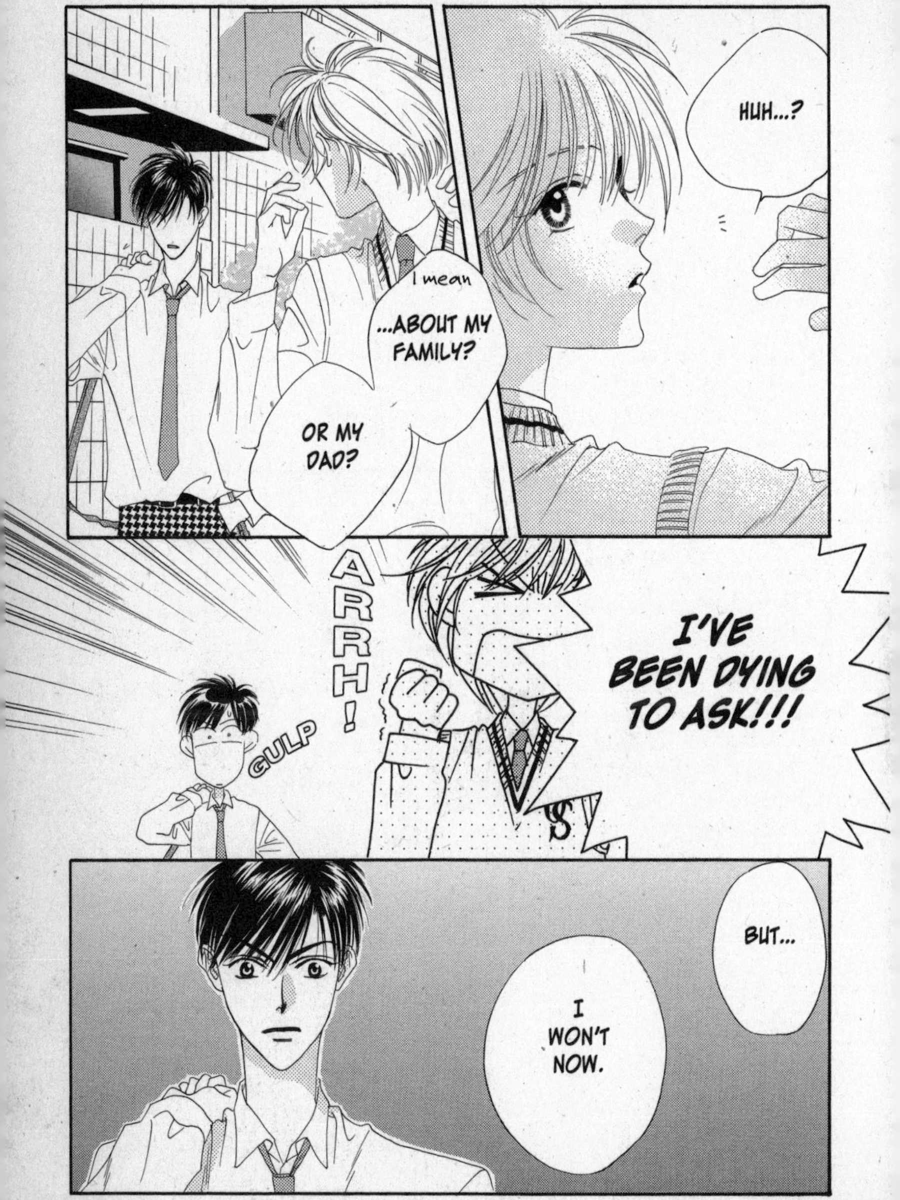
HUH...?
I mean
...ABOUT MY FAMILY?
OR MY DAD?
I'VE BEEN DYING TO ASK!!!
ARRH!
GULP
BUT...
I WON'T NOW.

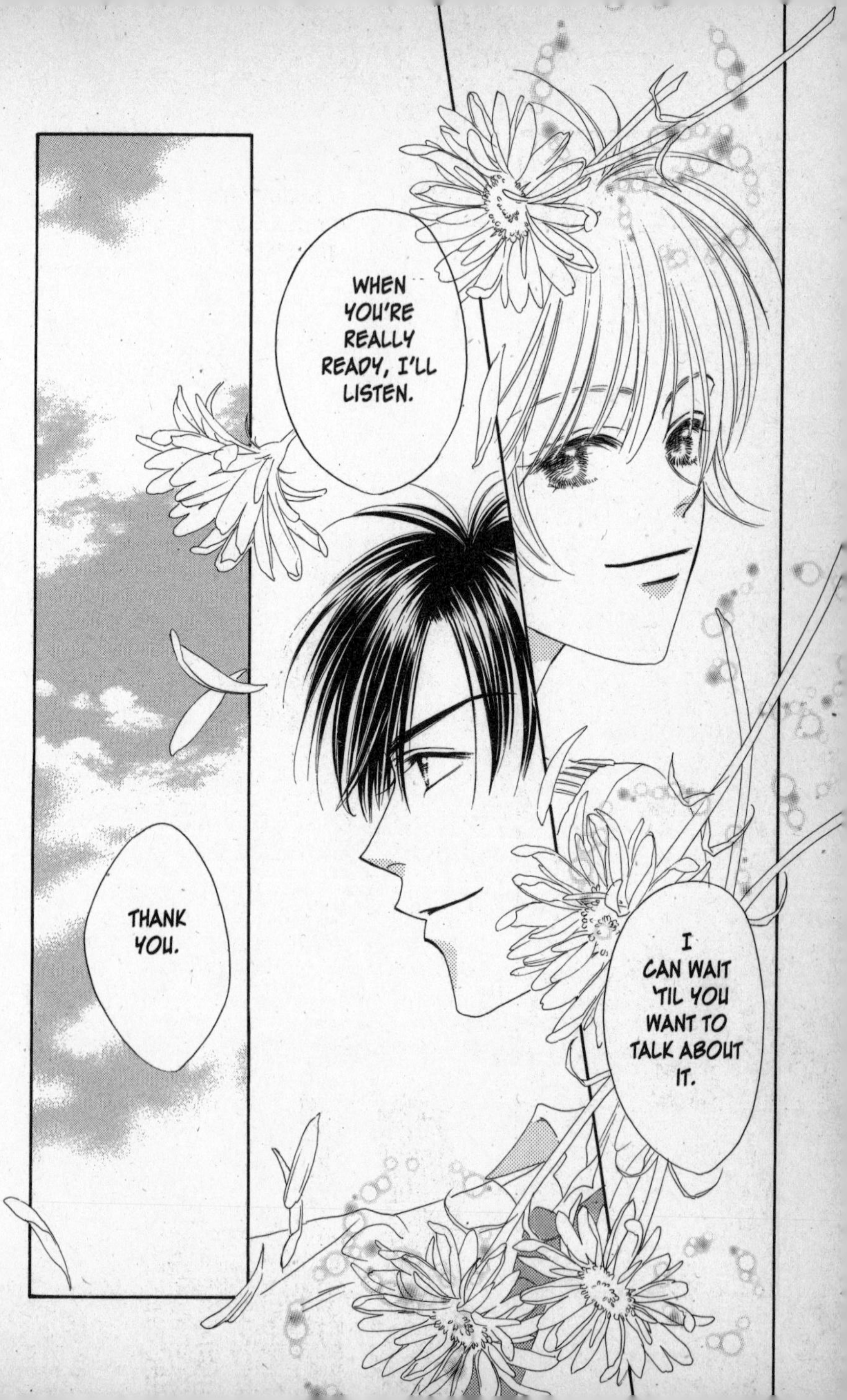
WHEN YOU'RE REALLY READY, I'LL LISTEN.
I CAN WAIT 'TIL YOU WANT TO TALK ABOUT IT.
THANK YOU.

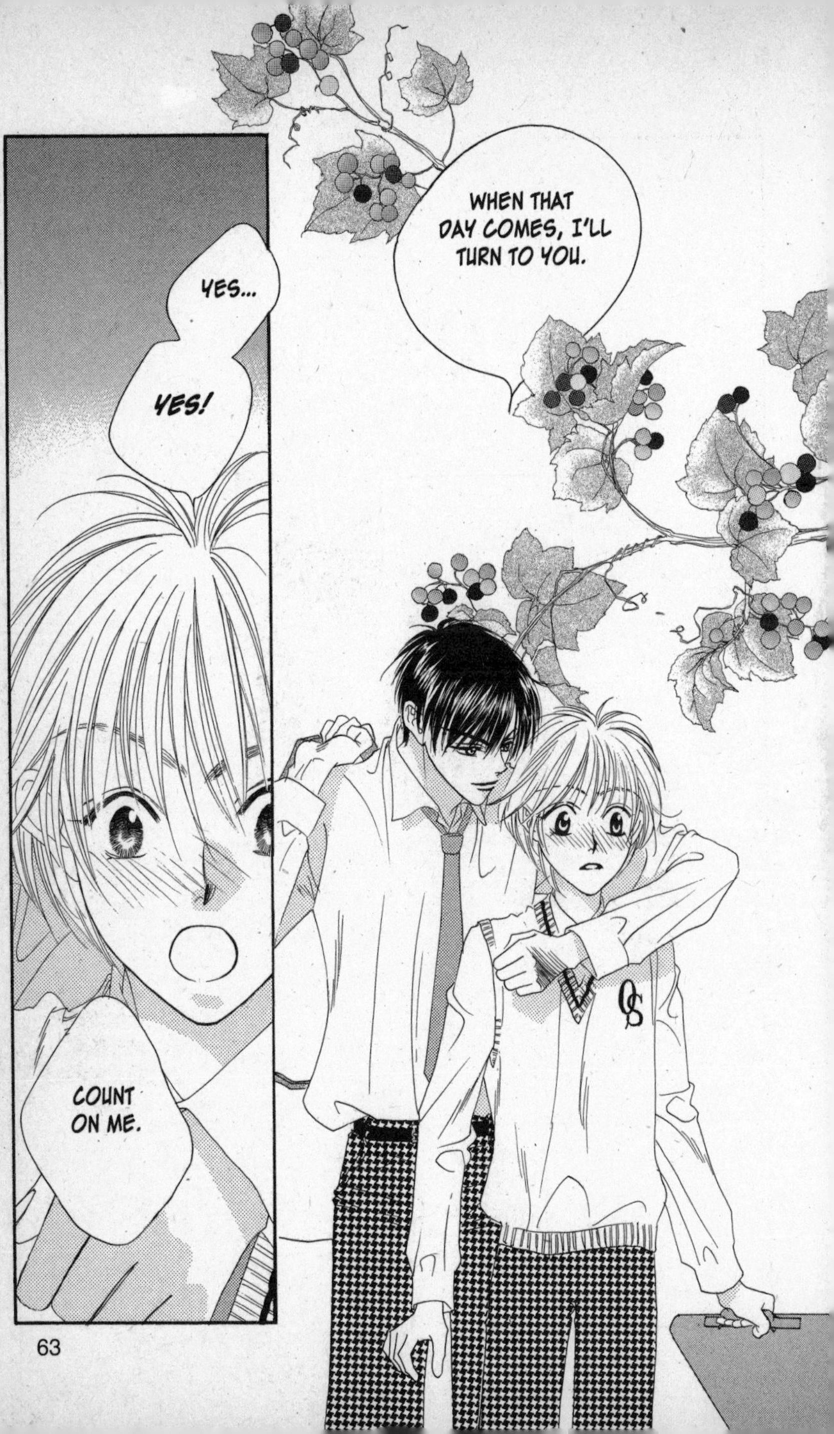
WHEN THAT DAY COMES, I'LL TURN TO YOU.
YES...
YES!
COUNT ON ME.

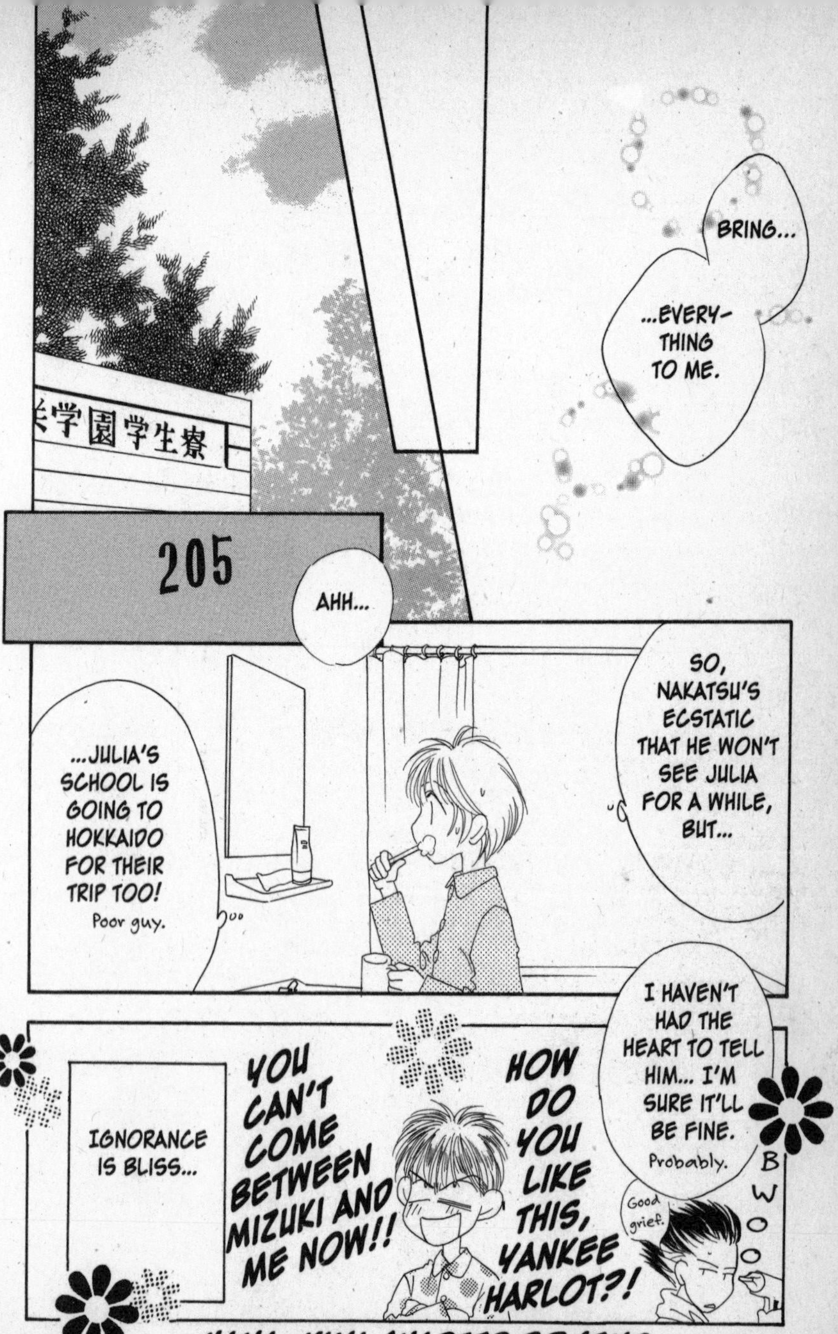
BRING...
...EVERYTHING TO ME.
学園学生寮
205
AHH...
SO, NAKATSU'S ECSTATIC THAT HE WON'T SEE JULIA FOR A WHILE, BUT...
...JULIA'S SCHOOL IS GOING TO HOKKAIDO FOR THEIR TRIP TOO!
Poor guy.
I HAVEN'T HAD THE HEART TO TELL HIM... I'M SURE IT'LL BE FINE.
Probably.
BWOOO
Good grief.
HOW DO YOU LIKE THIS, YANKEE HARLOT?!
YOU CAN'T COME BETWEEN MIZUKI AND ME NOW!!
IGNORANCE IS BLISS...

HANA-KIMI CHAPTER 32/END

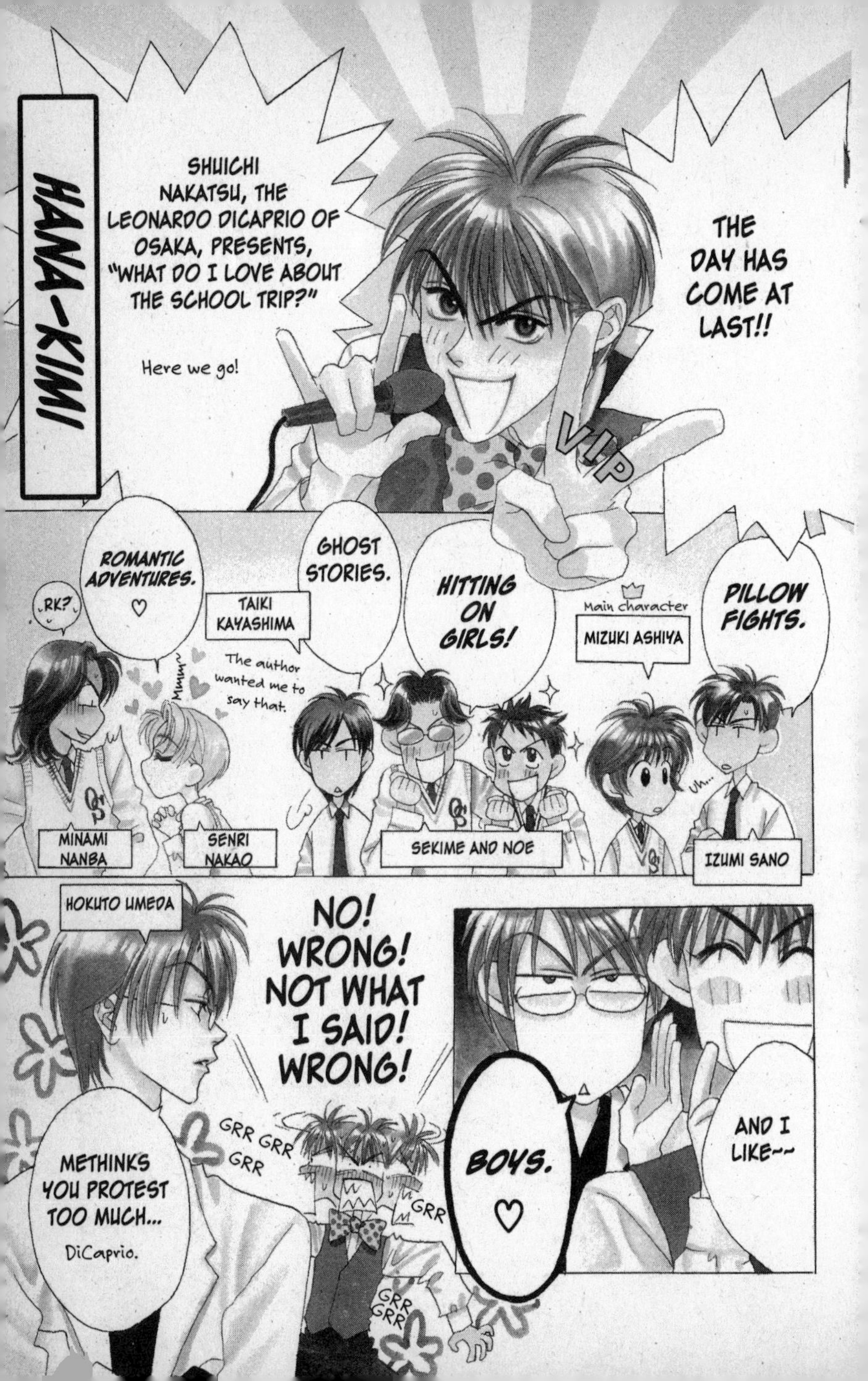

THE DAY HAS COME AT LAST!!
SHUICHI NAKATSU, THE LEONARDO DICAPRIO OF OSAKA, PRESENTS, "WHAT DO I LOVE ABOUT THE SCHOOL TRIP?"
Here we go!
VIP
HANA-KIMI
PILLOW FIGHTS.
IZUMI SANO
Main character
MIZUKI ASHIYA
Uh...
HITTING ON GIRLS!
SEKIME AND NOE
GHOST STORIES.
TAIKI KAYASHIMA
The author wanted me to say that.
ROMANTIC ADVENTURES. ♡
Mmm~
RK?
SENRI NAKAO
MINAMI NANBA
AND I LIKE~~
BOYS. ♡
NO! WRONG! NOT WHAT I SAID! WRONG!
GRR GRR GRR
GRR
HOKUTO UMEDA
METHINKS YOU PROTEST TOO MUCH...
DiCaprio.
GRR GRR

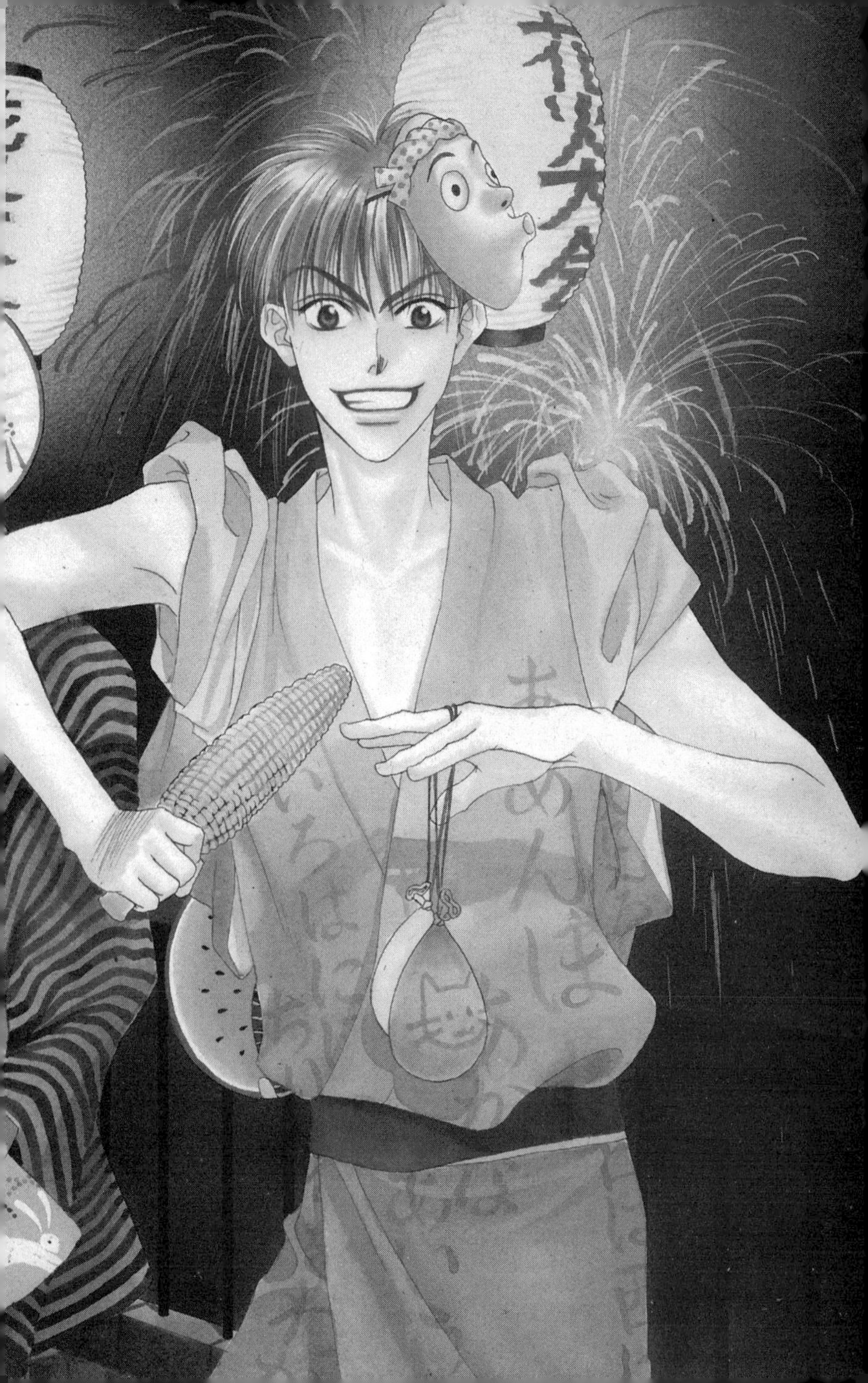

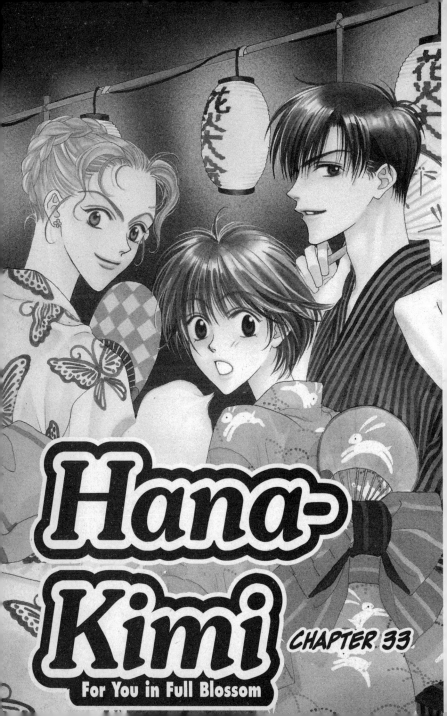

Hana-Kimi
For You in Full Blossom

CHAPTER 33

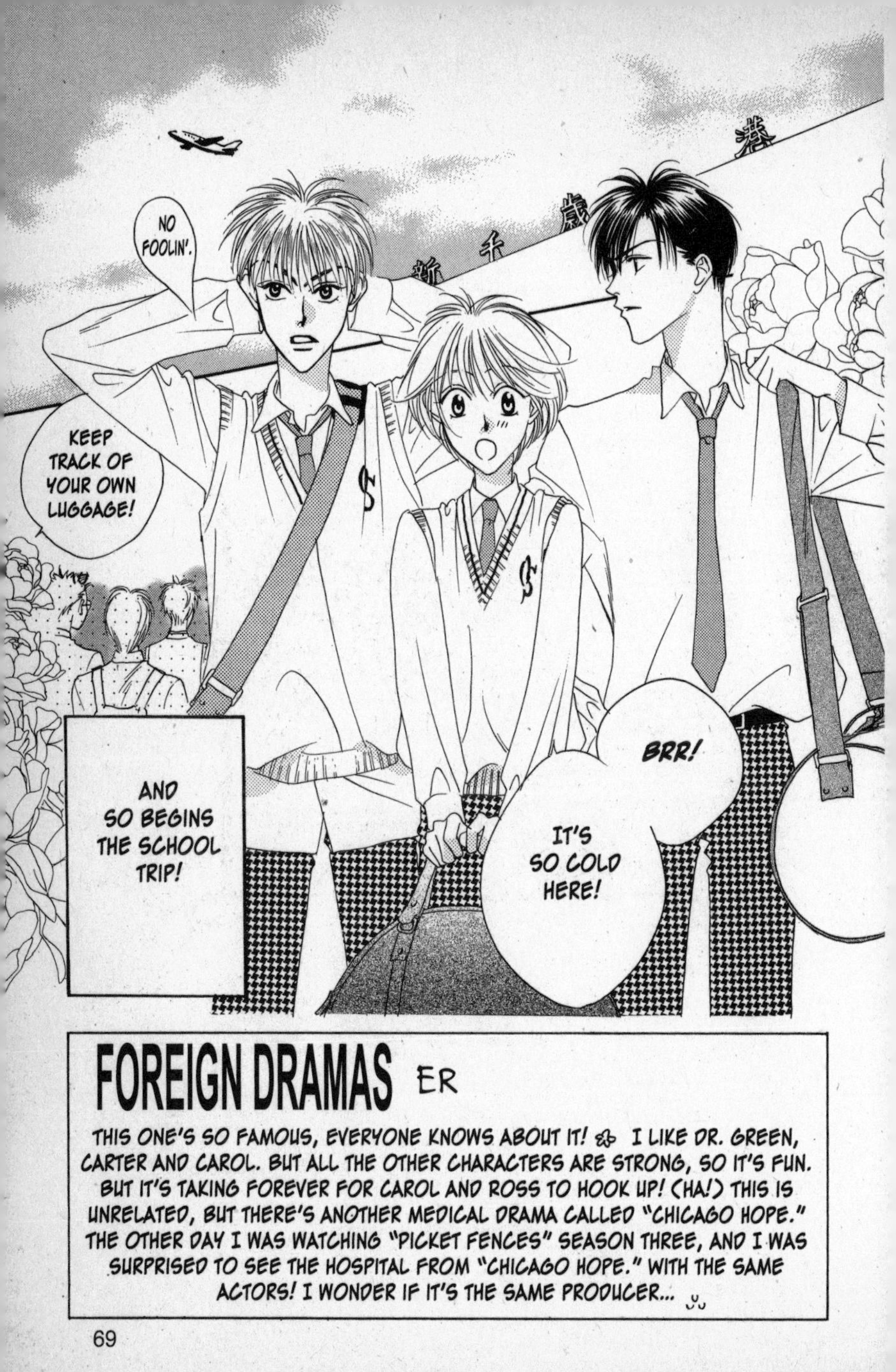
BRR!
IT'S SO COLD HERE!
NO FOOLIN'.
KEEP TRACK OF YOUR OWN LUGGAGE!
AND SO BEGINS THE SCHOOL TRIP!

FOREIGN DRAMAS ER

THIS ONE'S SO FAMOUS, EVERYONE KNOWS ABOUT IT! ✿ I LIKE DR. GREEN, CARTER AND CAROL. BUT ALL THE OTHER CHARACTERS ARE STRONG, SO IT'S FUN. BUT IT'S TAKING FOREVER FOR CAROL AND ROSS TO HOOK UP! (HA!) THIS IS UNRELATED, BUT THERE'S ANOTHER MEDICAL DRAMA CALLED "CHICAGO HOPE." THE OTHER DAY I WAS WATCHING "PICKET FENCES" SEASON THREE, AND I WAS SURPRISED TO SEE THE HOSPITAL FROM "CHICAGO HOPE." WITH THE SAME ACTORS! I WONDER IF IT'S THE SAME PRODUCER...

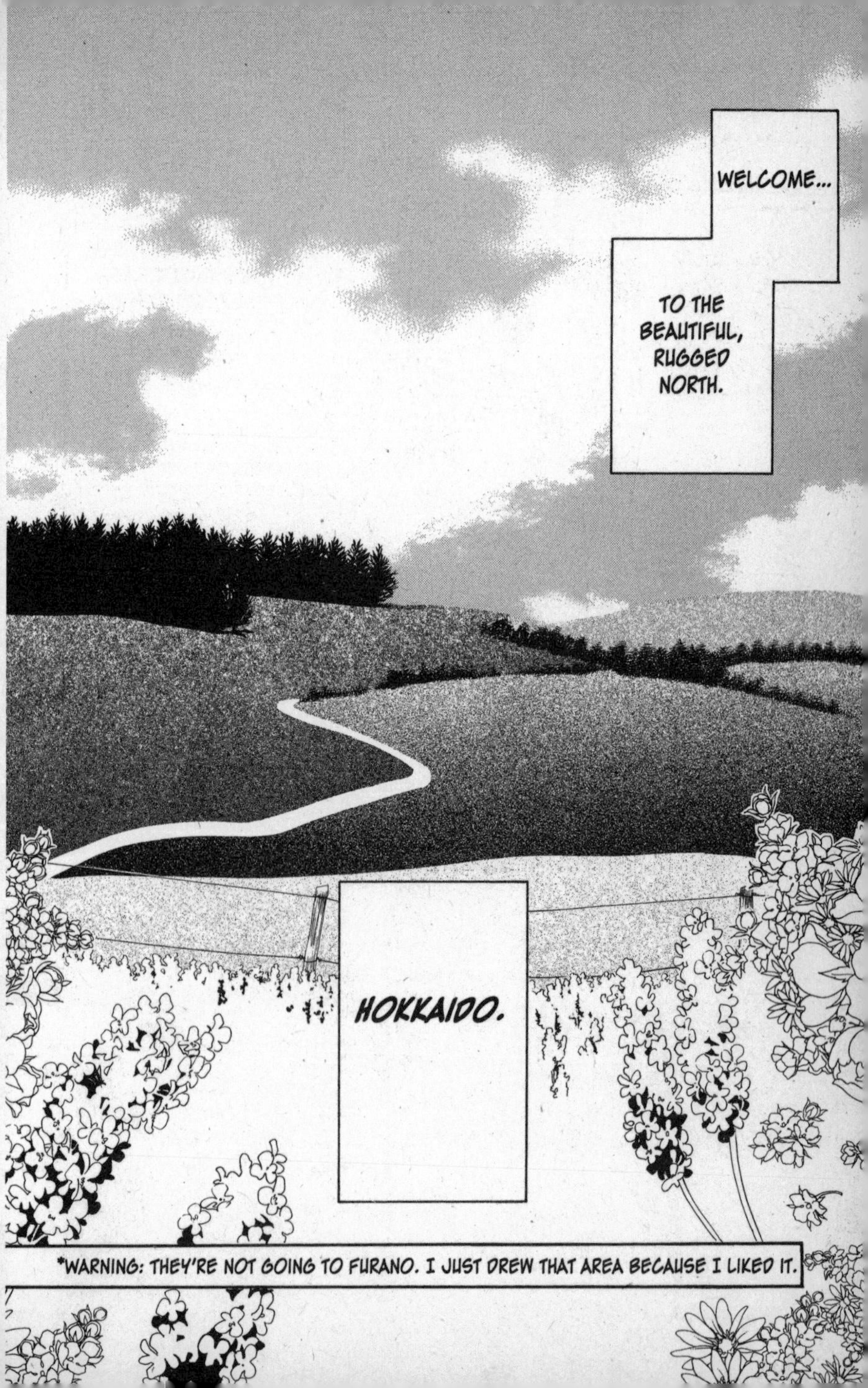
WELCOME...
TO THE BEAUTIFUL, RUGGED NORTH.
HOKKAIDO.
*WARNING: THEY'RE NOT GOING TO FURANO. I JUST DREW THAT AREA BECAUSE I LIKED IT.

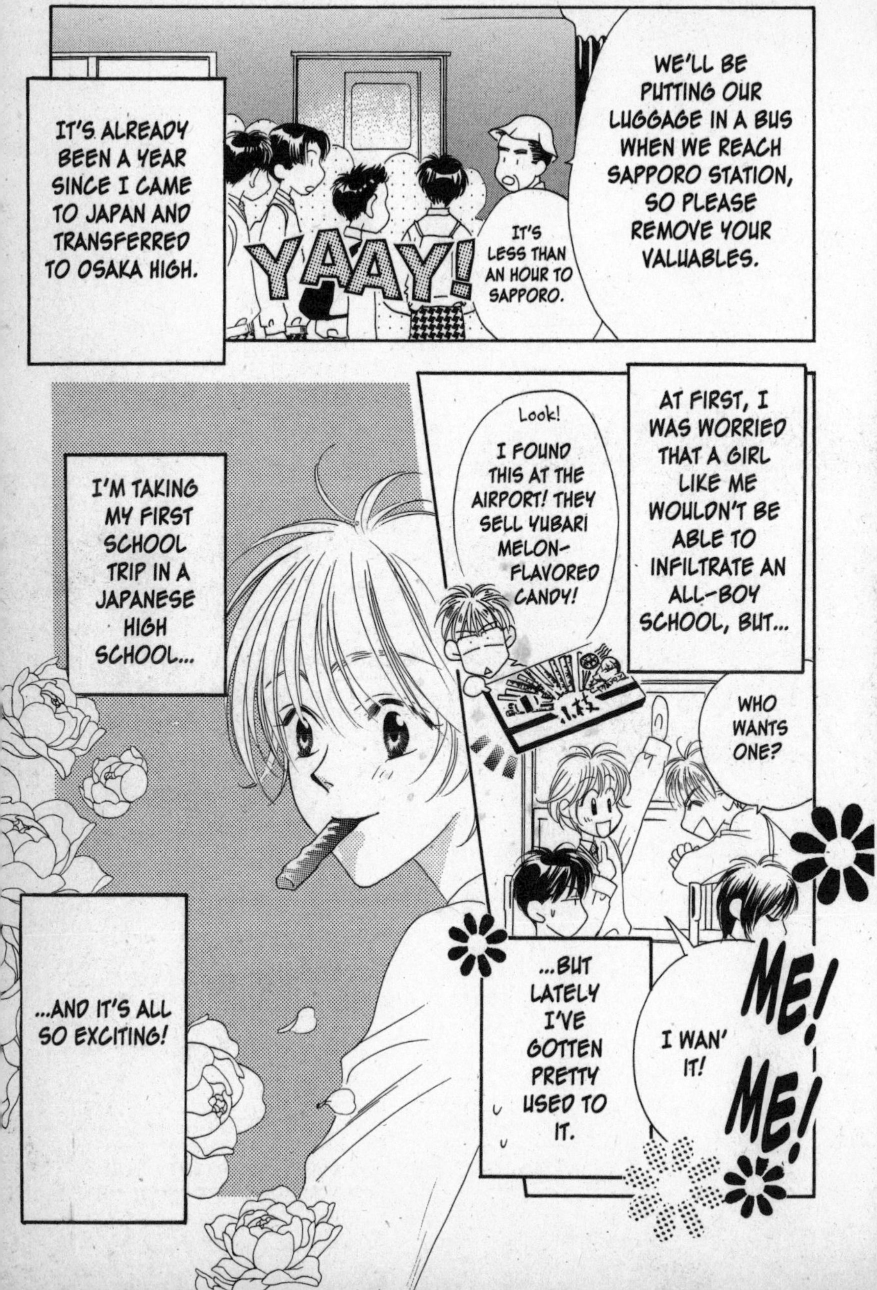
WE'LL BE PUTTING OUR LUGGAGE IN A BUS WHEN WE REACH SAPPORO STATION, SO PLEASE REMOVE YOUR VALUABLES.
IT'S LESS THAN AN HOUR TO SAPPORO.
YAAY!
IT'S ALREADY BEEN A YEAR SINCE I CAME TO JAPAN AND TRANSFERRED TO OSAKA HIGH.
AT FIRST, I WAS WORRIED THAT A GIRL LIKE ME WOULDN'T BE ABLE TO INFILTRATE AN ALL-BOY SCHOOL, BUT...
Look!
I FOUND THIS AT THE AIRPORT! THEY SELL YUBARI MELON-FLAVORED CANDY!
WHO WANTS ONE?
ME!
ME!
I WAN' IT!
...BUT LATELY I'VE GOTTEN PRETTY USED TO IT.
I'M TAKING MY FIRST SCHOOL TRIP IN A JAPANESE HIGH SCHOOL...
...AND IT'S ALL SO EXCITING!

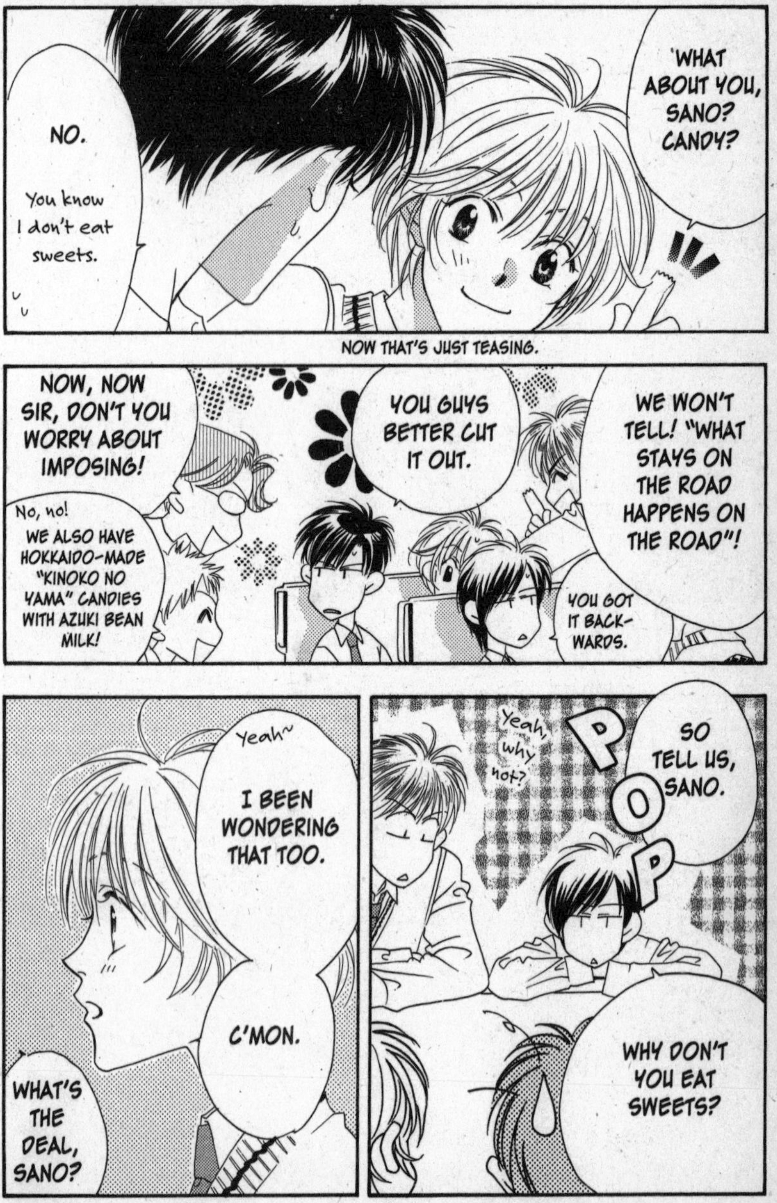
'WHAT ABOUT YOU, SANO? CANDY?
NO.
You know I don't eat sweets.
NOW THAT'S JUST TEASING.
WE WON'T TELL! "WHAT STAYS ON THE ROAD HAPPENS ON THE ROAD"!
YOU GOT IT BACK-WARDS.
YOU GUYS BETTER CUT IT OUT.
NOW, NOW SIR, DON'T YOU WORRY ABOUT IMPOSING!
No, no! WE ALSO HAVE HOKKAIDO-MADE "KINOKO NO YAMA" CANDIES WITH AZUKI BEAN MILK!
SO TELL US, SANO.
POP
Yeah, why not?
WHY DON'T YOU EAT SWEETS?
Yeah~
I BEEN WONDERING THAT TOO.
C'MON.
WHAT'S THE DEAL, SANO?

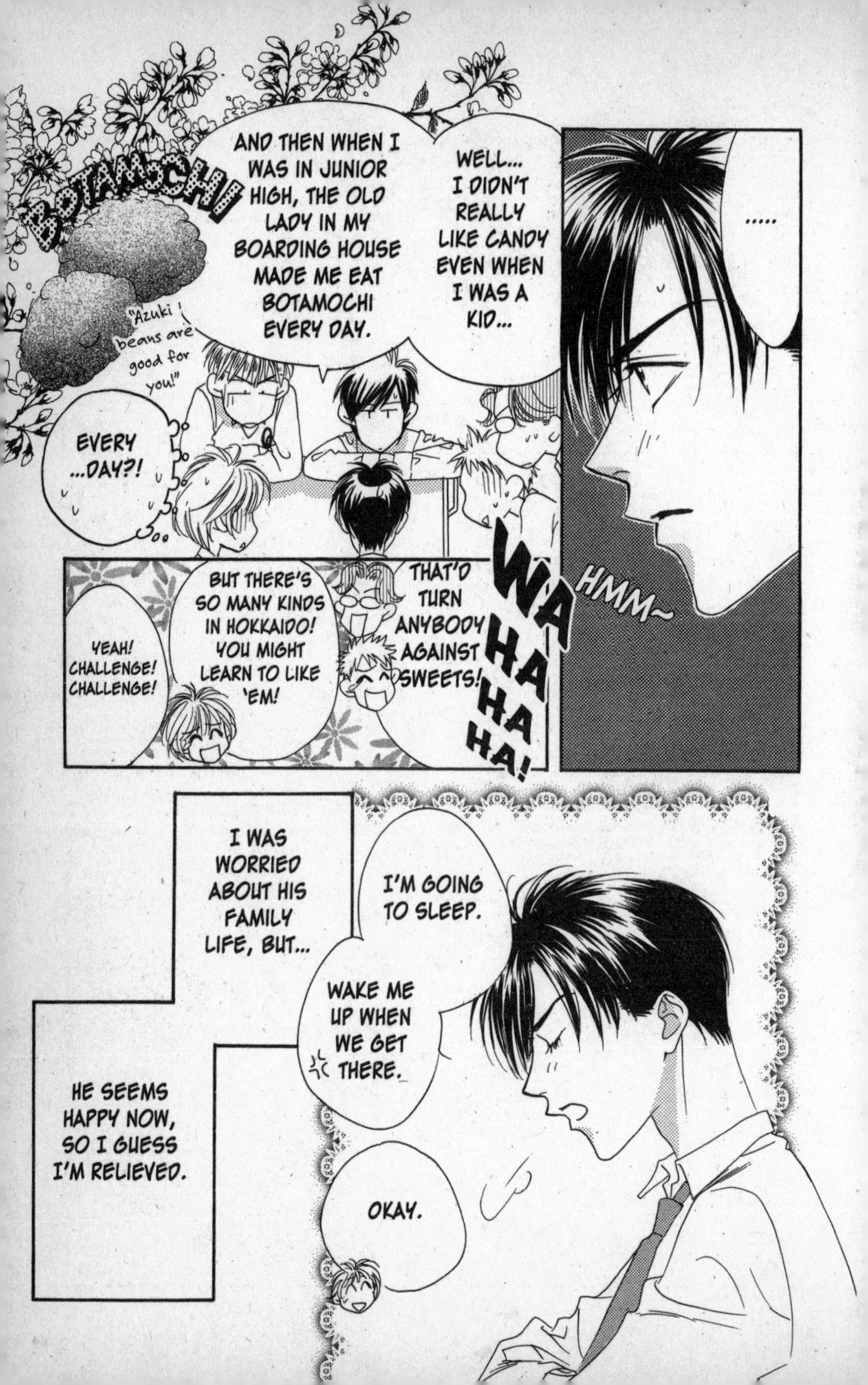
.....
HMM~
WELL... I DIDN'T REALLY LIKE CANDY EVEN WHEN I WAS A KID...
AND THEN WHEN I WAS IN JUNIOR HIGH, THE OLD LADY IN MY BOARDING HOUSE MADE ME EAT BOTAMOCHI EVERY DAY.
BOTAMOCHI
"Azuki beans are good for you!"
EVERY ...DAY?!
THAT'D TURN ANYBODY AGAINST SWEETS!
WA HA HA HA HA!
BUT THERE'S SO MANY KINDS IN HOKKAIDO! YOU MIGHT LEARN TO LIKE 'EM!
YEAH! CHALLENGE! CHALLENGE!
I'M GOING TO SLEEP.
WAKE ME UP WHEN WE GET THERE.
OKAY.
I WAS WORRIED ABOUT HIS FAMILY LIFE, BUT...
HE SEEMS HAPPY NOW, SO I GUESS I'M RELIEVED.

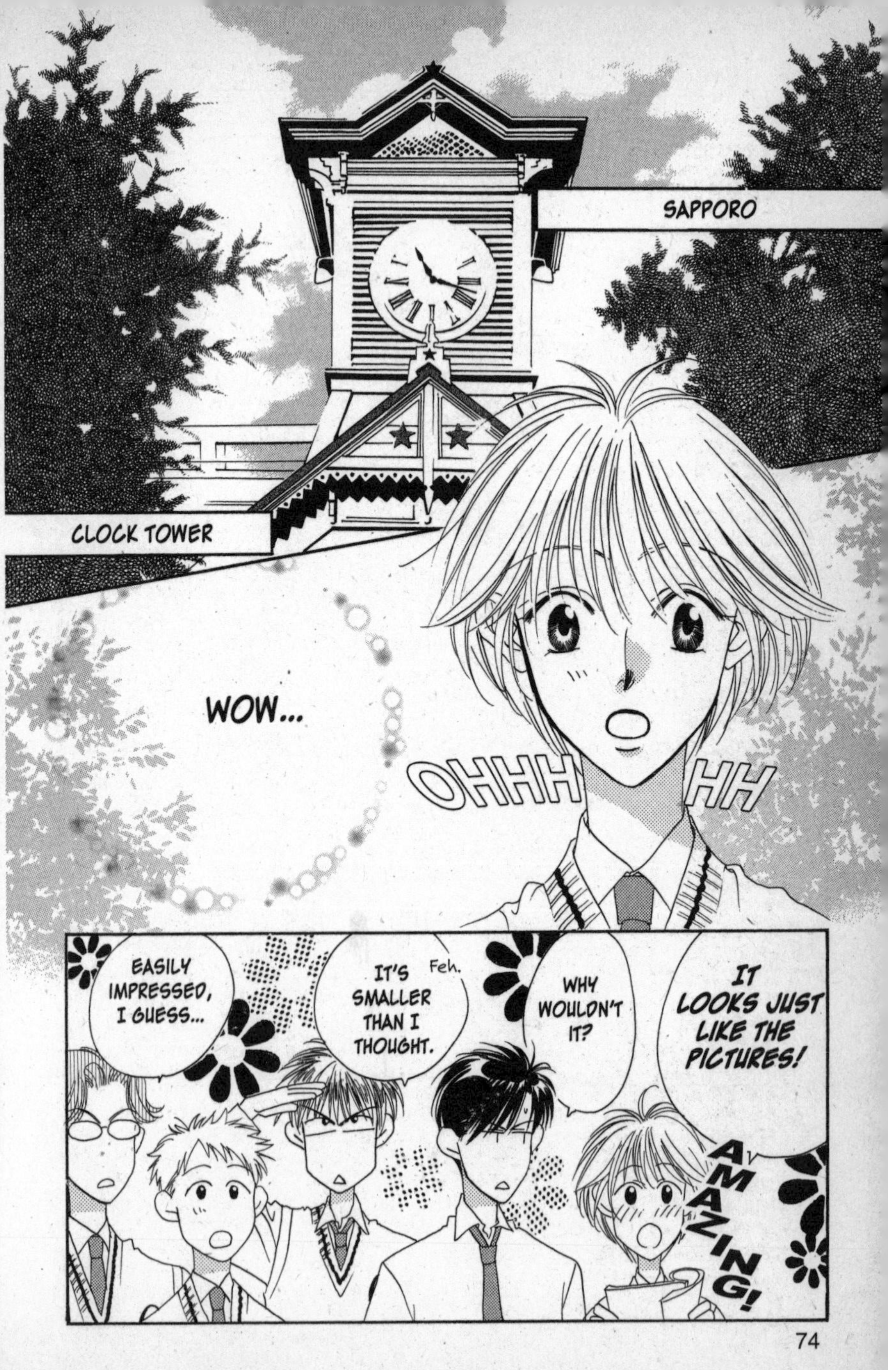
SAPPORO
CLOCK TOWER
WOW...
OHHHHH
IT LOOKS JUST LIKE THE PICTURES!
AMAZING!
WHY WOULDN'T IT?
IT'S SMALLER THAN I THOUGHT.
Feh.
EASILY IMPRESSED, I GUESS...

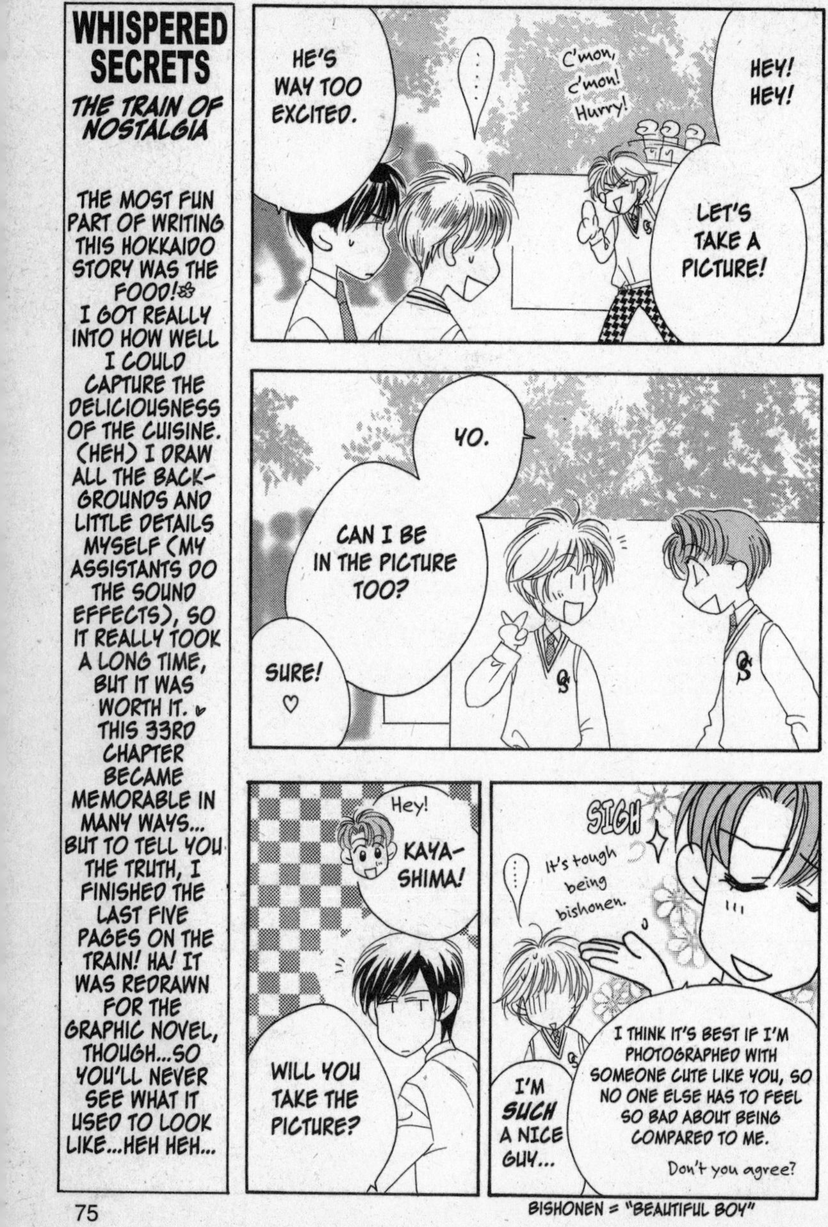
HEY! HEY!
LET'S TAKE A PICTURE!
C'mon, c'mon! Hurry!
...
HE'S WAY TOO EXCITED.
YO.
CAN I BE IN THE PICTURE TOO?
SURE! ♡
SIGH
It's tough being bishonen.
...
I THINK IT'S BEST IF I'M PHOTOGRAPHED WITH SOMEONE CUTE LIKE YOU, SO NO ONE ELSE HAS TO FEEL SO BAD ABOUT BEING COMPARED TO ME.
Don't you agree?
I'M *SUCH* A NICE GUY...
Hey!
KAYA-SHIMA!
WILL YOU TAKE THE PICTURE?

BISHONEN = "BEAUTIFUL BOY"

WHISPERED SECRETS

THE TRAIN OF NOSTALGIA

THE MOST FUN PART OF WRITING THIS HOKKAIDO STORY WAS THE FOOD!✿ I GOT REALLY INTO HOW WELL I COULD CAPTURE THE DELICIOUSNESS OF THE CUISINE. (HEH) I DRAW ALL THE BACK-GROUNDS AND LITTLE DETAILS MYSELF (MY ASSISTANTS DO THE SOUND EFFECTS), SO IT REALLY TOOK A LONG TIME, BUT IT WAS WORTH IT. ♥ THIS 33RD CHAPTER BECAME MEMORABLE IN MANY WAYS... BUT TO TELL YOU THE TRUTH, I FINISHED THE LAST FIVE PAGES ON THE TRAIN! HA! IT WAS REDRAWN FOR THE GRAPHIC NOVEL, THOUGH...SO YOU'LL NEVER SEE WHAT IT USED TO LOOK LIKE...HEH HEH...

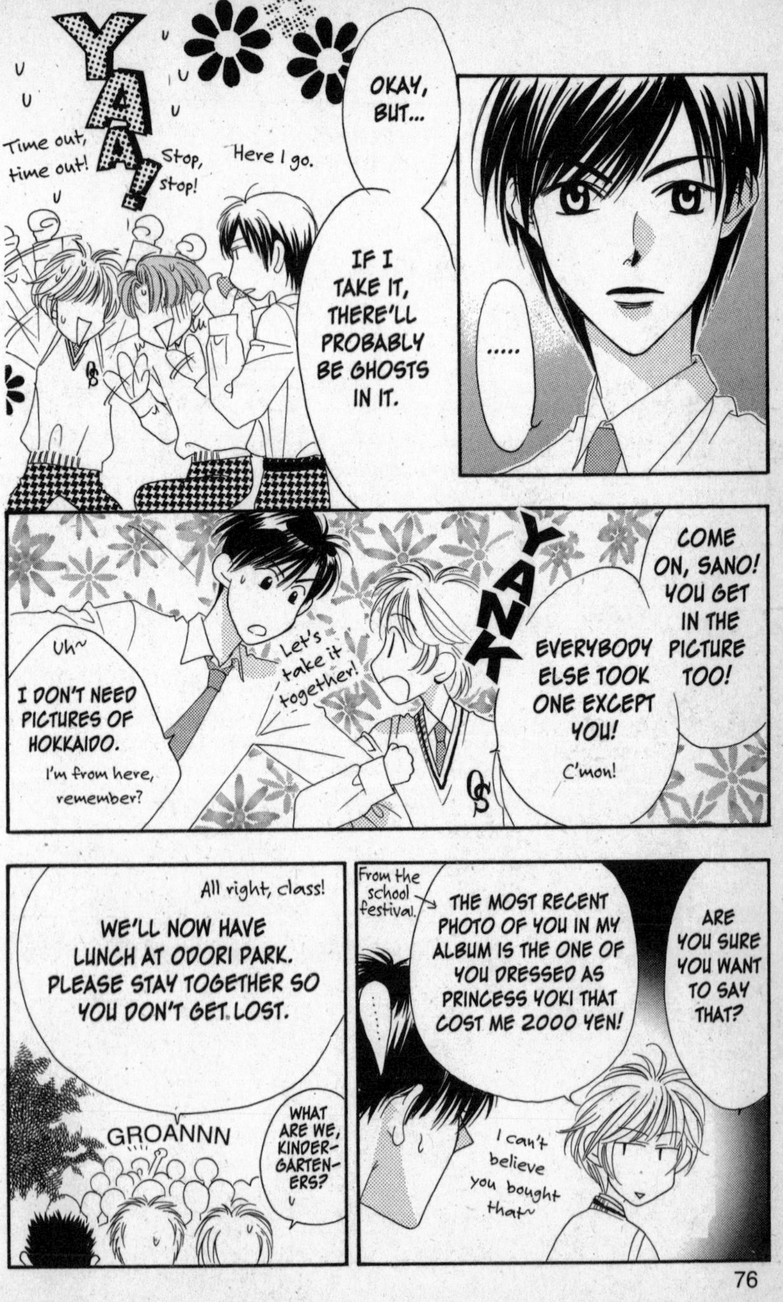
.....
OKAY, BUT...
IF I TAKE IT, THERE'LL PROBABLY BE GHOSTS IN IT.
YAA!
Here I go.
Stop, stop!
Time out, time out!
COME ON, SANO! YOU GET IN THE PICTURE TOO!
YANK
EVERYBODY ELSE TOOK ONE EXCEPT YOU!
C'mon!
Let's take it together!
Uh~
I DON'T NEED PICTURES OF HOKKAIDO.
I'm from here, remember?
ARE YOU SURE YOU WANT TO SAY THAT?
From the school festival.
THE MOST RECENT PHOTO OF YOU IN MY ALBUM IS THE ONE OF YOU DRESSED AS PRINCESS YOKI THAT COST ME 2000 YEN!
I can't believe you bought that~
All right, class!
WE'LL NOW HAVE LUNCH AT ODORI PARK. PLEASE STAY TOGETHER SO YOU DON'T GET LOST.
WHAT ARE WE, KINDER-GARTEN-ERS?
GROANNN

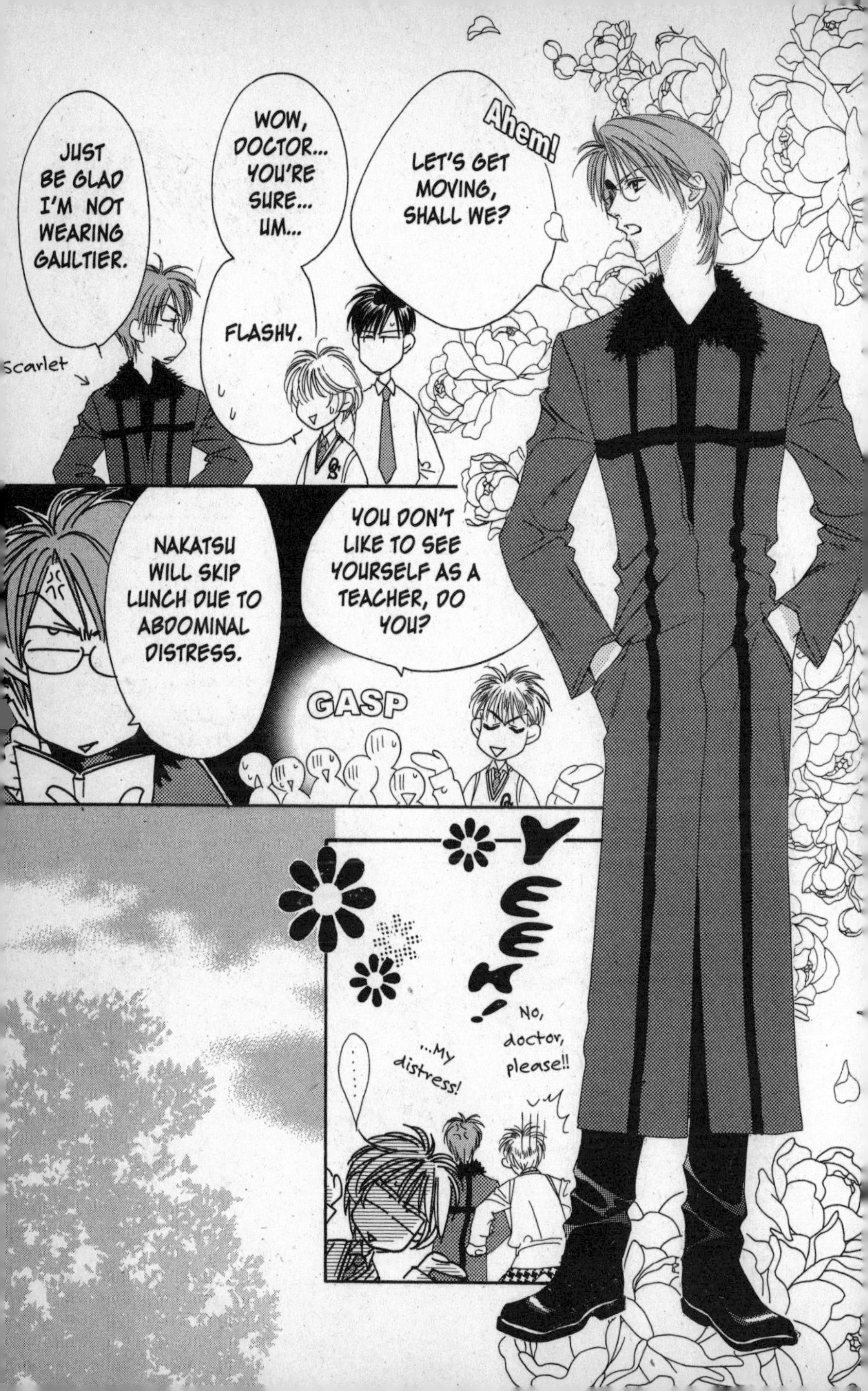
Ahem!
LET'S GET MOVING, SHALL WE?
WOW, DOCTOR... YOU'RE SURE... UM...
FLASHY.
JUST BE GLAD I'M NOT WEARING GAULTIER.
Scarlet
YOU DON'T LIKE TO SEE YOURSELF AS A TEACHER, DO YOU?
NAKATSU WILL SKIP LUNCH DUE TO ABDOMINAL DISTRESS.
GASP
YEEK!
No, doctor, please!!
...My distress!
......

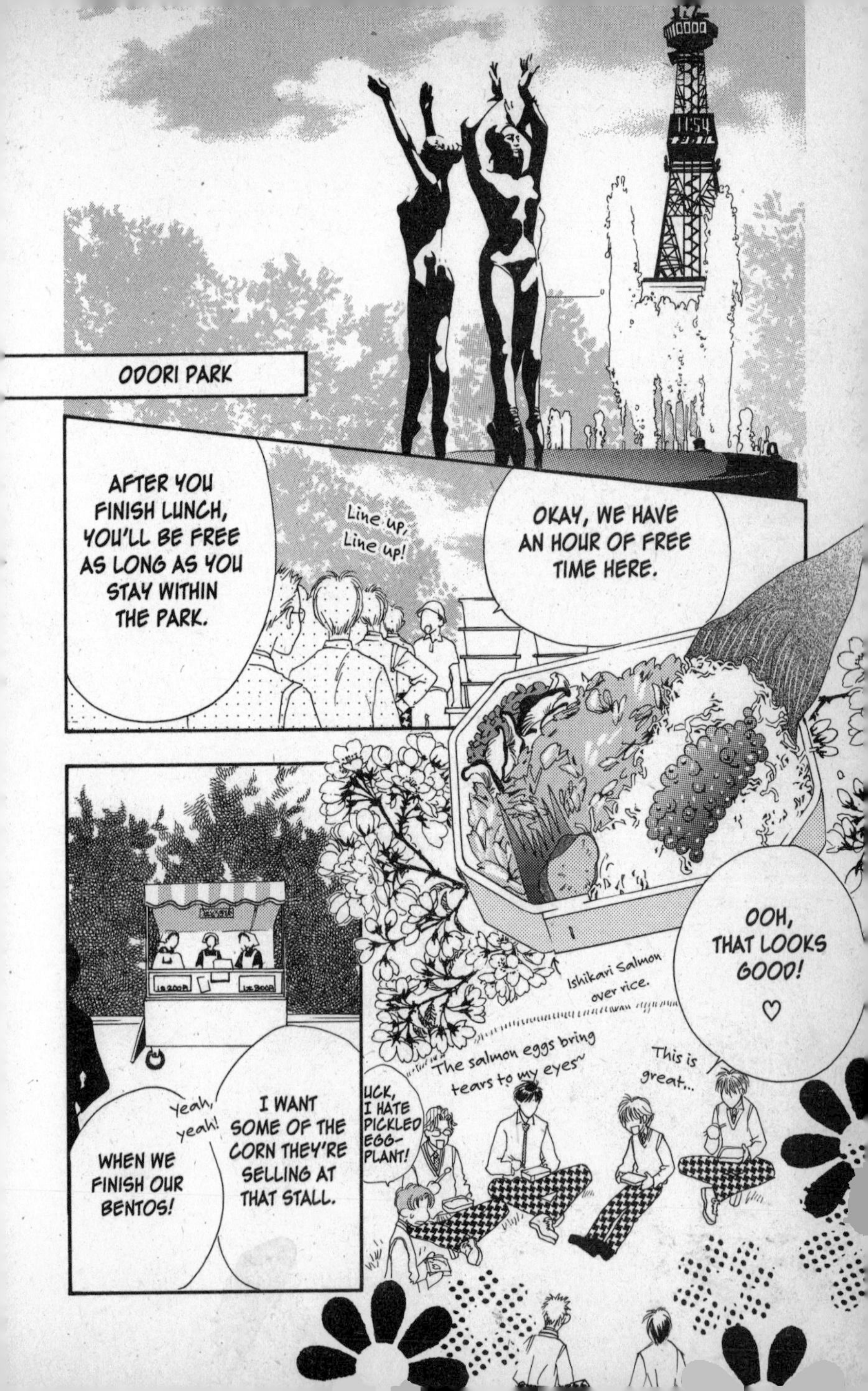
ODORI PARK
OKAY, WE HAVE AN HOUR OF FREE TIME HERE.
Line up, Line up!
AFTER YOU FINISH LUNCH, YOU'LL BE FREE AS LONG AS YOU STAY WITHIN THE PARK.
OOH, THAT LOOKS GOOD! ♡
Ishikari Salmon over rice.
This is great...
The salmon eggs bring tears to my eyes~
UCK, I HATE PICKLED EGG-PLANT!
I WANT SOME OF THE CORN THEY'RE SELLING AT THAT STALL.
Yeah, yeah!
WHEN WE FINISH OUR BENTOS!

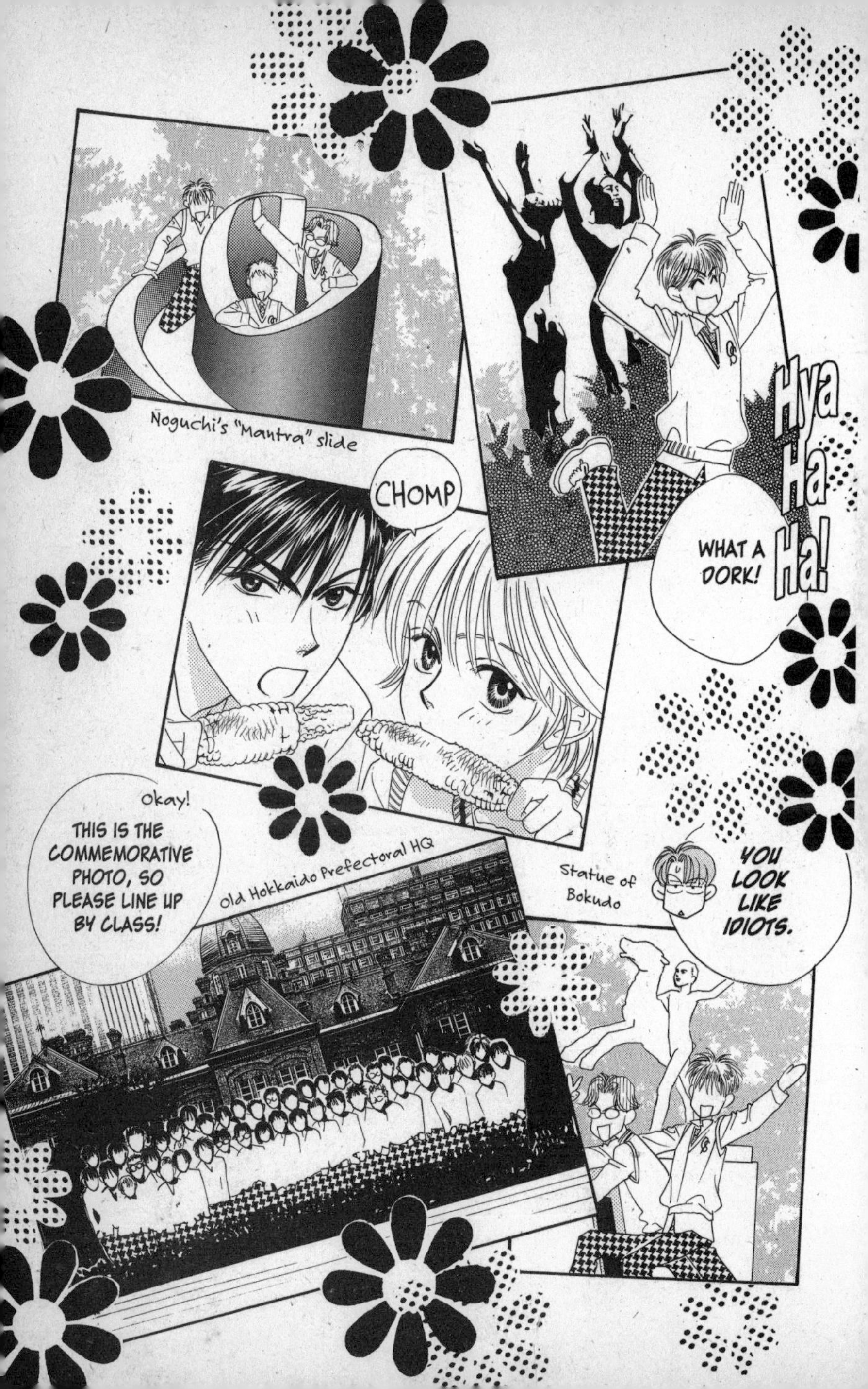
Hya Ha Ha!
WHAT A DORK!
Noguchi's "Mantra" slide
CHOMP
Statue of Bokudo
YOU LOOK LIKE IDIOTS.
Old Hokkaido Prefectoral HQ
Okay! THIS IS THE COMMEMORATIVE PHOTO, SO PLEASE LINE UP BY CLASS!

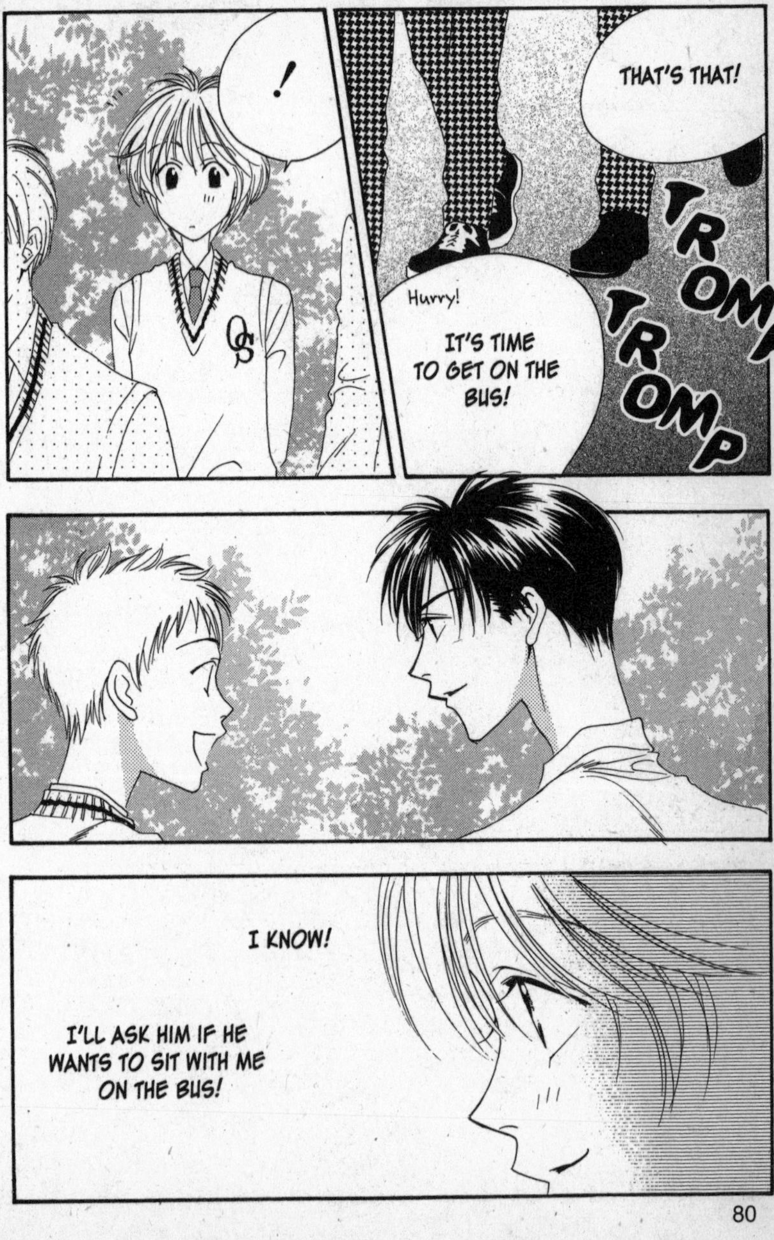

THAT'S THAT!
Hurry!
IT'S TIME TO GET ON THE BUS!
TROMP TROMP
!
I KNOW!
I'LL ASK HIM IF HE WANTS TO SIT WITH ME ON THE BUS!

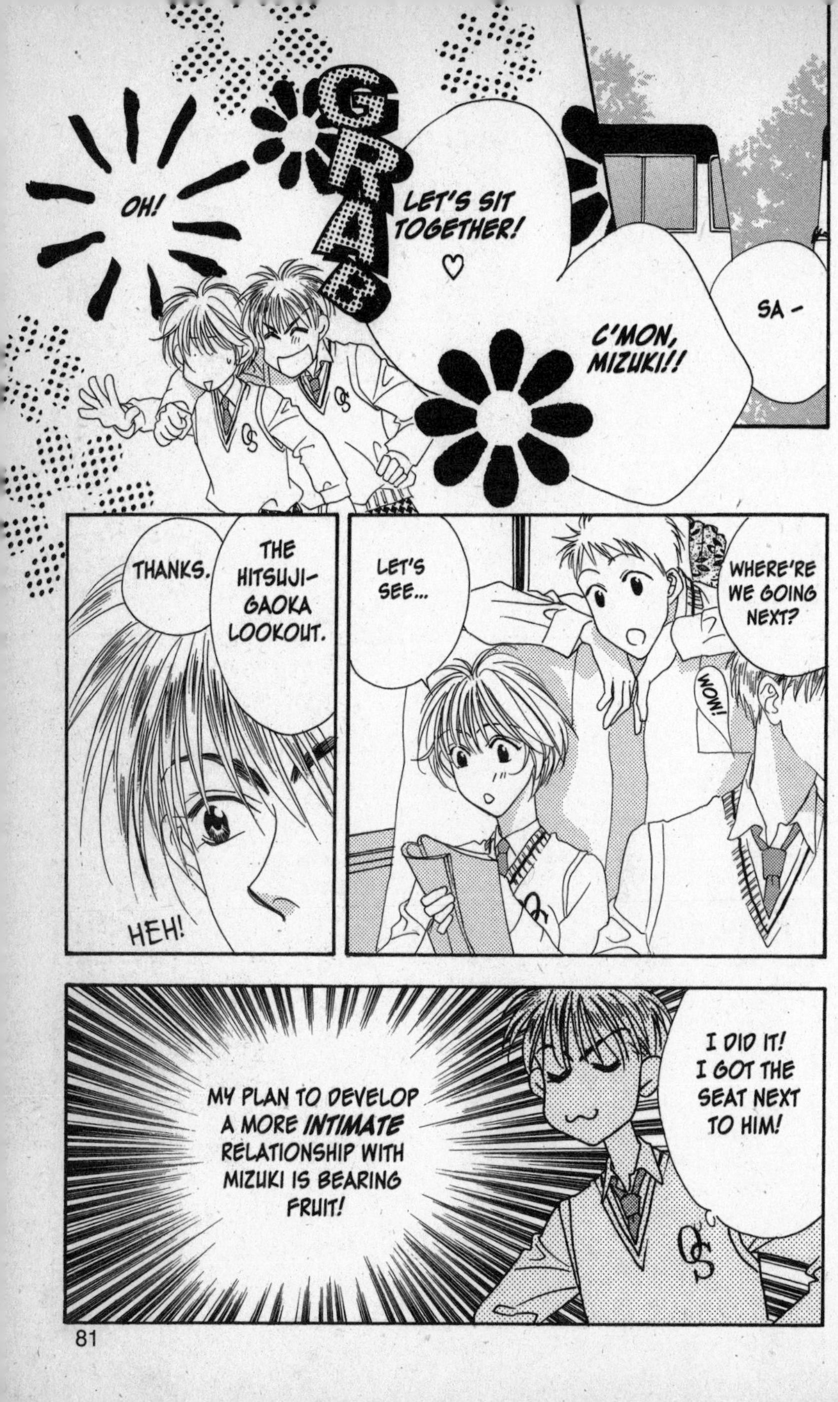
SA -
C'MON, MIZUKI!!
LET'S SIT TOGETHER! ♡
GRAB
OH!
WHERE'RE WE GOING NEXT?
WOW!
LET'S SEE...
THE HITSUJI-GAOKA LOOKOUT.
THANKS.
HEH!
I DID IT! I GOT THE SEAT NEXT TO HIM!
MY PLAN TO DEVELOP A MORE *INTIMATE* RELATIONSHIP WITH MIZUKI IS BEARING FRUIT!

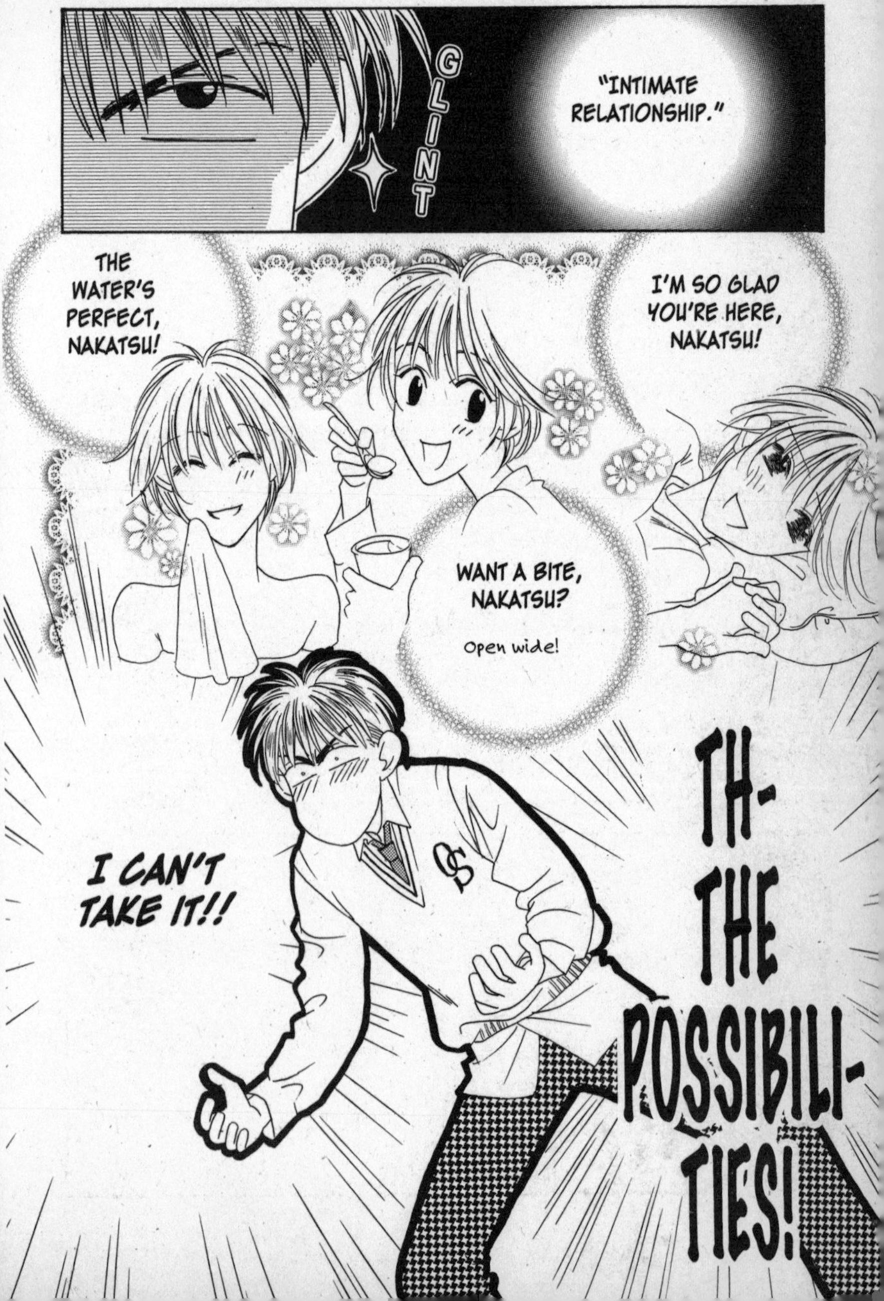
"INTIMATE RELATIONSHIP."
GLINT
I'M SO GLAD YOU'RE HERE, NAKATSU!
WANT A BITE, NAKATSU?
Open wide!
THE WATER'S PERFECT, NAKATSU!
TH- THE POSSIBILI- TIES!
I CAN'T TAKE IT!!

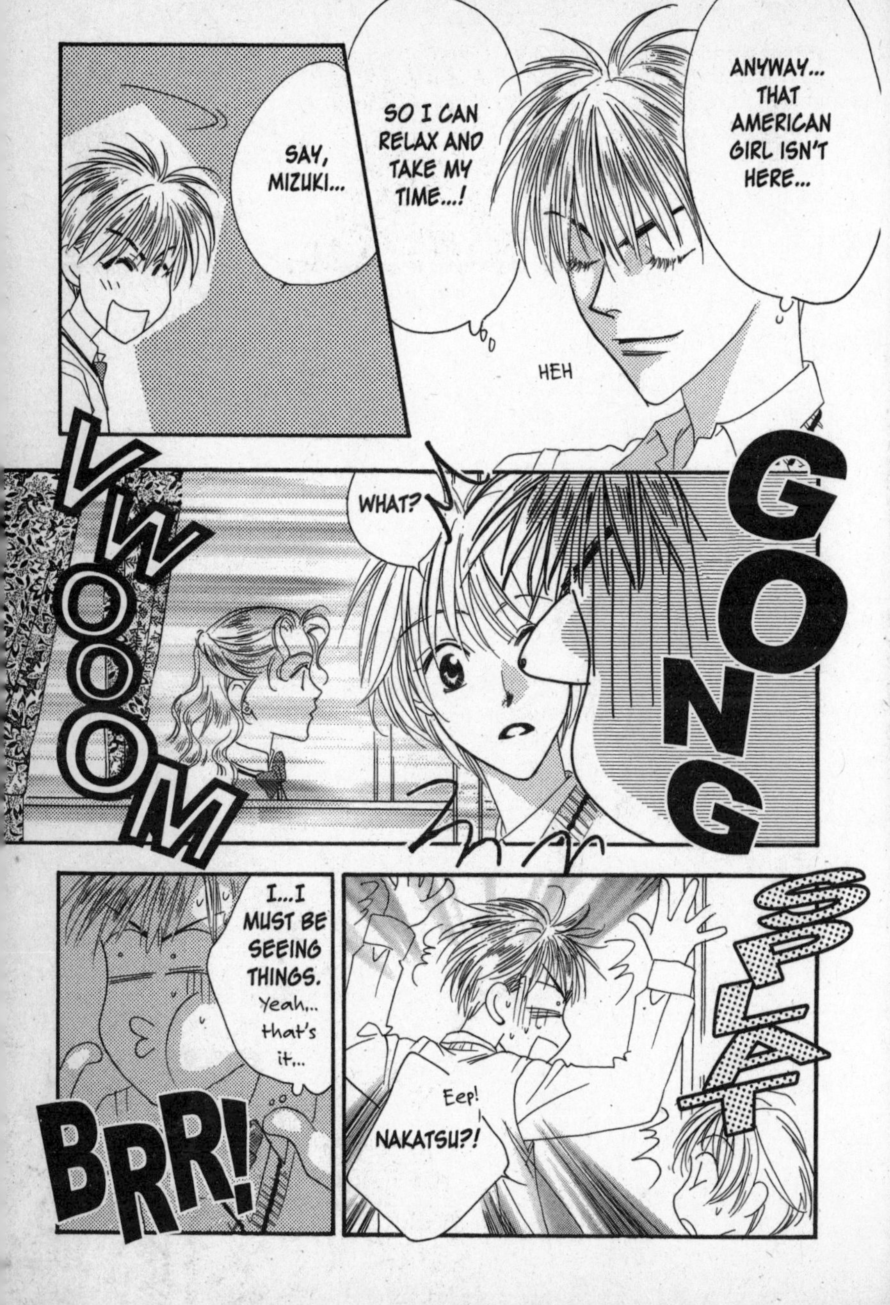
ANYWAY... THAT AMERICAN GIRL ISN'T HERE...
SO I CAN RELAX AND TAKE MY TIME...!
HEH
SAY, MIZUKI...
GONG
WHAT?
VWOOOOM
SPLAT
Eep!
NAKATSU?!
I...I MUST BE SEEING THINGS. Yeah... that's it...
BRR!

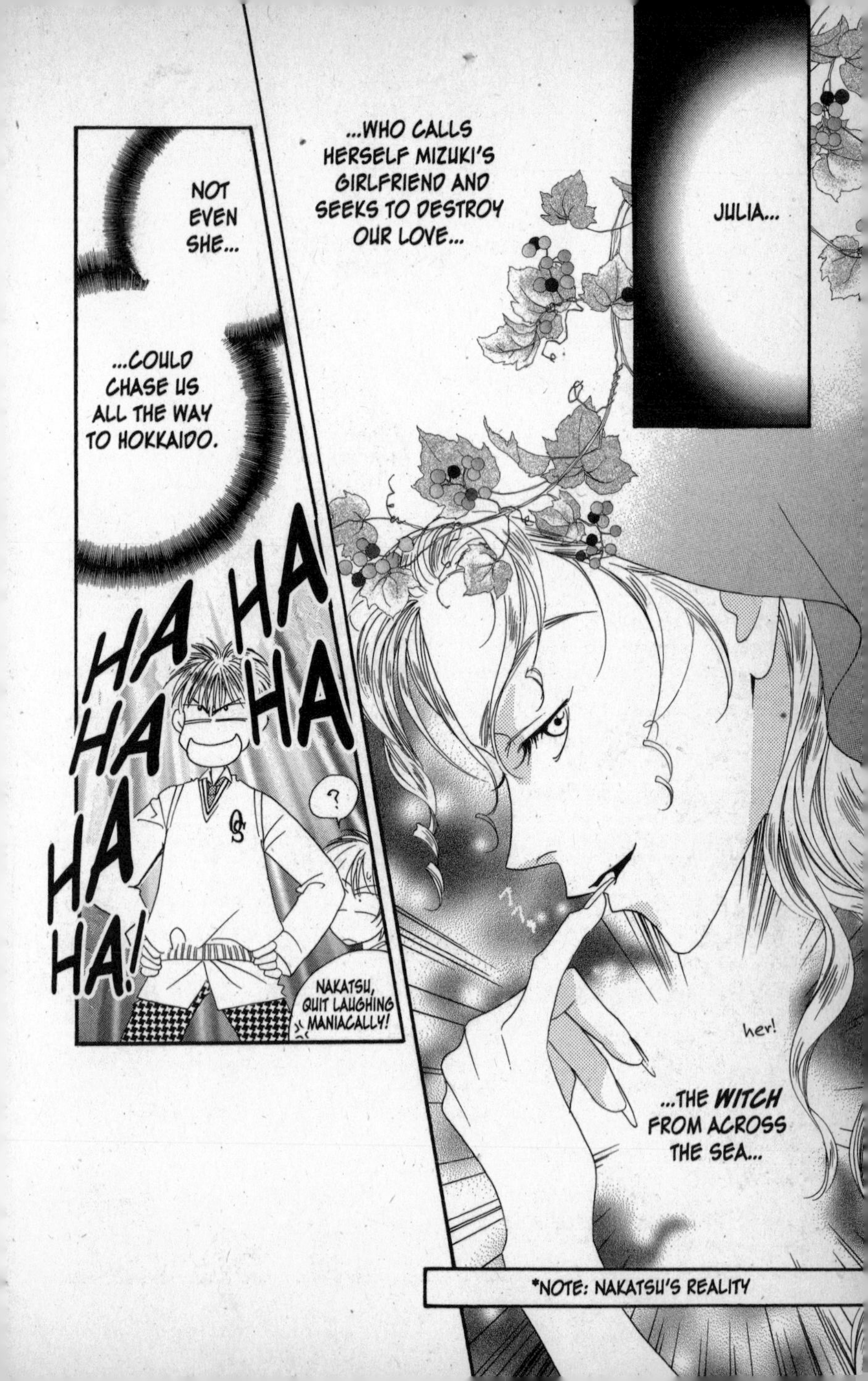
JULIA...
...WHO CALLS HERSELF MIZUKI'S GIRLFRIEND AND SEEKS TO DESTROY OUR LOVE...
...THE *WITCH* FROM ACROSS THE SEA...
her!
*NOTE: NAKATSU'S REALITY
NOT EVEN SHE...
...COULD CHASE US ALL THE WAY TO HOKKAIDO.
HA HA HA HA HA HA HA!
?
NAKATSU, QUIT LAUGHING MANIACALLY!

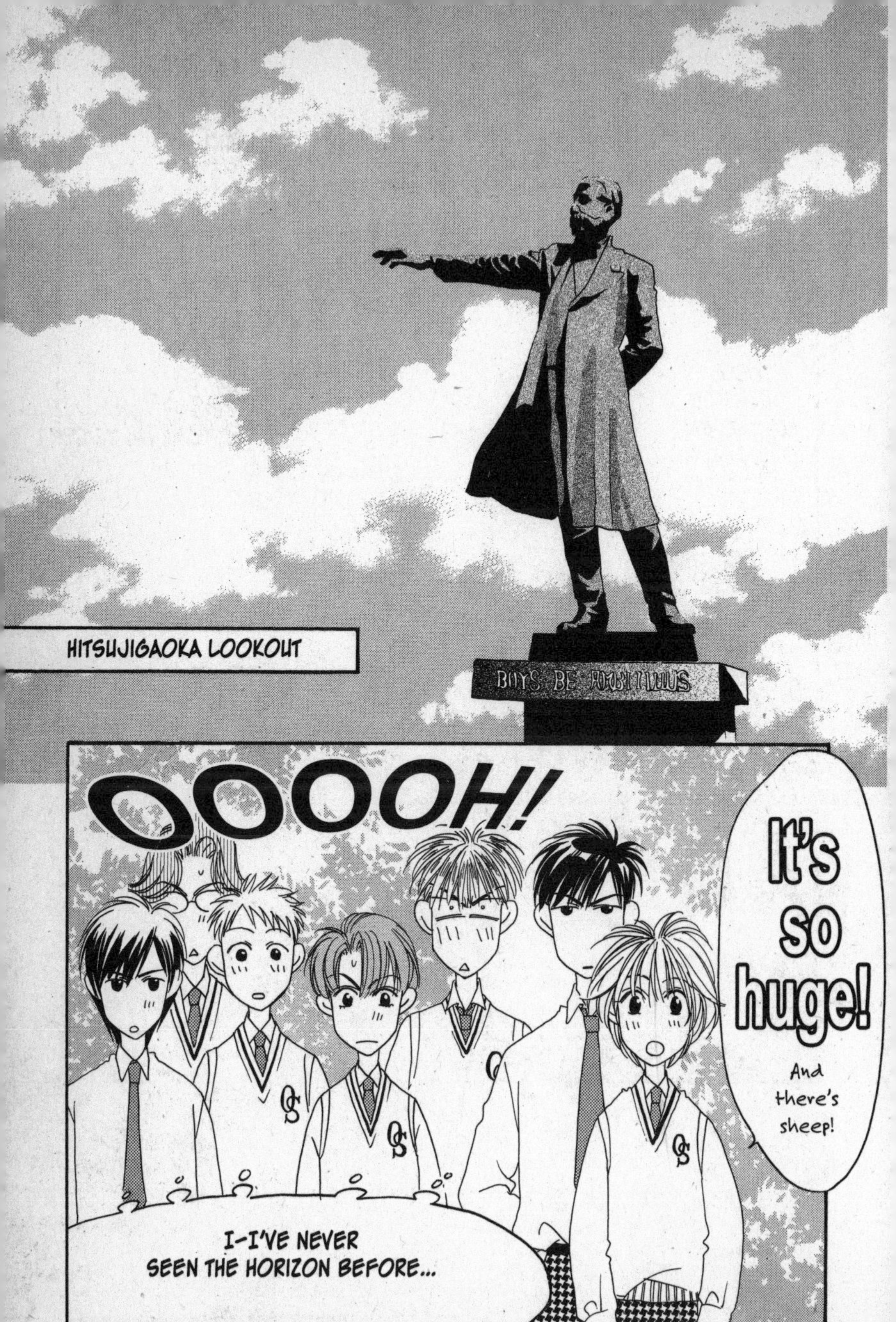
HITSUJIGAOKA LOOKOUT
BOYS BE AMBITIOUS
It's so huge!
And there's sheep!
OOOOH!
I-I'VE NEVER SEEN THE HORIZON BEFORE...

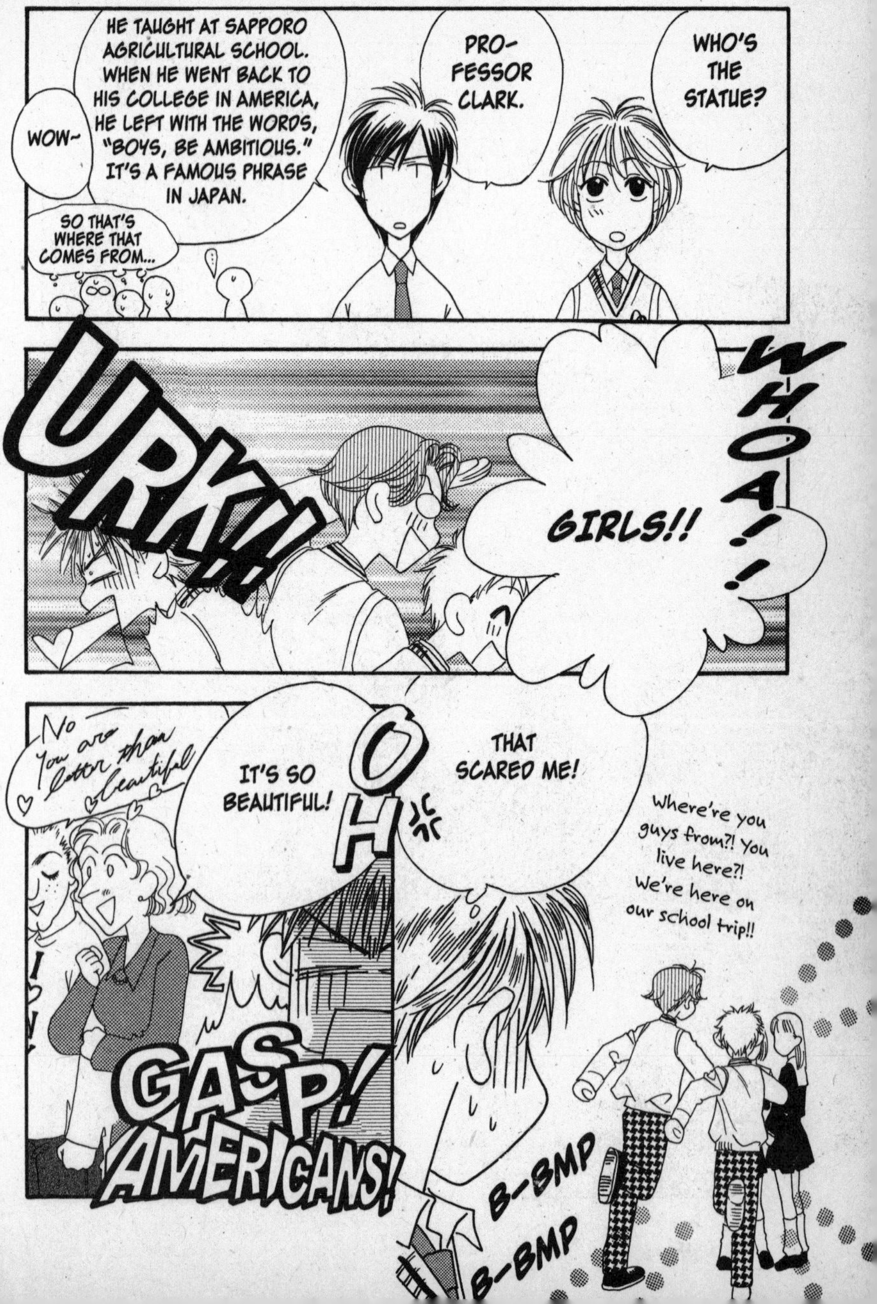
WHO'S THE STATUE?
PRO-FESSOR CLARK.
HE TAUGHT AT SAPPORO AGRICULTURAL SCHOOL. WHEN HE WENT BACK TO HIS COLLEGE IN AMERICA, HE LEFT WITH THE WORDS, "BOYS, BE AMBITIOUS." IT'S A FAMOUS PHRASE IN JAPAN.
WOW~
SO THAT'S WHERE THAT COMES FROM...
WHOA!!!
GIRLS!!
URK!!
Where're you guys from?! You live here?! We're here on our school trip!!
B-BMP
B-BMP
THAT SCARED ME!
OH
IT'S SO BEAUTIFUL!
No You are better than beautiful
GASP! AMERICANS!

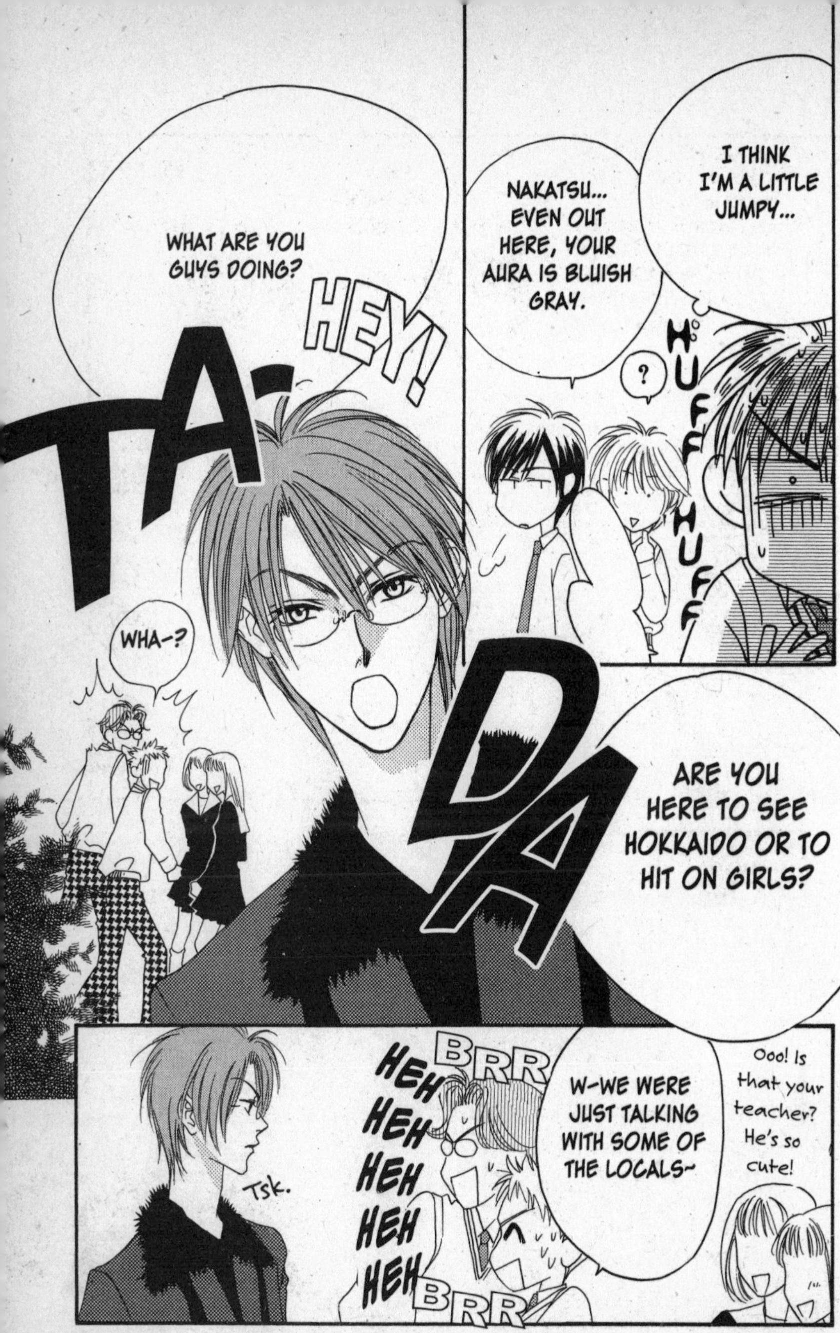
I THINK I'M A LITTLE JUMPY...
NAKATSU... EVEN OUT HERE, YOUR AURA IS BLUISH GRAY.
HUFF HUFF
?
WHAT ARE YOU GUYS DOING?
HEY!
TA-
DA
ARE YOU HERE TO SEE HOKKAIDO OR TO HIT ON GIRLS?
WHA-?
Ooo! Is that your teacher? He's so cute!
W-WE WERE JUST TALKING WITH SOME OF THE LOCALS~
BRR
HEH HEH HEH HEH HEH
BRR
TSK.

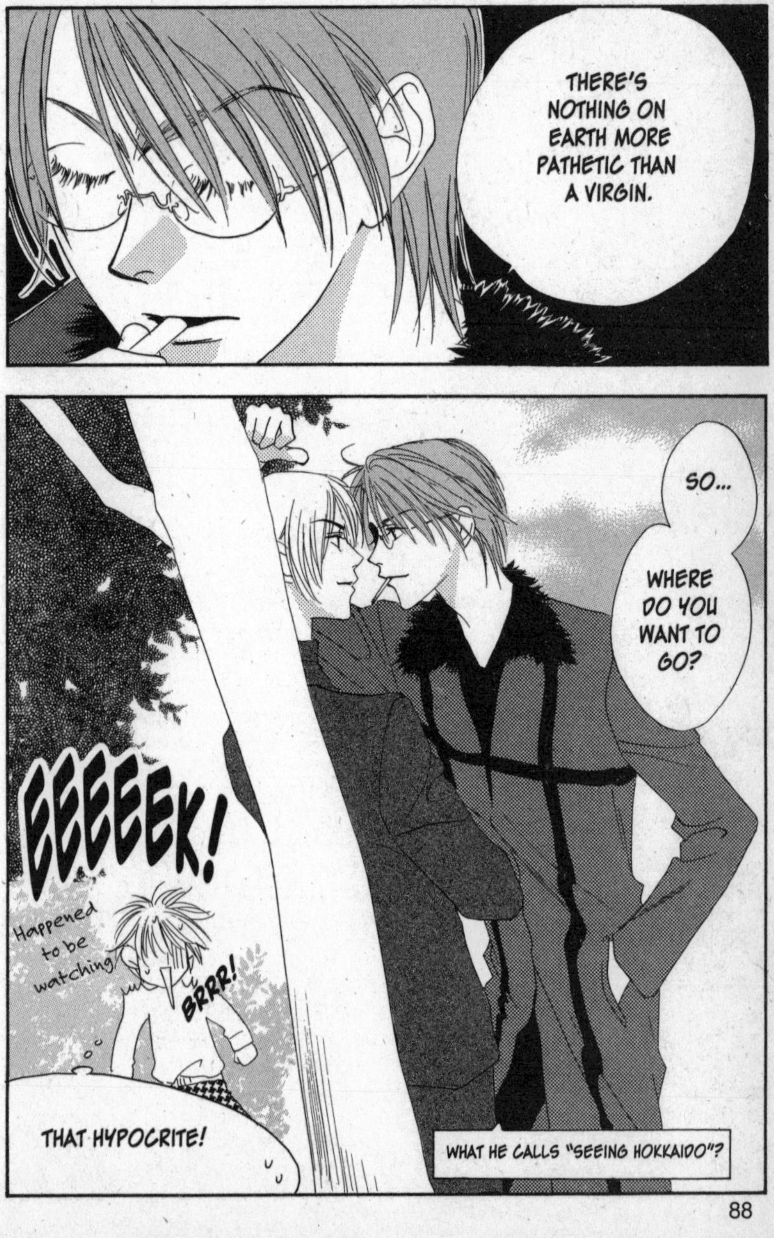
THERE'S NOTHING ON EARTH MORE PATHETIC THAN A VIRGIN.
SO...
WHERE DO YOU WANT TO GO?
WHAT HE CALLS "SEEING HOKKAIDO"?
EEEEEK!
Happened to be watching
BRRR!
THAT HYPOCRITE!

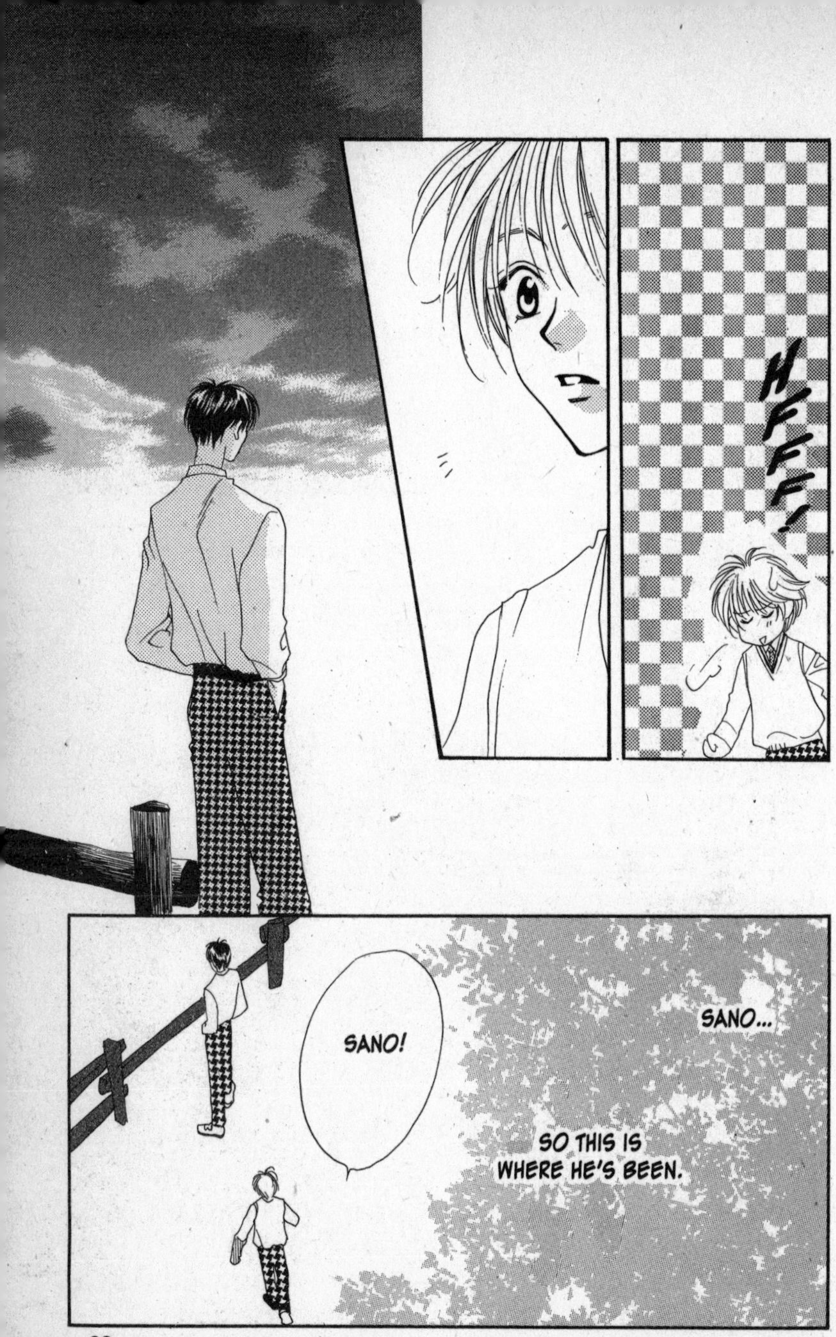
HFFF!
SANO...
SO THIS IS WHERE HE'S BEEN.
SANO!

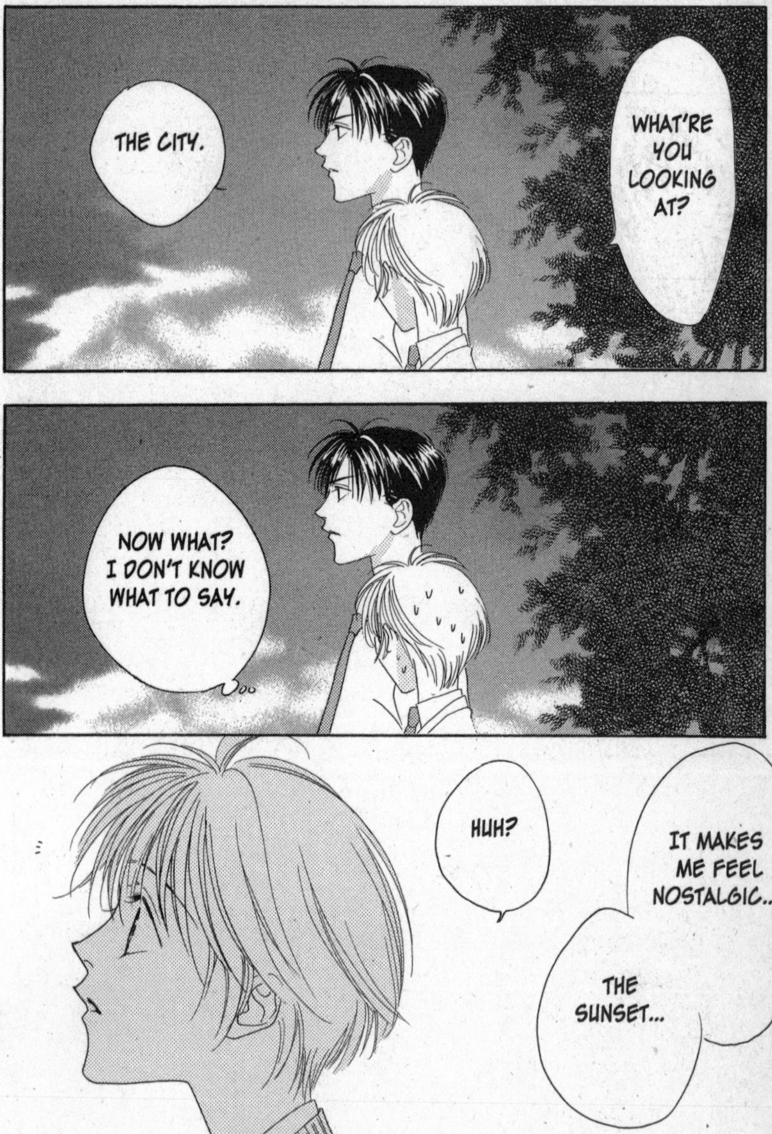
WHAT'RE YOU LOOKING AT?
THE CITY.
NOW WHAT? I DON'T KNOW WHAT TO SAY.
IT MAKES ME FEEL NOSTALGIC...
THE SUNSET...
HUH?

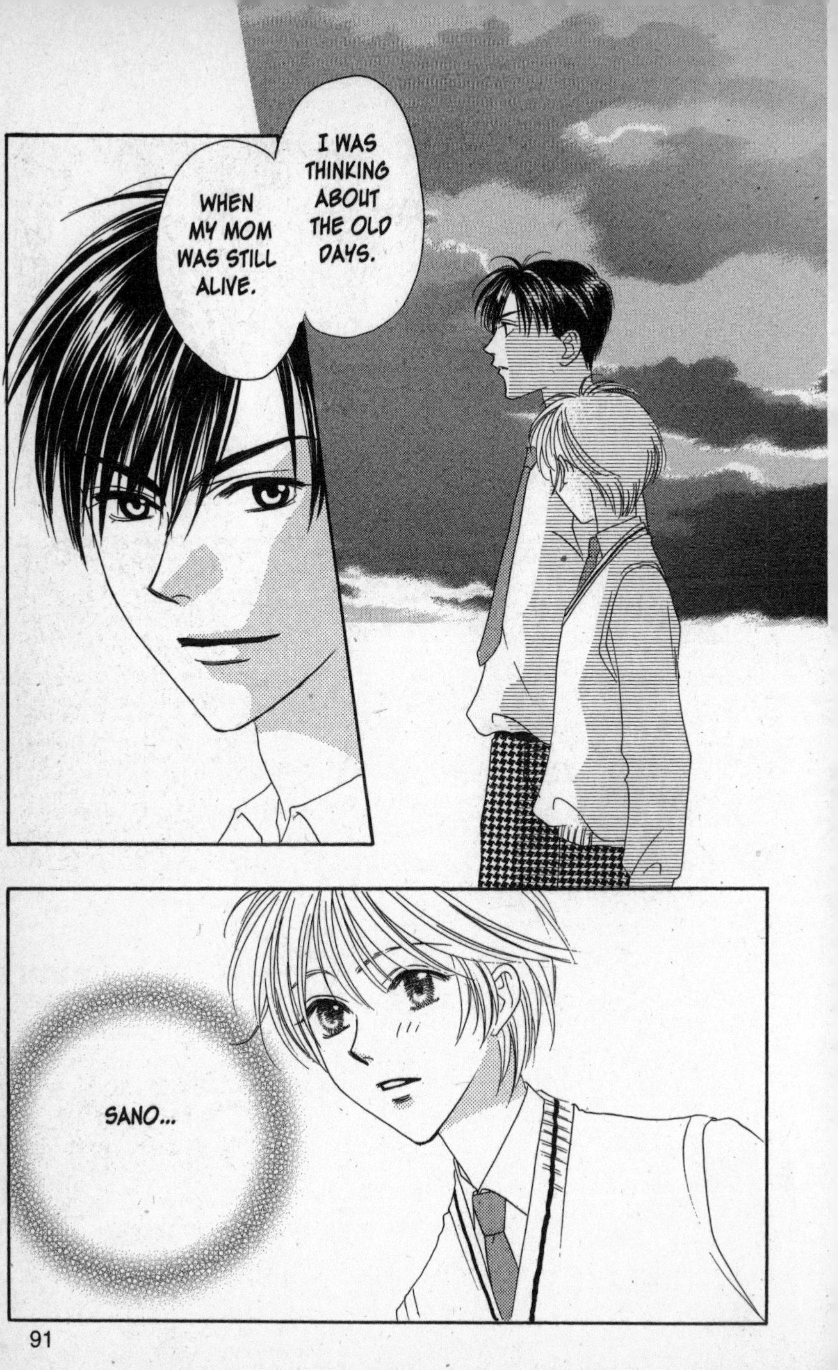
I WAS THINKING ABOUT THE OLD DAYS.
WHEN MY MOM WAS STILL ALIVE.
SANO...

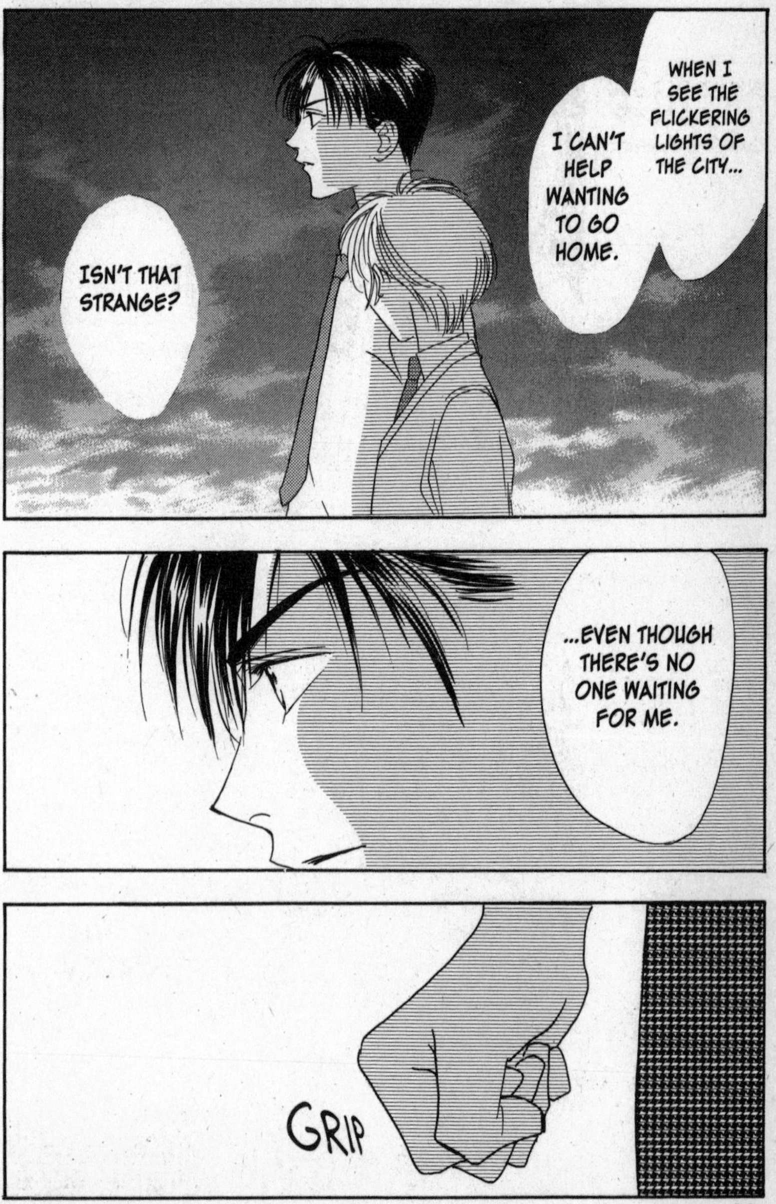
WHEN I SEE THE FLICKERING LIGHTS OF THE CITY...
I CAN'T HELP WANTING TO GO HOME.
ISN'T THAT STRANGE?
...EVEN THOUGH THERE'S NO ONE WAITING FOR ME.
GRIP

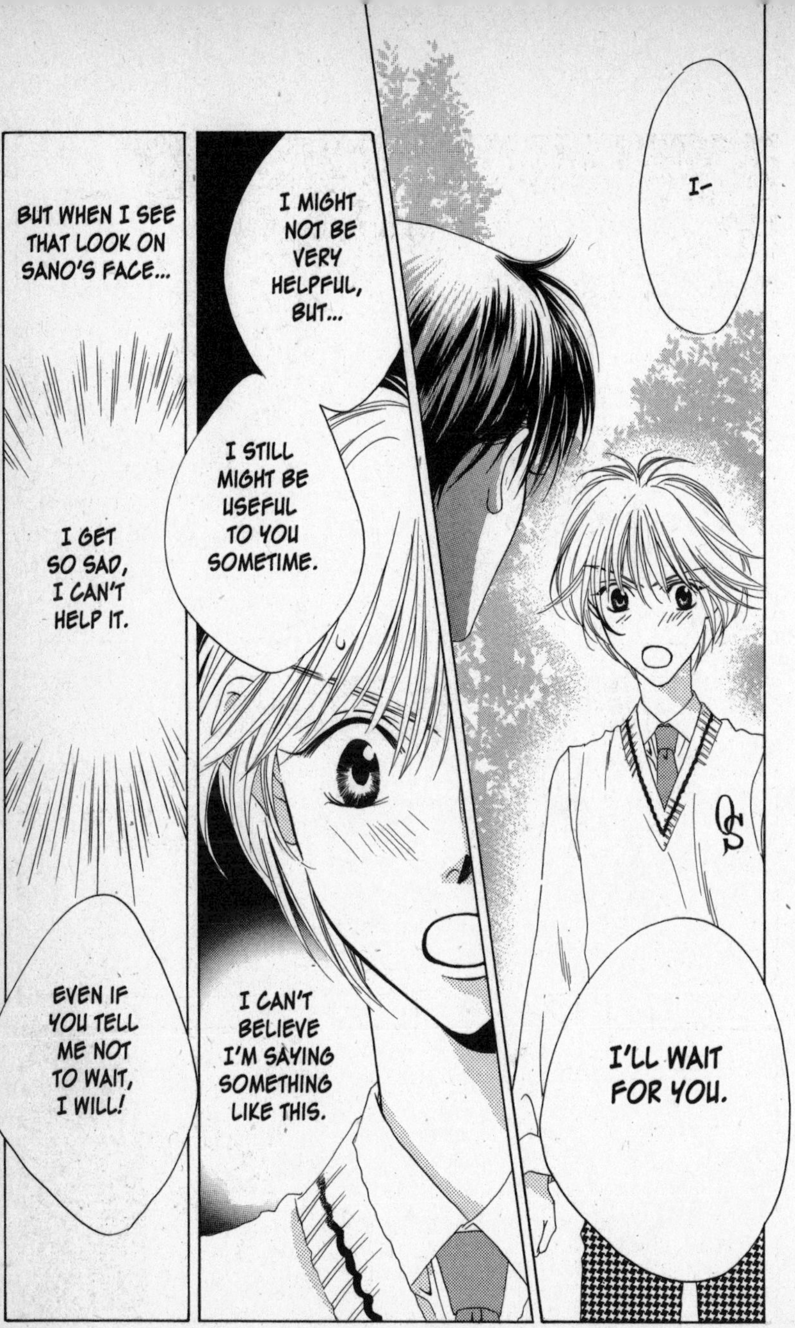
I-
I'LL WAIT FOR YOU.
I MIGHT NOT BE VERY HELPFUL, BUT...
I STILL MIGHT BE USEFUL TO YOU SOMETIME.
I CAN'T BELIEVE I'M SAYING SOMETHING LIKE THIS.
BUT WHEN I SEE THAT LOOK ON SANO'S FACE...
I GET SO SAD, I CAN'T HELP IT.
EVEN IF YOU TELL ME NOT TO WAIT, I WILL!

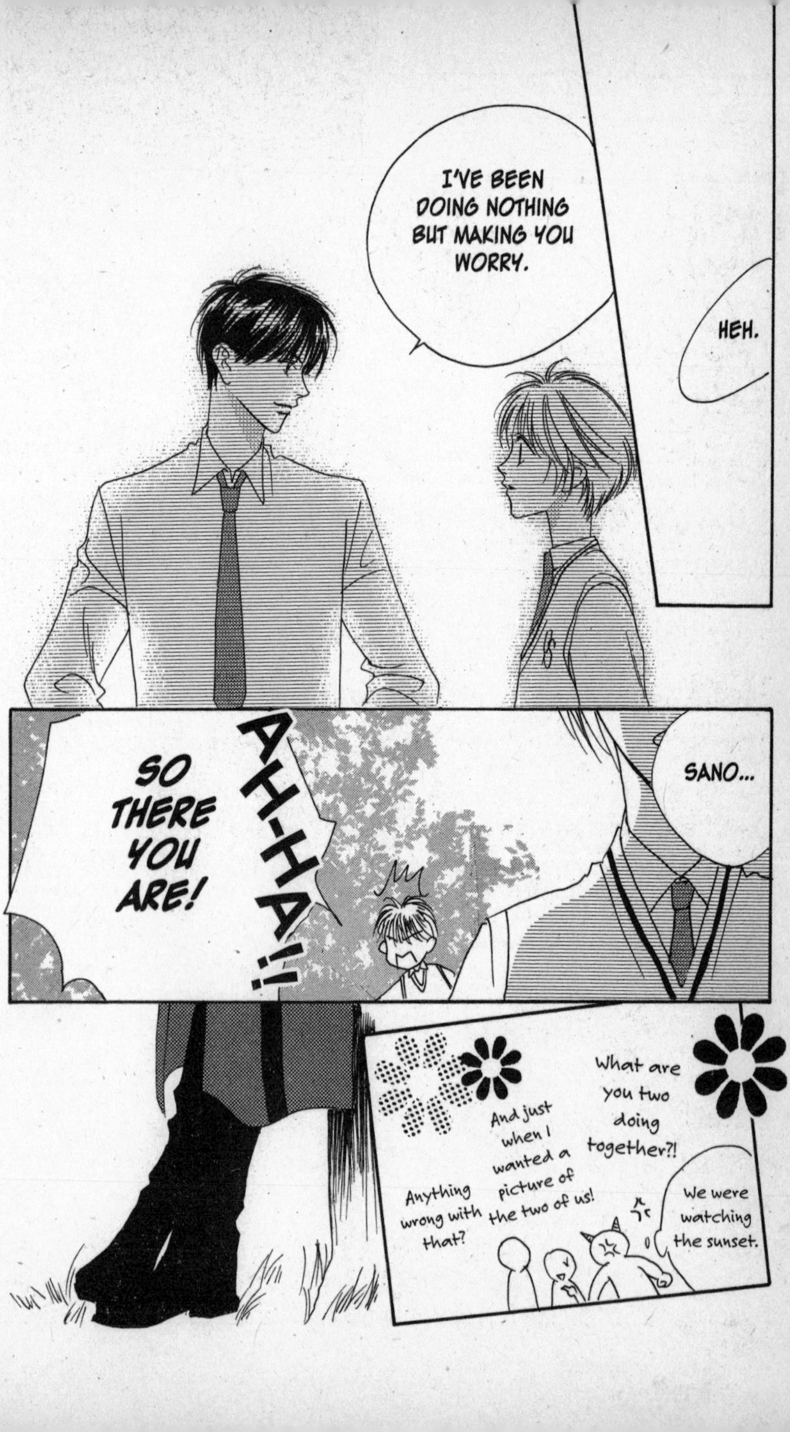
HEH.
I'VE BEEN DOING NOTHING BUT MAKING YOU WORRY.
SANO...
AH-HA!!
SO THERE YOU ARE!
What are you two doing together?!
We were watching the sunset.
And just when I wanted a picture of the two of us!
Anything wrong with that?

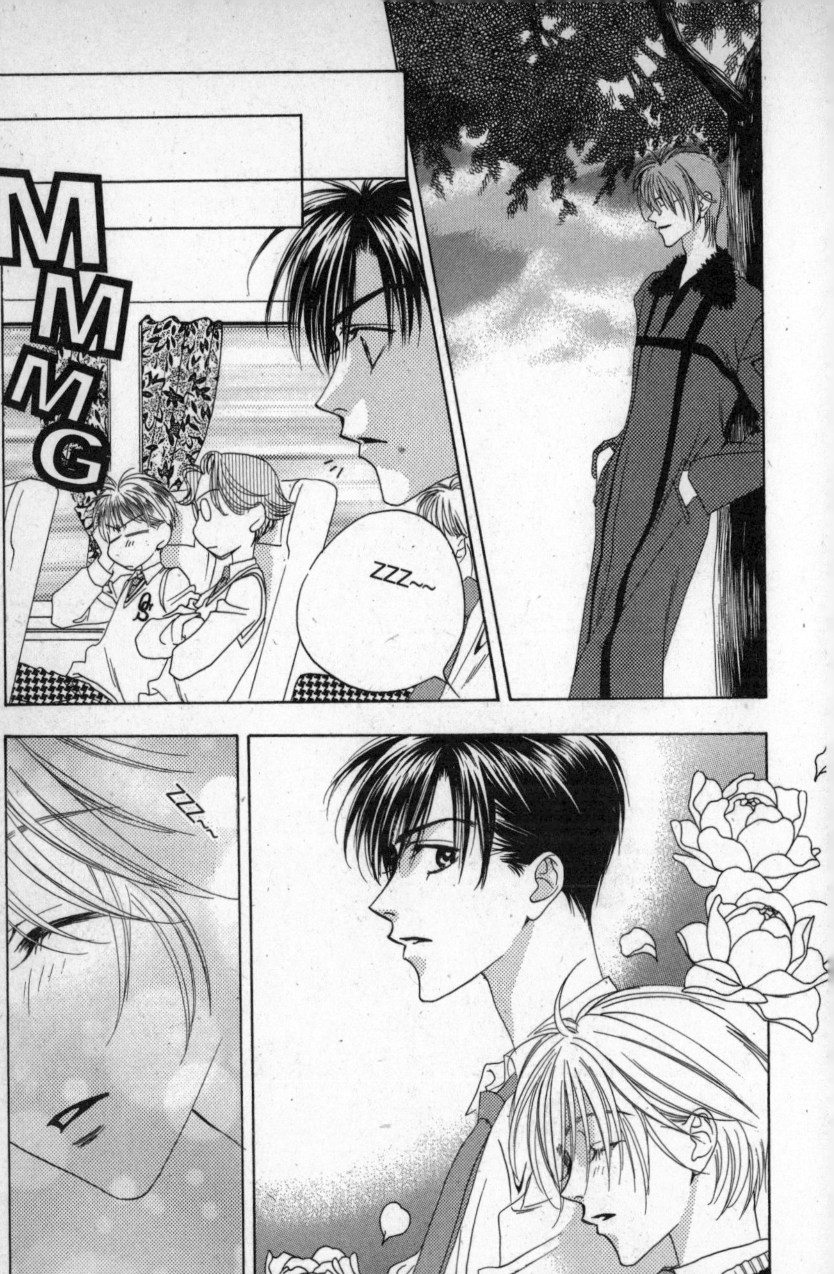
MMMG
ZZZ~~
ZZZ~~

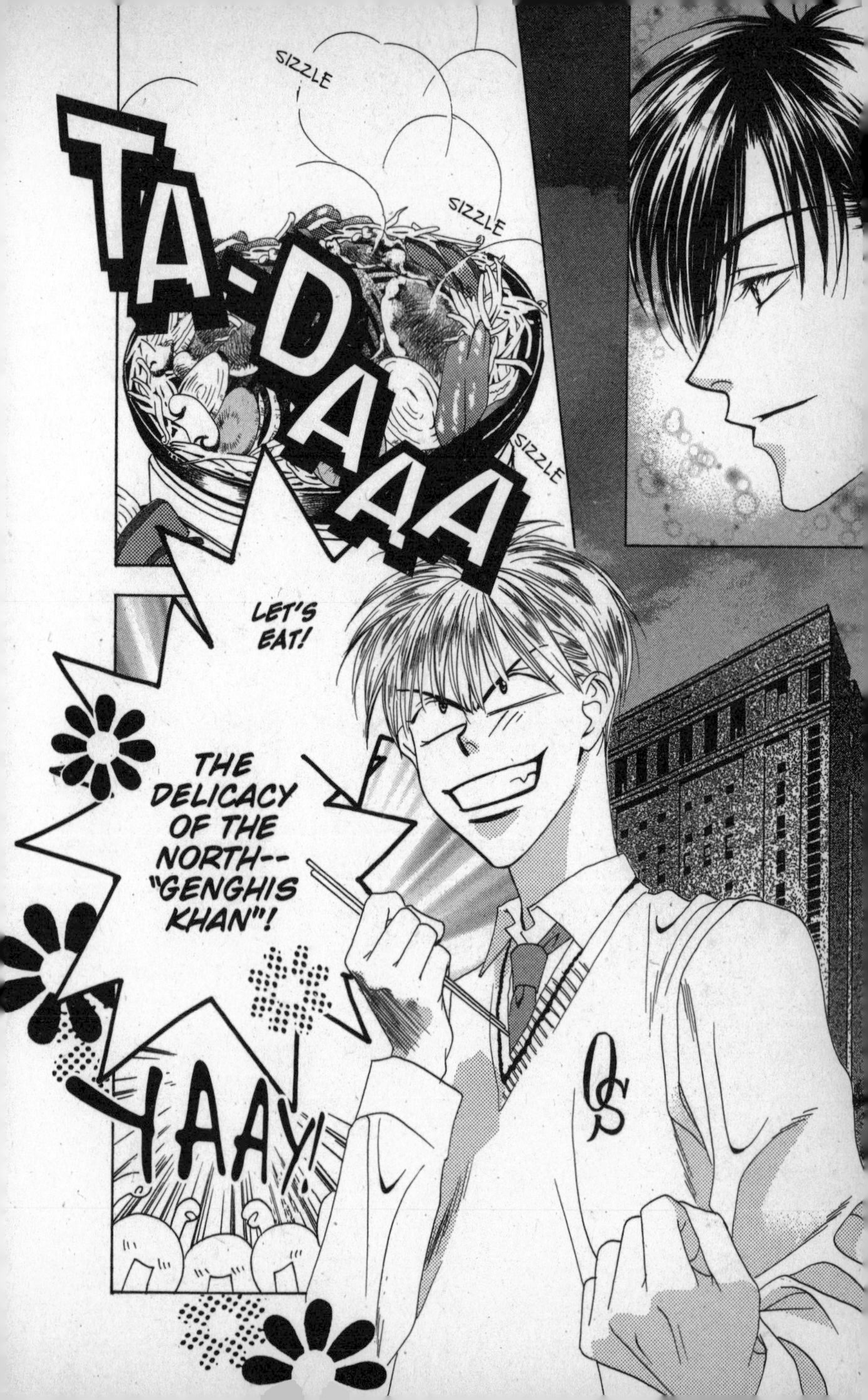
SIZZLE
SIZZLE
SIZZLE
TA-DAAA
LET'S EAT!
THE DELICACY OF THE NORTH-- "GENGHIS KHAN"!
YAAY!

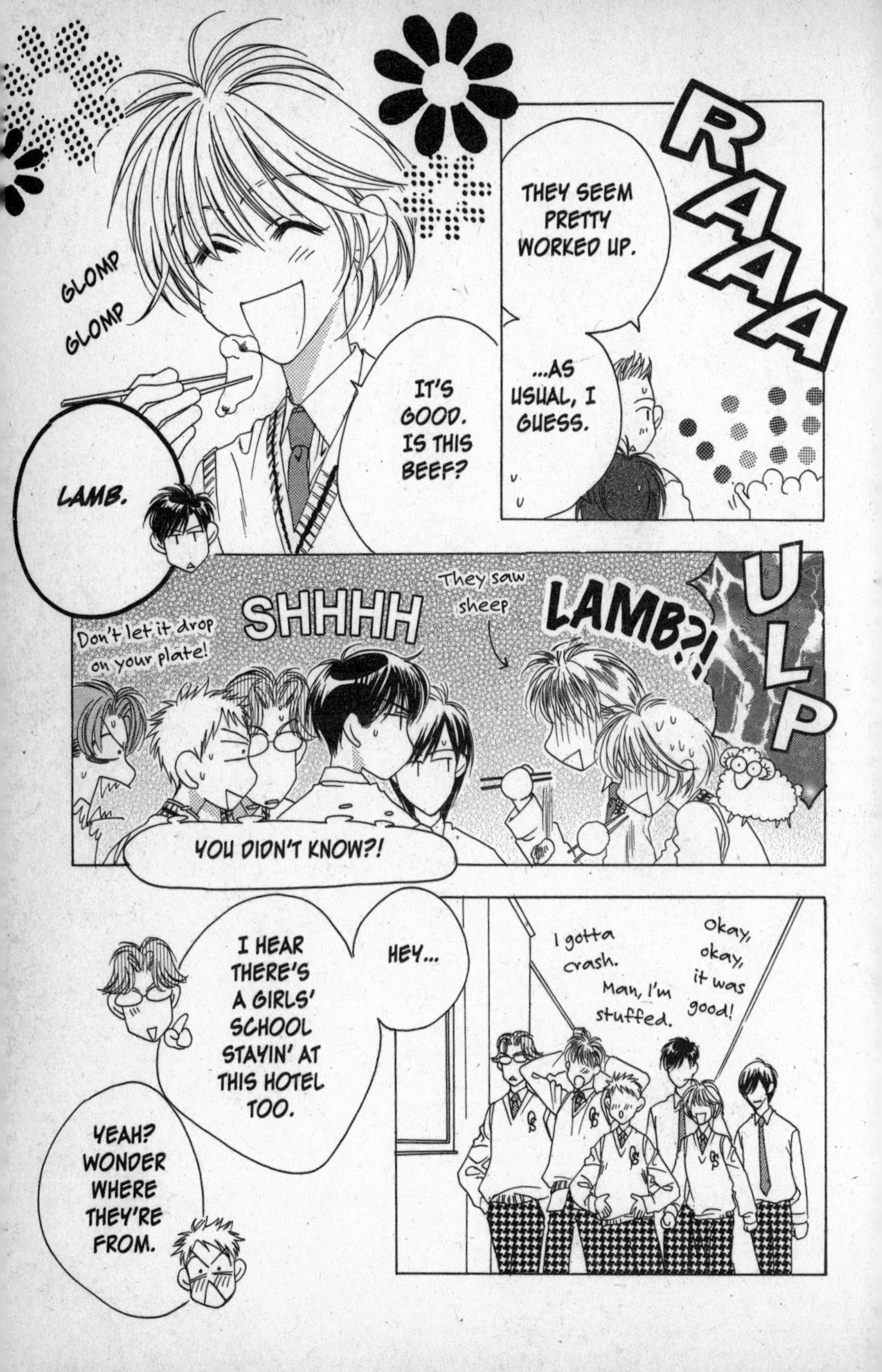
RAAA
THEY SEEM PRETTY WORKED UP.
...AS USUAL, I GUESS.
GLOMP GLOMP
IT'S GOOD. IS THIS BEEF?
LAMB.
ULP
LAMB?!
They saw sheep
SHHHH
Don't let it drop on your plate!
YOU DIDN'T KNOW?!
Okay, okay, it was good!
I gotta crash.
Man, I'm stuffed.
HEY...
I HEAR THERE'S A GIRLS' SCHOOL STAYIN' AT THIS HOTEL TOO.
YEAH? WONDER WHERE THEY'RE FROM.

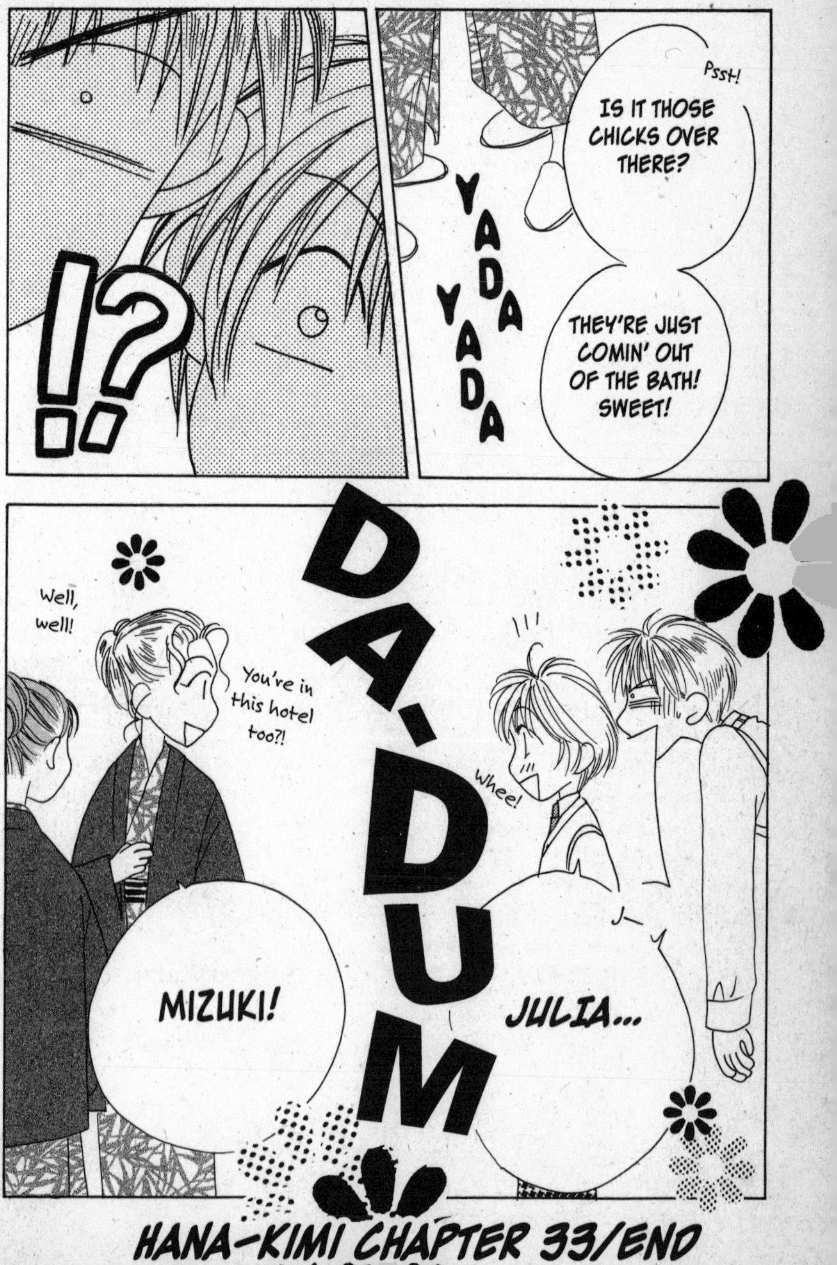
Psst!
IS IT THOSE CHICKS OVER THERE?
YADA YADA
YADA YADA
THEY'RE JUST COMIN' OUT OF THE BATH! SWEET!
!?
DA-DUM
Whee!
JULIA...
Well, well!
You're in this hotel too?!
MIZUKI!

HANA-KIMI CHAPTER 33/END

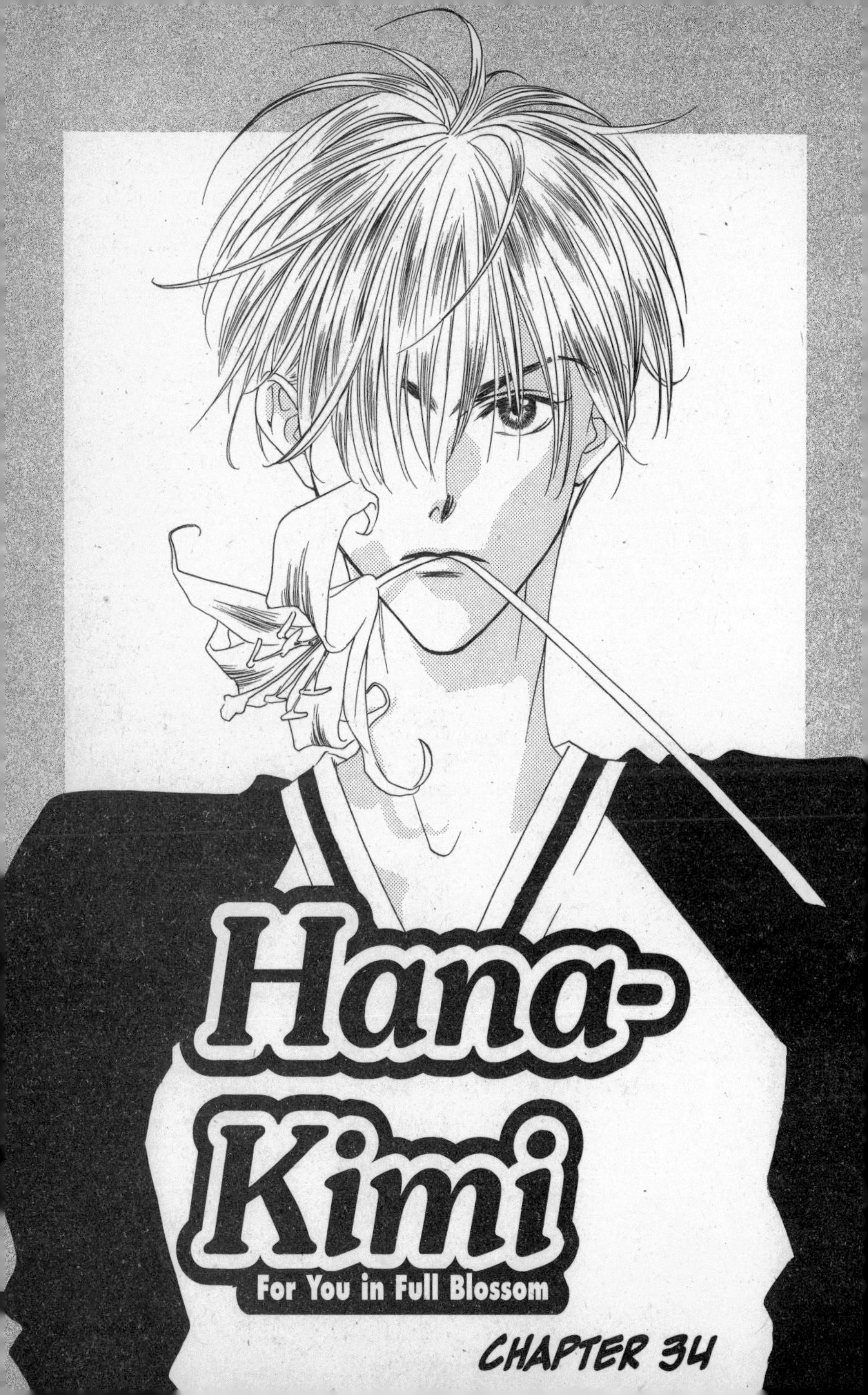
Hana-Kimi
For You in Full Blossom
CHAPTER 34

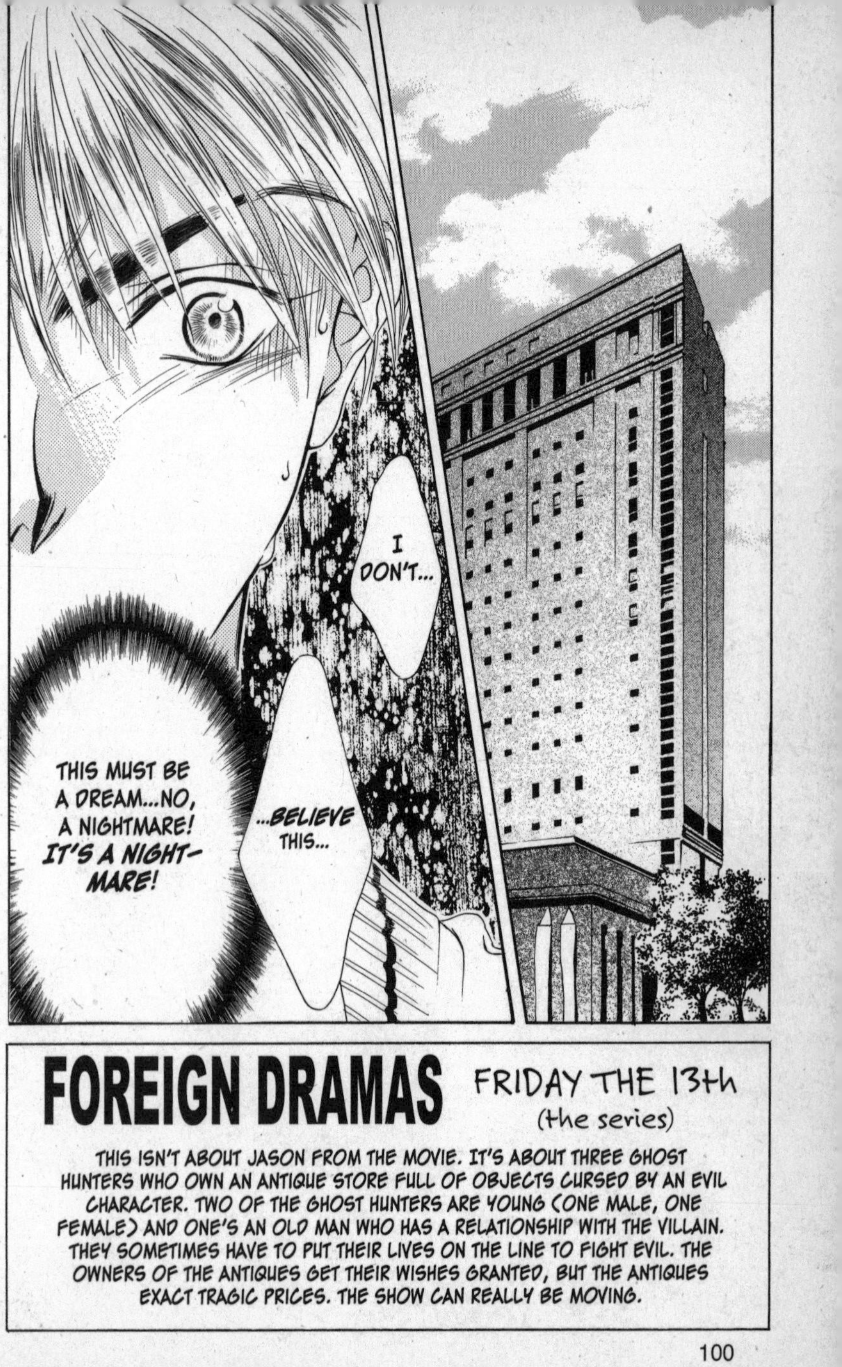
I DON'T...
...BELIEVE THIS...
THIS MUST BE A DREAM...NO, A NIGHTMARE! *IT'S A NIGHT-MARE!*

FOREIGN DRAMAS

FRIDAY THE 13th (the series)

THIS ISN'T ABOUT JASON FROM THE MOVIE. IT'S ABOUT THREE GHOST HUNTERS WHO OWN AN ANTIQUE STORE FULL OF OBJECTS CURSED BY AN EVIL CHARACTER. TWO OF THE GHOST HUNTERS ARE YOUNG (ONE MALE, ONE FEMALE) AND ONE'S AN OLD MAN WHO HAS A RELATIONSHIP WITH THE VILLAIN. THEY SOMETIMES HAVE TO PUT THEIR LIVES ON THE LINE TO FIGHT EVIL. THE OWNERS OF THE ANTIQUES GET THEIR WISHES GRANTED, BUT THE ANTIQUES EXACT TRAGIC PRICES. THE SHOW CAN REALLY BE MOVING.

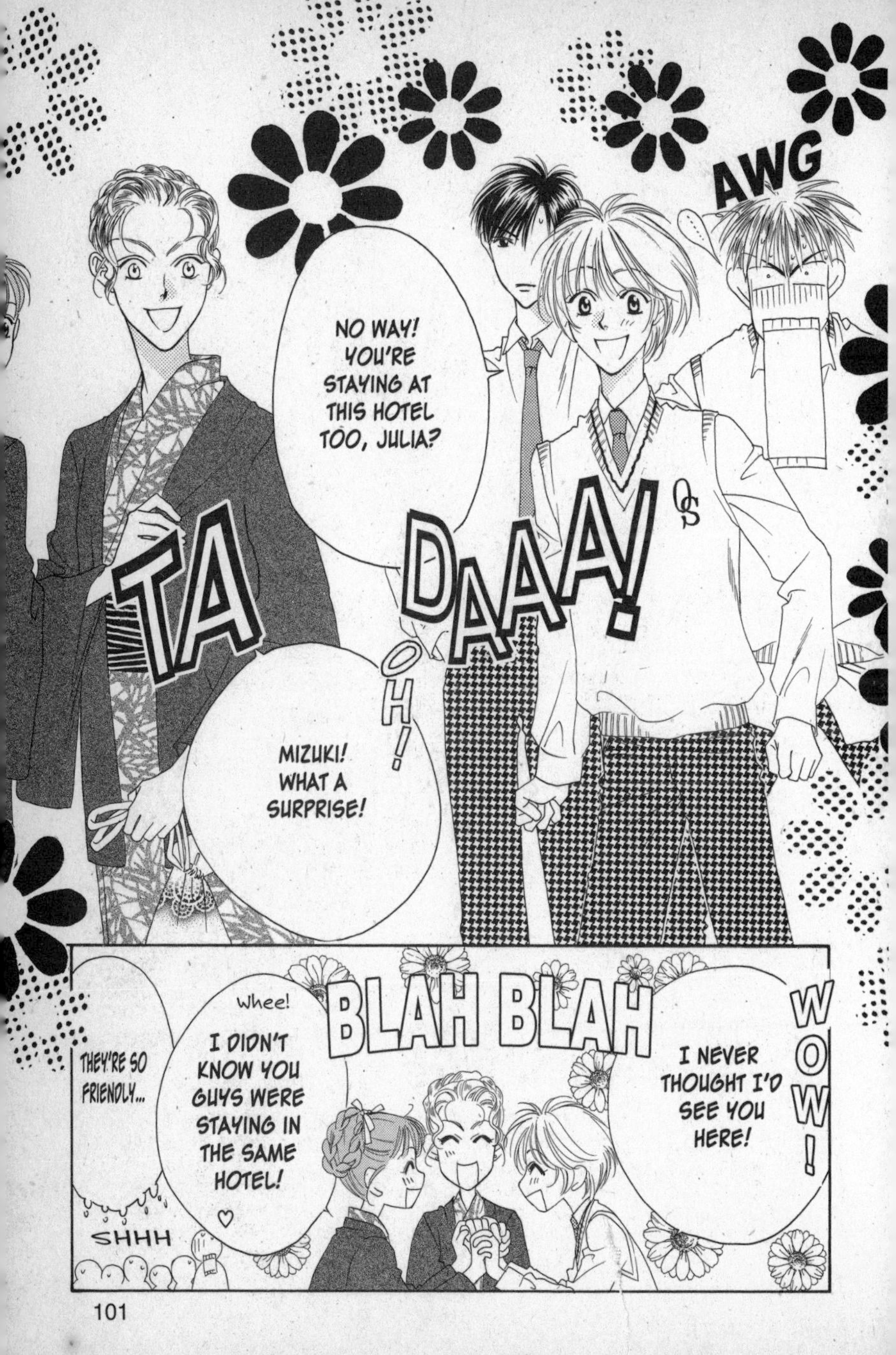
AWG
NO WAY! YOU'RE STAYING AT THIS HOTEL TOO, JULIA?
TA DAAA!
OH!
MIZUKI! WHAT A SURPRISE!
WOW!
I NEVER THOUGHT I'D SEE YOU HERE!
BLAH BLAH
Whee!
I DIDN'T KNOW YOU GUYS WERE STAYING IN THE SAME HOTEL! ♡
THEY'RE SO FRIENDLY...
SHHH

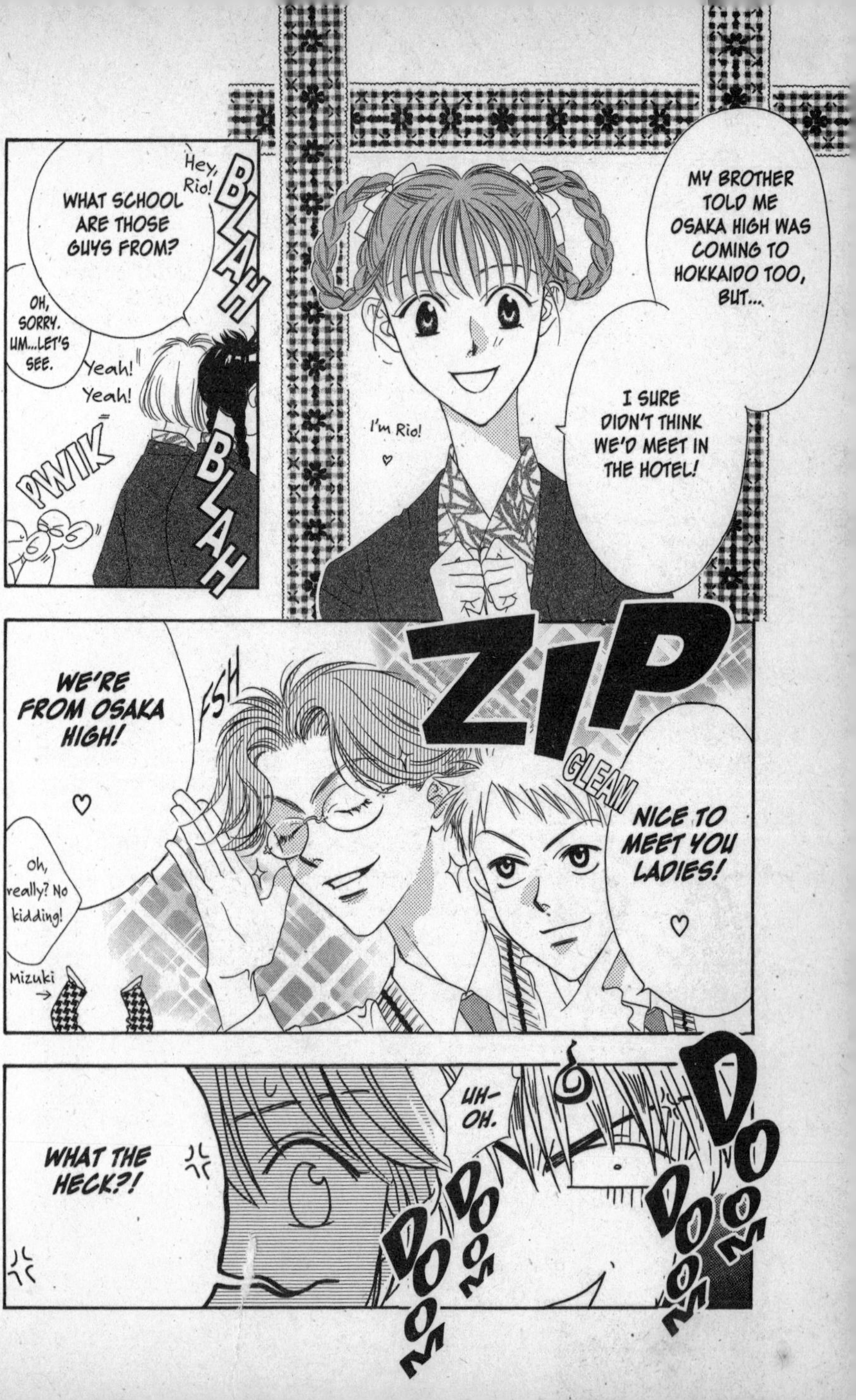
MY BROTHER TOLD ME OSAKA HIGH WAS COMING TO HOKKAIDO TOO, BUT...
I SURE DIDN'T THINK WE'D MEET IN THE HOTEL!
I'm Rio! ♡
Hey, Rio!
WHAT SCHOOL ARE THOSE GUYS FROM?
BLAH BLAH BLAH
OH, SORRY. UM...LET'S SEE.
Yeah! Yeah!
PWIK
ZIP
GLEAM
NICE TO MEET YOU LADIES! ♡
FSH
WE'RE FROM OSAKA HIGH! ♡
Oh, really? No kidding!
Mizuki →
DOOM DOOM DOOM
UH-OH.
DOOM DOOM DOOM
WHAT THE HECK?!

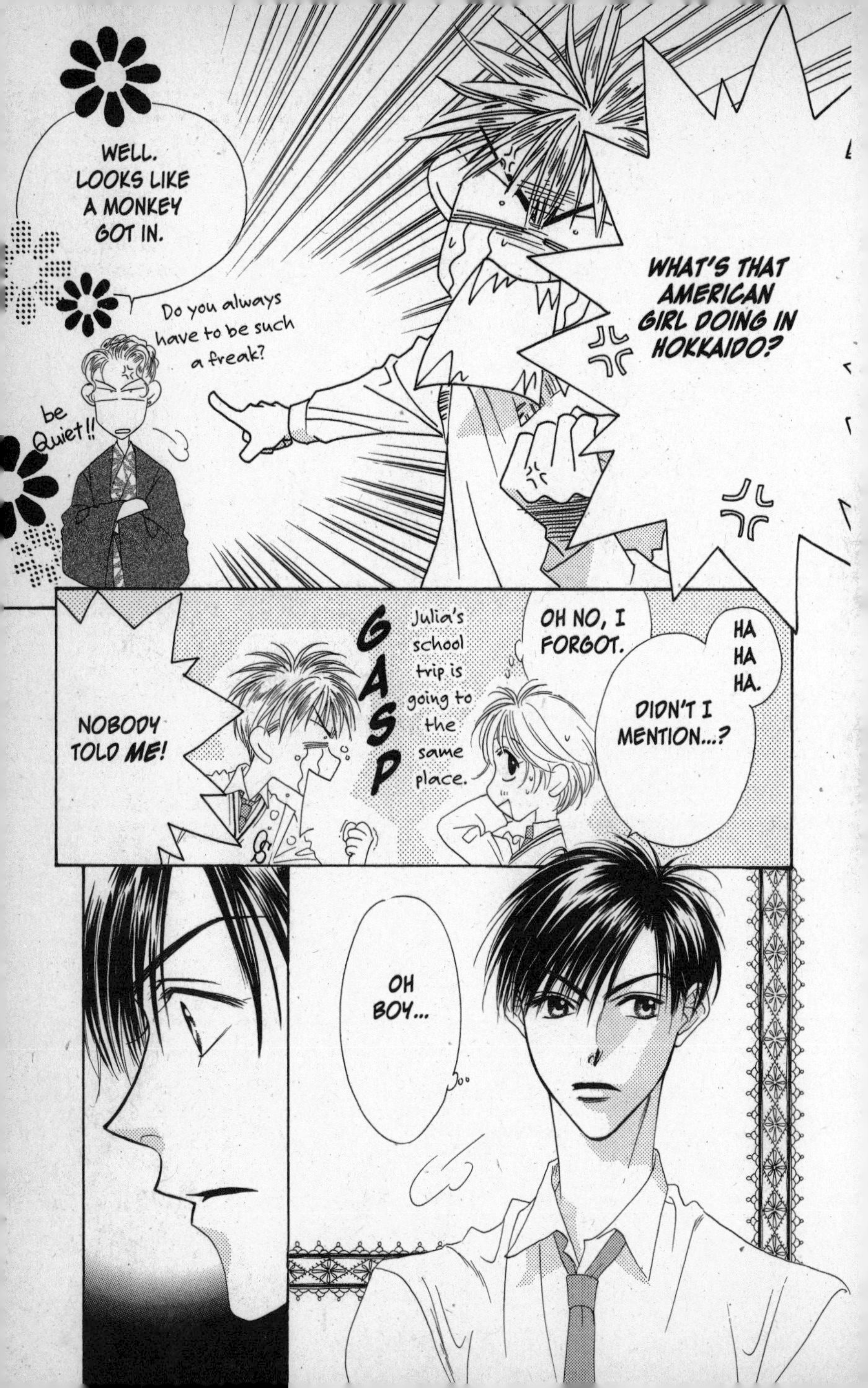
WHAT'S THAT AMERICAN GIRL DOING IN HOKKAIDO?
WELL. LOOKS LIKE A MONKEY GOT IN.
Do you always have to be such a freak?
be Quiet!!
HA HA HA.
DIDN'T I MENTION...?
OH NO, I FORGOT.
Julia's school trip is going to the same place.
GASP
NOBODY TOLD ME!
OH BOY...

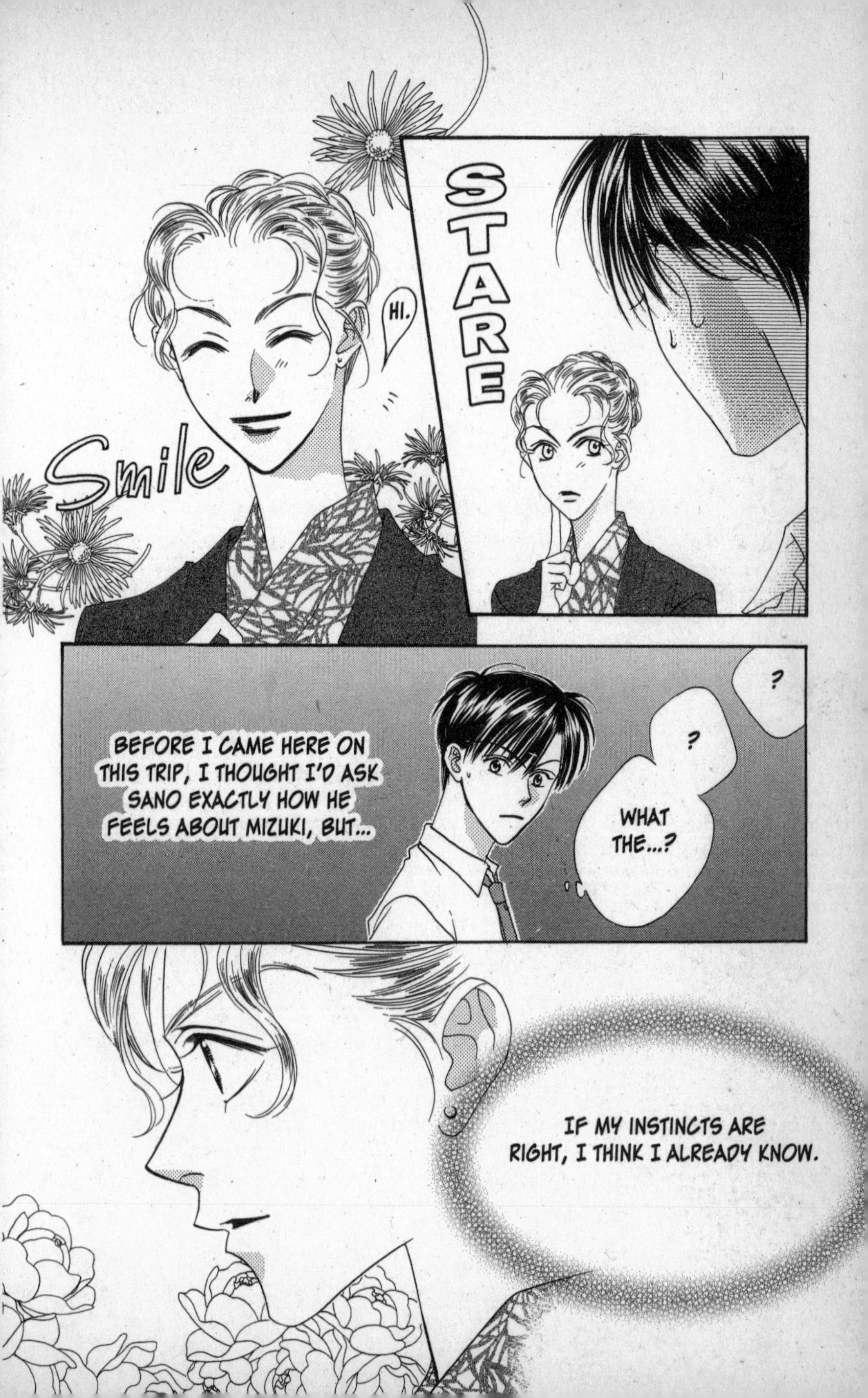
STARE
HI.
Smile
?
?
WHAT THE...?
BEFORE I CAME HERE ON THIS TRIP, I THOUGHT I'D ASK SANO EXACTLY HOW HE FEELS ABOUT MIZUKI, BUT...
IF MY INSTINCTS ARE RIGHT, I THINK I ALREADY KNOW.

WHISPERED SECRETS

DRAWING MANGA ON THE TRAIN

THIS IS A CONTINUATION OF THE LAST QUARTER-PAGE COLUMN. ANYWAY...WE HAD TO DRAW THE LAST FEW PAGES OF THE LAST CHAPTER ON THE TRAIN. THOSE POOR READERS WHO READ THE ORIGINAL ***HANA TO YUME*** VERSION WERE PROBABLY THINKING, "WHAT THE HECK IS THIS?" I'M SORRY! I WAS RUNNING OUT OF TIME AND I DIDN'T HAVE ANY OTHER CHOICE. IT WAS A MILITARY-LIKE SCHEDULE. THREE OF US GIRLS SAT IN THE THREE-SEAT SECTION AND QUIETLY WORKED ON MANGA AS IF OUR LIVES DEPENDED ON IT! WE WERE COMPLETELY SURROUNDED BY BUSINESSMEN. IT WAS TOTALLY WEIRD. (EVEN THOUGH WE WERE ON THE SUPER-FAST NOZOMI TRAIN, IT WAS REALLY WOBBLY. HOW WERE WE SUPPOSED TO DRAW? NOT THAT THAT'S ANY EXCUSE...) NOW WE'RE ON CHAPTER 34. TO ME, THE BIG EVENT IS THAT SANO'S BROTHER FINALLY APPEARS. BUT WHAT REALLY BECAME A HOT TOPIC WAS "THAT SCENE" WITH DR. UMEDA! ***WAAGGH!***

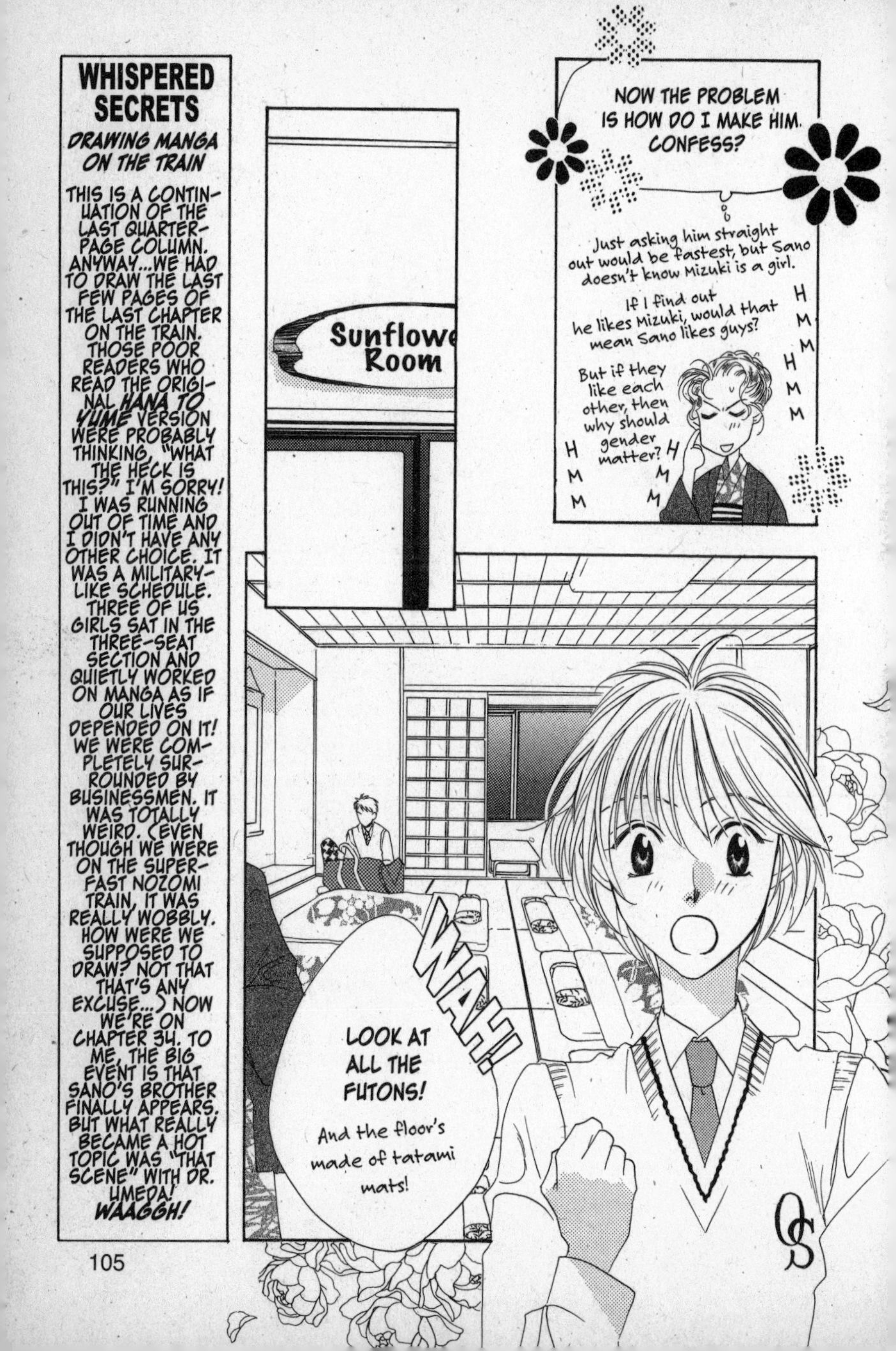
NOW THE PROBLEM IS HOW DO I MAKE HIM CONFESS?
Just asking him straight out would be fastest, but Sano doesn't know Mizuki is a girl.
If I find out he likes Mizuki, would that mean Sano likes guys?
But if they like each other, then why should gender matter?
HMM HMM HMM HMM
Sunflowe Room
WAH!
LOOK AT ALL THE FUTONS!
And the floor's made of tatami mats!
OS

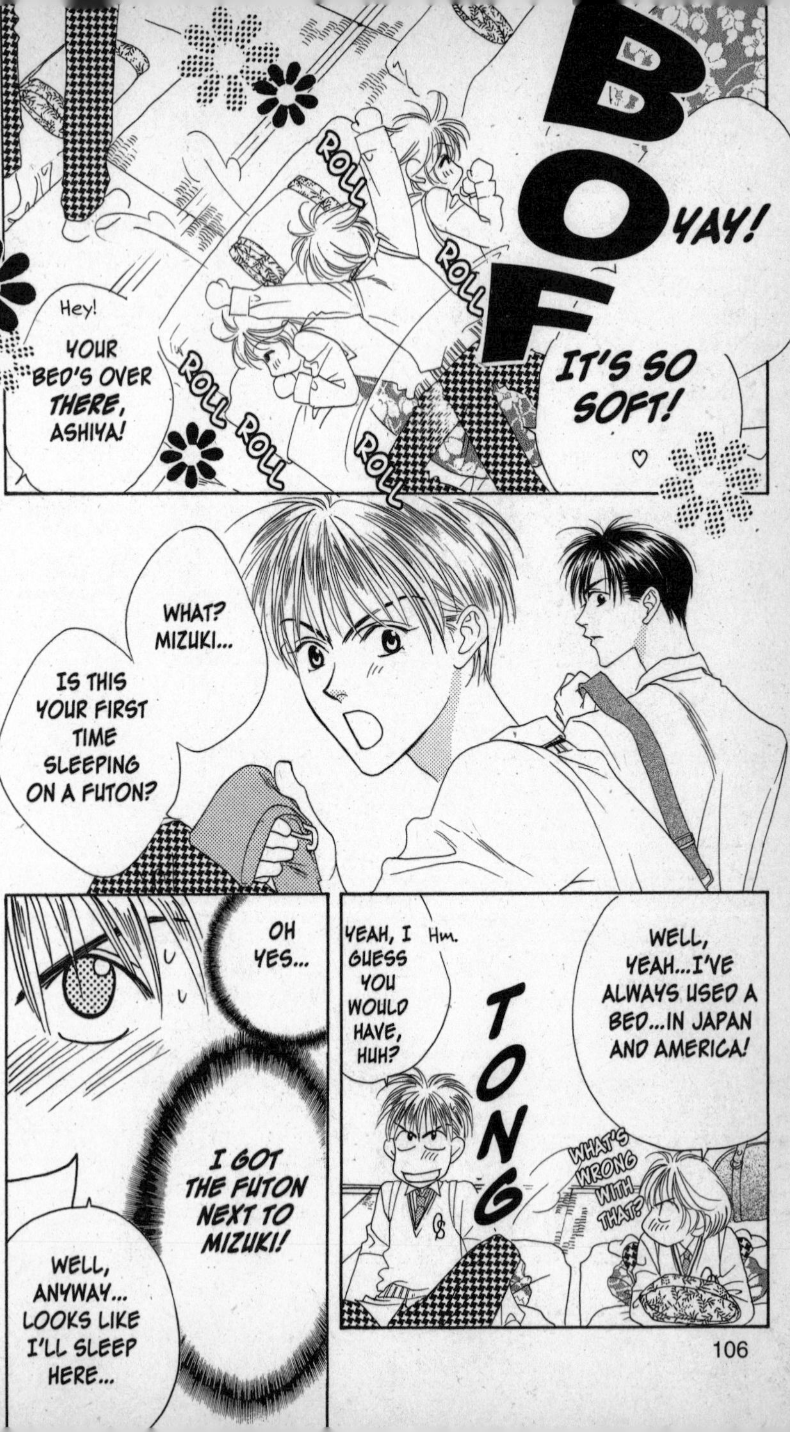

BOF
YAY!
IT'S SO SOFT!
ROLL
ROLL
ROLL
ROLL ROLL
Hey!
YOUR BED'S OVER THERE, ASHIYA!
WHAT? MIZUKI...
IS THIS YOUR FIRST TIME SLEEPING ON A FUTON?
WELL, YEAH...I'VE ALWAYS USED A BED...IN JAPAN AND AMERICA!
TONG
WHAT'S WRONG WITH THAT?
Hm.
YEAH, I GUESS YOU WOULD HAVE, HUH?
OH YES...
I GOT THE FUTON NEXT TO MIZUKI!
WELL, ANYWAY... LOOKS LIKE I'LL SLEEP HERE...

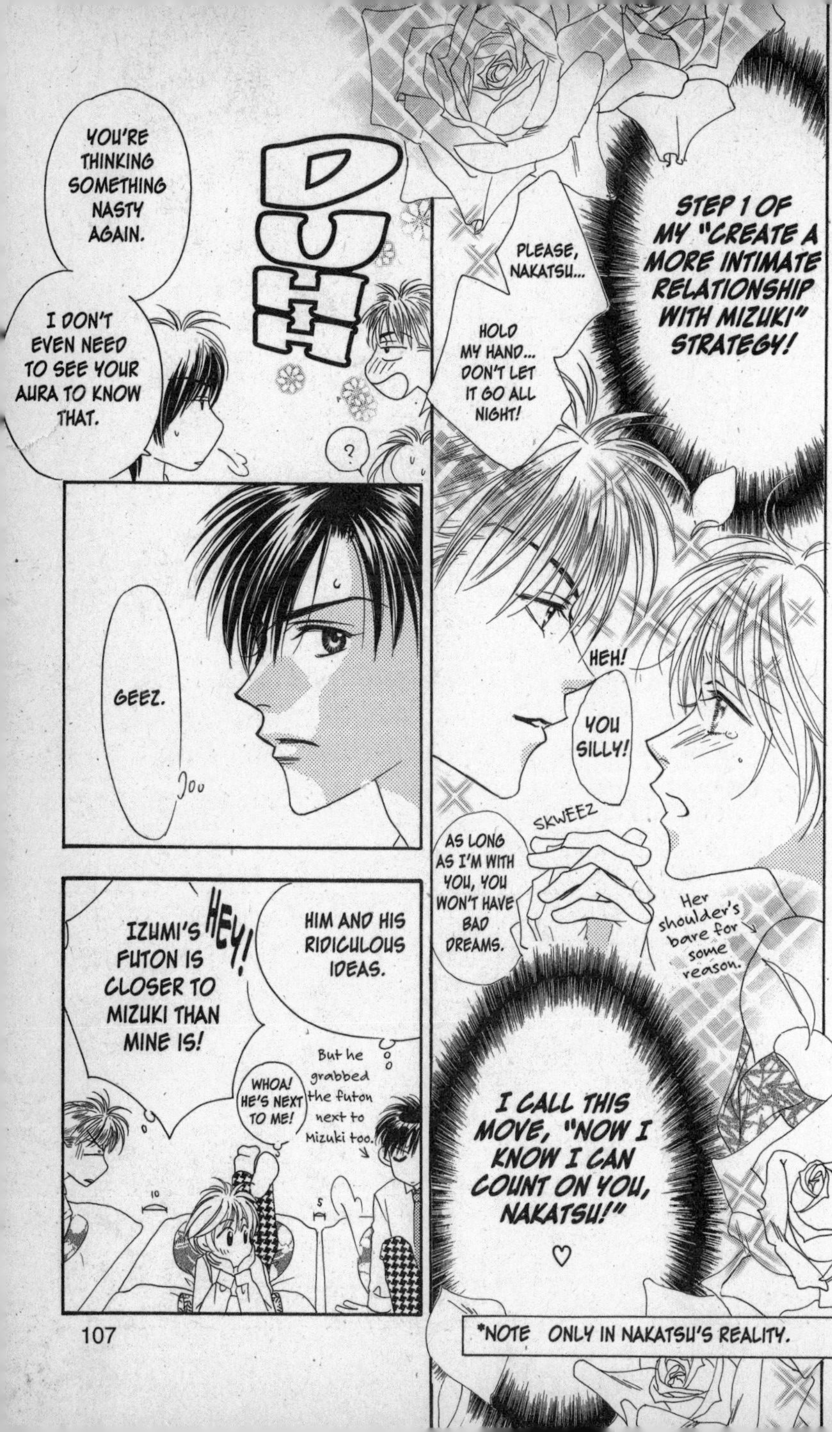
STEP 1 OF MY "CREATE A MORE INTIMATE RELATIONSHIP WITH MIZUKI" STRATEGY!
PLEASE, NAKATSU...
HOLD MY HAND... DON'T LET IT GO ALL NIGHT!
HEH!
YOU SILLY!
SKWEEZ
AS LONG AS I'M WITH YOU, YOU WON'T HAVE BAD DREAMS.
Her shoulder's bare for some reason.
I CALL THIS MOVE, "NOW I KNOW I CAN COUNT ON YOU, NAKATSU!" ♥
*NOTE ONLY IN NAKATSU'S REALITY.
DUH
YOU'RE THINKING SOMETHING NASTY AGAIN.
I DON'T EVEN NEED TO SEE YOUR AURA TO KNOW THAT.
?
GEEZ.
HIM AND HIS RIDICULOUS IDEAS.
HEY!
IZUMI'S FUTON IS CLOSER TO MIZUKI THAN MINE IS!
But he grabbed the futon next to Mizuki too.
WHOA! HE'S NEXT TO ME!

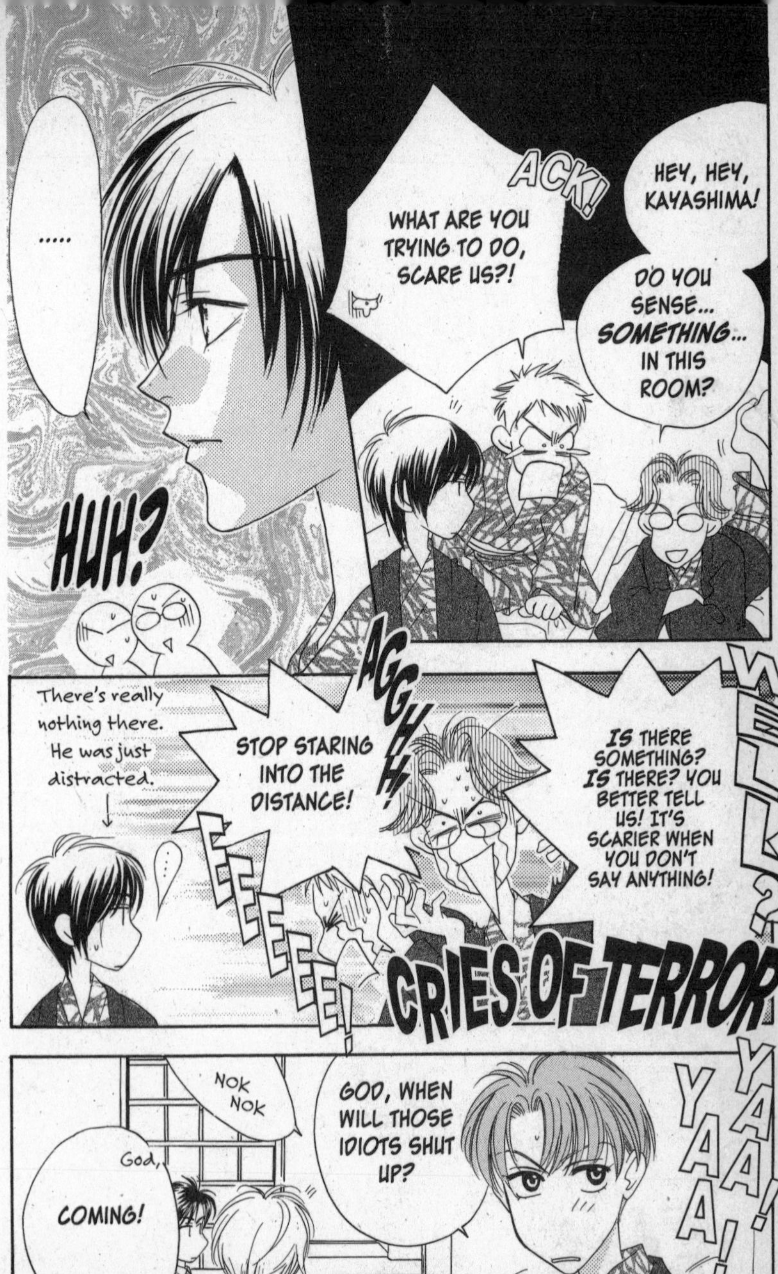
HEY, HEY, KAYASHIMA!
DO YOU SENSE... SOMETHING... IN THIS ROOM?
ACK!
WHAT ARE YOU TRYING TO DO, SCARE US?!
.....
HUH?
WELL?
IS THERE SOMETHING? IS THERE? YOU BETTER TELL US! IT'S SCARIER WHEN YOU DON'T SAY ANYTHING!
AGGHH!
STOP STARING INTO THE DISTANCE!
EEEEEEE!
CRIES OF TERROR
There's really nothing there. He was just distracted.
YAAA!
YAAA!
GOD, WHEN WILL THOSE IDIOTS SHUT UP?
NOK NOK
God,
COMING!

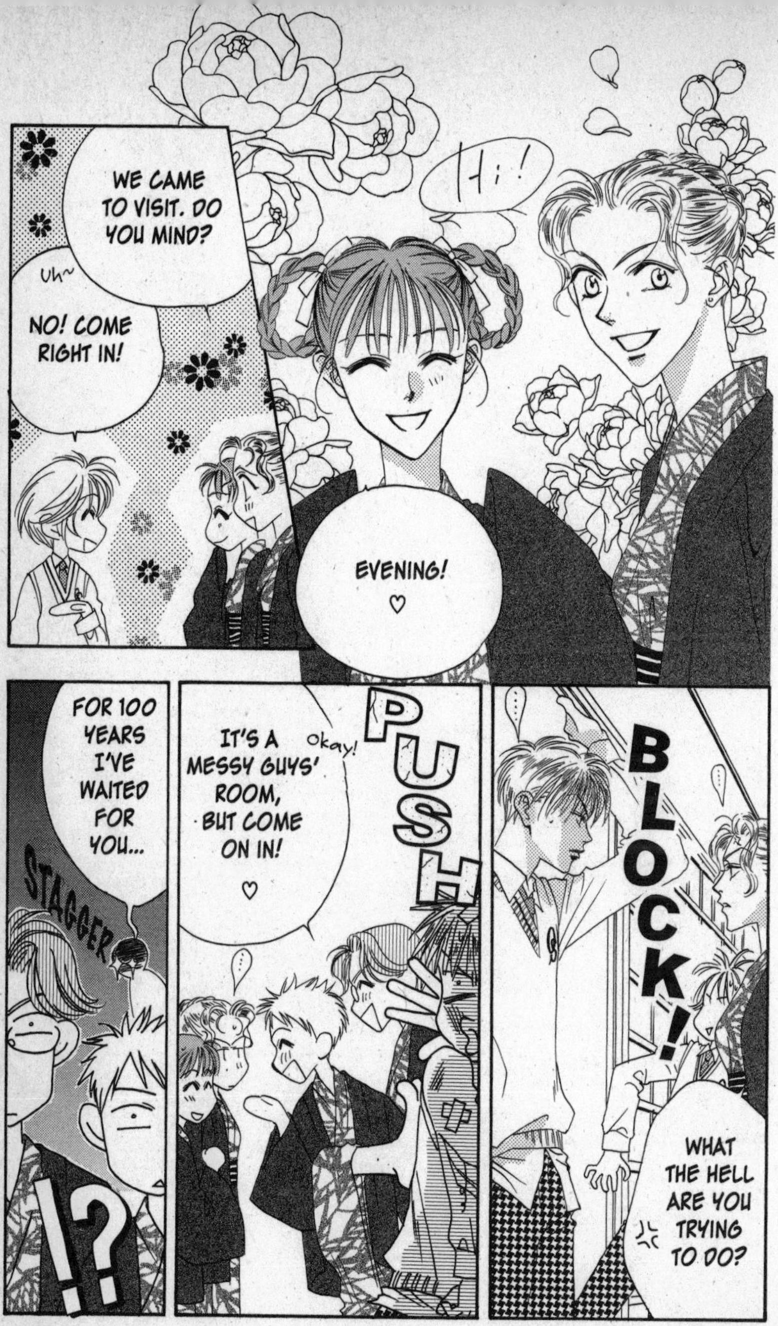
Hi!
EVENING! ♡
WE CAME TO VISIT. DO YOU MIND?
Uh~
NO! COME RIGHT IN!
BLOCK!
WHAT THE HELL ARE YOU TRYING TO DO?
PUSH
IT'S A MESSY GUYS' ROOM, BUT COME ON IN! ♡
Okay!
FOR 100 YEARS I'VE WAITED FOR YOU...
STAGGER
!?

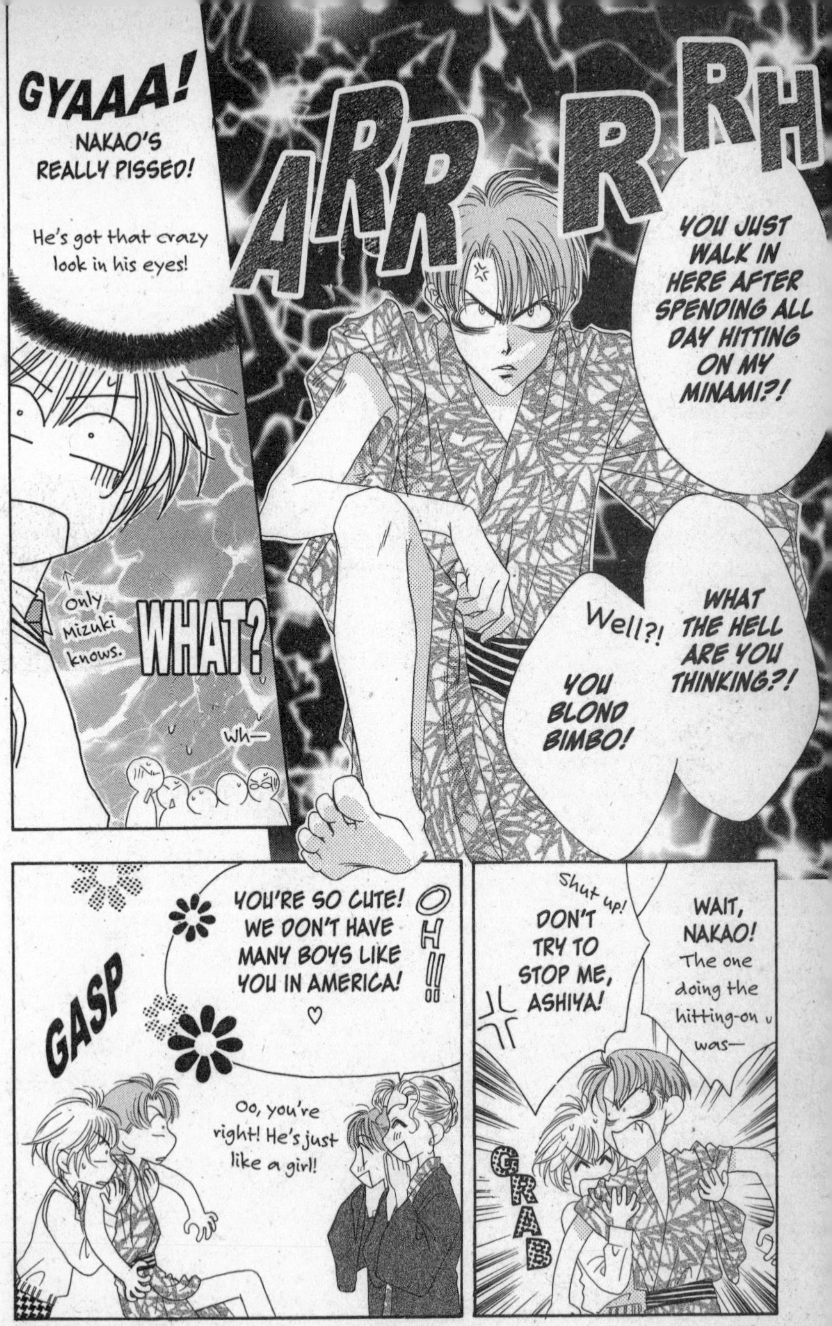
ARRRRRH
YOU JUST WALK IN HERE AFTER SPENDING ALL DAY HITTING ON MY MINAMI?!
WHAT THE HELL ARE YOU THINKING?!
Well?!
YOU BLOND BIMBO!
GYAAA!
NAKAO'S REALLY PISSED!
He's got that crazy look in his eyes!
Only Mizuki knows.
WHAT?
Wh—
WAIT, NAKAO!
The one doing the hitting-on was—
Shut up!
DON'T TRY TO STOP ME, ASHIYA!
GRAB
YOU'RE SO CUTE! WE DON'T HAVE MANY BOYS LIKE YOU IN AMERICA! ♡
OH!!
GASP
Oo, you're right! He's just like a girl!

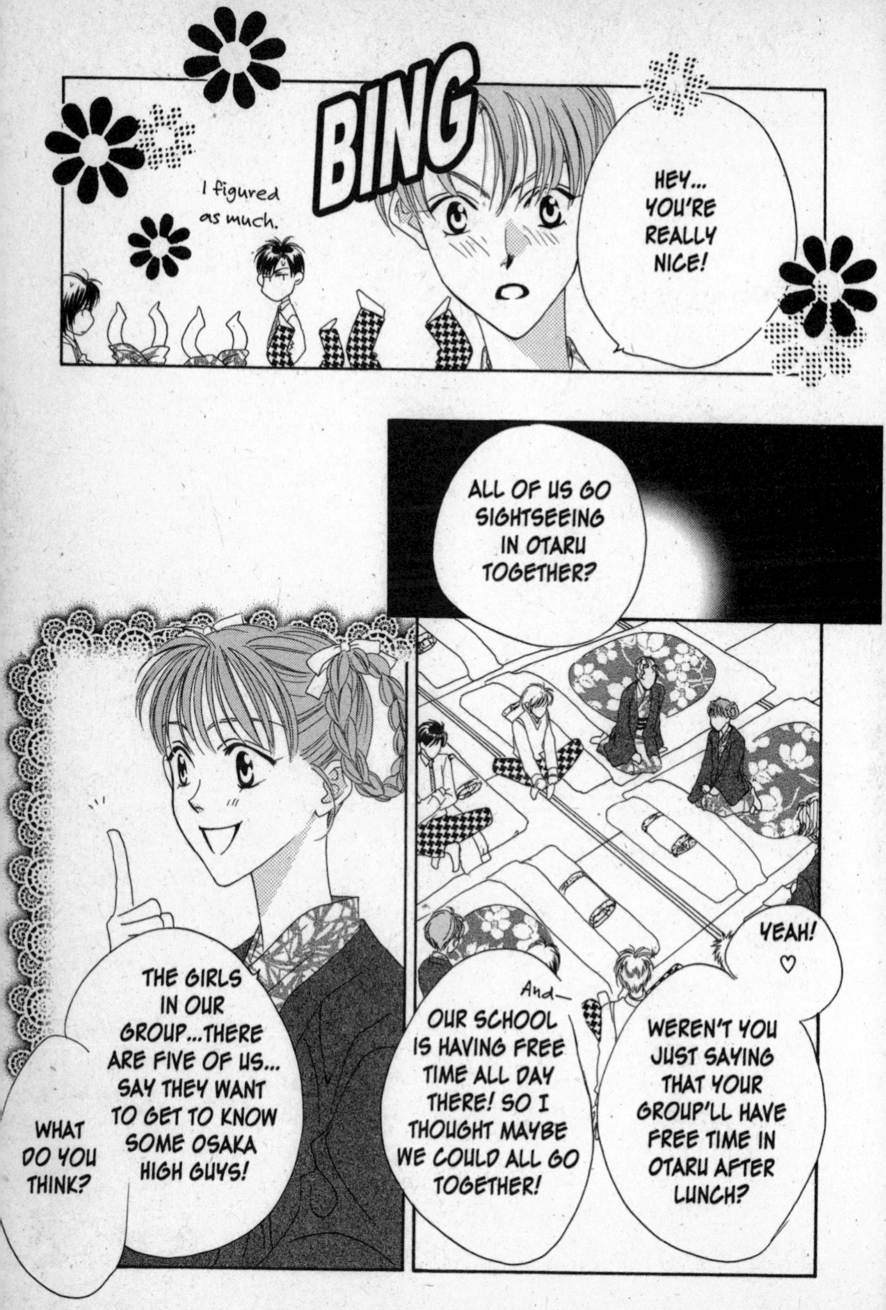
HEY... YOU'RE REALLY NICE!
BING
I figured as much.
WEREN'T YOU JUST SAYING THAT YOUR GROUP'LL HAVE FREE TIME IN OTARU AFTER LUNCH?
YEAH! ♡
And—
OUR SCHOOL IS HAVING FREE TIME ALL DAY THERE! SO I THOUGHT MAYBE WE COULD ALL GO TOGETHER!
THE GIRLS IN OUR GROUP...THERE ARE FIVE OF US... SAY THEY WANT TO GET TO KNOW SOME OSAKA HIGH GUYS!
WHAT DO YOU THINK?
ALL OF US GO SIGHTSEEING IN OTARU TOGETHER?

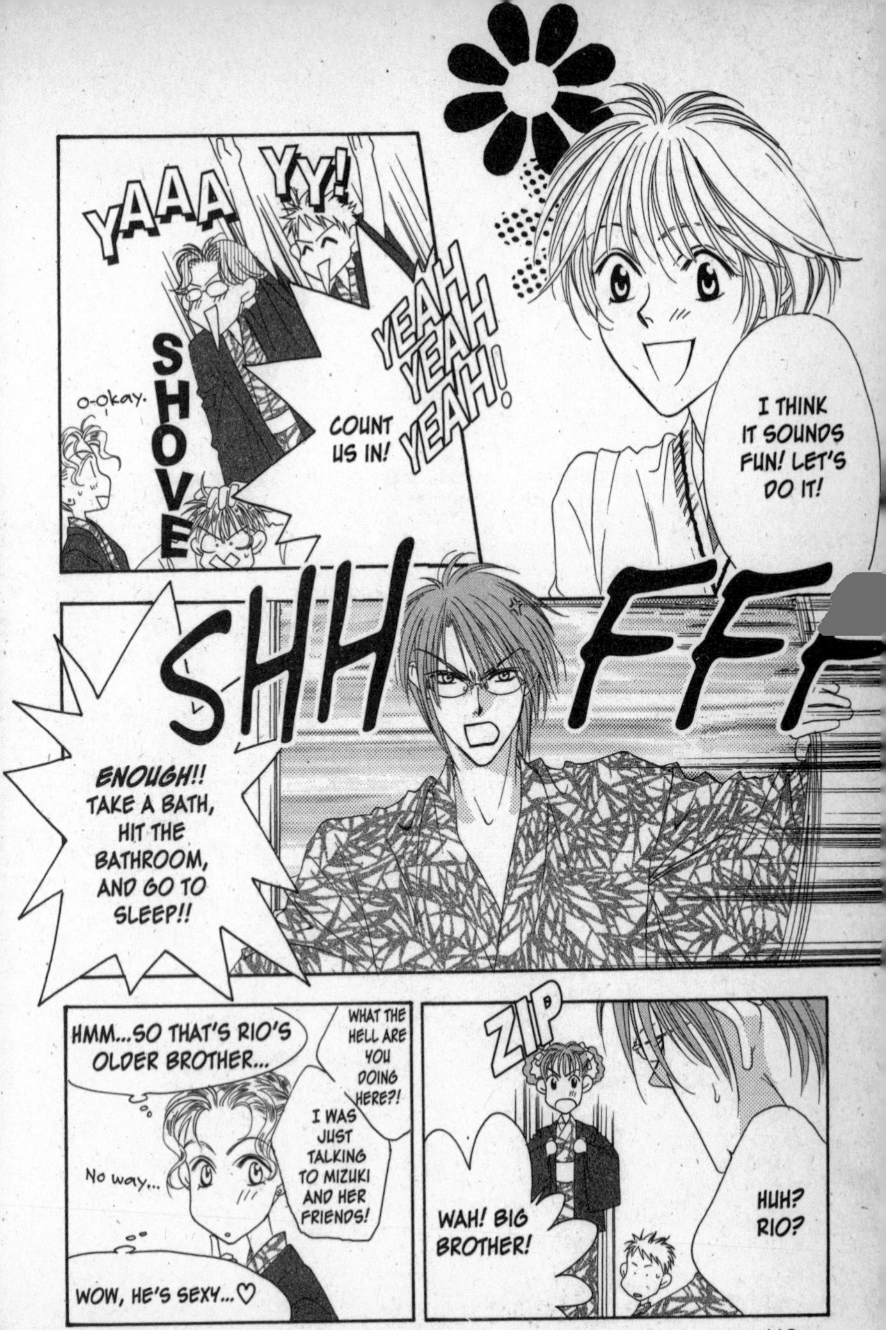
I THINK IT SOUNDS FUN! LET'S DO IT!
YAAAYY!
YEAH YEAH YEAH!
COUNT US IN!
SHOVE
o-okay.
SHHFFF
ENOUGH!! TAKE A BATH, HIT THE BATHROOM, AND GO TO SLEEP!!
ZIP
HUH? RIO?
WAH! BIG BROTHER!
WHAT THE HELL ARE YOU DOING HERE?!
HMM...SO THAT'S RIO'S OLDER BROTHER...
I WAS JUST TALKING TO MIZUKI AND HER FRIENDS!
No way...
WOW, HE'S SEXY...♡

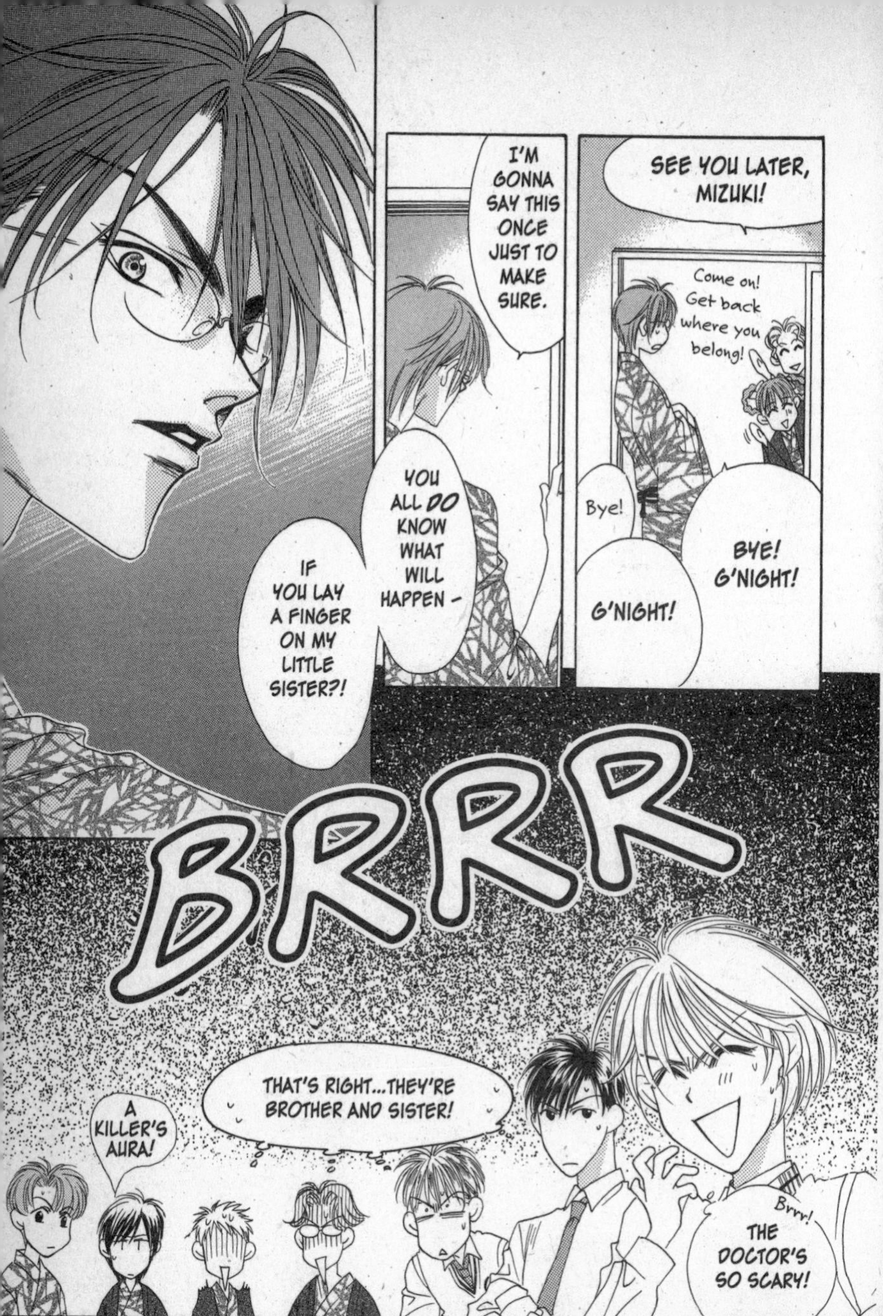
SEE YOU LATER, MIZUKI!
Come on! Get back where you belong!
BYE! G'NIGHT!
Bye!
G'NIGHT!
I'M GONNA SAY THIS ONCE JUST TO MAKE SURE.
YOU ALL *DO* KNOW WHAT WILL HAPPEN –
IF YOU LAY A FINGER ON MY LITTLE SISTER?!
BRRR
Brrr!
THE DOCTOR'S SO SCARY!
THAT'S RIGHT...THEY'RE BROTHER AND SISTER!
A KILLER'S AURA!

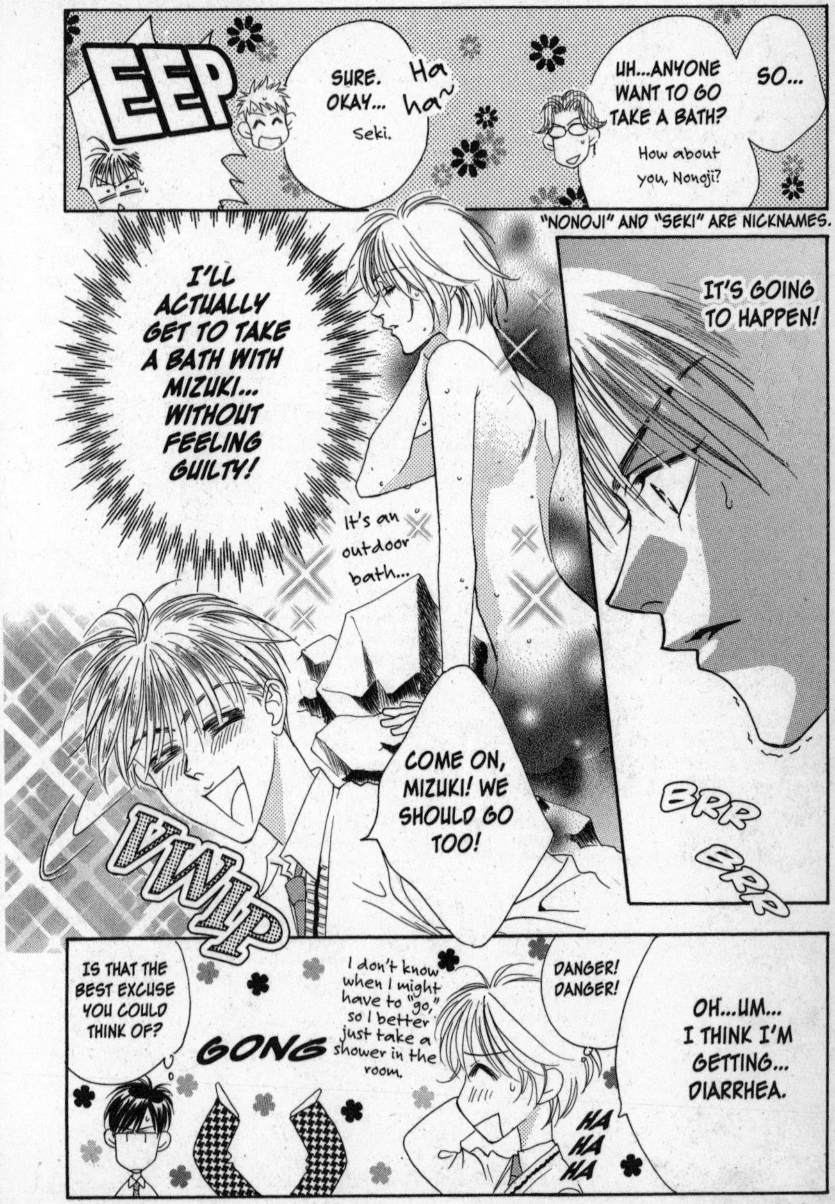
SO...
UH...ANYONE WANT TO GO TAKE A BATH?
How about you, Nonoji?
SURE. OKAY...
Ha ha~
Seki.
EEP
"NONOJI" AND "SEKI" ARE NICKNAMES.
IT'S GOING TO HAPPEN!
BRR BRR
I'LL ACTUALLY GET TO TAKE A BATH WITH MIZUKI... WITHOUT FEELING GUILTY!
It's an outdoor bath...
COME ON, MIZUKI! WE SHOULD GO TOO!
VWIP
OH...UM... I THINK I'M GETTING... DIARRHEA.
DANGER! DANGER!
HA HA HA
I don't know when I might have to "go," so I better just take a shower in the room.
GONG
IS THAT THE BEST EXCUSE YOU COULD THINK OF?

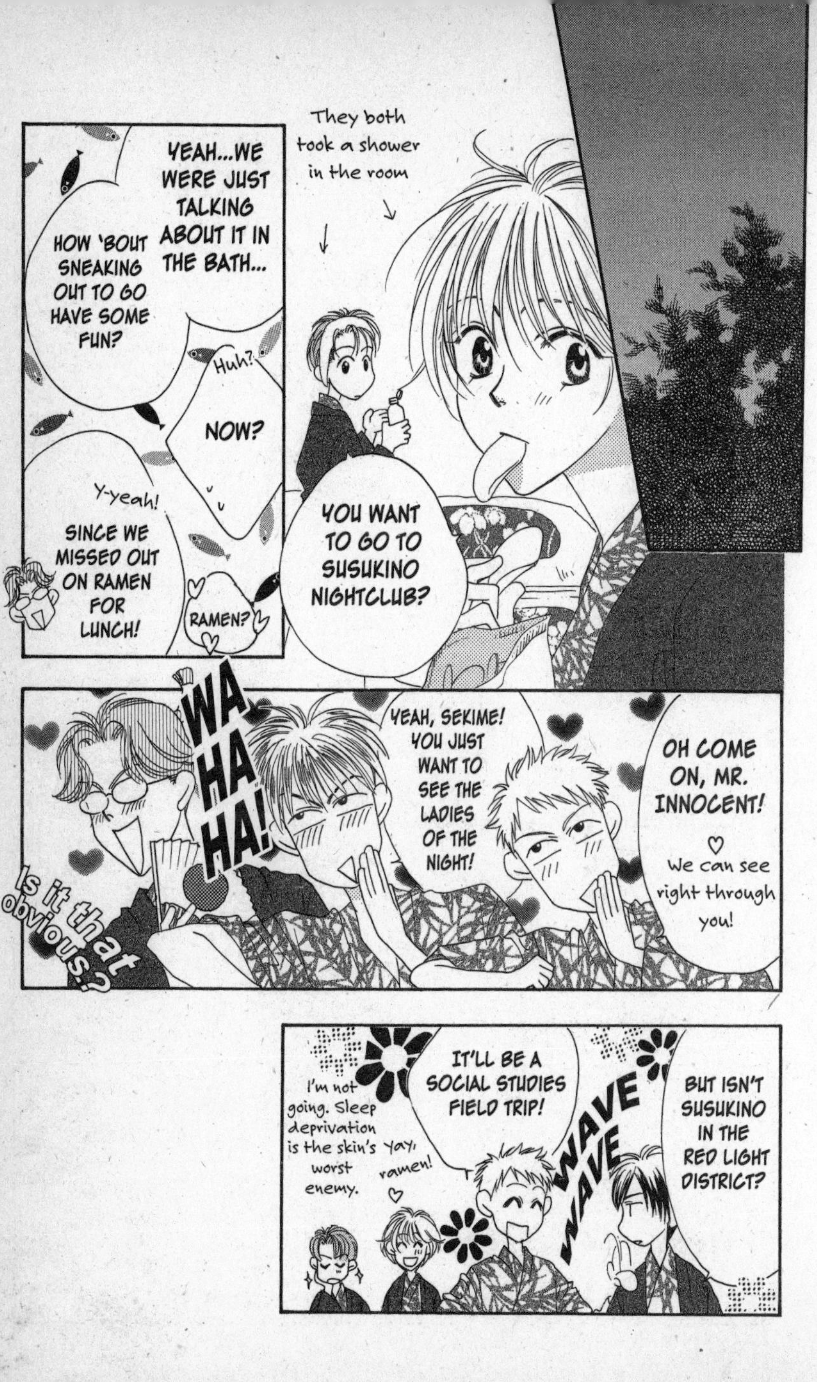
They both took a shower in the room
YOU WANT TO GO TO SUSUKINO NIGHTCLUB?
YEAH...WE WERE JUST TALKING ABOUT IT IN THE BATH...
HOW 'BOUT SNEAKING OUT TO GO HAVE SOME FUN?
Huh?
NOW?
RAMEN?
Y-yeah!
SINCE WE MISSED OUT ON RAMEN FOR LUNCH!
OH COME ON, MR. INNOCENT!
We can see right through you!
YEAH, SEKIME! YOU JUST WANT TO SEE THE LADIES OF THE NIGHT!
WA HA HA!
Is it that obvious..?
BUT ISN'T SUSUKINO IN THE RED LIGHT DISTRICT?
WAVE WAVE
IT'LL BE A SOCIAL STUDIES FIELD TRIP!
Yay, ramen!
I'm not going. Sleep deprivation is the skin's worst enemy.

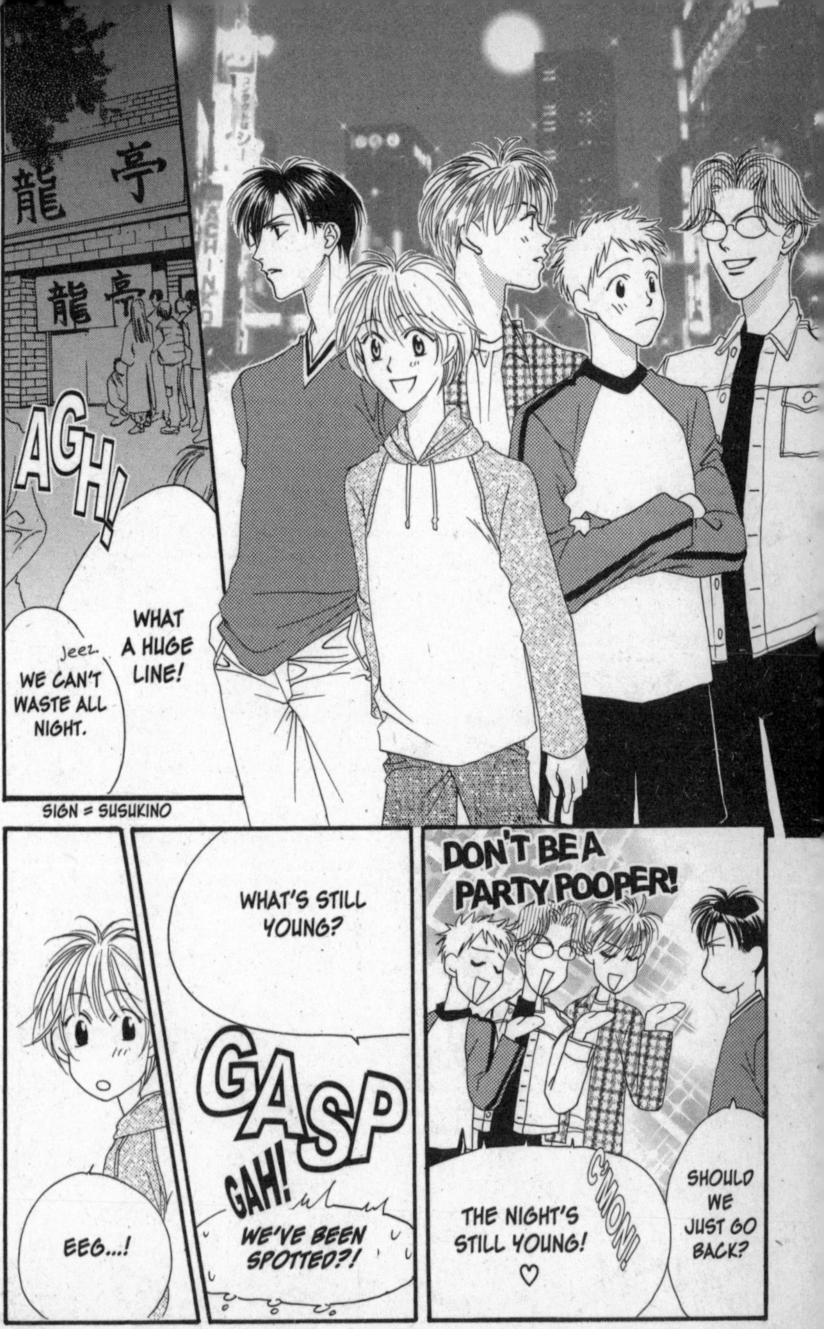
AGH!
WHAT A HUGE LINE!
Jeez. WE CAN'T WASTE ALL NIGHT.
DON'T BE A PARTY POOPER!
SHOULD WE JUST GO BACK?
C'MON!
THE NIGHT'S STILL YOUNG! ♡
WHAT'S STILL YOUNG?
GASP
GAH!
WE'VE BEEN SPOTTED?!
EEG...!

SIGN = SUSUKINO

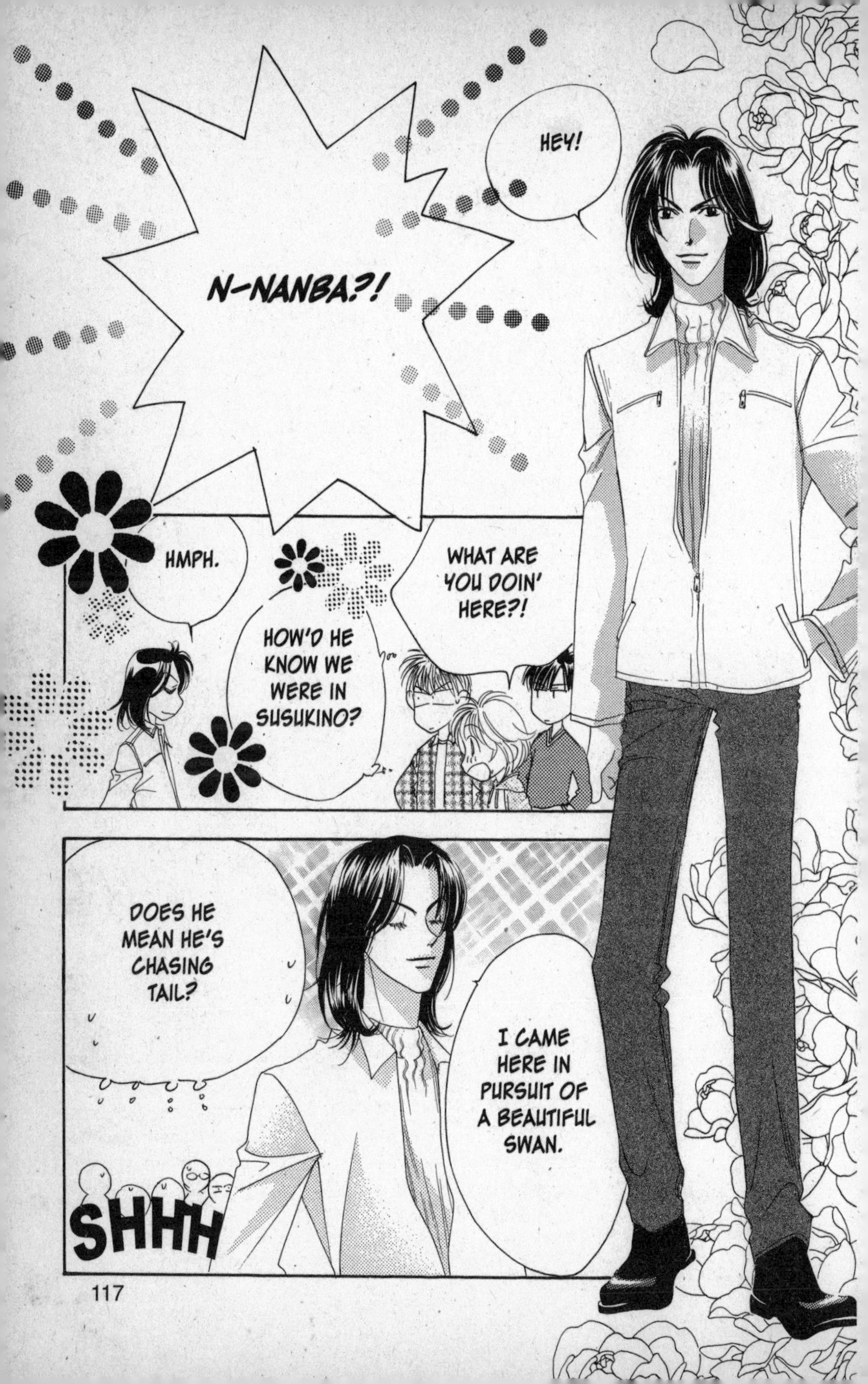
HEY!
N-NANBA?!
WHAT ARE YOU DOIN' HERE?!
HOW'D HE KNOW WE WERE IN SUSUKINO?
HMPH.
I CAME HERE IN PURSUIT OF A BEAUTIFUL SWAN.
DOES HE MEAN HE'S CHASING TAIL?
SHHH

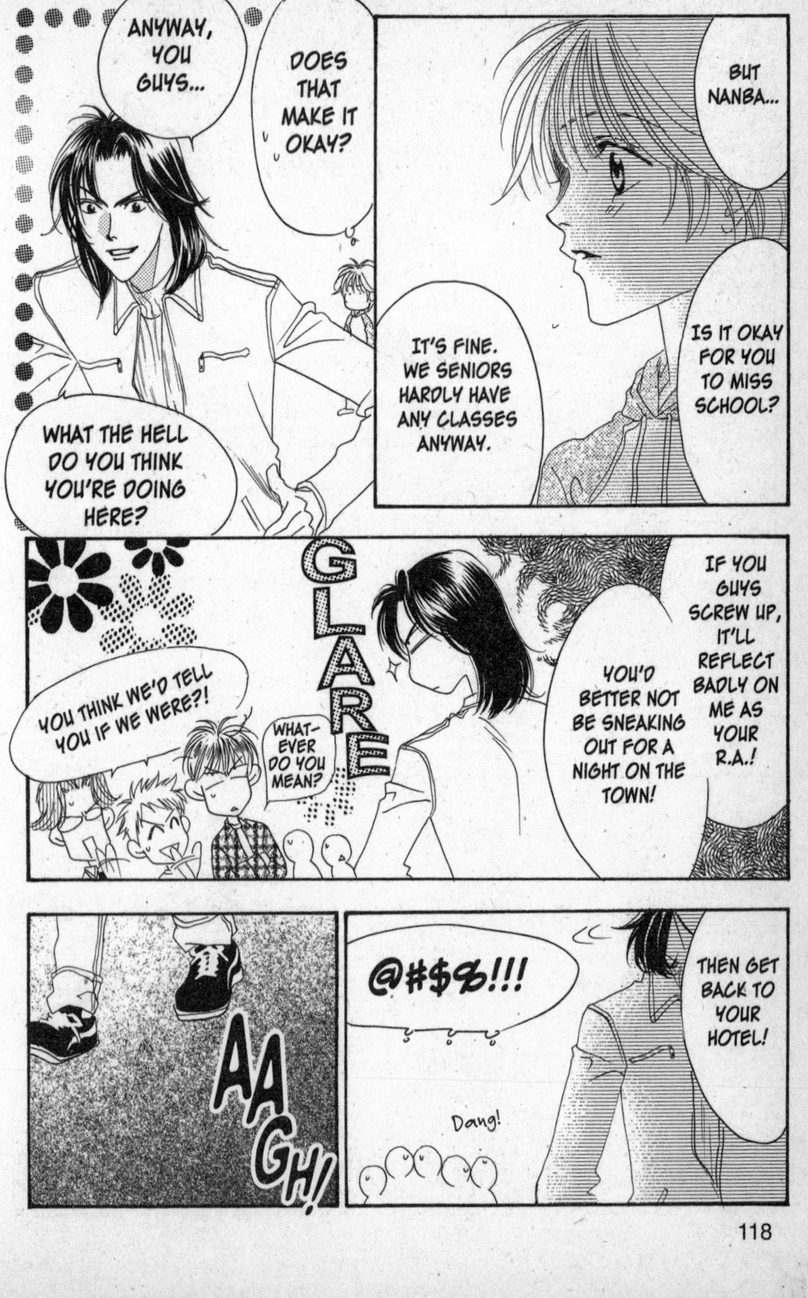
BUT NANBA...
IS IT OKAY FOR YOU TO MISS SCHOOL?
IT'S FINE. WE SENIORS HARDLY HAVE ANY CLASSES ANYWAY.
DOES THAT MAKE IT OKAY?
ANYWAY, YOU GUYS...
WHAT THE HELL DO YOU THINK YOU'RE DOING HERE?
IF YOU GUYS SCREW UP, IT'LL REFLECT BADLY ON ME AS YOUR R.A.!
YOU'D BETTER NOT BE SNEAKING OUT FOR A NIGHT ON THE TOWN!
GLARE
WHAT-EVER DO YOU MEAN?
YOU THINK WE'D TELL YOU IF WE WERE?!
THEN GET BACK TO YOUR HOTEL!
@#$%!!!
Dang!
AAGH!

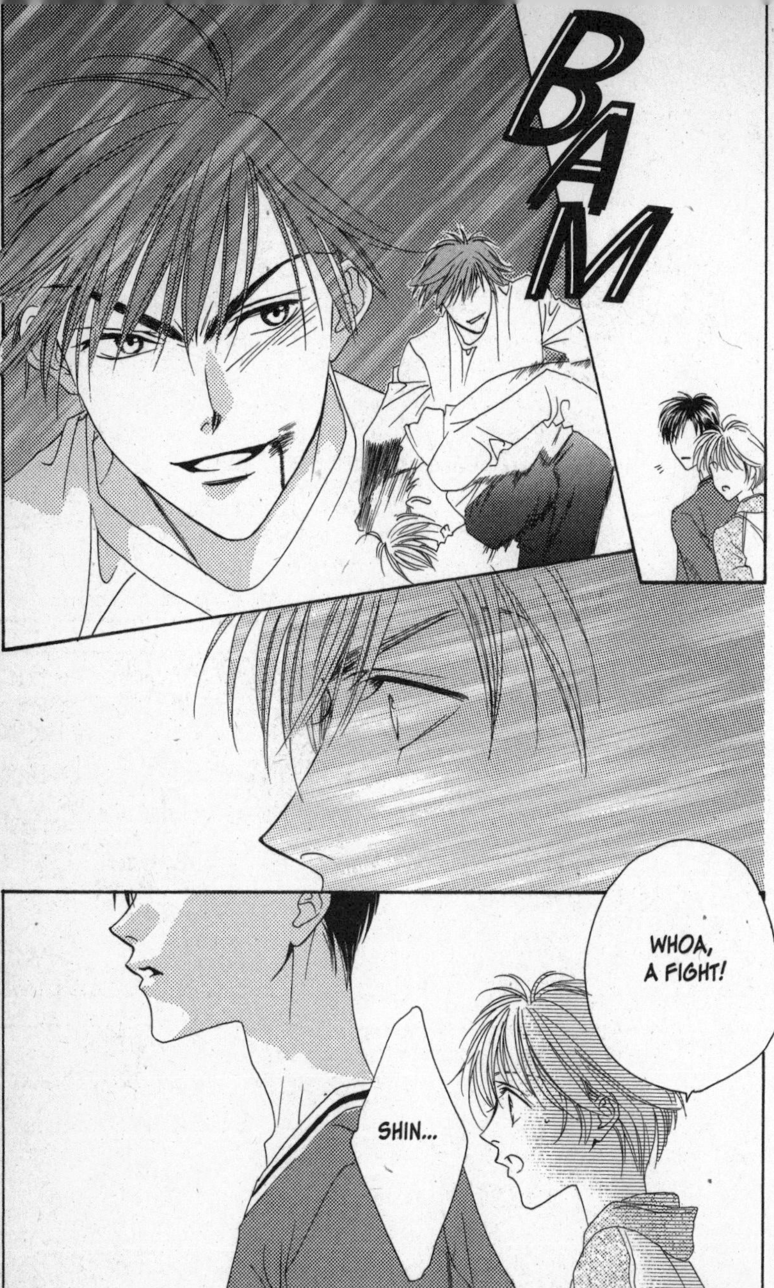
BAM
WHOA, A FIGHT!
SHIN...

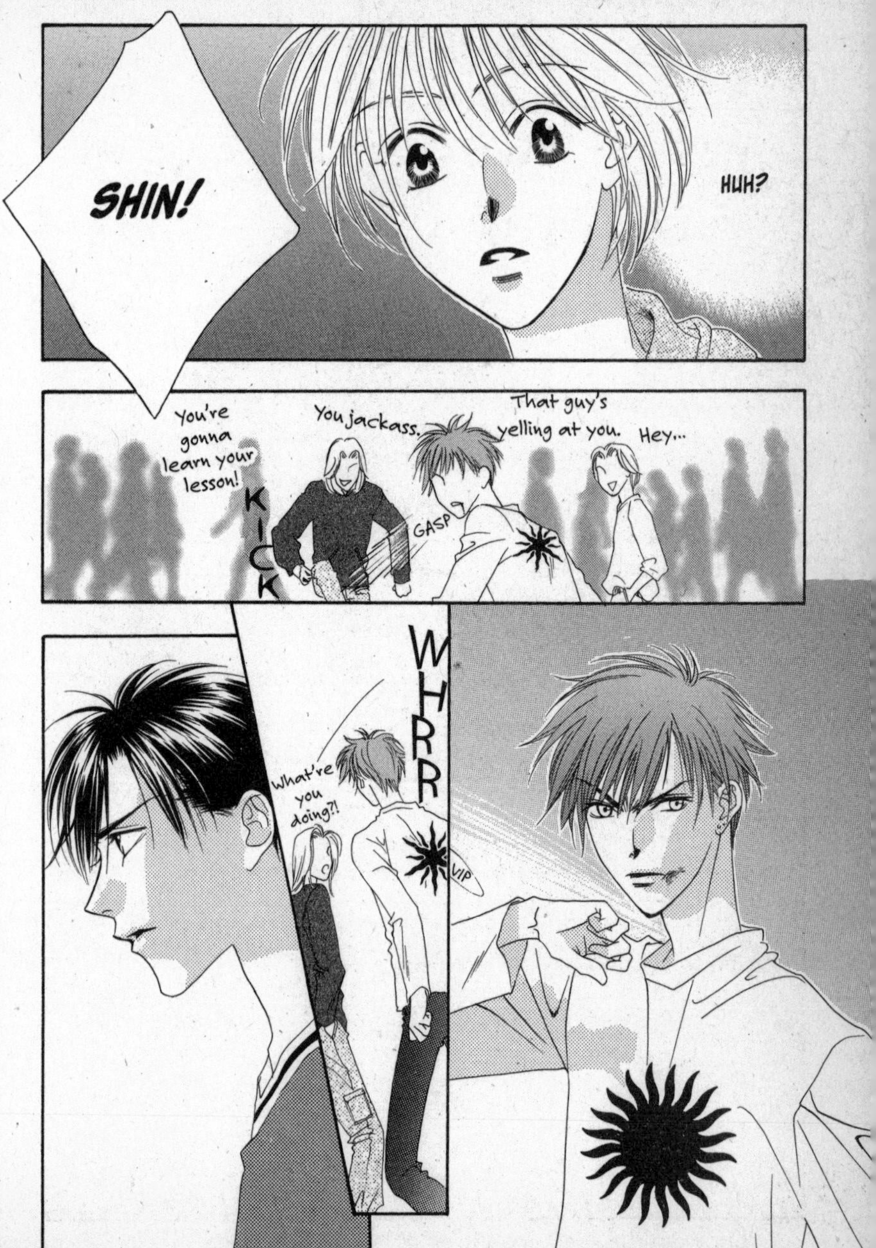
HUH?
SHIN!
Hey...
That guy's yelling at you.
You jackass.
You're gonna learn your lesson!
GASP
KICK
WHRR
What're you doing?!
VIP

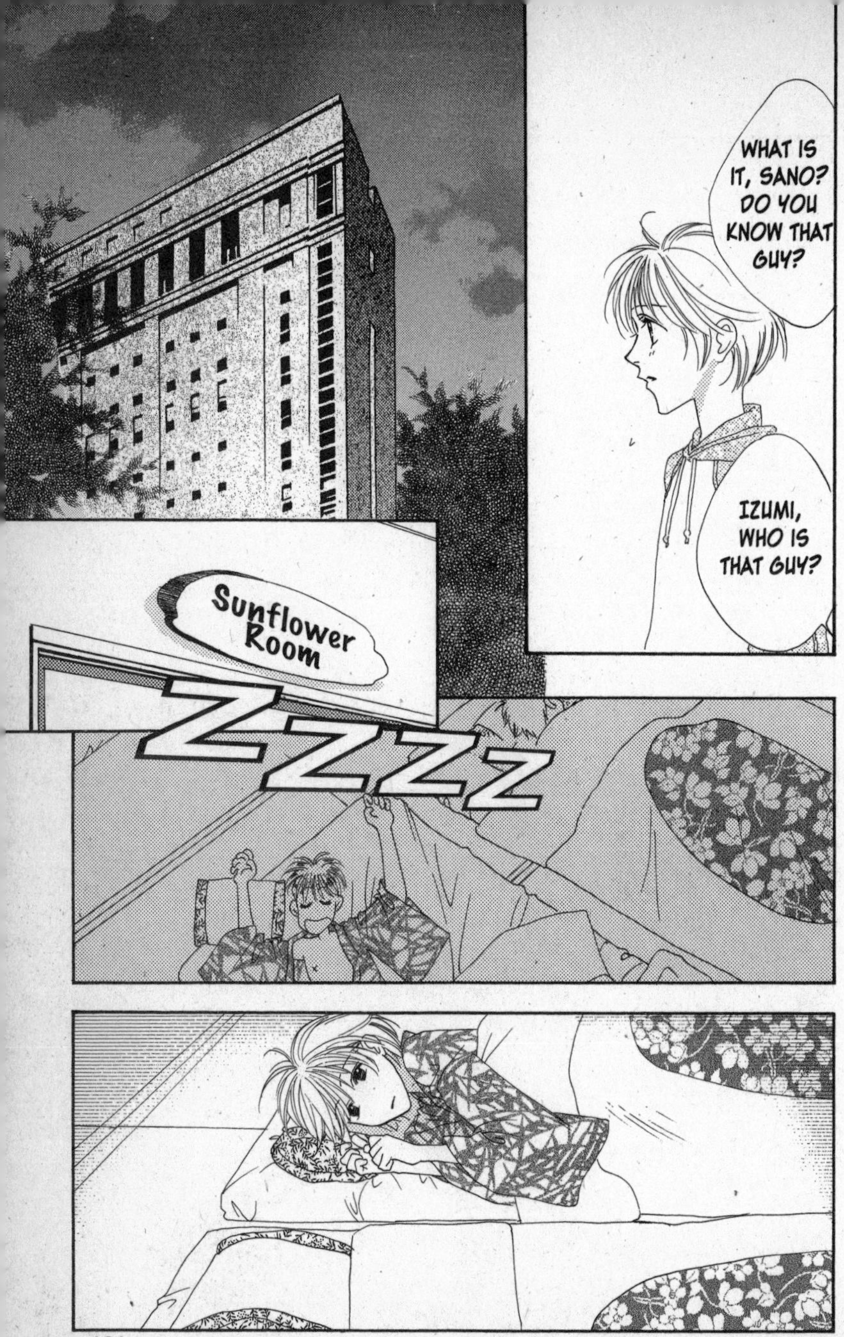
WHAT IS IT, SANO? DO YOU KNOW THAT GUY?
IZUMI, WHO IS THAT GUY?
Sunflower Room
ZZZZ

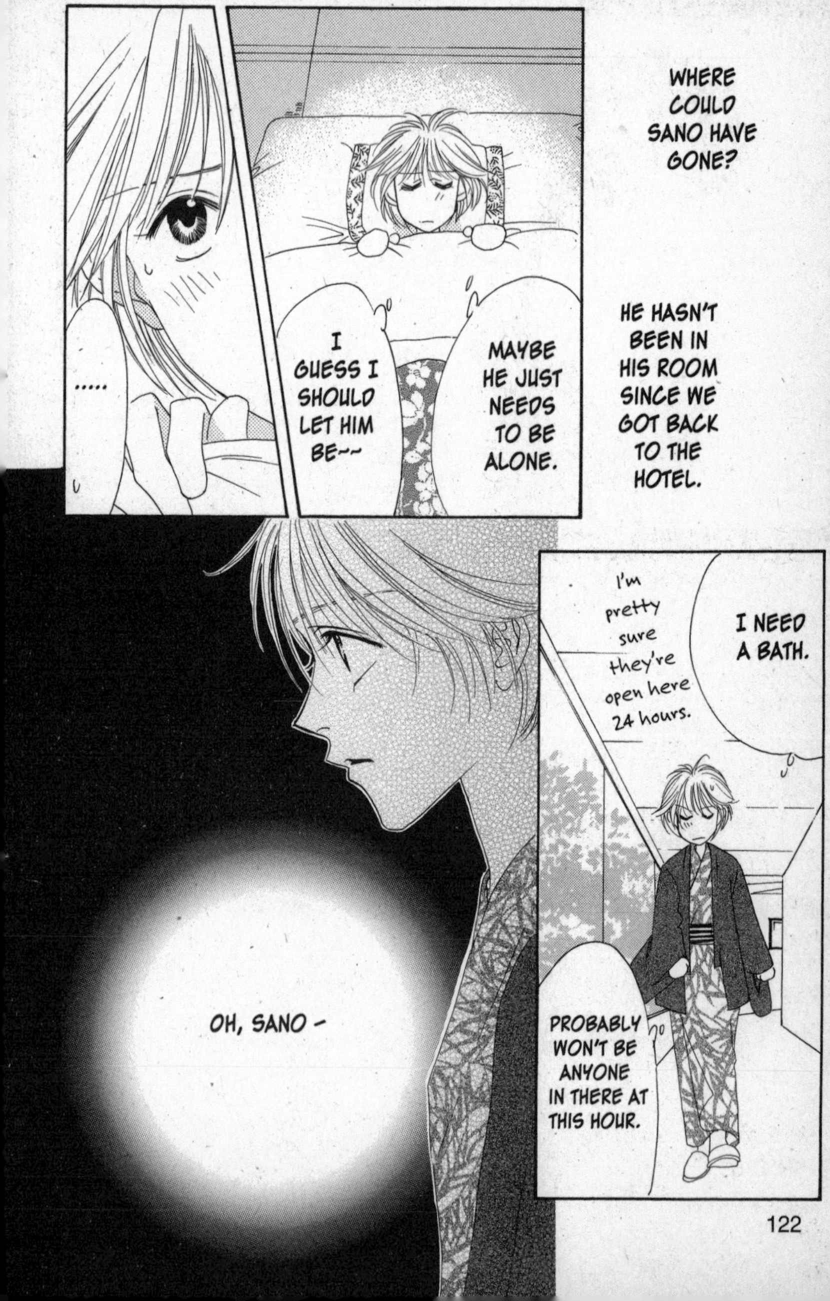
WHERE COULD SANO HAVE GONE?
HE HASN'T BEEN IN HIS ROOM SINCE WE GOT BACK TO THE HOTEL.
MAYBE HE JUST NEEDS TO BE ALONE.
I GUESS I SHOULD LET HIM BE--
.....
I NEED A BATH.
I'm pretty sure they're open here 24 hours.
PROBABLY WON'T BE ANYONE IN THERE AT THIS HOUR.
OH, SANO -

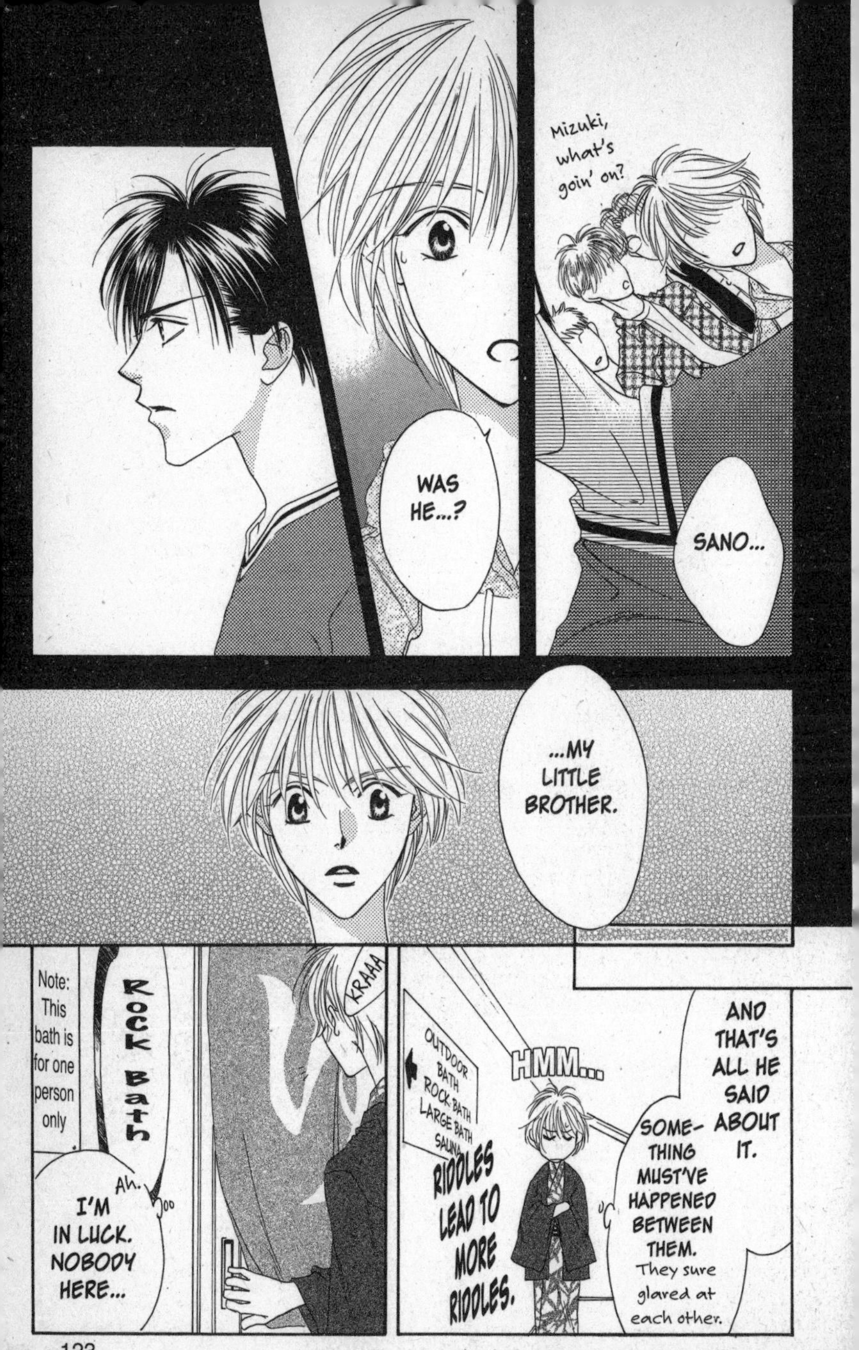

Mizuki, what's goin' on?
SANO...
WAS HE...?
...MY LITTLE BROTHER.
AND THAT'S ALL HE SAID ABOUT IT.
HMM...
SOME-THING MUST'VE HAPPENED BETWEEN THEM.
They sure glared at each other.
OUTDOOR BATH
ROCK BATH
LARGE BATH
SAUNA
RIDDLES LEAD TO MORE RIDDLES.
KRAAA
Rock Bath
Note: This bath is for one person only
Ah.
I'M IN LUCK. NOBODY HERE...

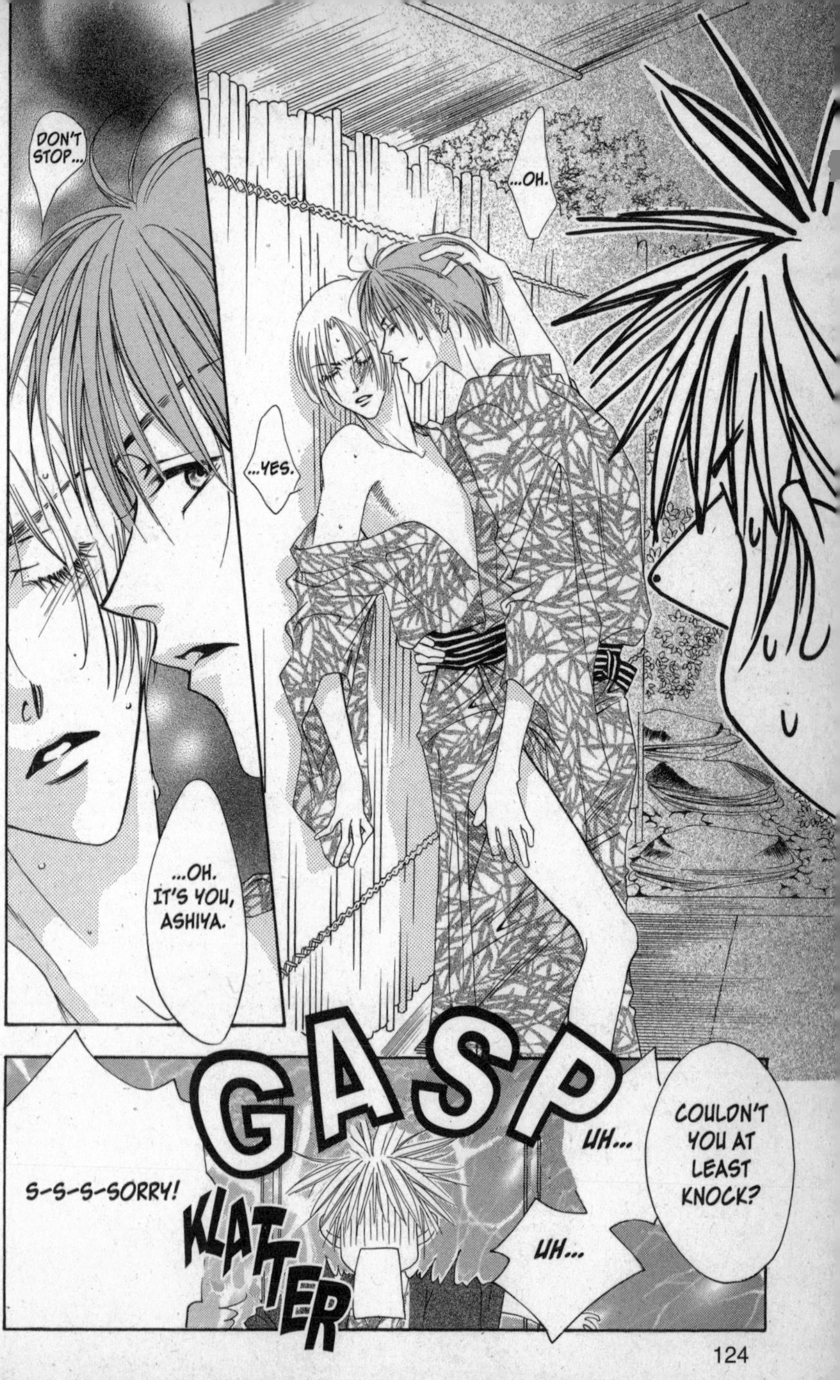
...OH.
...YES.
DON'T STOP...
...OH. IT'S YOU, ASHIYA.
COULDN'T YOU AT LEAST KNOCK?
UH...
UH...
GASP
S-S-S-SORRY!
KLATTER

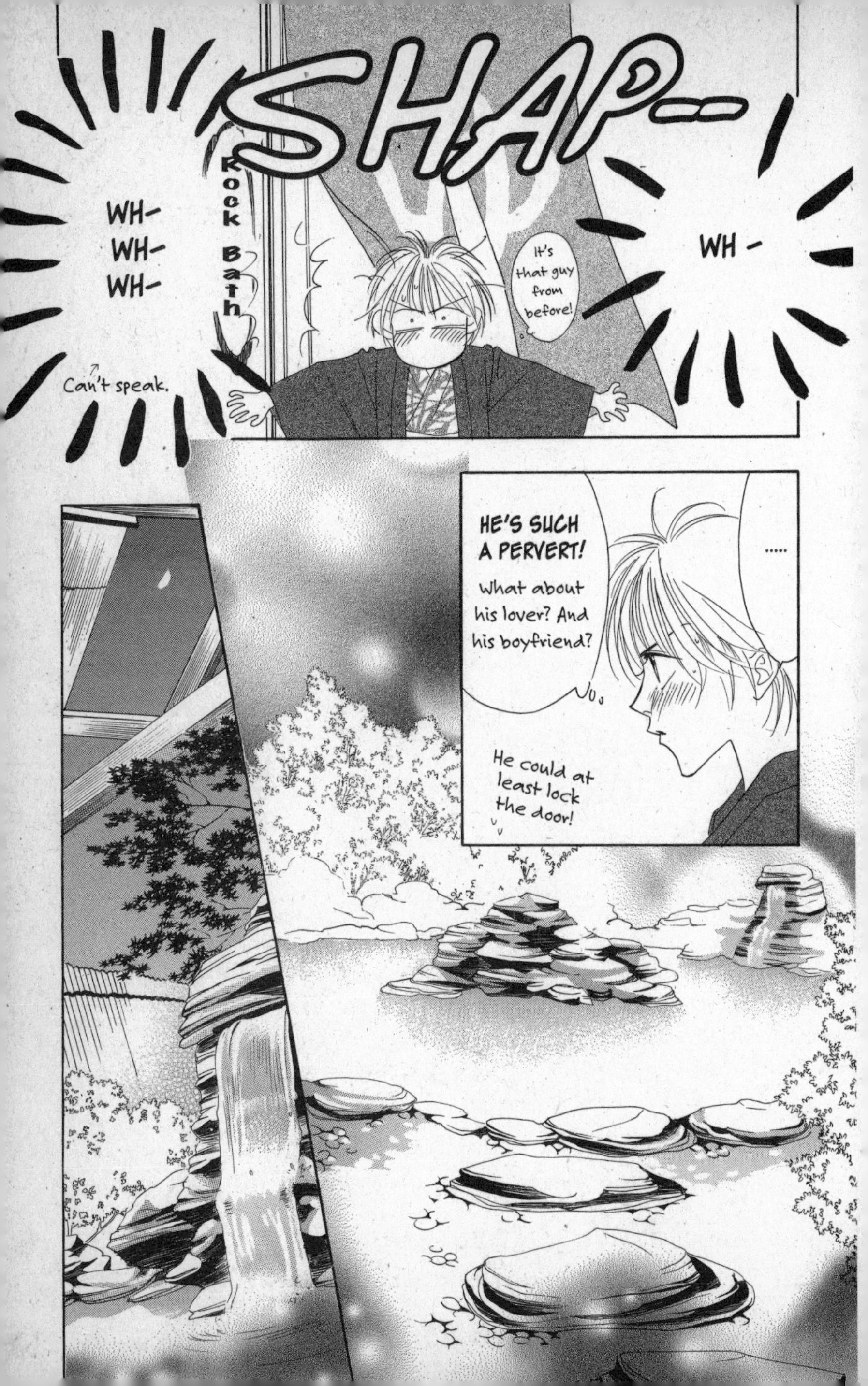
SHAP--
WH -
It's that guy from before!
Rock Bath
WH- WH- WH-
Can't speak.
.....
HE'S SUCH A PERVERT!
What about his lover? And his boyfriend?
He could at least lock the door!

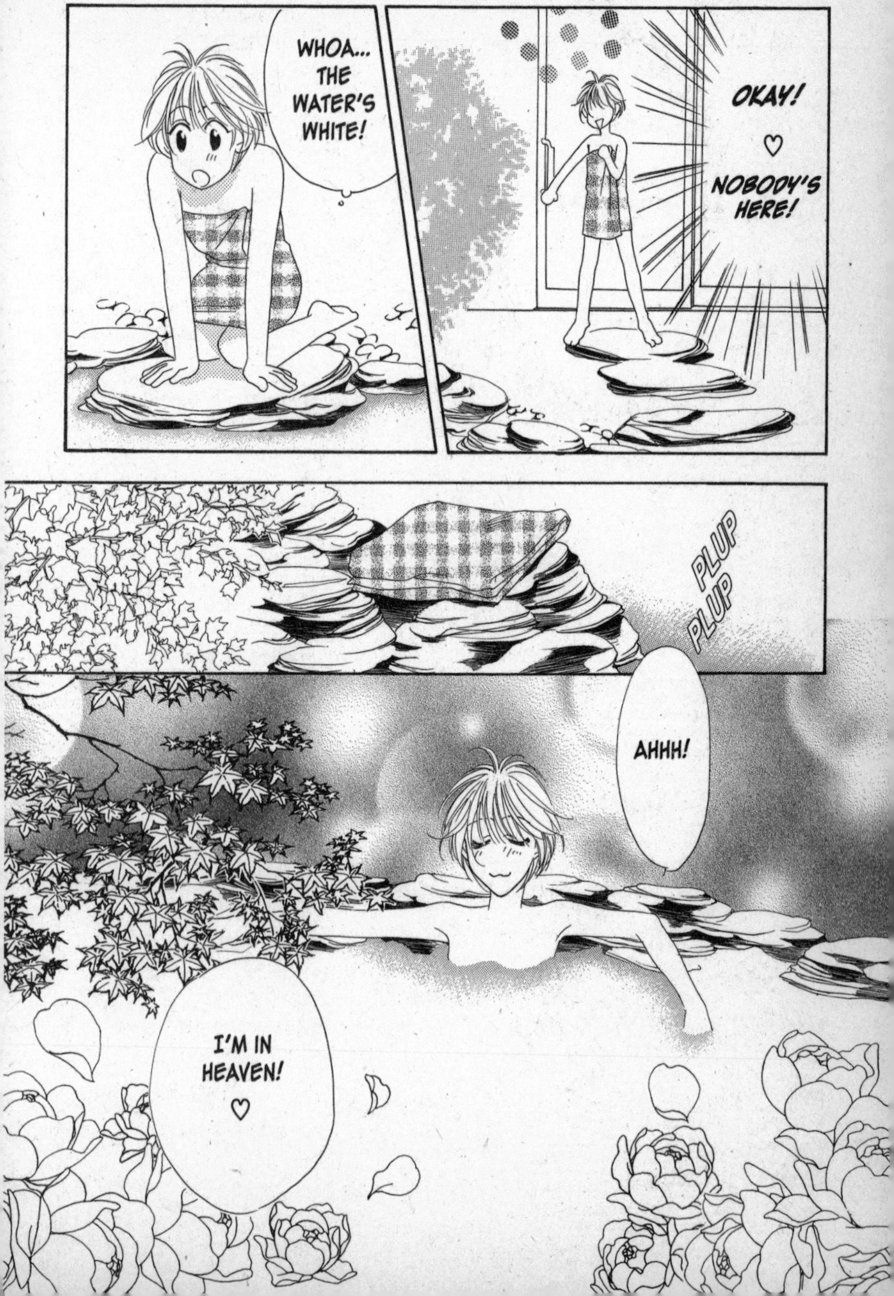
OKAY! ♡ NOBODY'S HERE!
WHOA... THE WATER'S WHITE!
PLUP PLUP
AHHH!
I'M IN HEAVEN! ♡

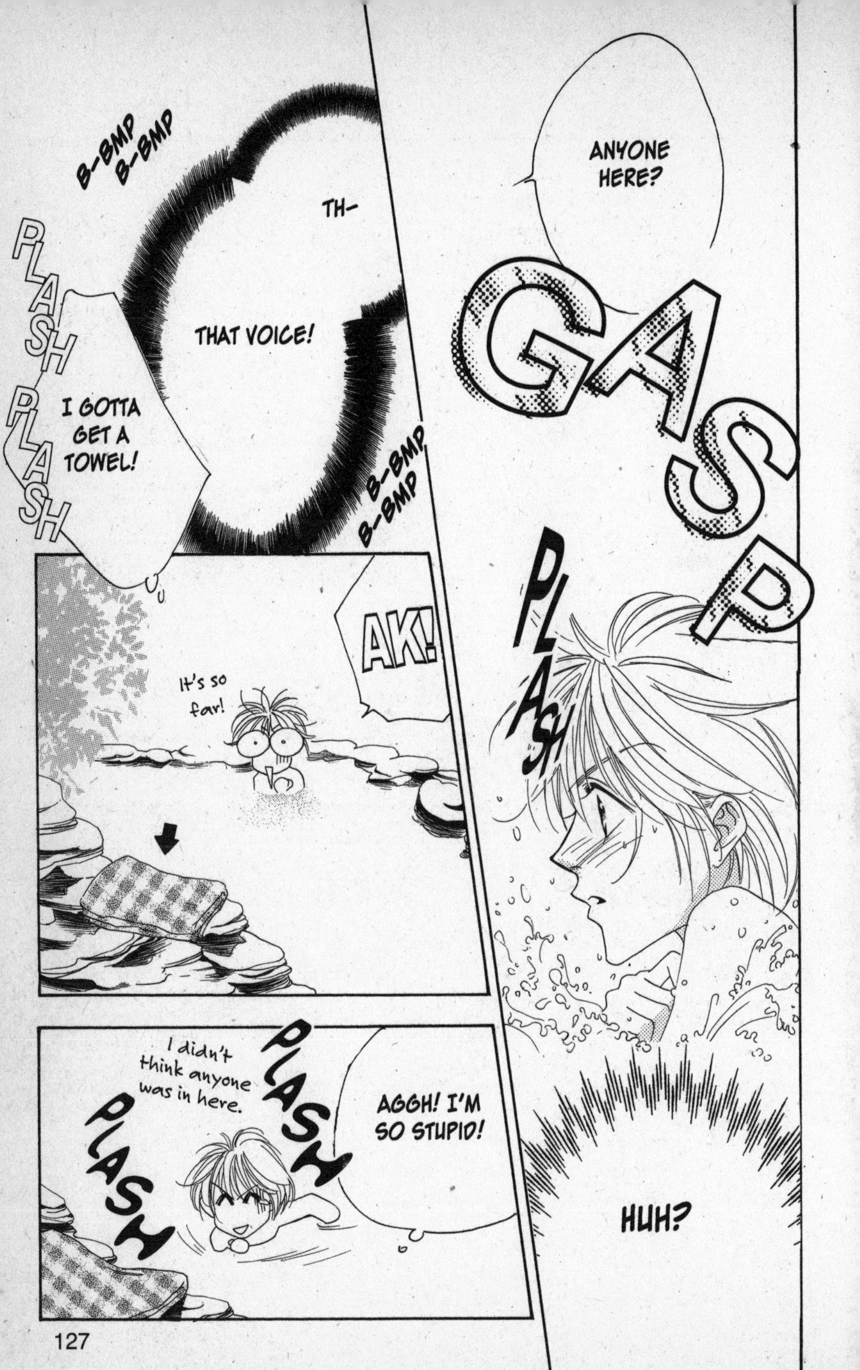
ANYONE HERE?
GASP
PLASH
HUH?
B-BMP B-BMP
TH-
THAT VOICE!
B-BMP B-BMP
I GOTTA GET A TOWEL!
PLASH PLASH
AK!
It's so far!
AGGH! I'M SO STUPID!
I didn't think anyone was in here.
PLASH
PLASH

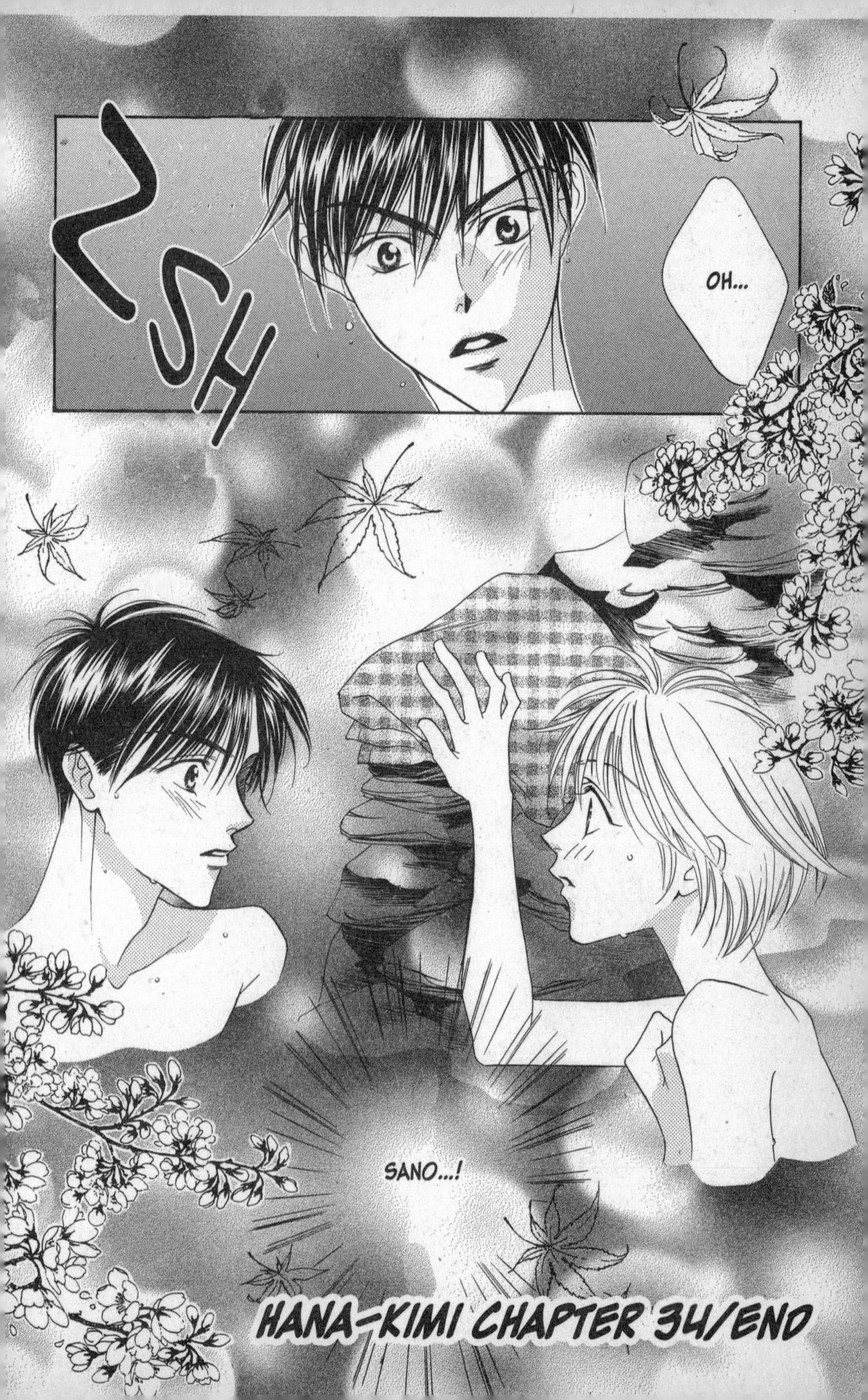
OH...
SWSH
SANO...!
HANA-KIMI CHAPTER 34/END

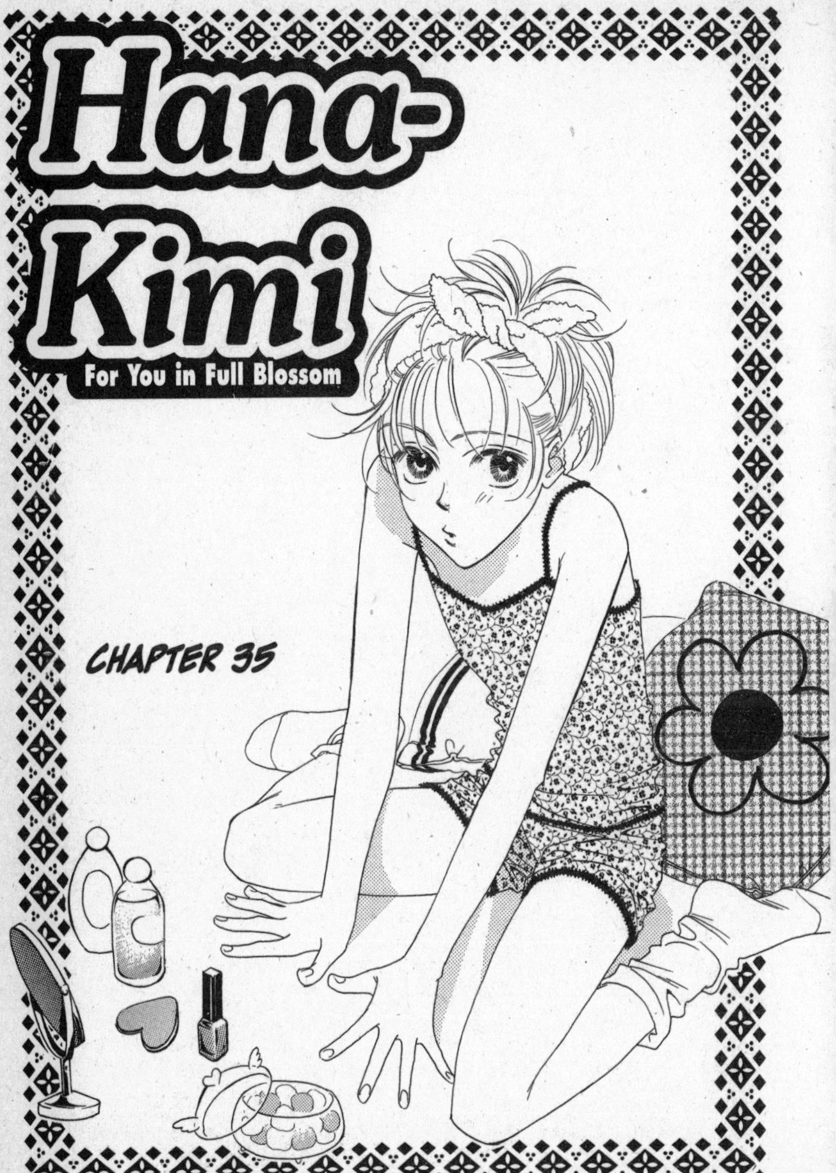
Hana-Kimi
For You in Full Blossom
CHAPTER 35

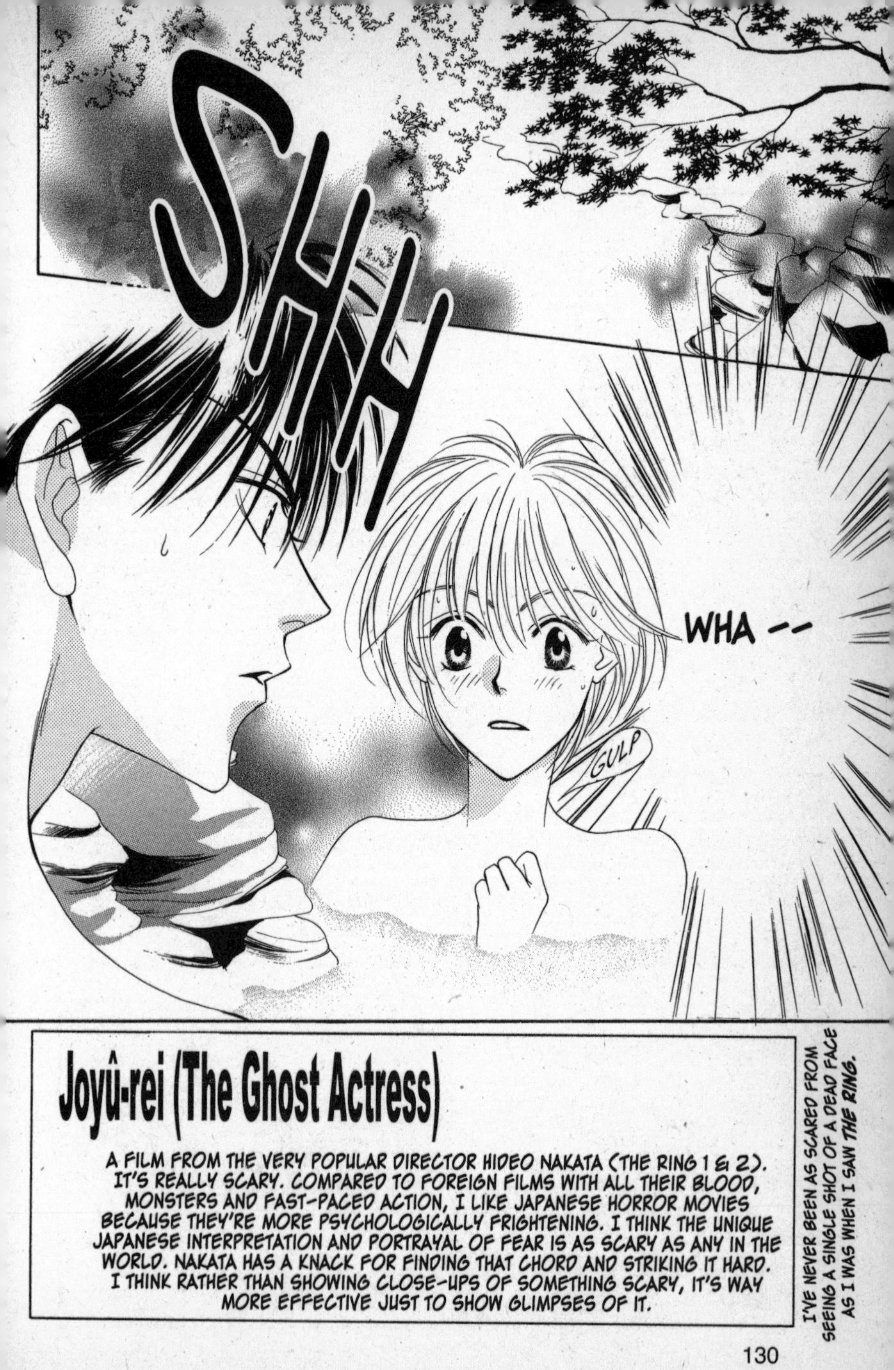
SHHH
WHA --
GULP

Joyû-rei (The Ghost Actress)

A FILM FROM THE VERY POPULAR DIRECTOR HIDEO NAKATA (THE RING 1 & 2). IT'S REALLY SCARY. COMPARED TO FOREIGN FILMS WITH ALL THEIR BLOOD, MONSTERS AND FAST-PACED ACTION, I LIKE JAPANESE HORROR MOVIES BECAUSE THEY'RE MORE PSYCHOLOGICALLY FRIGHTENING. I THINK THE UNIQUE JAPANESE INTERPRETATION AND PORTRAYAL OF FEAR IS AS SCARY AS ANY IN THE WORLD. NAKATA HAS A KNACK FOR FINDING THAT CHORD AND STRIKING IT HARD. I THINK RATHER THAN SHOWING CLOSE-UPS OF SOMETHING SCARY, IT'S WAY MORE EFFECTIVE JUST TO SHOW GLIMPSES OF IT.

I'VE NEVER BEEN AS SCARED FROM SEEING A SINGLE SHOT OF A DEAD FACE AS I WAS WHEN I SAW *THE RING.*

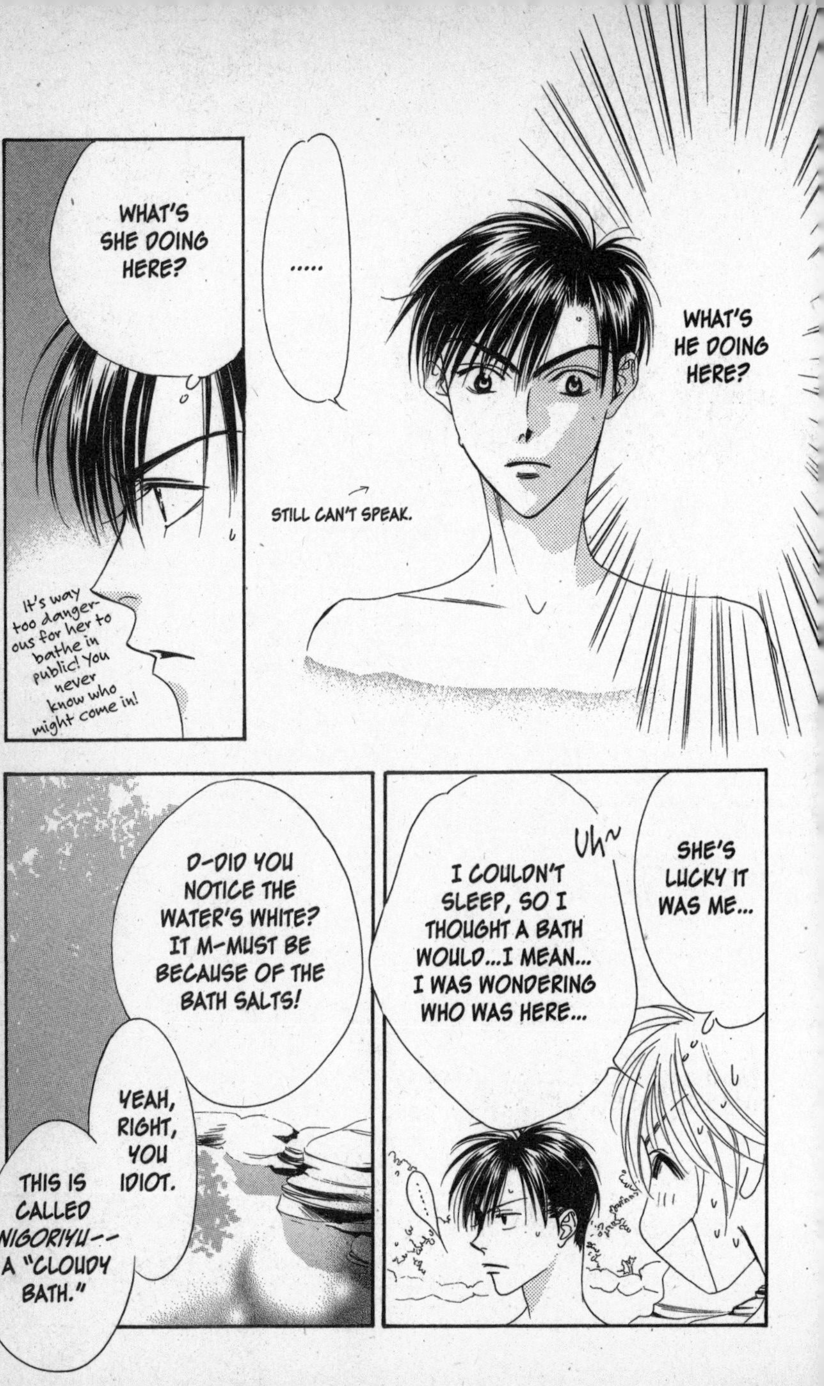
WHAT'S HE DOING HERE?
.....
STILL CAN'T SPEAK.
WHAT'S SHE DOING HERE?
It's way too dangerous for her to bathe in public! You never know who might come in!
SHE'S LUCKY IT WAS ME...
Uh~
I COULDN'T SLEEP, SO I THOUGHT A BATH WOULD...I MEAN... I WAS WONDERING WHO WAS HERE...
D-DID YOU NOTICE THE WATER'S WHITE? IT M-MUST BE BECAUSE OF THE BATH SALTS!
YEAH, RIGHT, YOU IDIOT.
THIS IS CALLED NIGORIYU-- A "CLOUDY BATH."

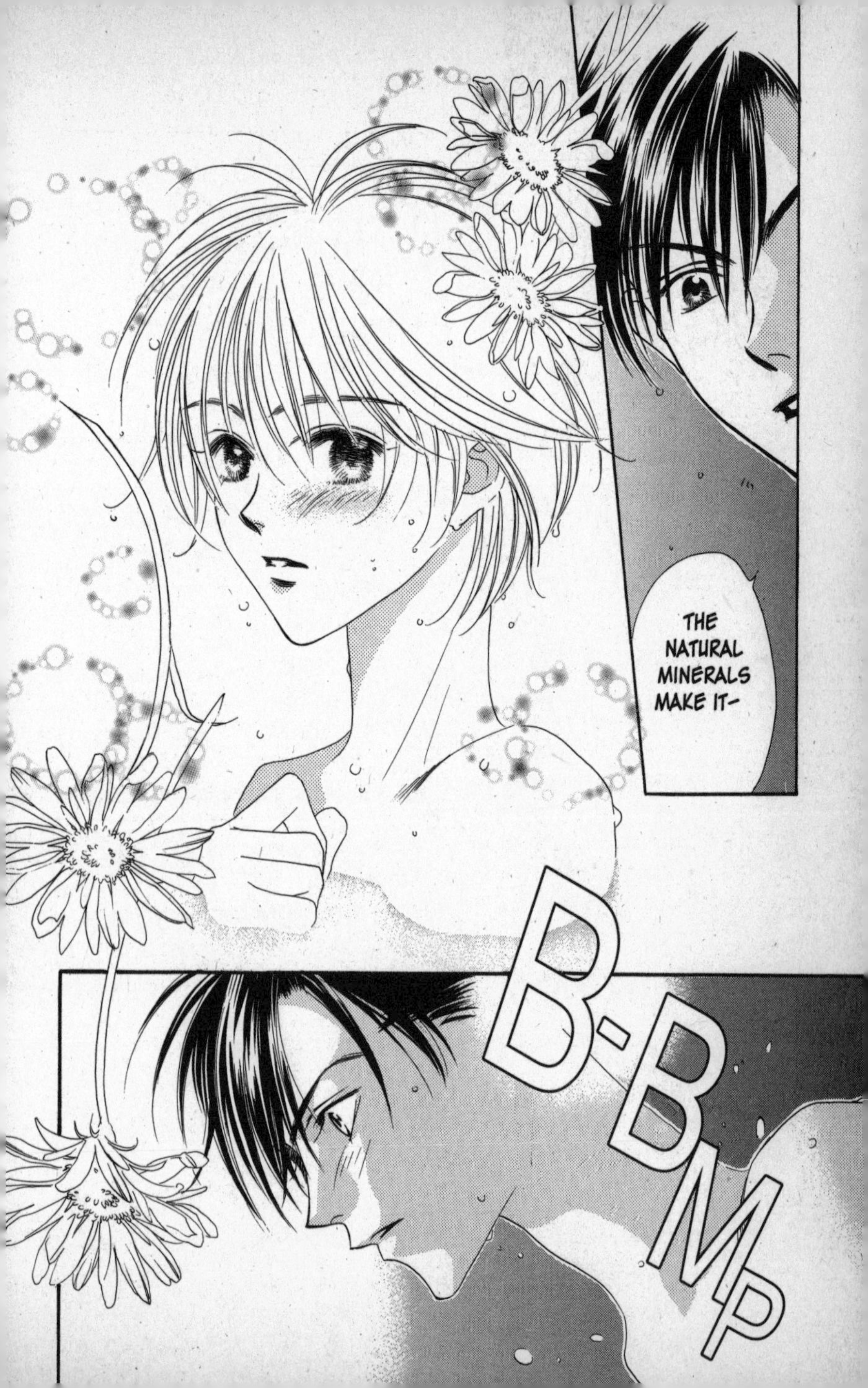
THE NATURAL MINERALS MAKE IT-
B-BMP

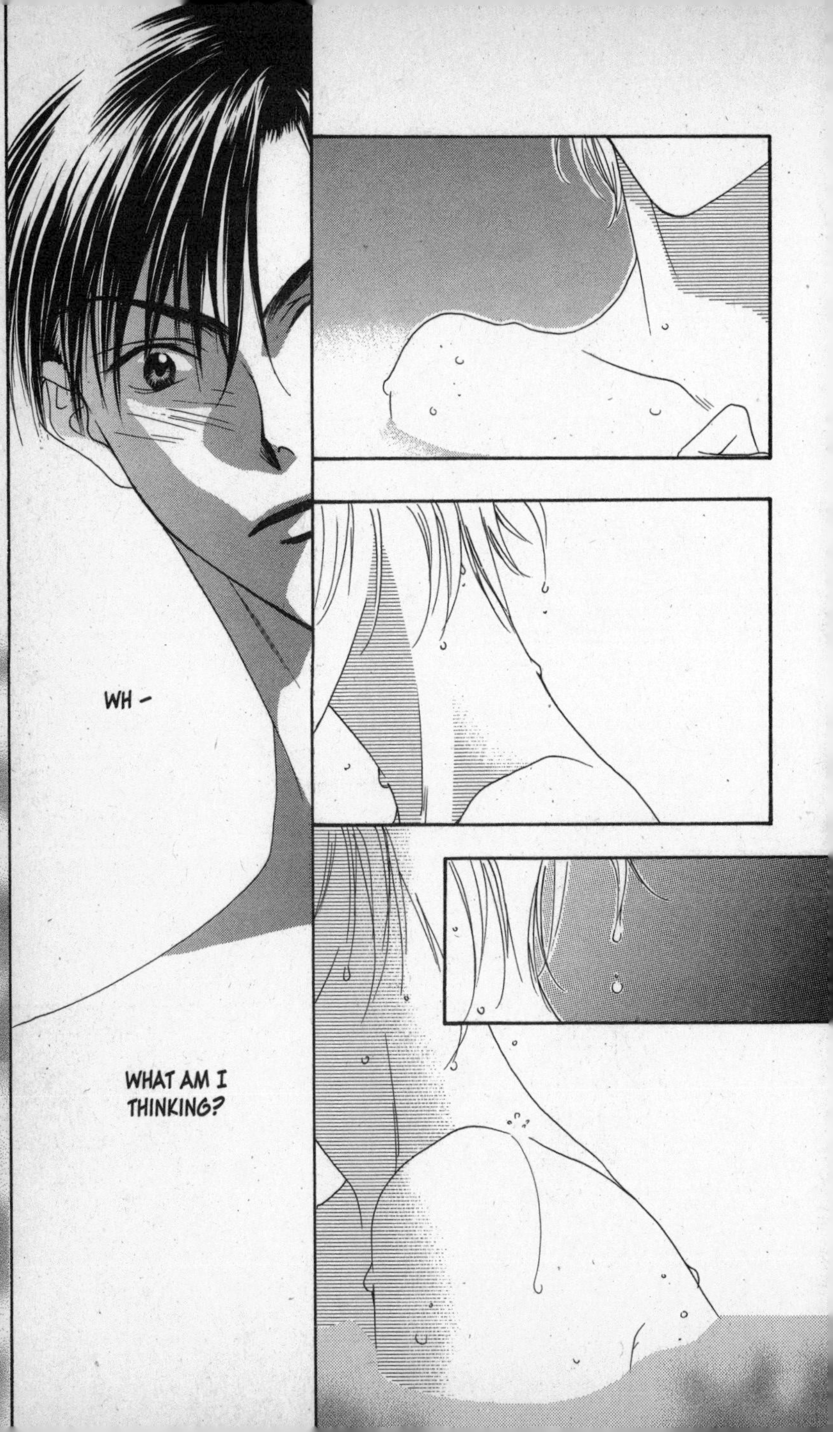
WH -
WHAT AM I THINKING?

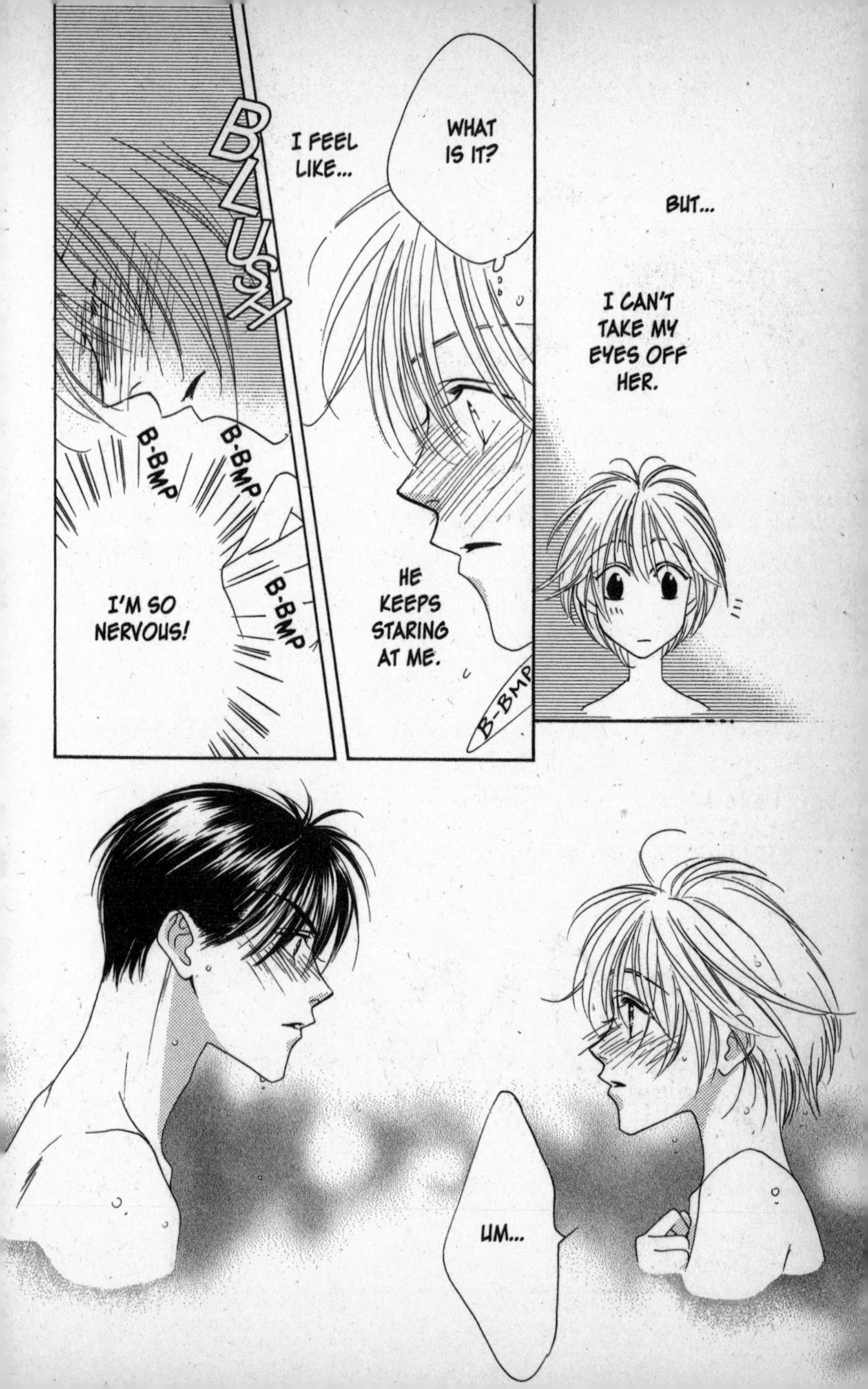
BUT...
I CAN'T TAKE MY EYES OFF HER.
WHAT IS IT?
I FEEL LIKE...
HE KEEPS STARING AT ME.
B-BMP
BLUSH
B-BMP
B-BMP
B-BMP
I'M SO NERVOUS!
UM...

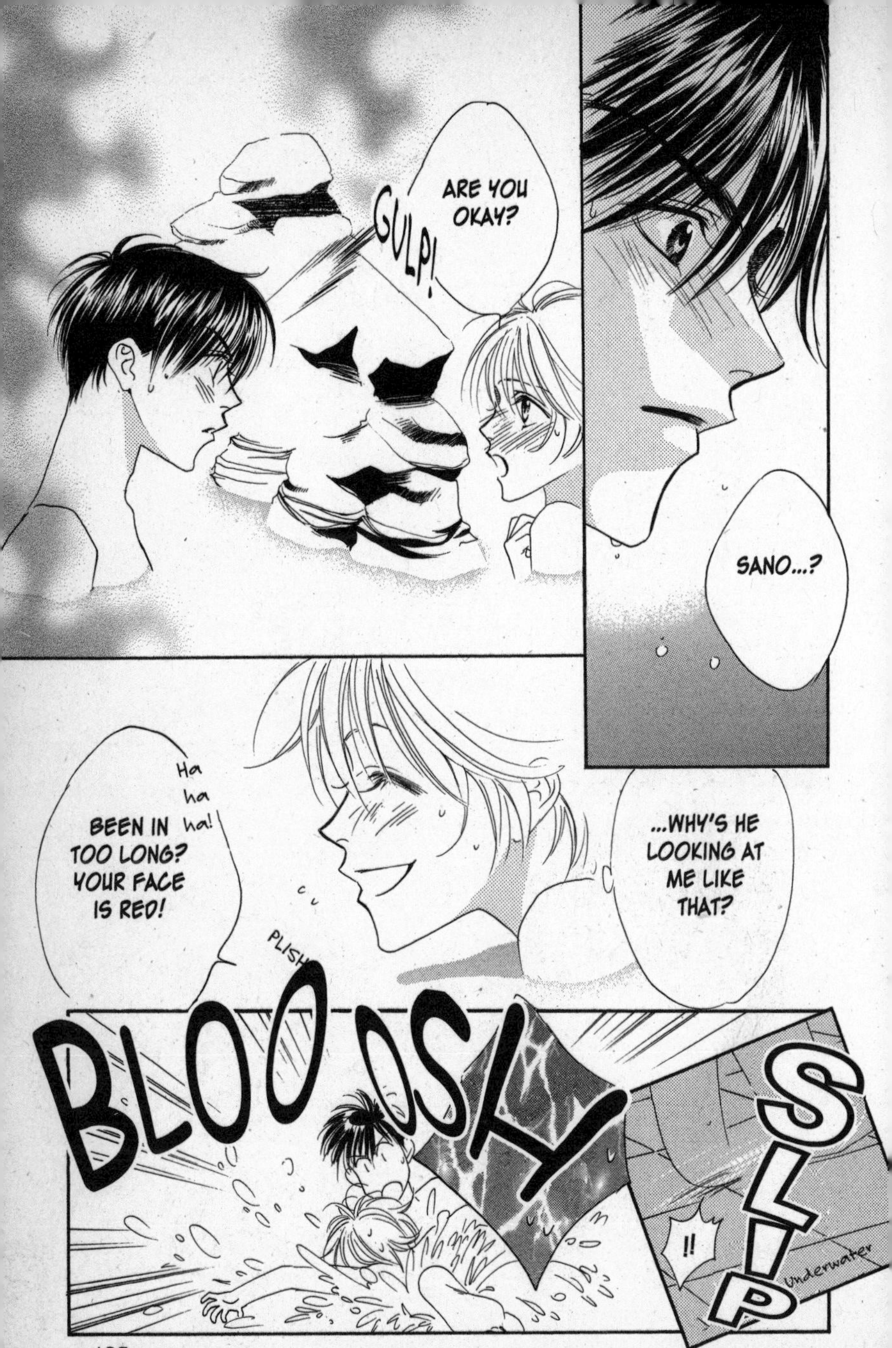
SANO...?
ARE YOU OKAY?
GULP!
...WHY'S HE LOOKING AT ME LIKE THAT?
Ha ha ha!
BEEN IN TOO LONG? YOUR FACE IS RED!
PLISH
SLIP
!!
Underwater
BLOOOSH

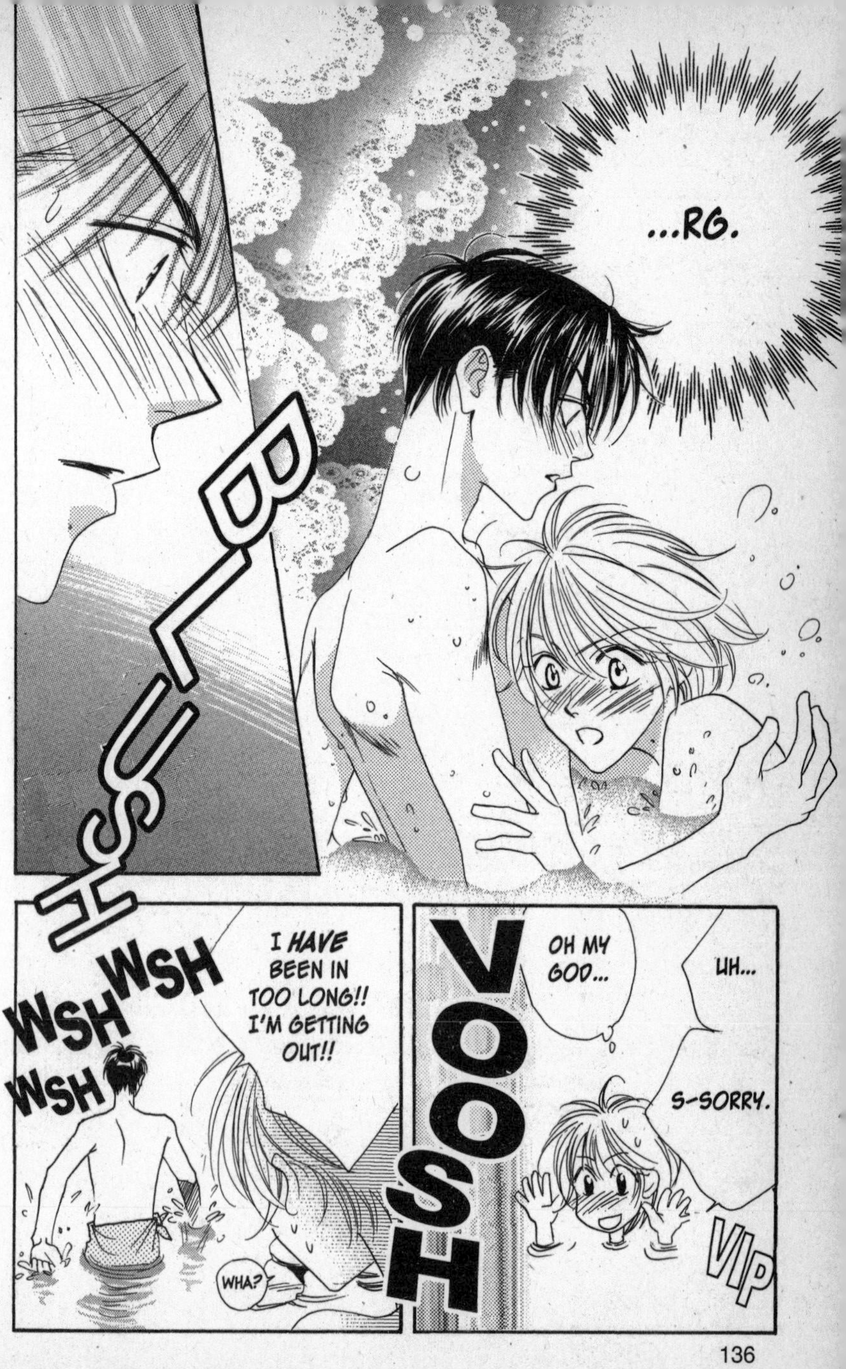
...RG.
BLUSH
UH...
OH MY GOD...
S-SORRY.
VIP
VOOSH
I *HAVE* BEEN IN TOO LONG!! I'M GETTING OUT!!
WSH WSH WSH
WHA?

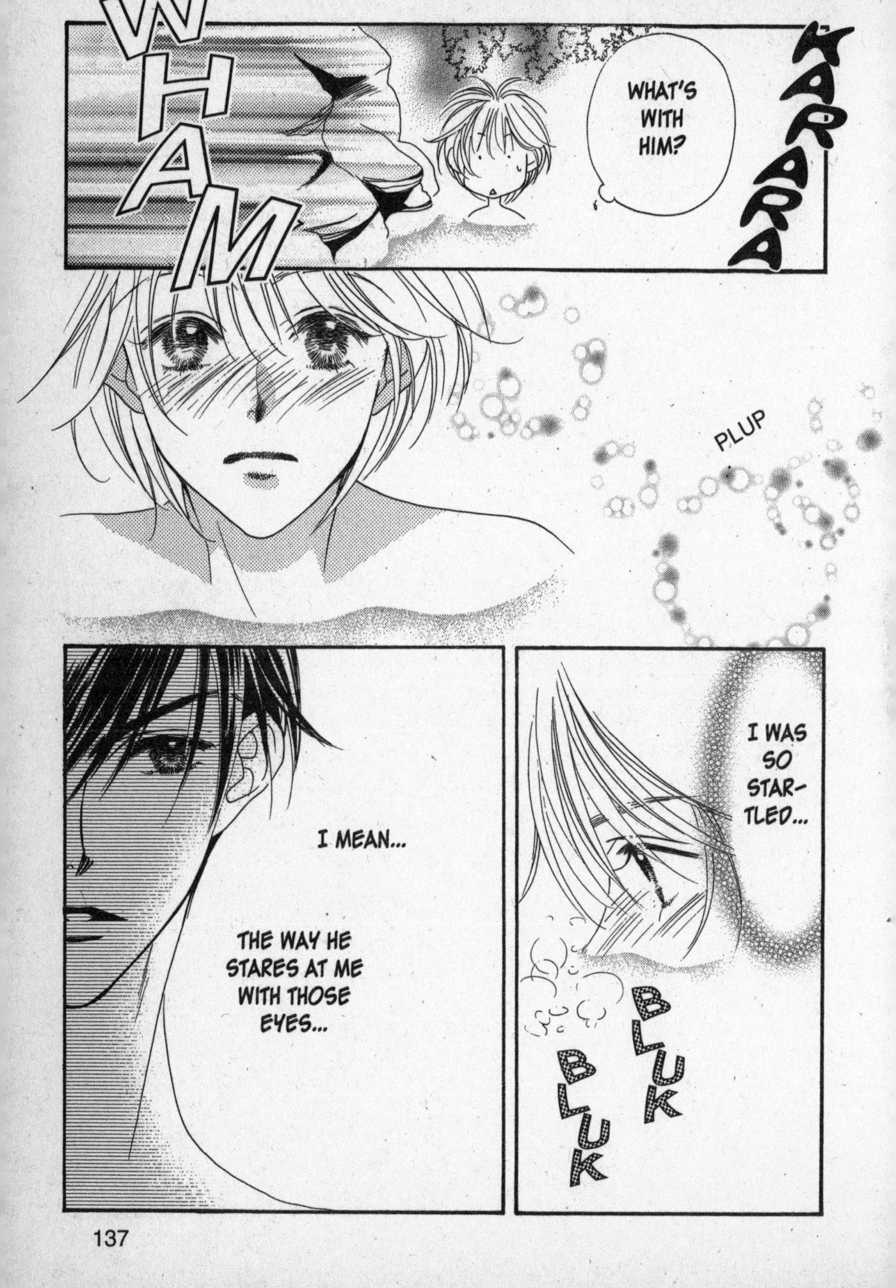
KARARA
WHAT'S WITH HIM?
WHAM
PLUP
I WAS SO STARTLED...
BLUK BLUK
I MEAN...
THE WAY HE STARES AT ME WITH THOSE EYES...

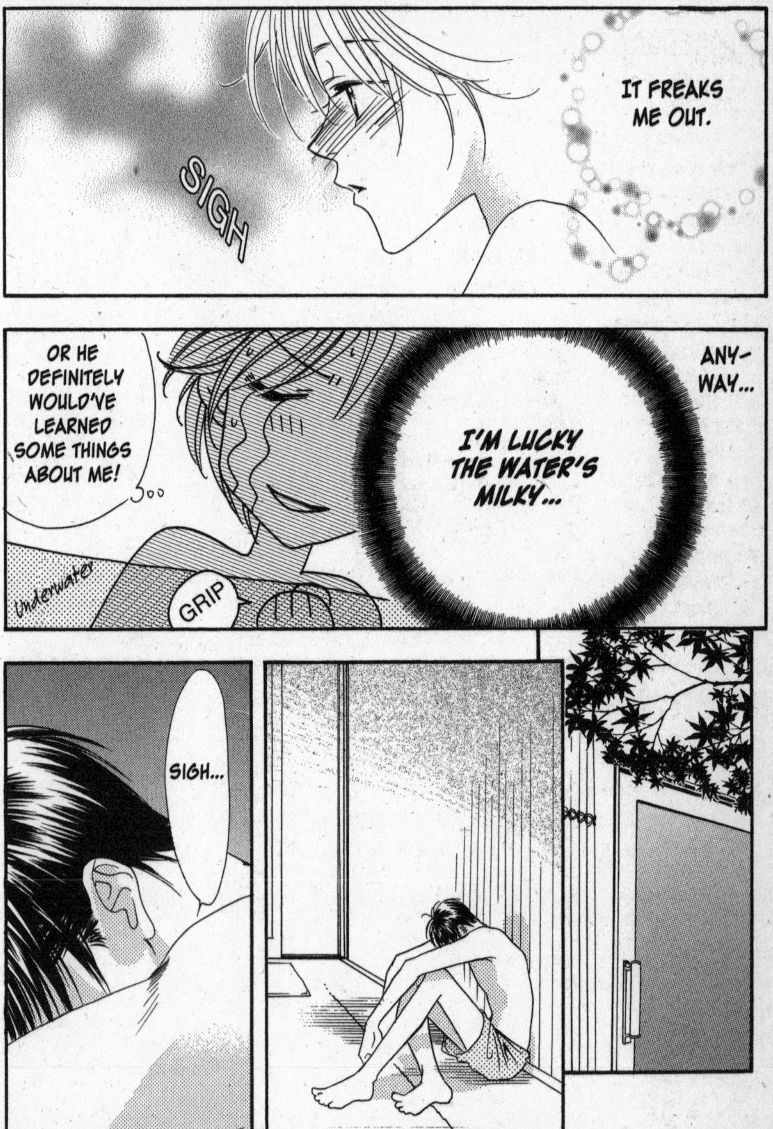
IT FREAKS ME OUT.
SIGH
ANY-WAY...
I'M LUCKY THE WATER'S MILKY...
OR HE DEFINITELY WOULD'VE LEARNED SOME THINGS ABOUT ME!
GRIP
Underwater
SIGH...

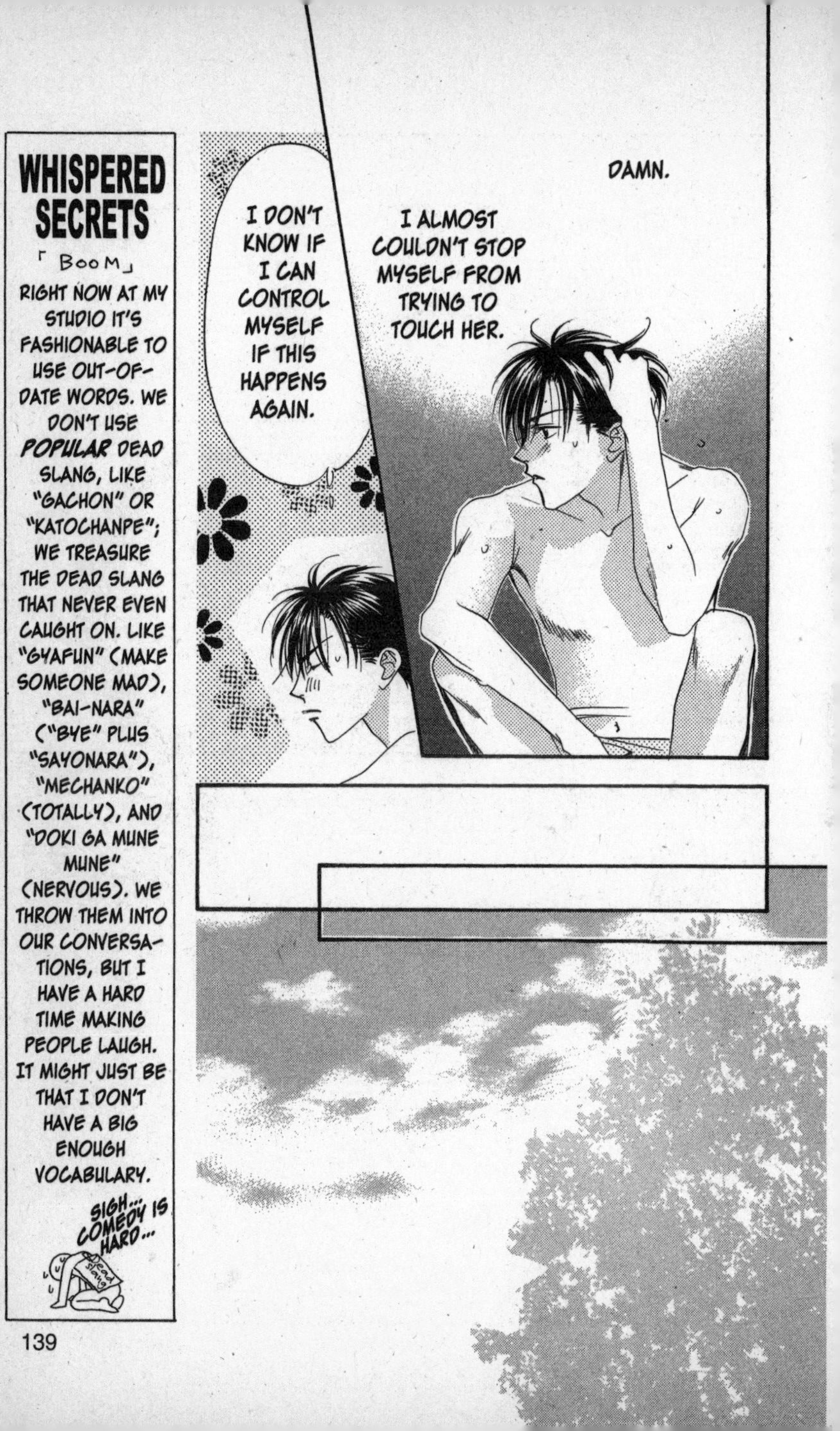
DAMN.
I ALMOST COULDN'T STOP MYSELF FROM TRYING TO TOUCH HER.
I DON'T KNOW IF I CAN CONTROL MYSELF IF THIS HAPPENS AGAIN.

WHISPERED SECRETS

「BooM」

RIGHT NOW AT MY STUDIO IT'S FASHIONABLE TO USE OUT-OF-DATE WORDS. WE DON'T USE *POPULAR* DEAD SLANG, LIKE "GACHON" OR "KATOCHANPE"; WE TREASURE THE DEAD SLANG THAT NEVER EVEN CAUGHT ON. LIKE "GYAFUN" (MAKE SOMEONE MAD), "BAI-NARA" ("BYE" PLUS "SAYONARA"), "MECHANKO" (TOTALLY), AND "DOKI GA MUNE MUNE" (NERVOUS). WE THROW THEM INTO OUR CONVERSATIONS, BUT I HAVE A HARD TIME MAKING PEOPLE LAUGH. IT MIGHT JUST BE THAT I DON'T HAVE A BIG ENOUGH VOCABULARY.

SIGH... COMEDY IS HARD...

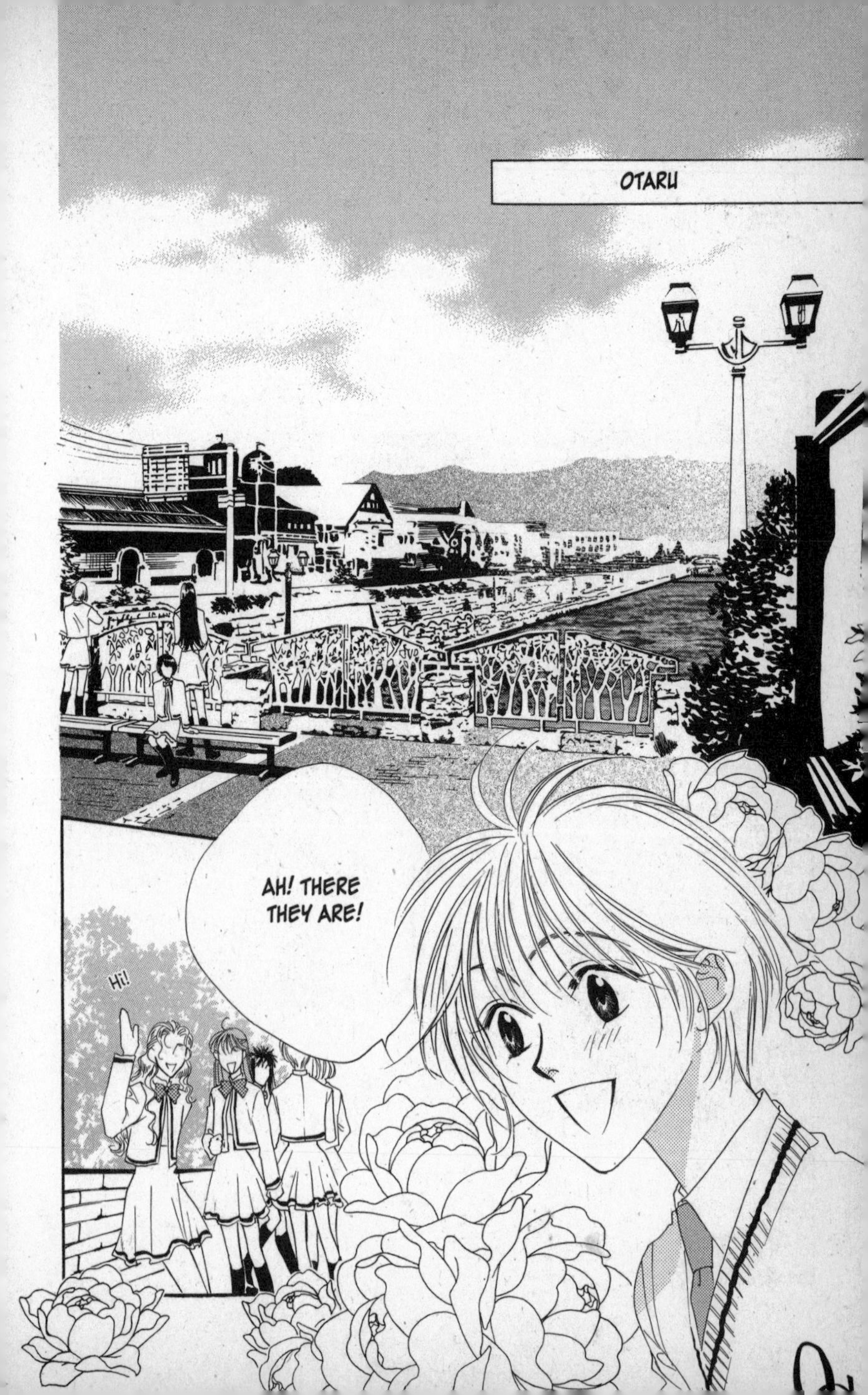

OTARU
AH! THERE THEY ARE!
Hi!

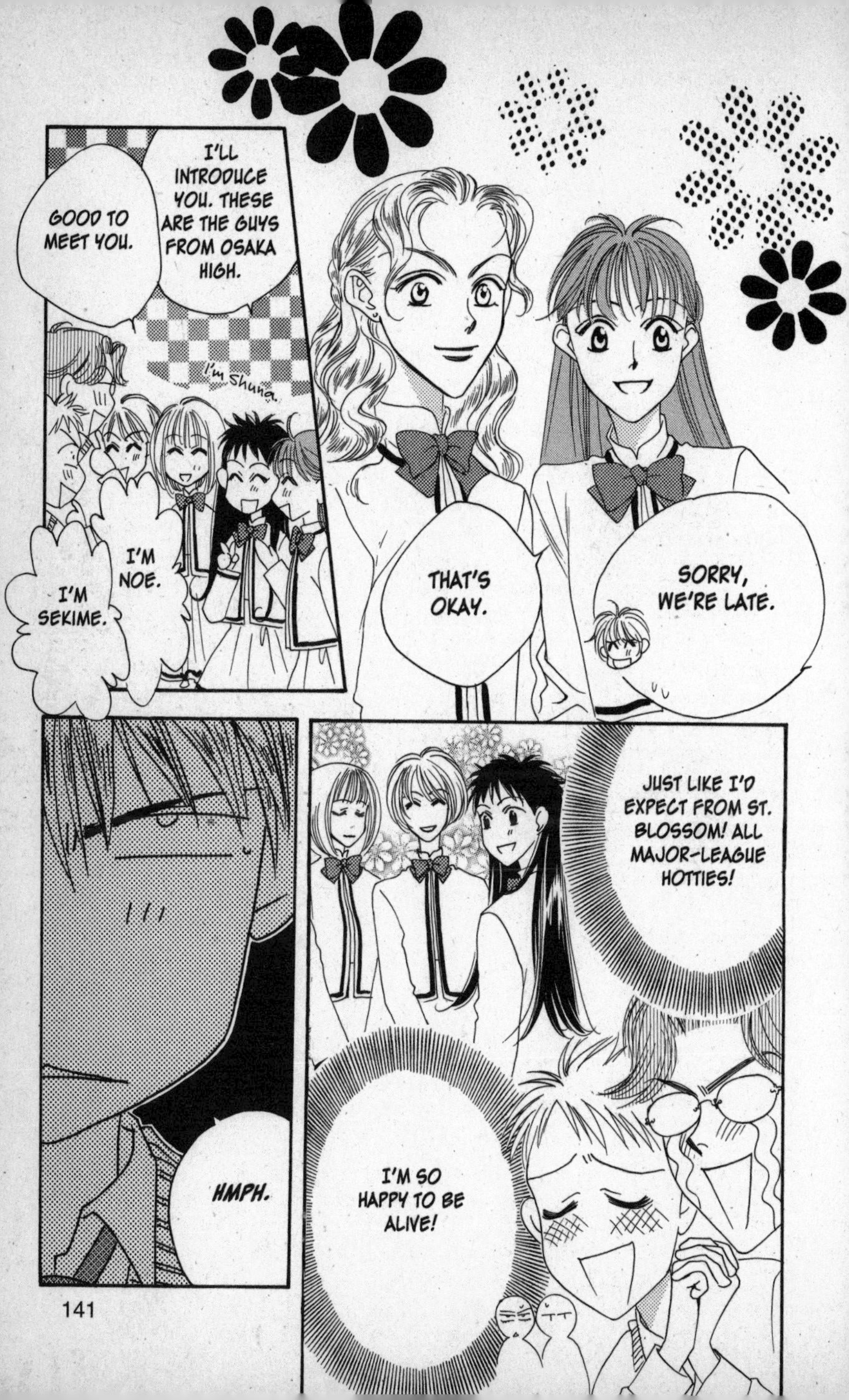
SORRY, WE'RE LATE.
THAT'S OKAY.
I'LL INTRODUCE YOU. THESE ARE THE GUYS FROM OSAKA HIGH.
GOOD TO MEET YOU.
I'm Shuna.
I'M NOE.
I'M SEKIME.
JUST LIKE I'D EXPECT FROM ST. BLOSSOM! ALL MAJOR-LEAGUE HOTTIES!
I'M SO HAPPY TO BE ALIVE!
HMPH.

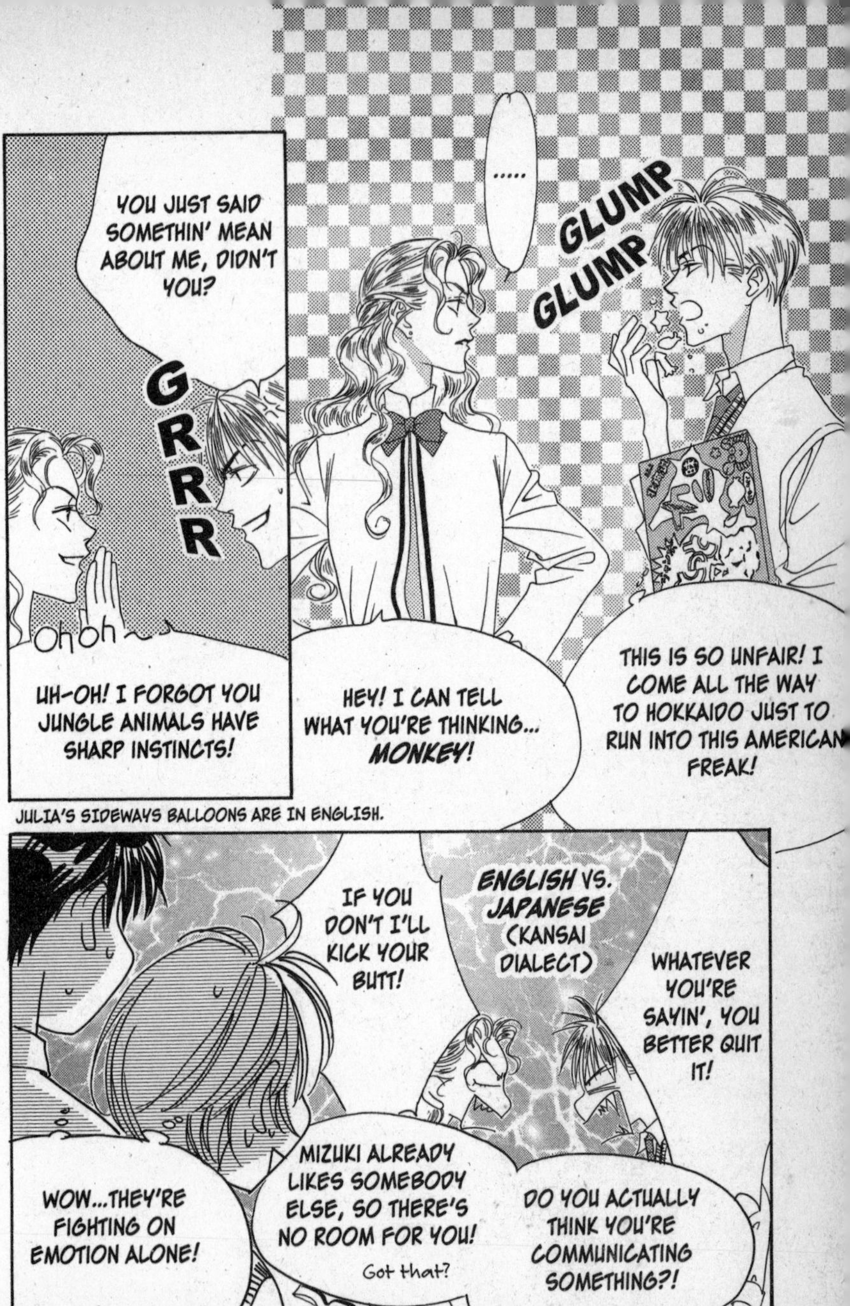
.....
GLUMP GLUMP
THIS IS SO UNFAIR! I COME ALL THE WAY TO HOKKAIDO JUST TO RUN INTO THIS AMERICAN FREAK!
HEY! I CAN TELL WHAT YOU'RE THINKING... MONKEY!
YOU JUST SAID SOMETHIN' MEAN ABOUT ME, DIDN'T YOU?
GRRR
Oh oh
UH-OH! I FORGOT YOU JUNGLE ANIMALS HAVE SHARP INSTINCTS!
JULIA'S SIDEWAYS BALLOONS ARE IN ENGLISH.
ENGLISH VS. JAPANESE (KANSAI DIALECT)
WHATEVER YOU'RE SAYIN', YOU BETTER QUIT IT!
IF YOU DON'T I'LL KICK YOUR BUTT!
DO YOU ACTUALLY THINK YOU'RE COMMUNICATING SOMETHING?!
MIZUKI ALREADY LIKES SOMEBODY ELSE, SO THERE'S NO ROOM FOR YOU!
Got that?
WOW...THEY'RE FIGHTING ON EMOTION ALONE!

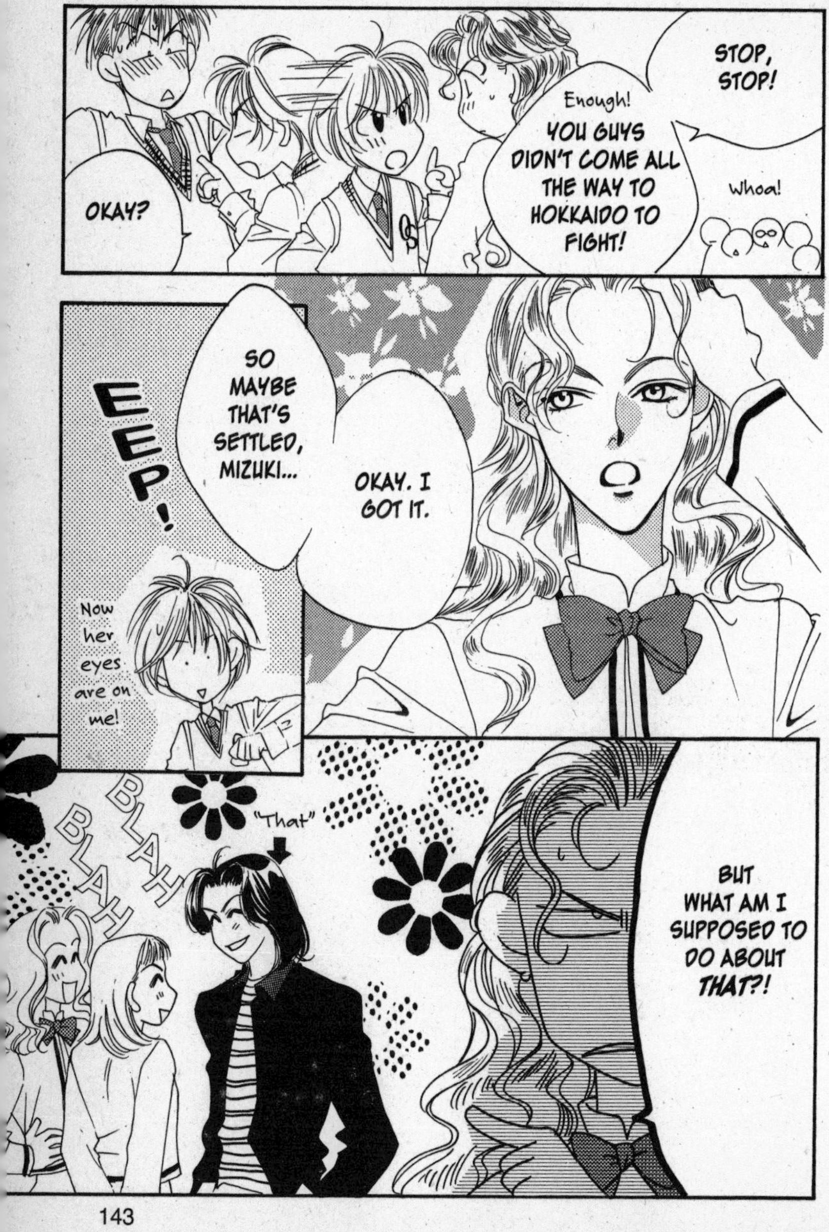
STOP, STOP!
Whoa!
Enough!
YOU GUYS DIDN'T COME ALL THE WAY TO HOKKAIDO TO FIGHT!
OKAY?
SO MAYBE THAT'S SETTLED, MIZUKI...
OKAY. I GOT IT.
EEP!
Now her eyes are on me!
BUT WHAT AM I SUPPOSED TO DO ABOUT *THAT*?!
"That"
BLAH BLAH

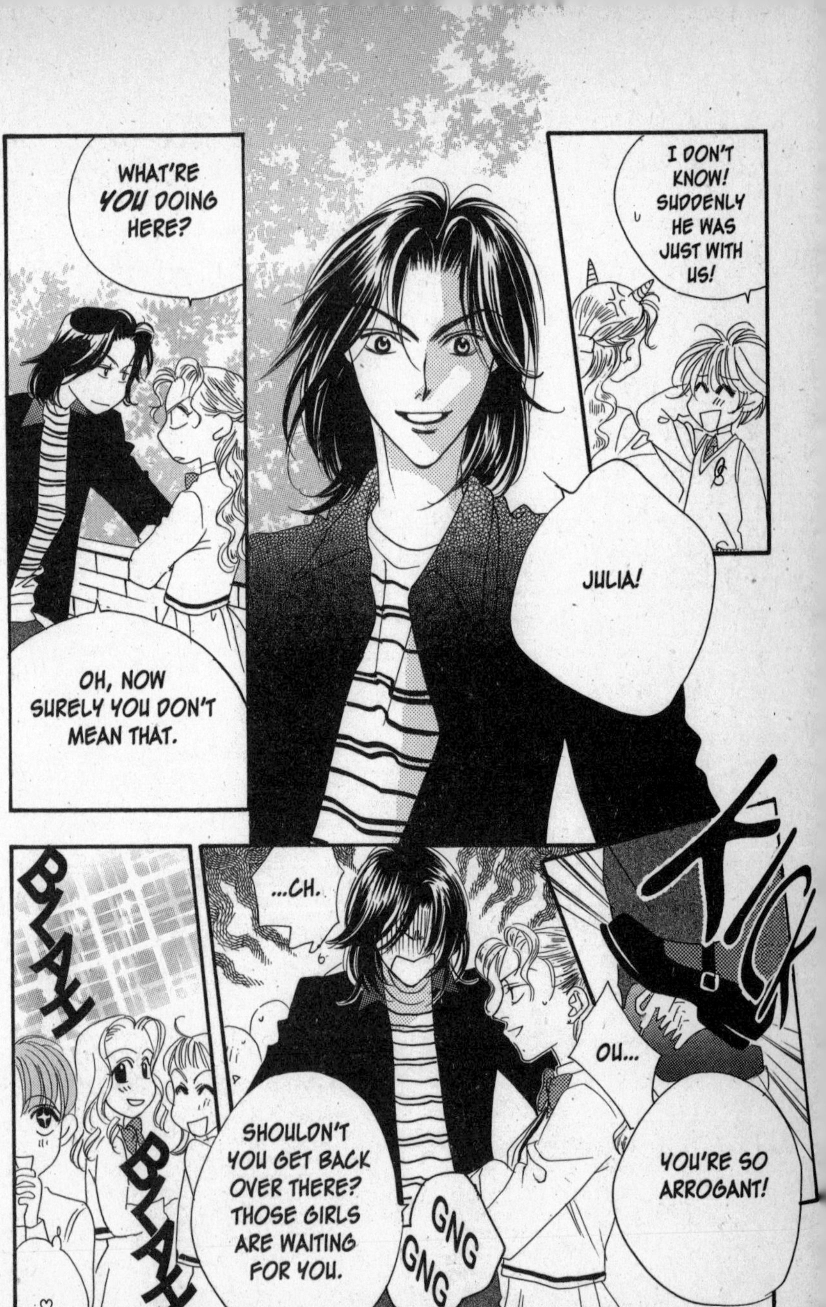
I DON'T KNOW! SUDDENLY HE WAS JUST WITH US!
JULIA!
WHAT'RE YOU DOING HERE?
OH, NOW SURELY YOU DON'T MEAN THAT.
KICK
OU...
YOU'RE SO ARROGANT!
...CH.
SHOULDN'T YOU GET BACK OVER THERE? THOSE GIRLS ARE WAITING FOR YOU.
GNG GNG
BLAH BLAH

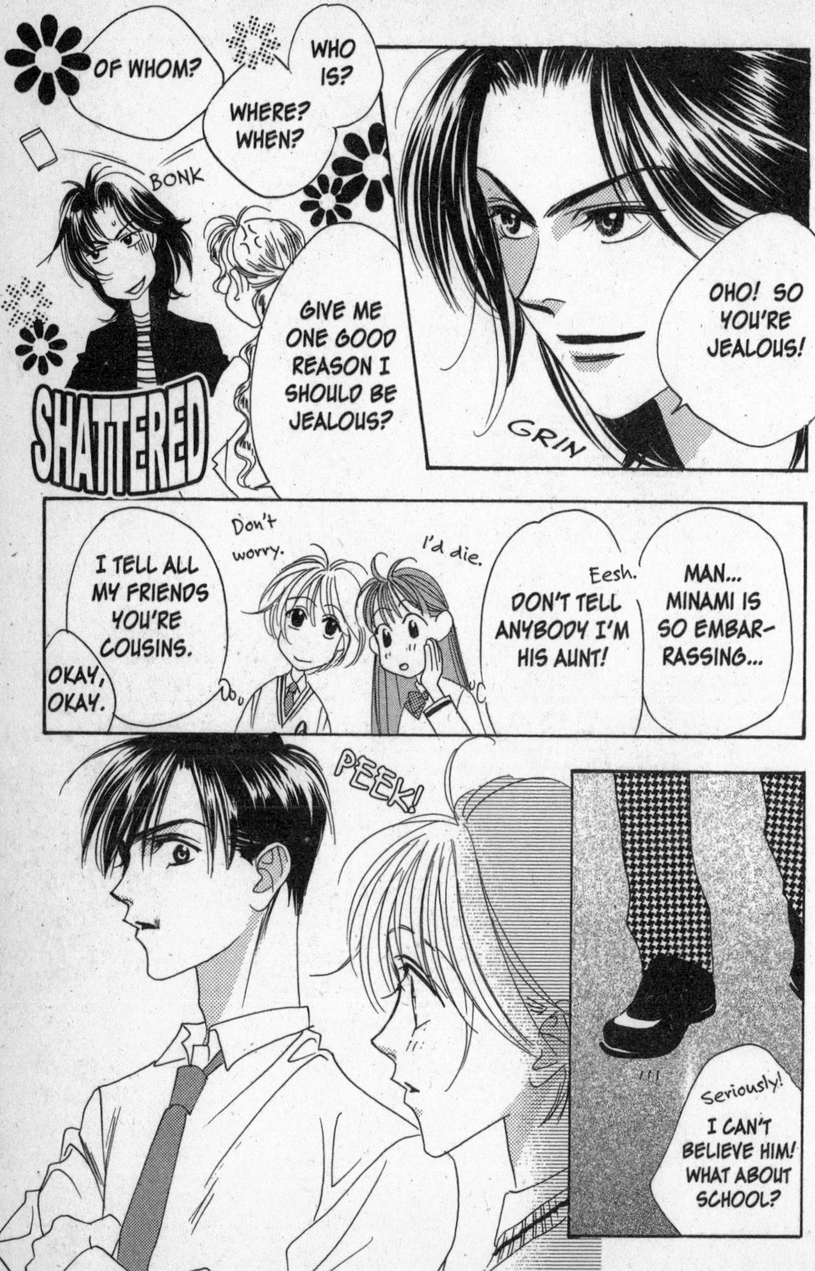
OHO! SO YOU'RE JEALOUS!
GRIN
GIVE ME ONE GOOD REASON I SHOULD BE JEALOUS?
WHO IS?
WHERE? WHEN?
OF WHOM?
BONK
SHATTERED
MAN... MINAMI IS SO EMBARRASSING...
DON'T TELL ANYBODY I'M HIS AUNT!
Eesh.
I'd die.
Don't worry.
I TELL ALL MY FRIENDS YOU'RE COUSINS.
OKAY, OKAY.
Seriously!
I CAN'T BELIEVE HIM! WHAT ABOUT SCHOOL?
PEEK!

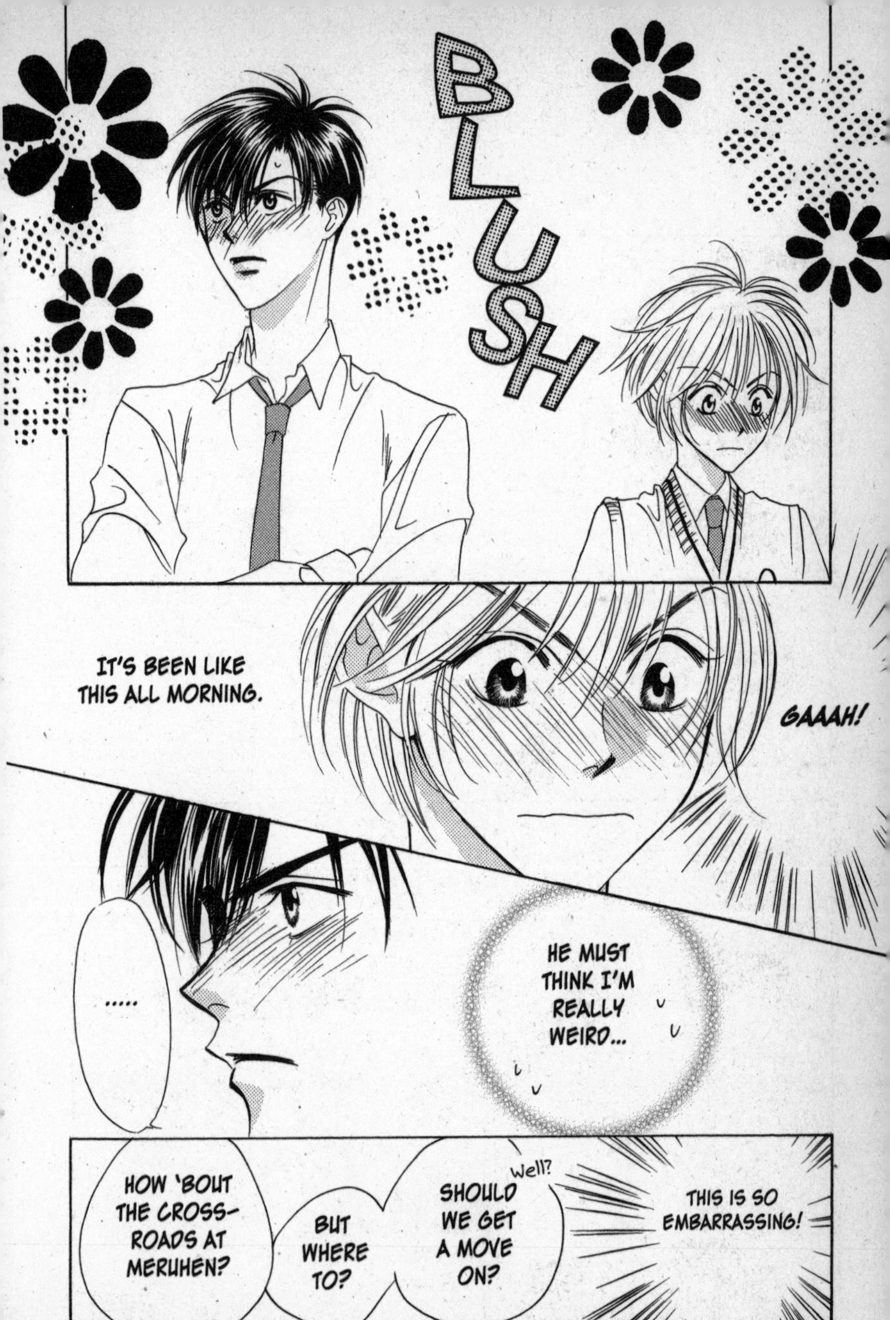
BLUSH
GAAAH!
IT'S BEEN LIKE THIS ALL MORNING.
HE MUST THINK I'M REALLY WEIRD...
.....
THIS IS SO EMBARRASSING!
Well?
SHOULD WE GET A MOVE ON?
BUT WHERE TO?
HOW 'BOUT THE CROSS-ROADS AT MERUHEN?

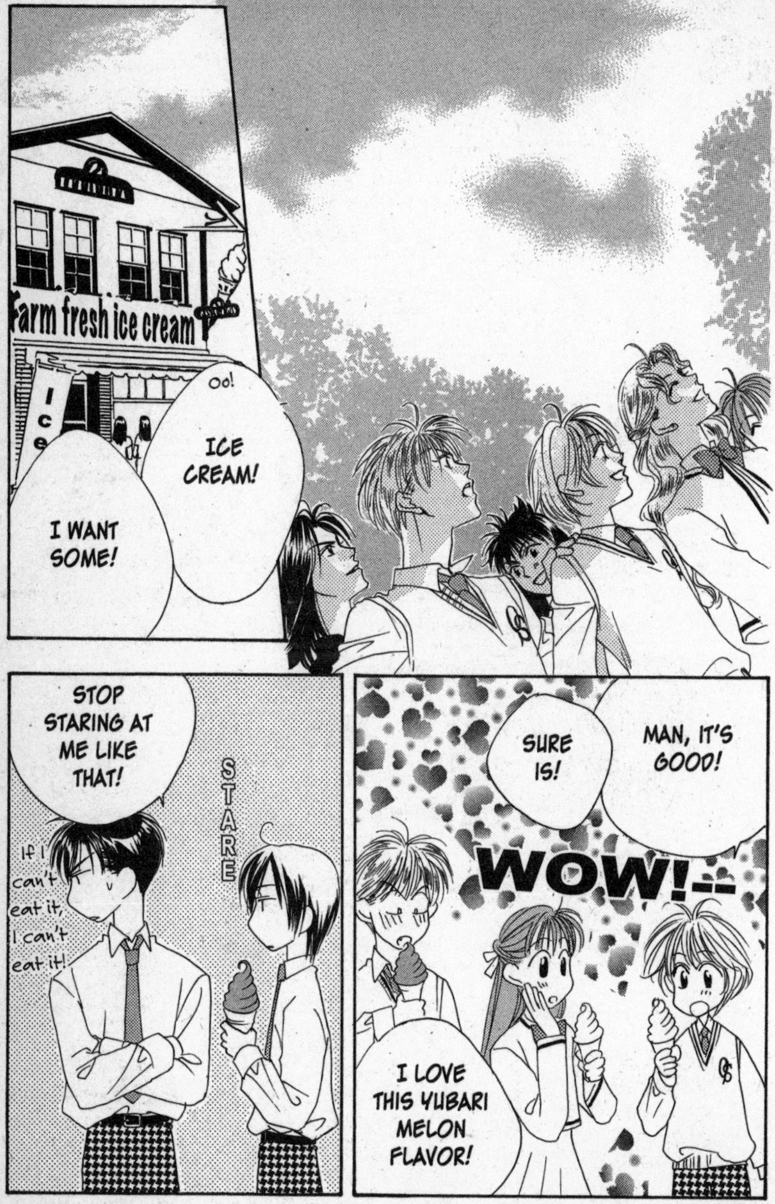
Farm fresh ice cream
Oo! ICE CREAM!
I WANT SOME!
MAN, IT'S GOOD!
SURE IS!
WOW!..
I LOVE THIS YUBARI MELON FLAVOR!
STARE
STOP STARING AT ME LIKE THAT!
If I can't eat it, I can't eat it!

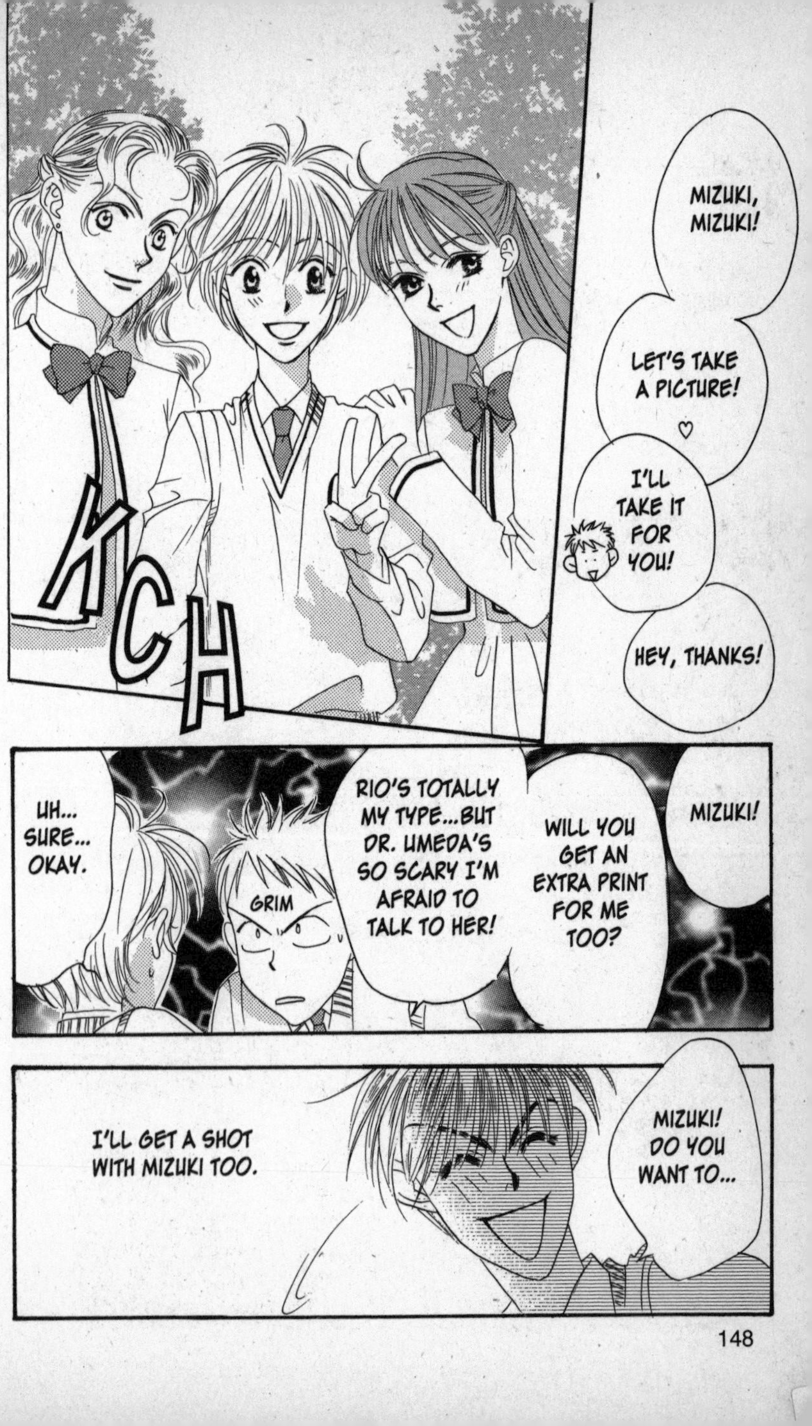
MIZUKI, MIZUKI!
LET'S TAKE A PICTURE! ♡
I'LL TAKE IT FOR YOU!
HEY, THANKS!
KCH
MIZUKI!
WILL YOU GET AN EXTRA PRINT FOR ME TOO?
RIO'S TOTALLY MY TYPE...BUT DR. UMEDA'S SO SCARY I'M AFRAID TO TALK TO HER!
GRIM
UH... SURE... OKAY.
MIZUKI! DO YOU WANT TO...
I'LL GET A SHOT WITH MIZUKI TOO.

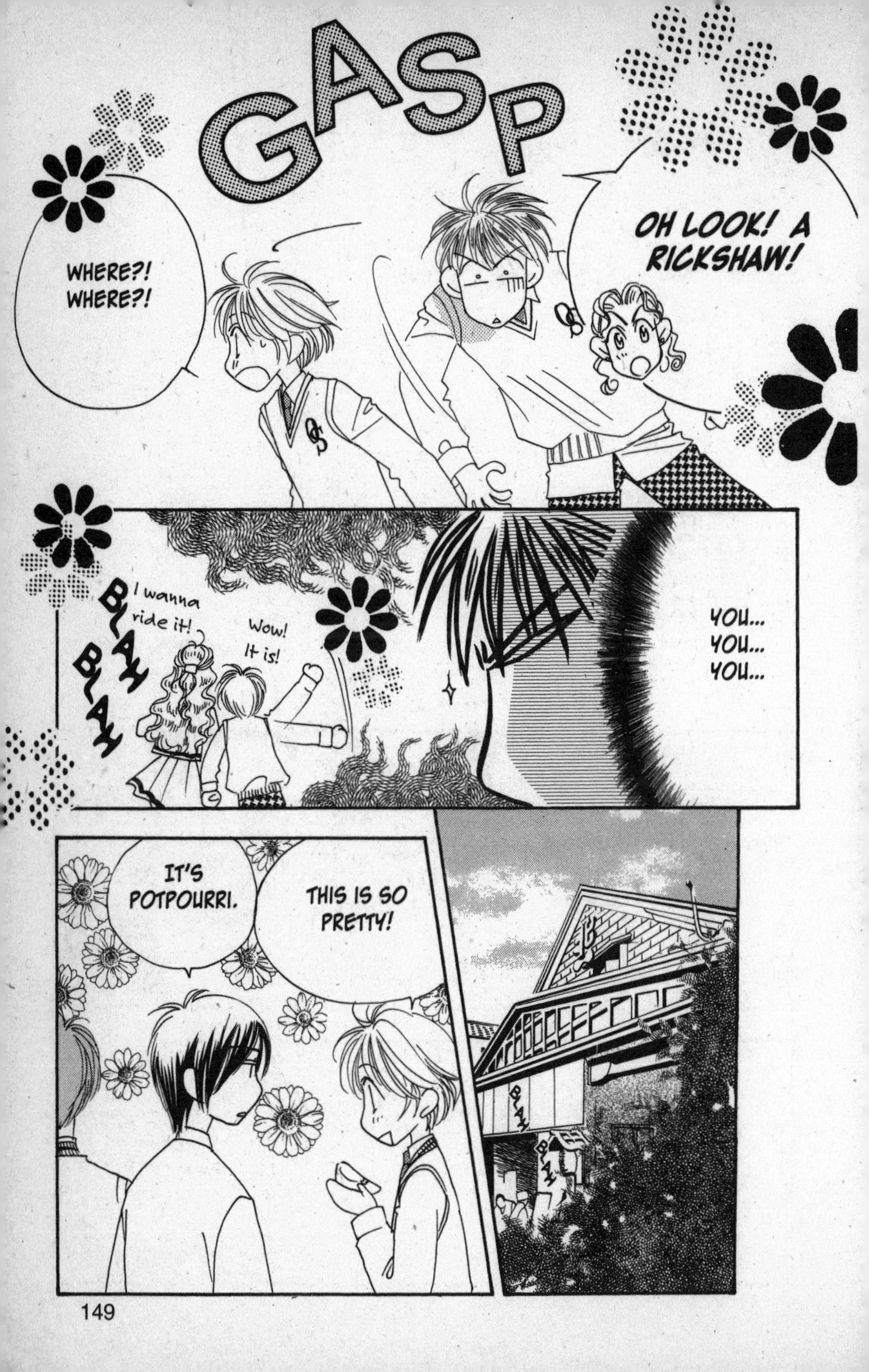
GASP
OH LOOK! A RICKSHAW!
WHERE?! WHERE?!
YOU... YOU... YOU...
Wow! It is!
I wanna ride it!
BLAH BLAH BLAH
BLAH
BLAH
BLAH
THIS IS SO PRETTY!
IT'S POTPOURRI.

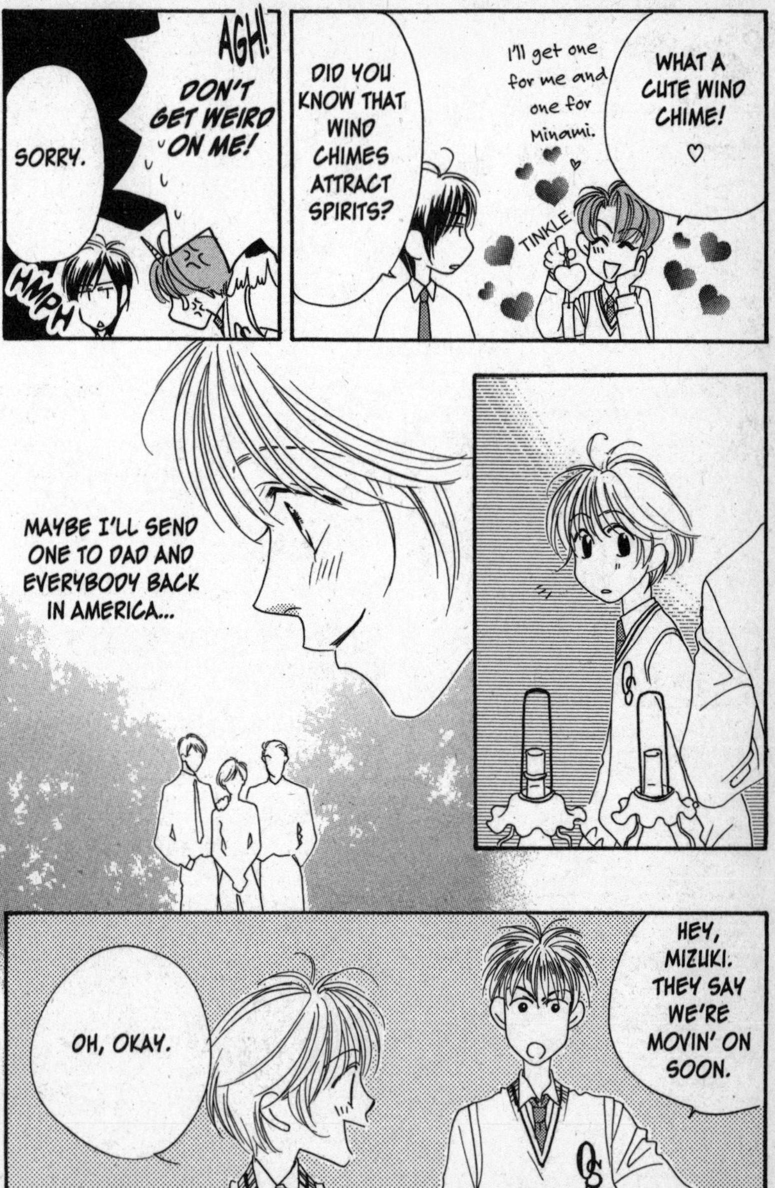
WHAT A CUTE WIND CHIME! ♡
I'll get one for me and one for Minami.
TINKLE
DID YOU KNOW THAT WIND CHIMES ATTRACT SPIRITS?
AGH!
DON'T GET WEIRD ON ME!
SORRY.
HMPH
MAYBE I'LL SEND ONE TO DAD AND EVERYBODY BACK IN AMERICA...
HEY, MIZUKI. THEY SAY WE'RE MOVIN' ON SOON.
OH, OKAY.

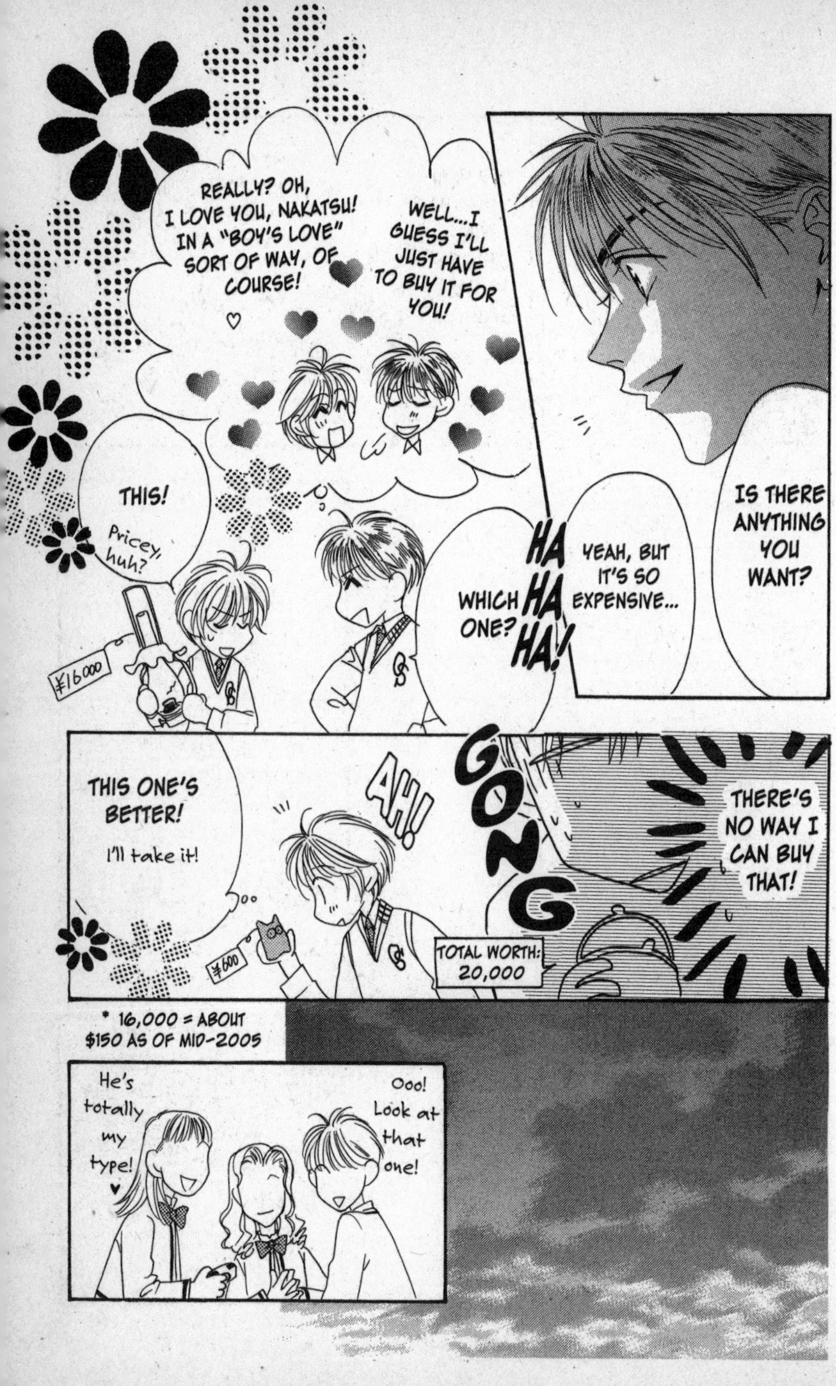
IS THERE ANYTHING YOU WANT?
YEAH, BUT IT'S SO EXPENSIVE...
HA HA HA!
WHICH ONE?
THIS!
Pricey, huh?
¥16,000
WELL...I GUESS I'LL JUST HAVE TO BUY IT FOR YOU!
REALLY? OH, I LOVE YOU, NAKATSU! IN A "BOY'S LOVE" SORT OF WAY, OF COURSE!
GONG
THERE'S NO WAY I CAN BUY THAT!
TOTAL WORTH: 20,000
AH!
THIS ONE'S BETTER!
I'll take it!
¥600
Ooo! Look at that one!
He's totally my type!

* 16,000 = ABOUT $150 AS OF MID-2005

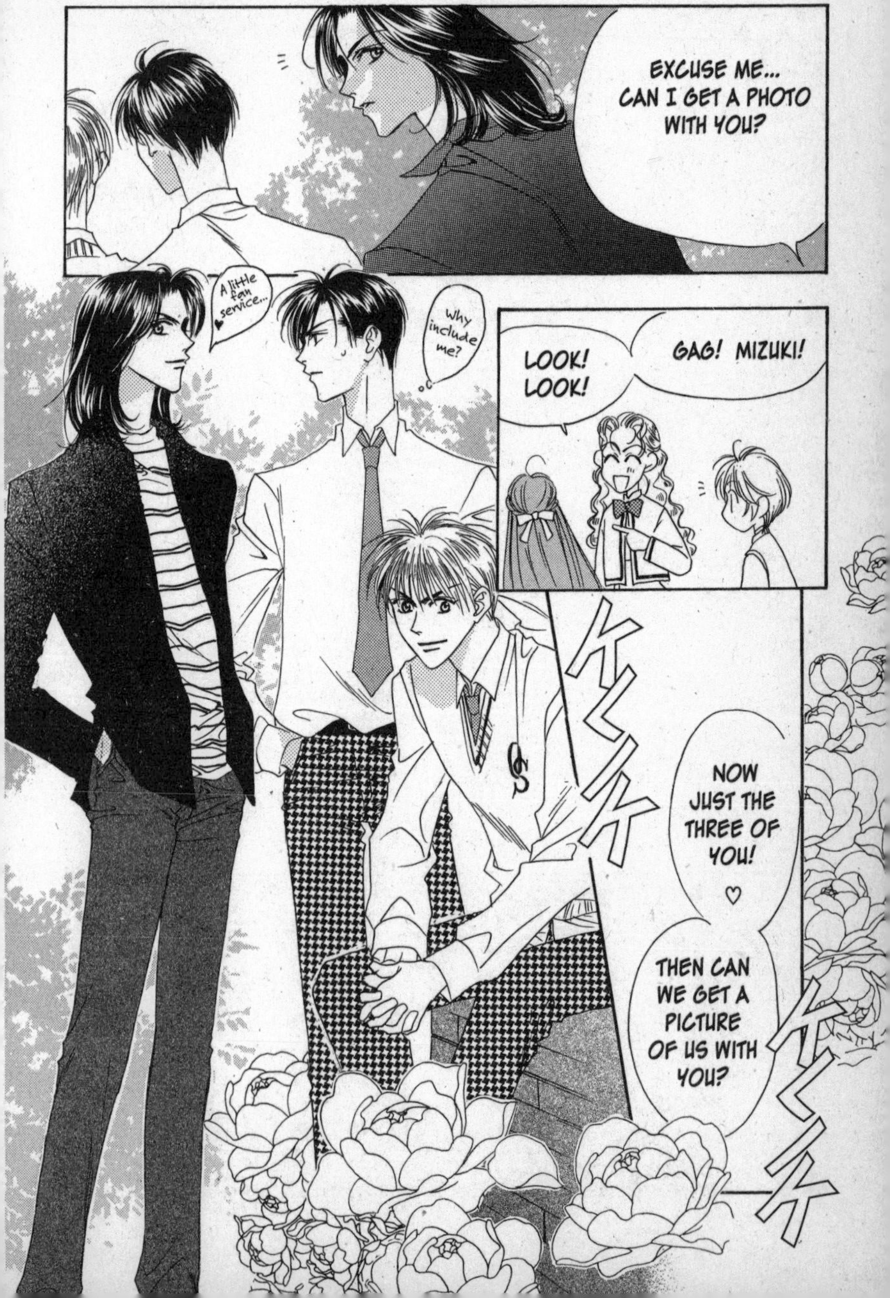
EXCUSE ME... CAN I GET A PHOTO WITH YOU?
GAG! MIZUKI!
LOOK! LOOK!
Why include me?
A little fan service...
KLIK
NOW JUST THE THREE OF YOU! ♡
THEN CAN WE GET A PICTURE OF US WITH YOU?
KLIK

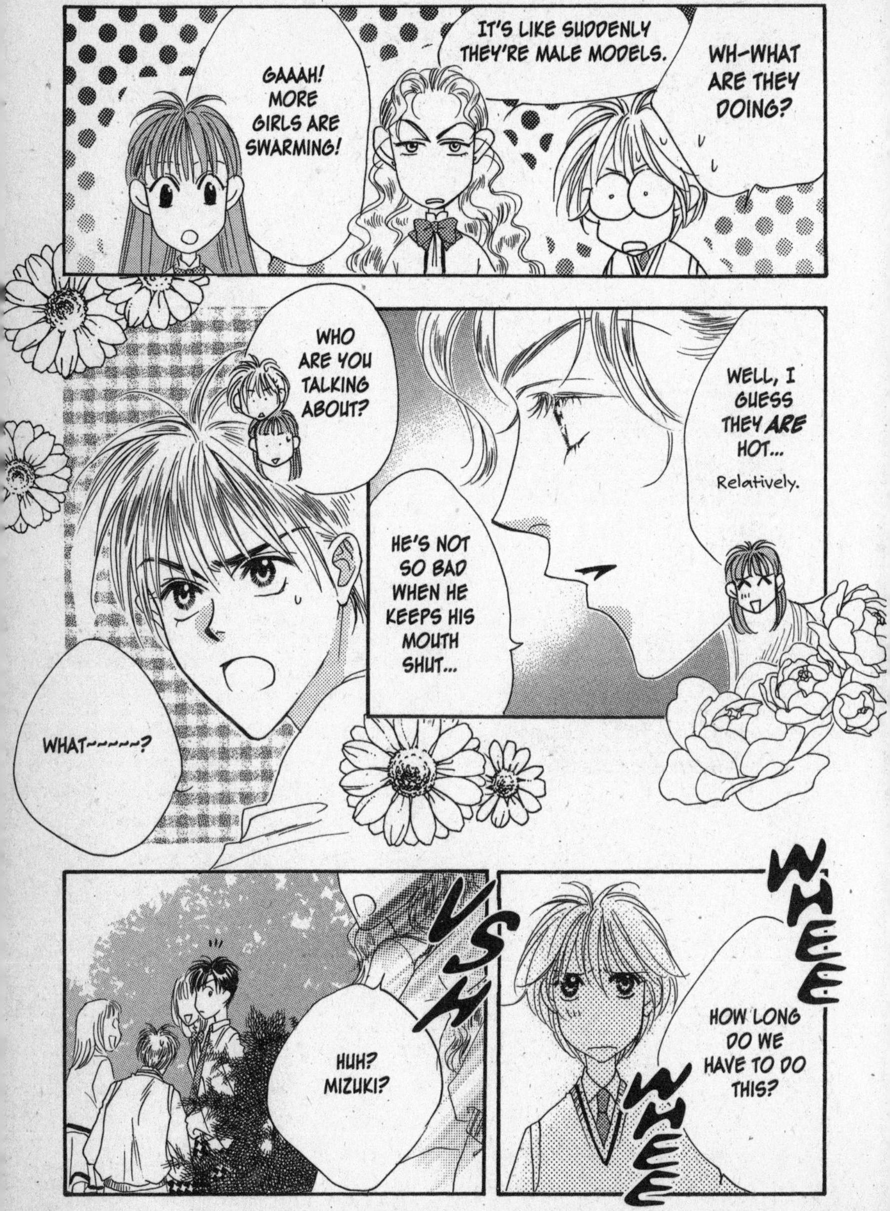
WH-WHAT ARE THEY DOING?
IT'S LIKE SUDDENLY THEY'RE MALE MODELS.
GAAAH! MORE GIRLS ARE SWARMING!
WELL, I GUESS THEY ARE HOT...
Relatively.
HE'S NOT SO BAD WHEN HE KEEPS HIS MOUTH SHUT...
WHO ARE YOU TALKING ABOUT?
WHAT~~~~~?
WHEE
HOW LONG DO WE HAVE TO DO THIS?
WHEE
VSH
HUH? MIZUKI?

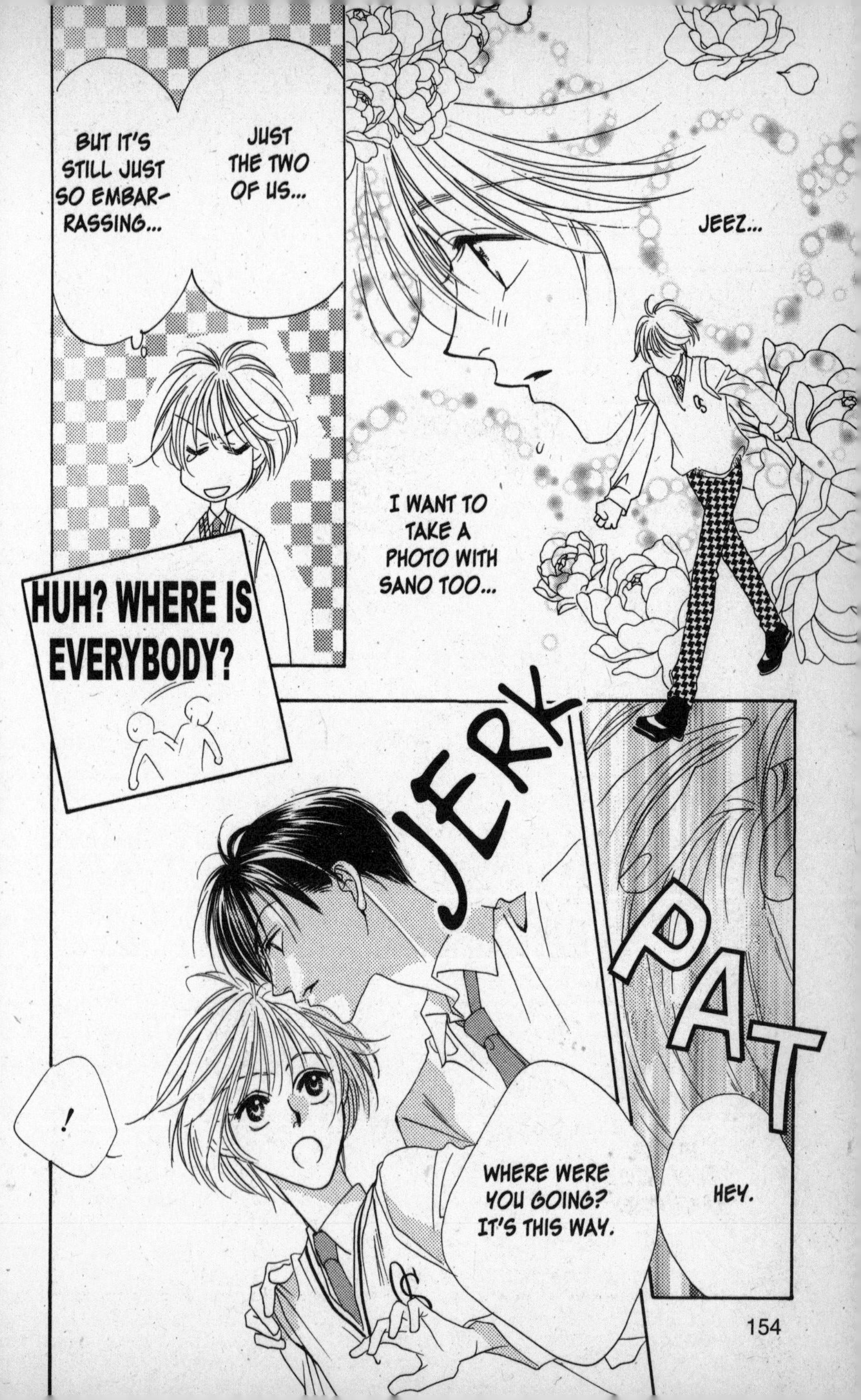
JEEZ...
I WANT TO TAKE A PHOTO WITH SANO TOO...
JUST THE TWO OF US...
BUT IT'S STILL JUST SO EMBARRASSING...
HUH? WHERE IS EVERYBODY?
JERK
PAT
HEY.
WHERE WERE YOU GOING? IT'S THIS WAY.
!

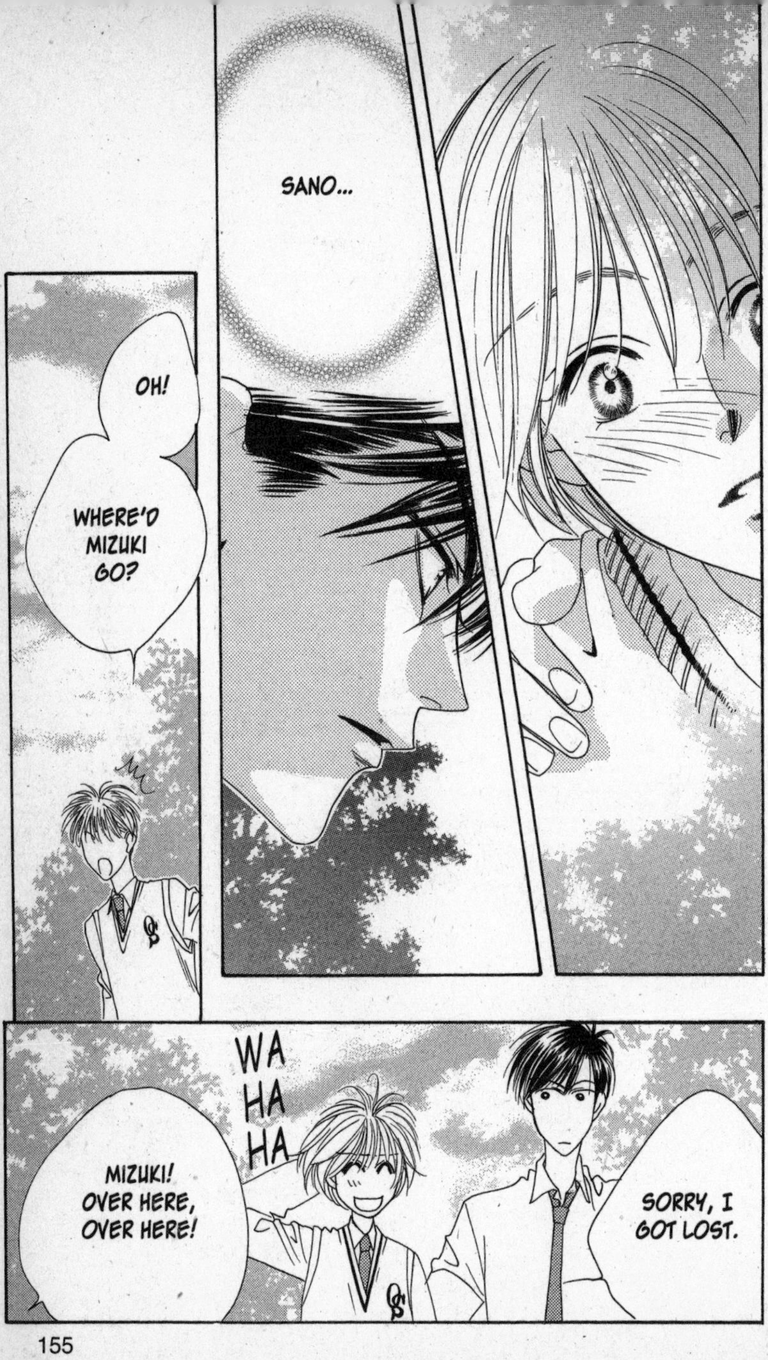
SANO...
OH!
WHERE'D MIZUKI GO?
SORRY, I GOT LOST.
WA HA HA
MIZUKI! OVER HERE, OVER HERE!

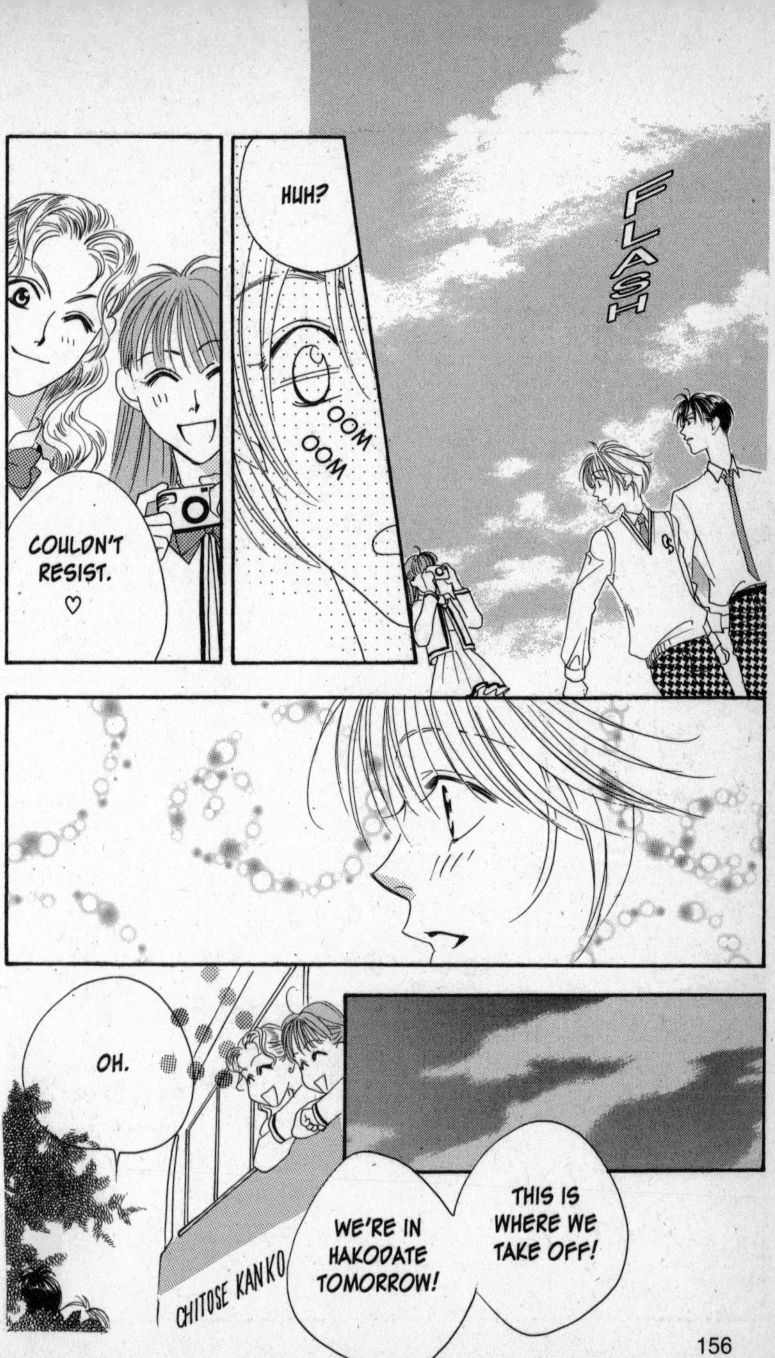
FLASH
HUH?
MOOM MOOM
COULDN'T RESIST. ♡
THIS IS WHERE WE TAKE OFF!
WE'RE IN HAKODATE TOMORROW!
OH.
CHITOSE KANKO

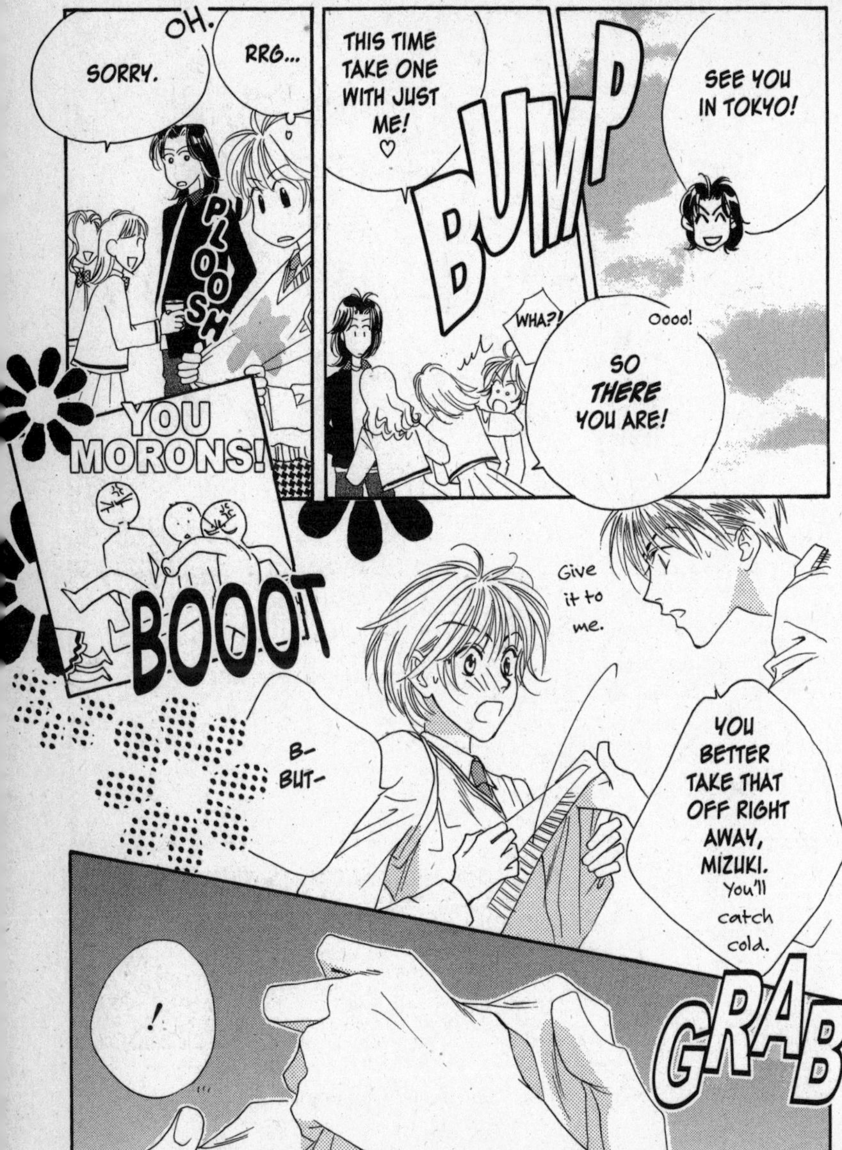
SEE YOU IN TOKYO!
THIS TIME TAKE ONE WITH JUST ME! ♡
BUMP
WHA?!
Oooo!
SO THERE YOU ARE!
RRG...
OH.
SORRY.
PLOSH
YOU MORONS!
BOOOT
Give it to me.
YOU BETTER TAKE THAT OFF RIGHT AWAY, MIZUKI.
You'll catch cold.
B-BUT-
GRAB
!

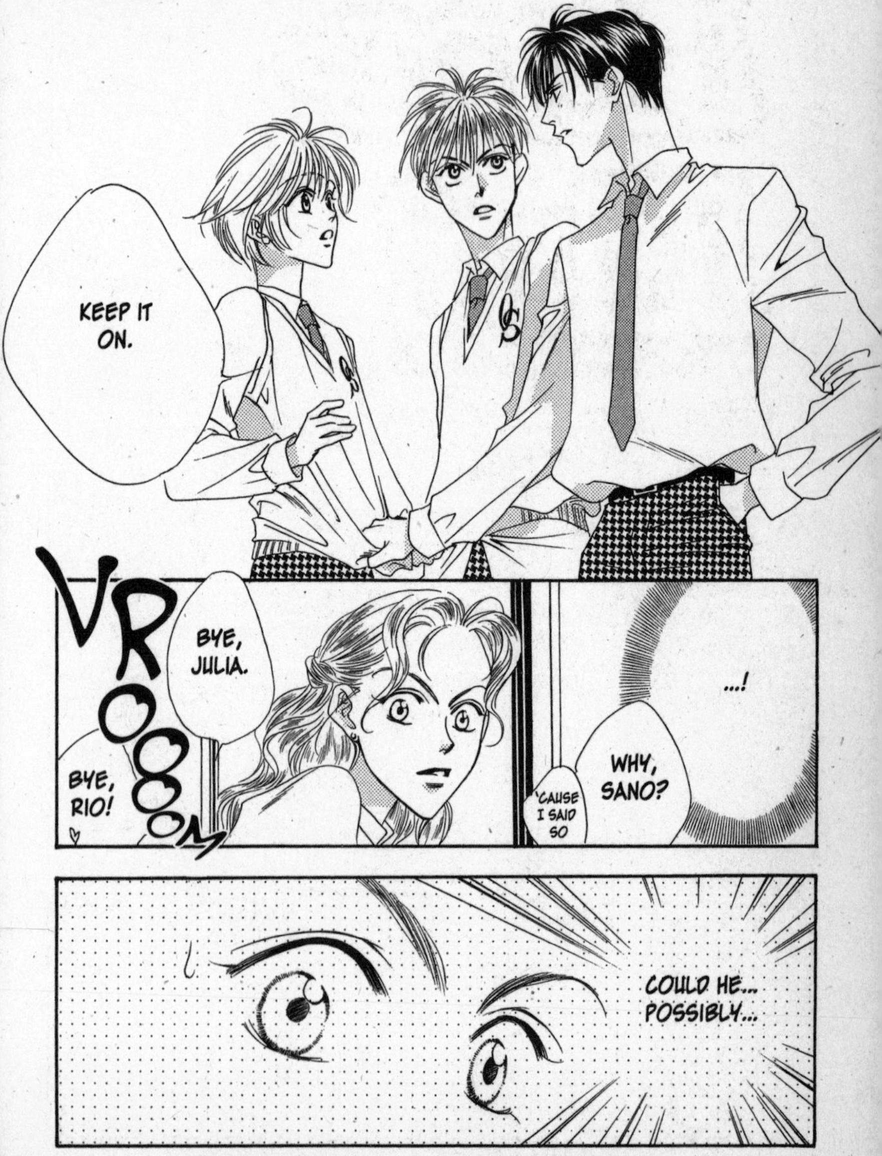
KEEP IT ON.
...!
WHY, SANO?
'CAUSE I SAID SO
VROOOOOM
BYE, JULIA.
BYE, RIO! ♡
COULD HE... POSSIBLY...

HANA-KIMI CHAPTER 35/END

Hana-Kimi

For You in Full Blossom

CHAPTER 36

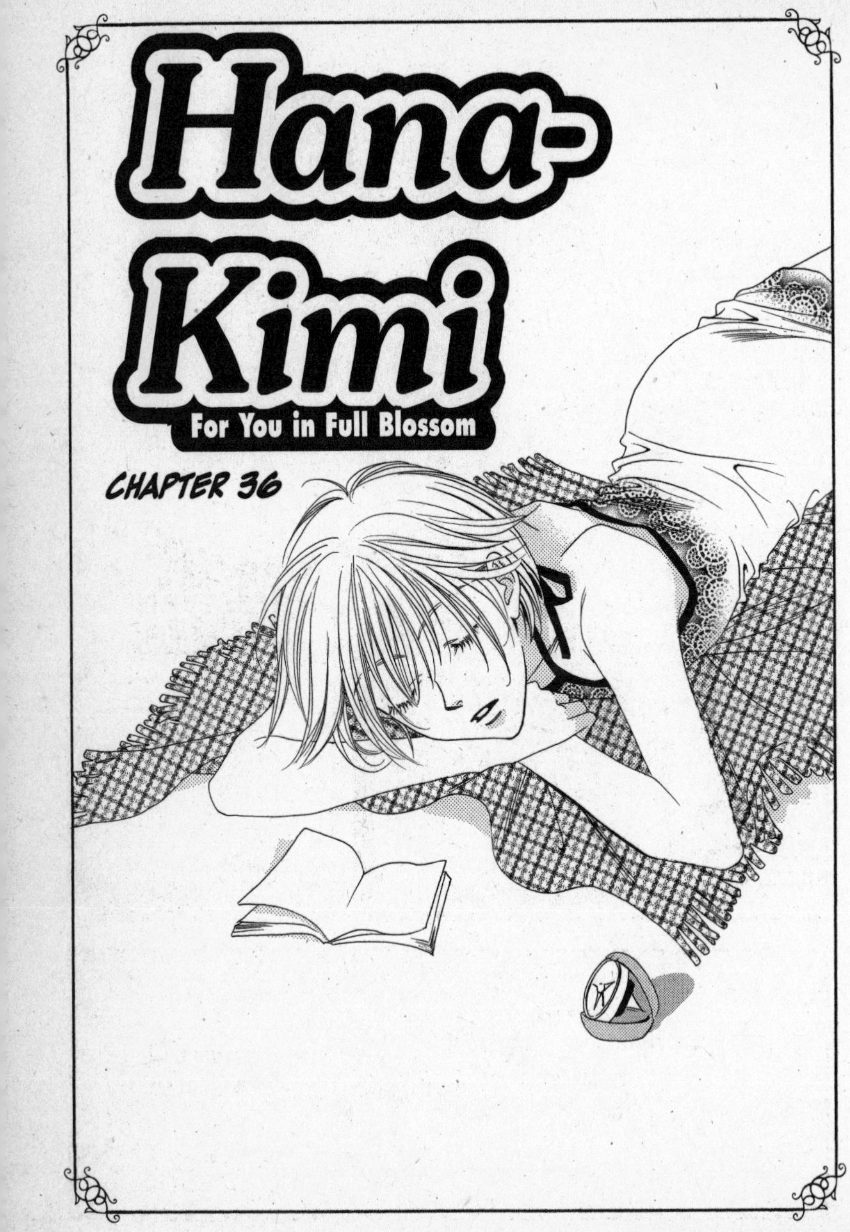

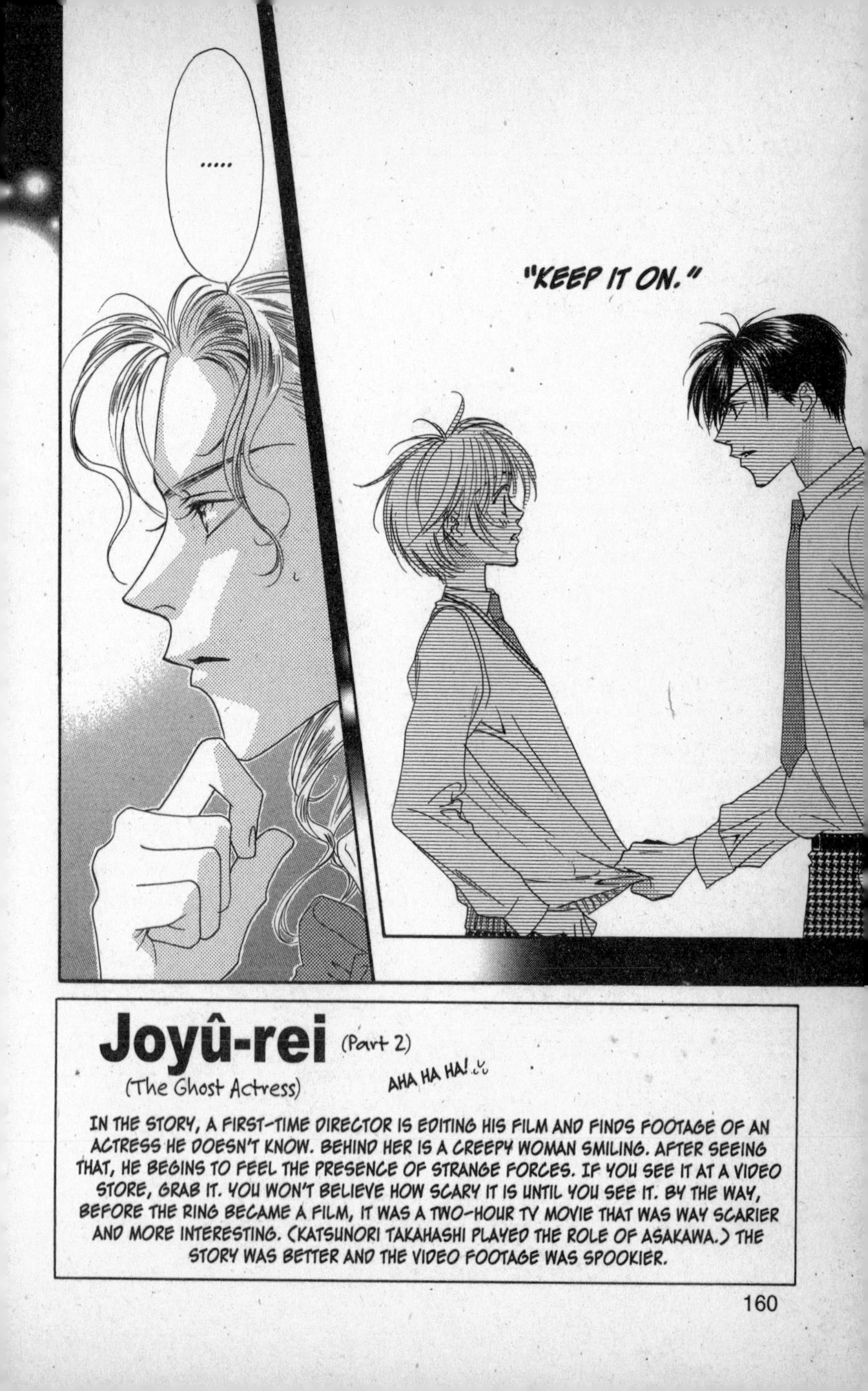
"KEEP IT ON."
.....

Joyû-rei (Part 2)

(The Ghost Actress)

AHA HA HA!

IN THE STORY, A FIRST-TIME DIRECTOR IS EDITING HIS FILM AND FINDS FOOTAGE OF AN ACTRESS HE DOESN'T KNOW. BEHIND HER IS A CREEPY WOMAN SMILING. AFTER SEEING THAT, HE BEGINS TO FEEL THE PRESENCE OF STRANGE FORCES. IF YOU SEE IT AT A VIDEO STORE, GRAB IT. YOU WON'T BELIEVE HOW SCARY IT IS UNTIL YOU SEE IT. BY THE WAY, BEFORE THE RING BECAME A FILM, IT WAS A TWO-HOUR TV MOVIE THAT WAS WAY SCARIER AND MORE INTERESTING. (KATSUNORI TAKAHASHI PLAYED THE ROLE OF ASAKAWA.) THE STORY WAS BETTER AND THE VIDEO FOOTAGE WAS SPOOKIER.

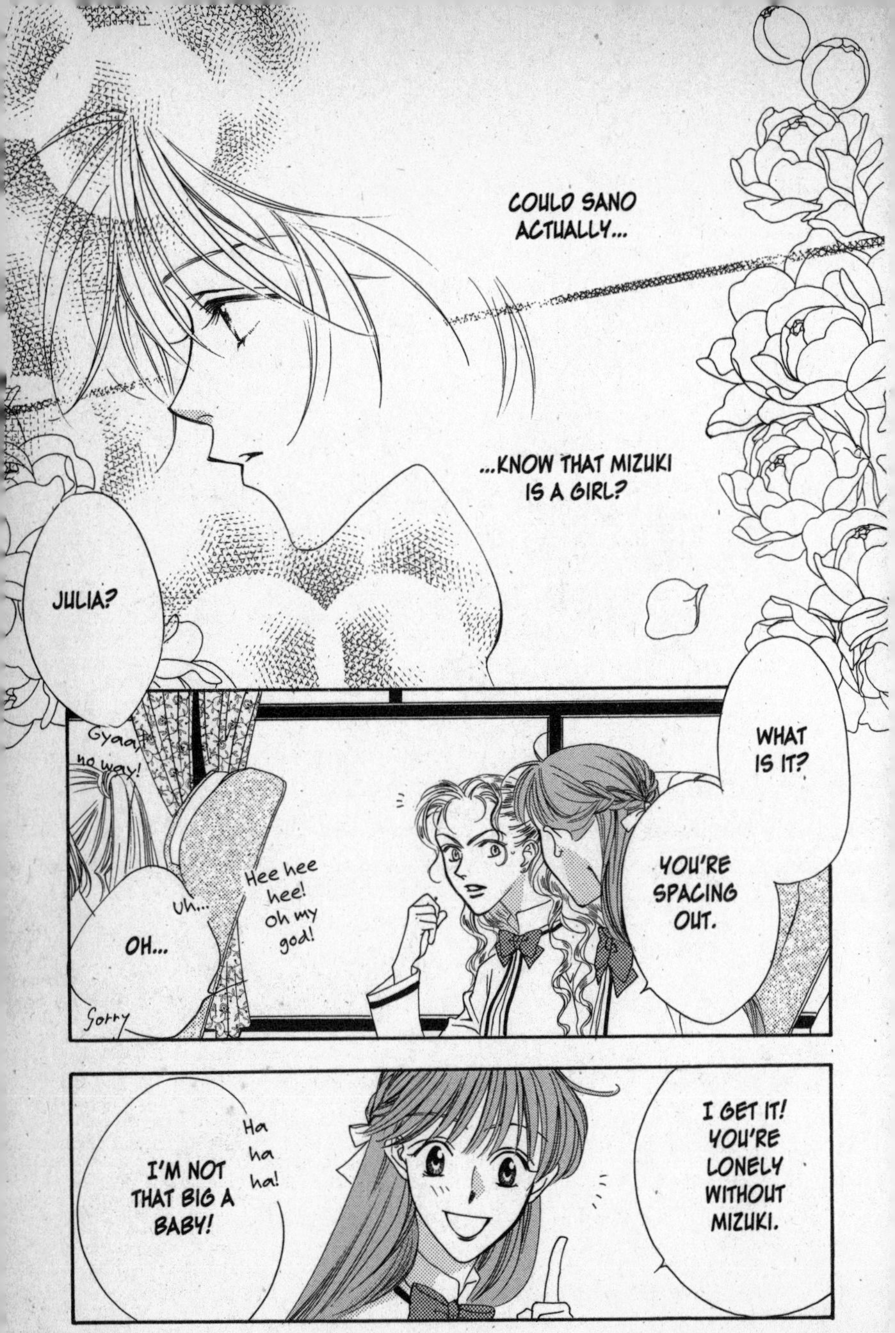
COULD SANO ACTUALLY...
...KNOW THAT MIZUKI IS A GIRL?
JULIA?
WHAT IS IT?
YOU'RE SPACING OUT.
Hee hee hee! oh my god!
Uh...
OH...
Gyaa, no way!
Sorry
I GET IT! YOU'RE LONELY WITHOUT MIZUKI.
Ha ha ha!
I'M NOT THAT BIG A BABY!

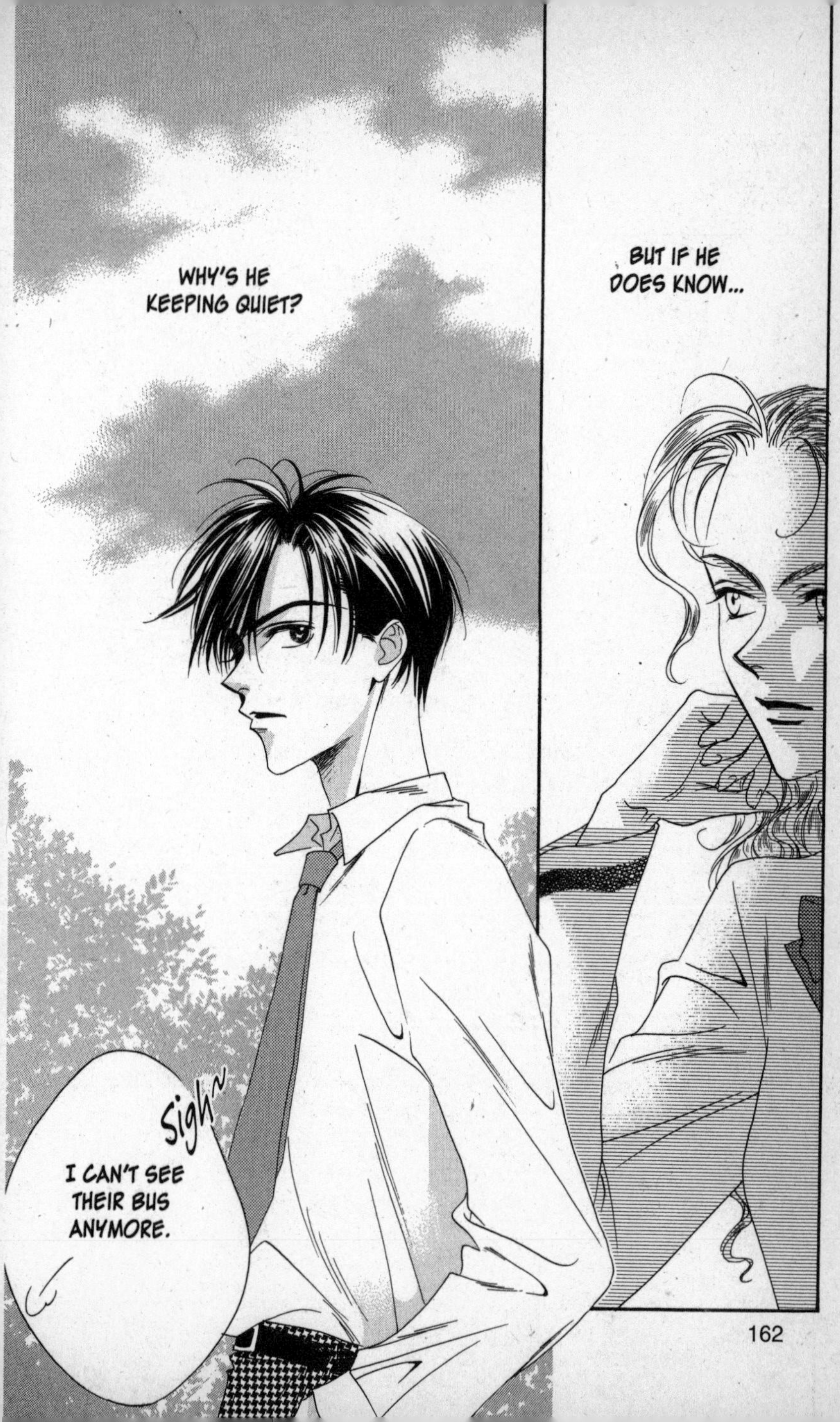
BUT IF HE DOES KNOW...
WHY'S HE KEEPING QUIET?
Sigh~
I CAN'T SEE THEIR BUS ANYMORE.

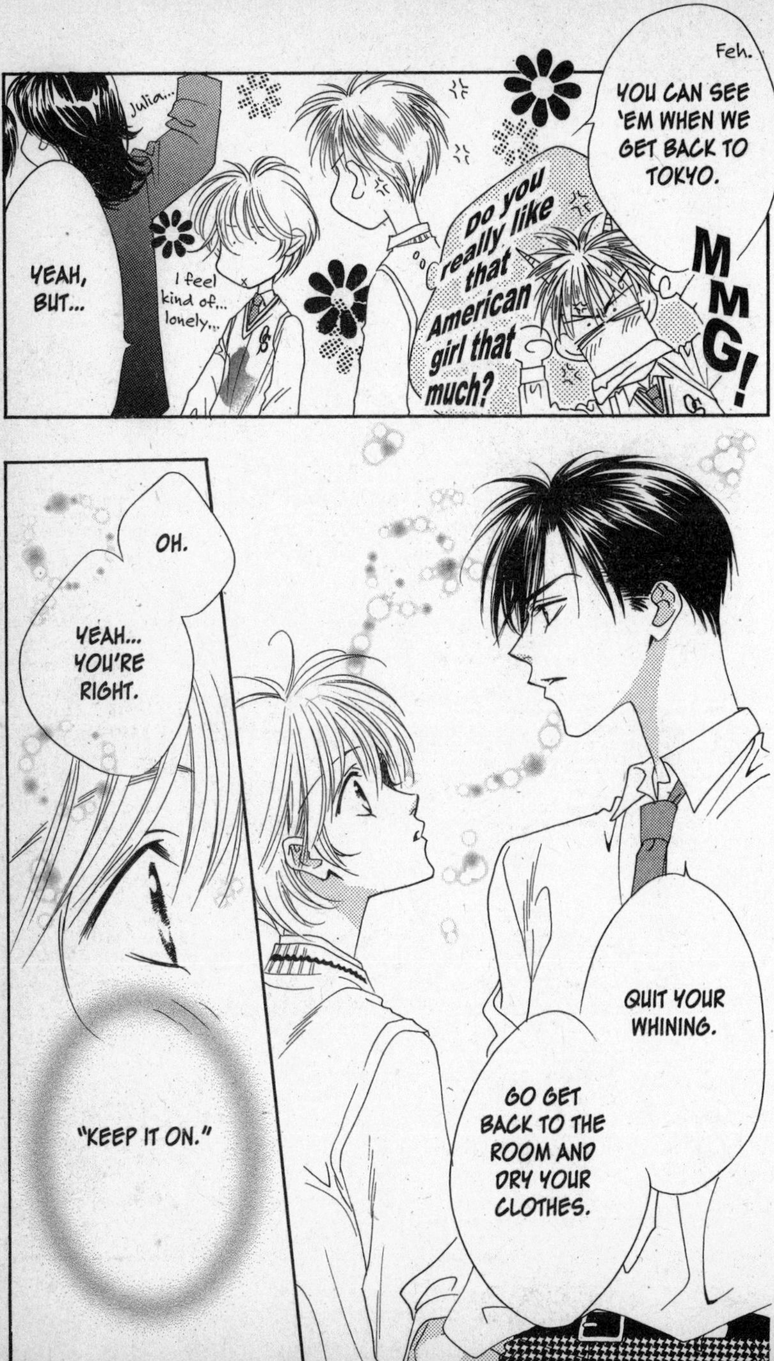
Feh.
YOU CAN SEE 'EM WHEN WE GET BACK TO TOKYO.
MMG!
Do you really like that American girl that much?
Julia...
I feel kind of... lonely...
YEAH, BUT...
QUIT YOUR WHINING.
GO GET BACK TO THE ROOM AND DRY YOUR CLOTHES.
OH.
YEAH... YOU'RE RIGHT.
"KEEP IT ON."

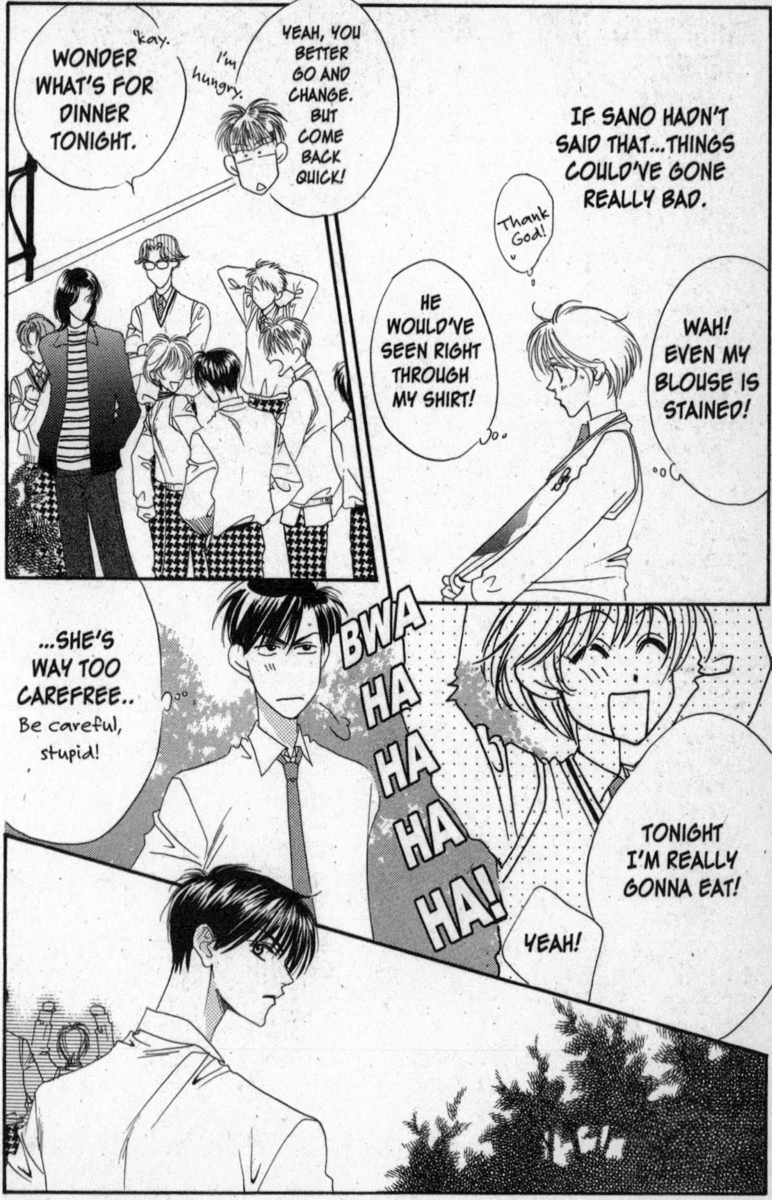
IF SANO HADN'T SAID THAT...THINGS COULD'VE GONE REALLY BAD.
Thank God!
WAH! EVEN MY BLOUSE IS STAINED!
HE WOULD'VE SEEN RIGHT THROUGH MY SHIRT!
YEAH, YOU BETTER GO AND CHANGE. BUT COME BACK QUICK!
I'm hungry.
'kay.
WONDER WHAT'S FOR DINNER TONIGHT.
BWA HA HA HA HA!
TONIGHT I'M REALLY GONNA EAT!
YEAH!
...SHE'S WAY TOO CAREFREE..
Be careful, stupid!

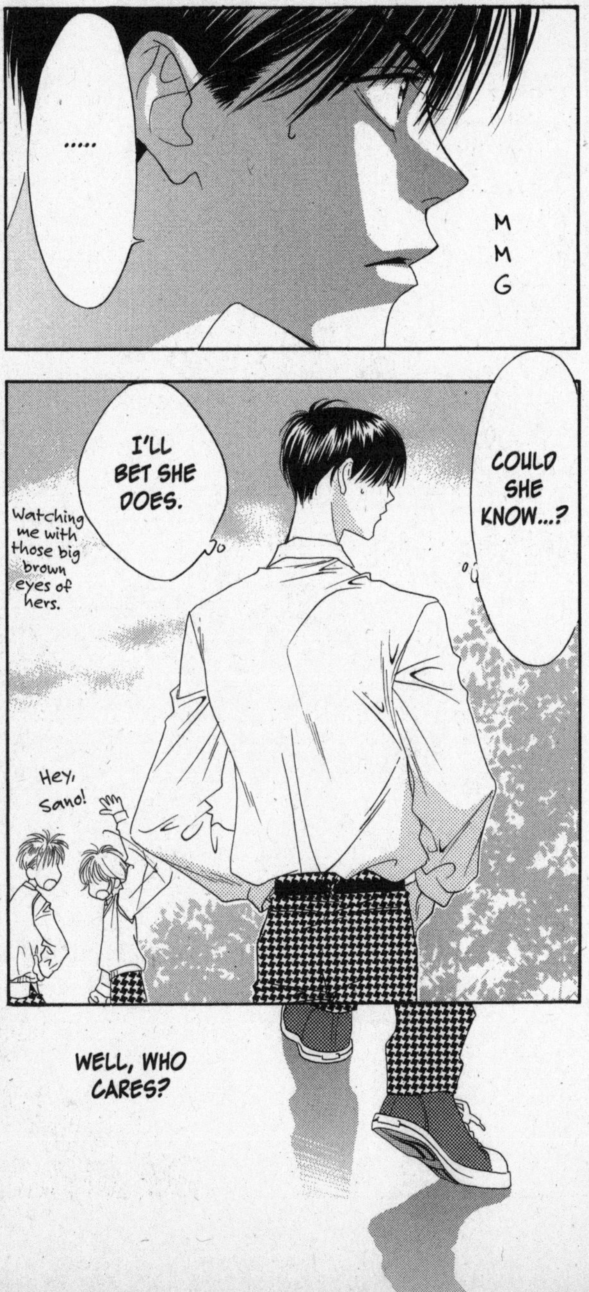
.....
MMG
COULD SHE KNOW...?
I'LL BET SHE DOES.
Watching me with those big brown eyes of hers.
Hey, Sano!
WELL, WHO CARES?

WHISPERED SECRETS

FAN MAIL

SORRY THIS VOLUME WAS SO FULL OF TEXT BUT THIS IS THE LAST COLUMN! AFTER I LISTED AN ADDRESS FOR FAN MAIL IN THE JAPANESE VERSION OF VOL. 6, I WAS SURPRISED TO GET SO MANY RESPONSES FROM READERS SAYING, "I'VE BEEN WAITING FOR THIS." APPARENTLY THERE WERE A LOT OF PEOPLE THINKING, "I WANT TO SEND A LETTER, BUT I DON'T KNOW WHERE TO SEND IT." WHICH IS GREAT!

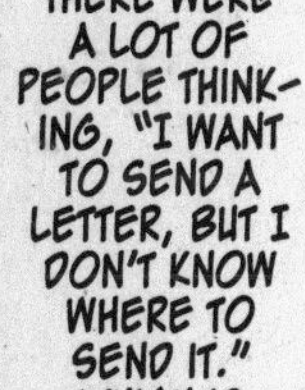
Yay!

So see you in Vol. 8!

BGM: Pierrot
Yoko Kanno
Kuroyuri Shimai

I like Pierrot's "Mad Sky."

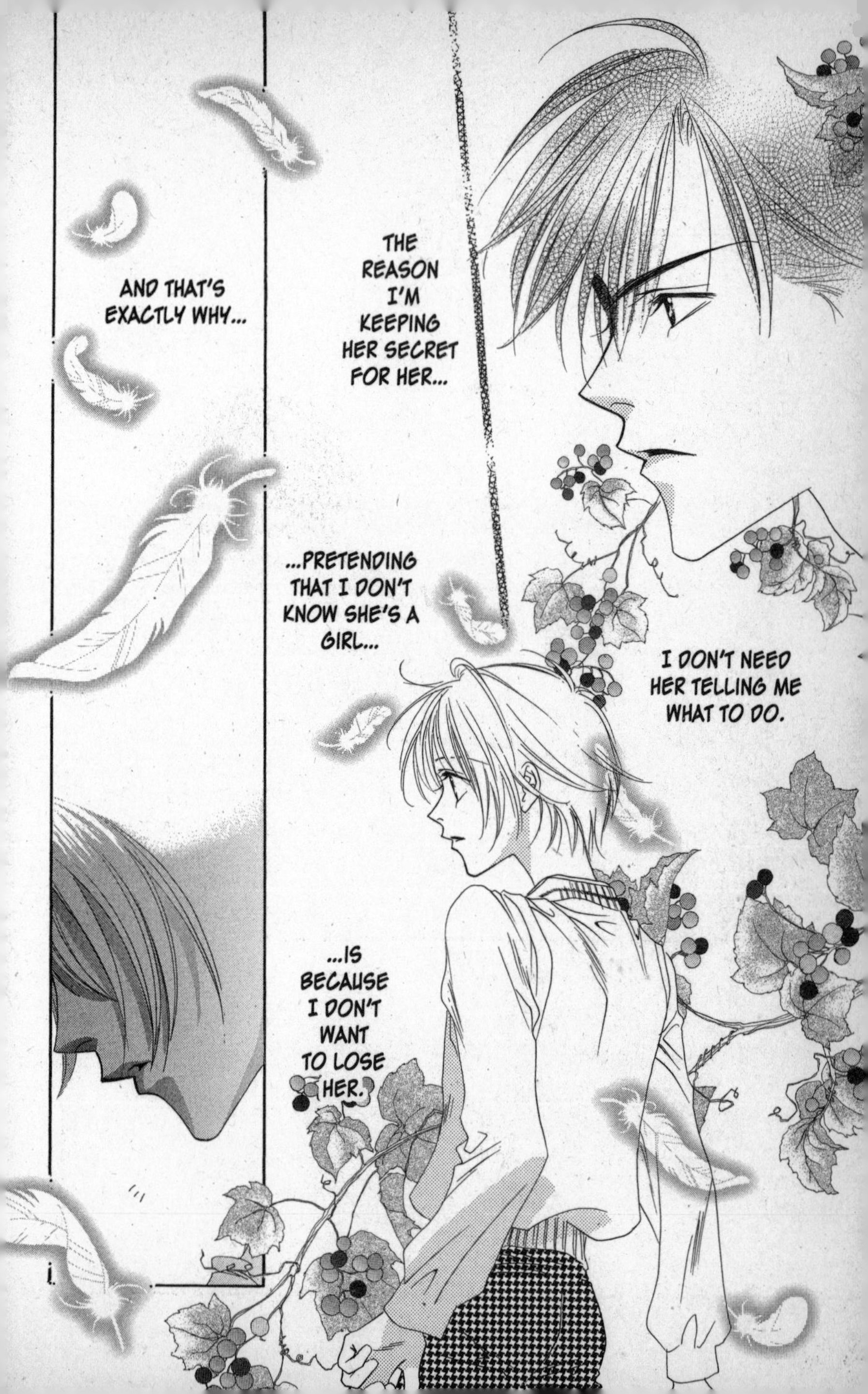
THE REASON I'M KEEPING HER SECRET FOR HER...
...PRETENDING THAT I DON'T KNOW SHE'S A GIRL...
...IS BECAUSE I DON'T WANT TO LOSE HER.
I DON'T NEED HER TELLING ME WHAT TO DO.
AND THAT'S EXACTLY WHY...

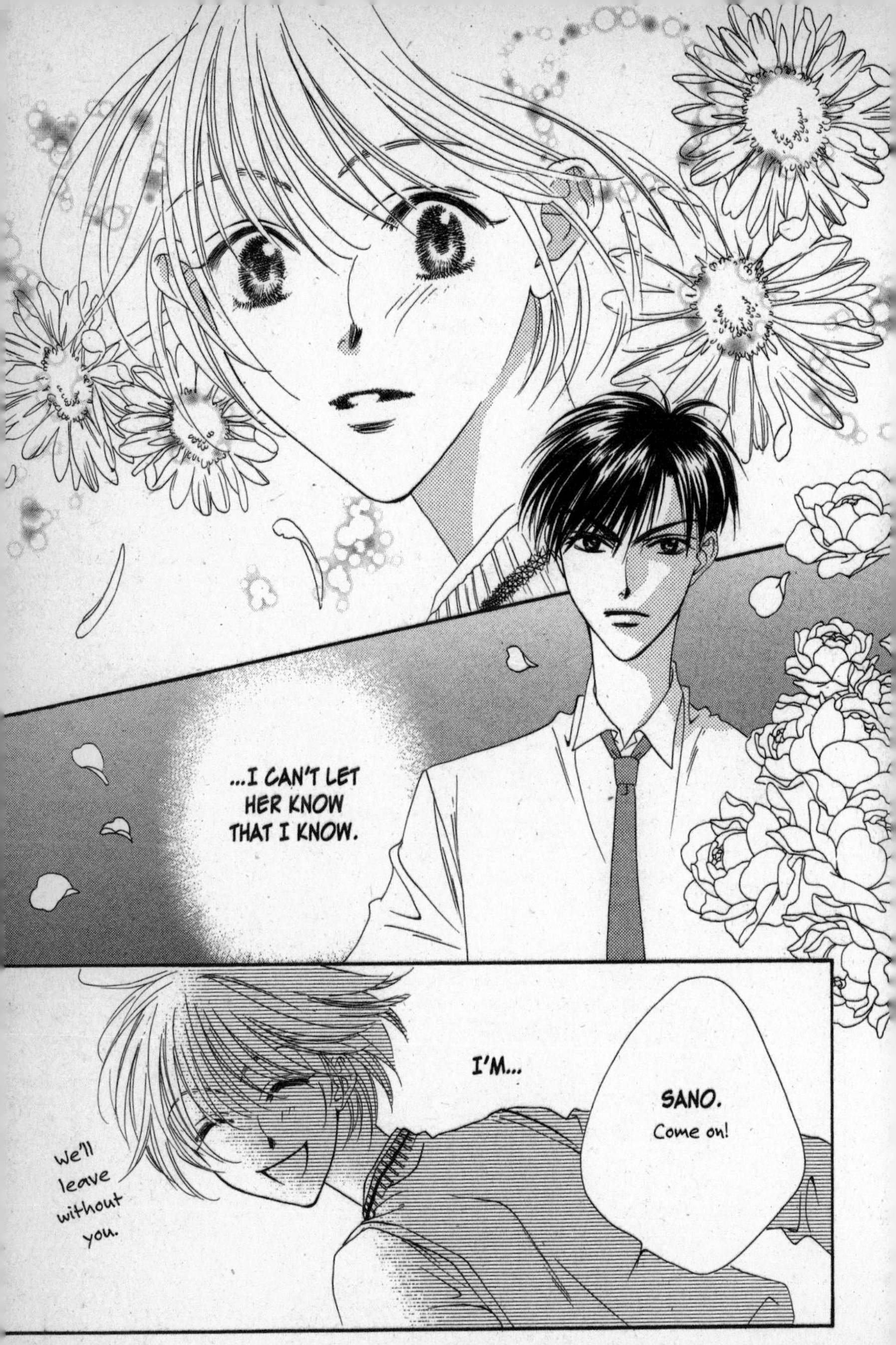
...I CAN'T LET HER KNOW THAT I KNOW.
SANO.
Come on!
I'M...
We'll leave without you.

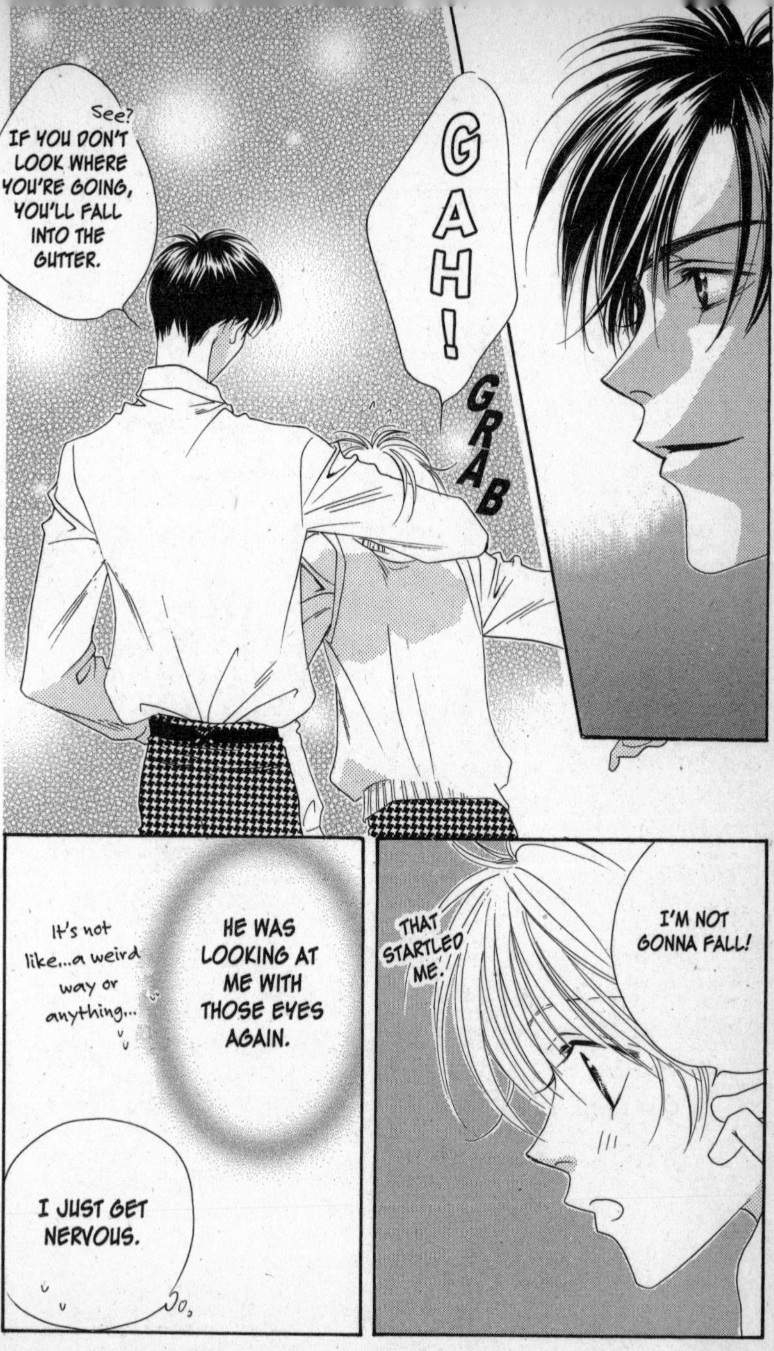
GAH!
GRAB
See? IF YOU DON'T LOOK WHERE YOU'RE GOING, YOU'LL FALL INTO THE GUTTER.
I'M NOT GONNA FALL!
THAT STARTLED ME.
HE WAS LOOKING AT ME WITH THOSE EYES AGAIN.
It's not like...a weird way or anything...
I JUST GET NERVOUS.

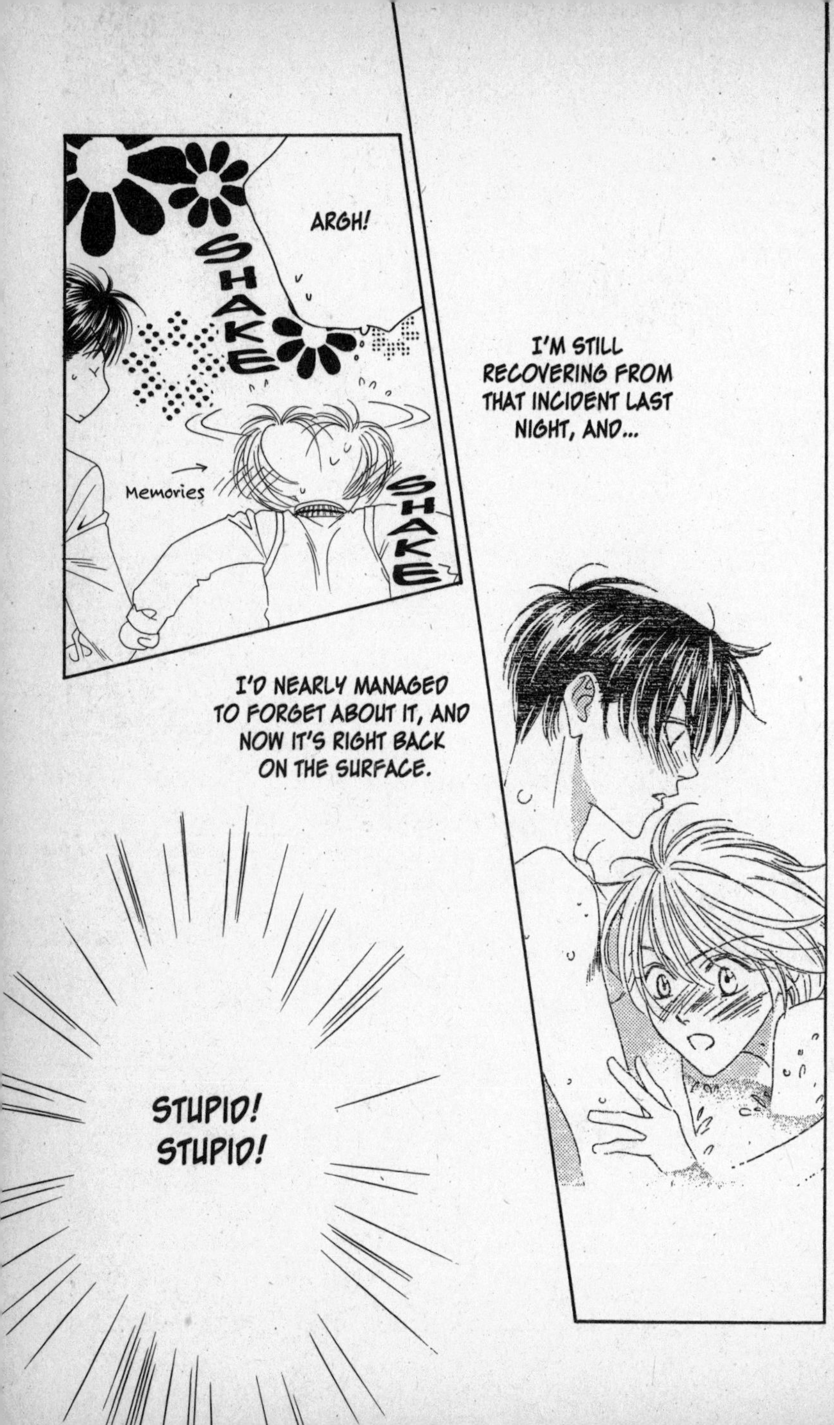
I'M STILL RECOVERING FROM THAT INCIDENT LAST NIGHT, AND...
ARGH!
SHAKE
SHAKE
Memories
I'D NEARLY MANAGED TO FORGET ABOUT IT, AND NOW IT'S RIGHT BACK ON THE SURFACE.
STUPID! STUPID!

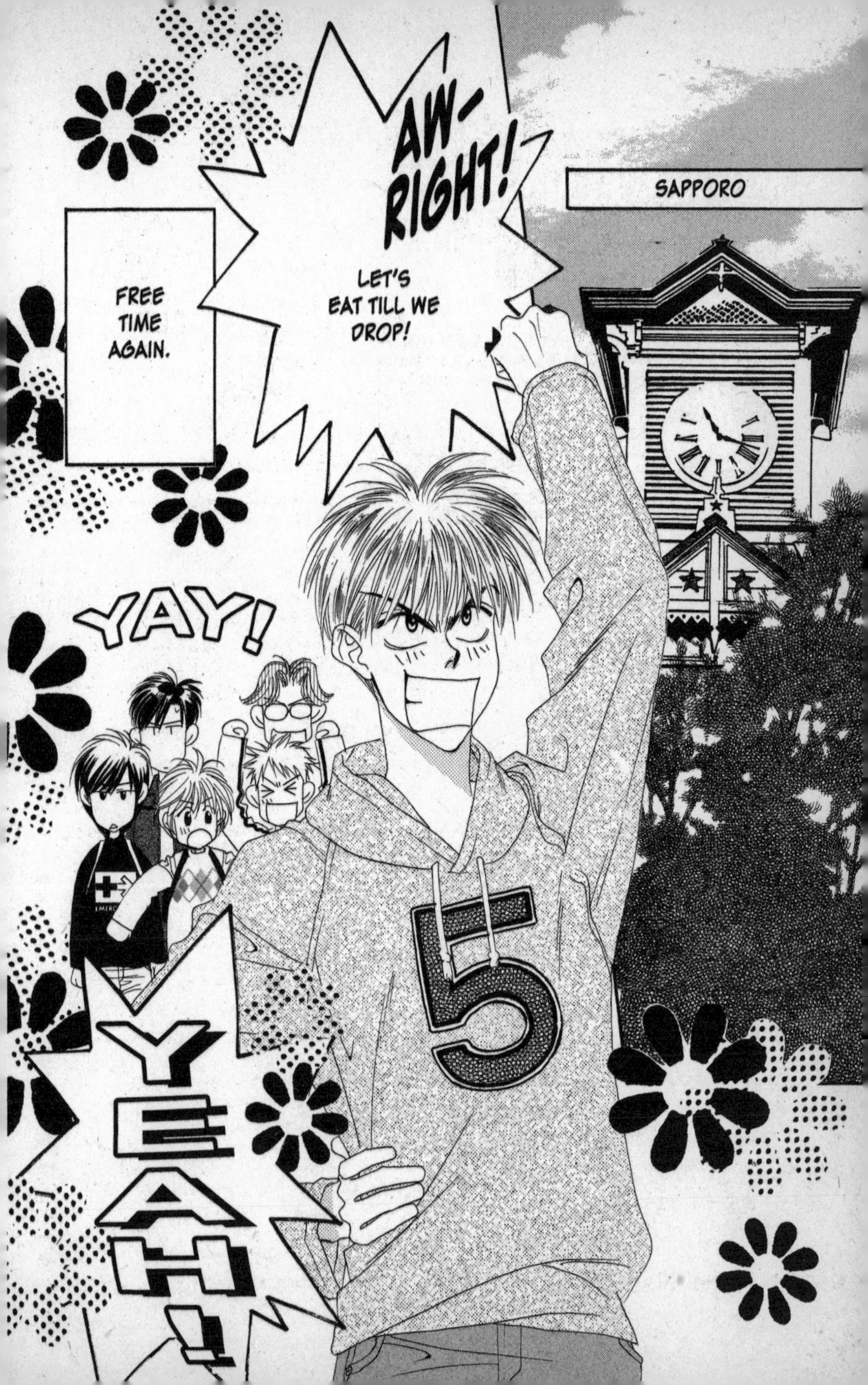
SAPPORO
AW-RIGHT!
LET'S EAT TILL WE DROP!
FREE TIME AGAIN.
YAY!
YEAH!

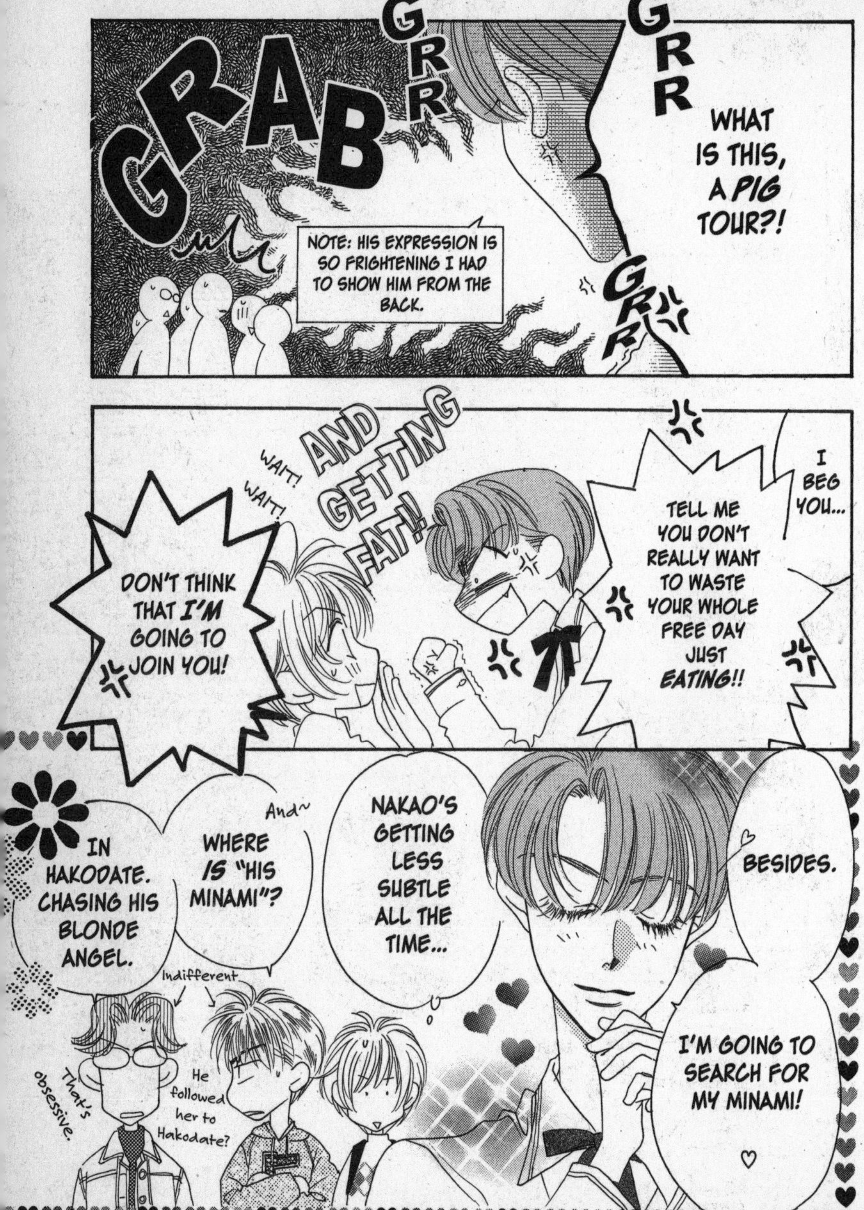
GRR
GRR
WHAT IS THIS, A PIG TOUR?!
GRR
NOTE: HIS EXPRESSION IS SO FRIGHTENING I HAD TO SHOW HIM FROM THE BACK.
GRAB
I BEG YOU...
TELL ME YOU DON'T REALLY WANT TO WASTE YOUR WHOLE FREE DAY JUST EATING!!
AND GETTING FAT!
WAIT! WAIT!
DON'T THINK THAT I'M GOING TO JOIN YOU!
BESIDES.
I'M GOING TO SEARCH FOR MY MINAMI! ♡
NAKAO'S GETTING LESS SUBTLE ALL THE TIME...
And~
WHERE IS "HIS MINAMI"?
IN HAKODATE. CHASING HIS BLONDE ANGEL.
Indifferent
He followed her to Hakodate?
That's obsessive.

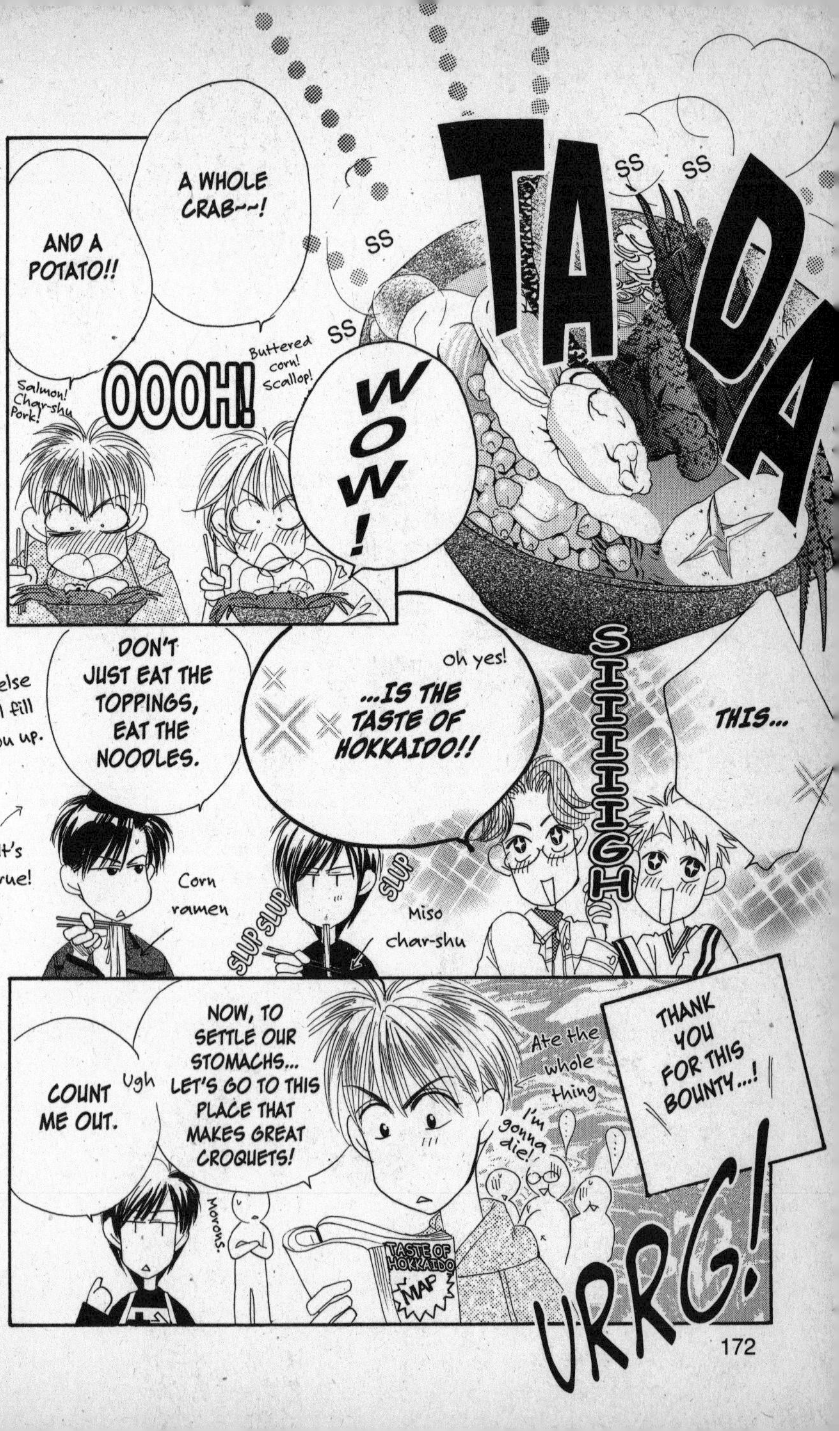
TA DA
SS SS
SS
SS
A WHOLE CRAB~~!
AND A POTATO!!
OOOH!
Buttered corn! Scallop!
Salmon! Char-shu Pork!
WOW!
THIS...
SIIIIIGH
...IS THE TASTE OF HOKKAIDO!!
Oh yes!
Miso char-shu
SLUP SLUP SLUP
Corn ramen
DON'T JUST EAT THE TOPPINGS, EAT THE NOODLES.
Or else it'll fill you up.
It's true!
THANK YOU FOR THIS BOUNTY...!
URRG!
Ate the whole thing
I'm gonna die!
TASTE OF HOKKAIDO MAP
NOW, TO SETTLE OUR STOMACHS... LET'S GO TO THIS PLACE THAT MAKES GREAT CROQUETS!
Ugh
COUNT ME OUT.
Morons.

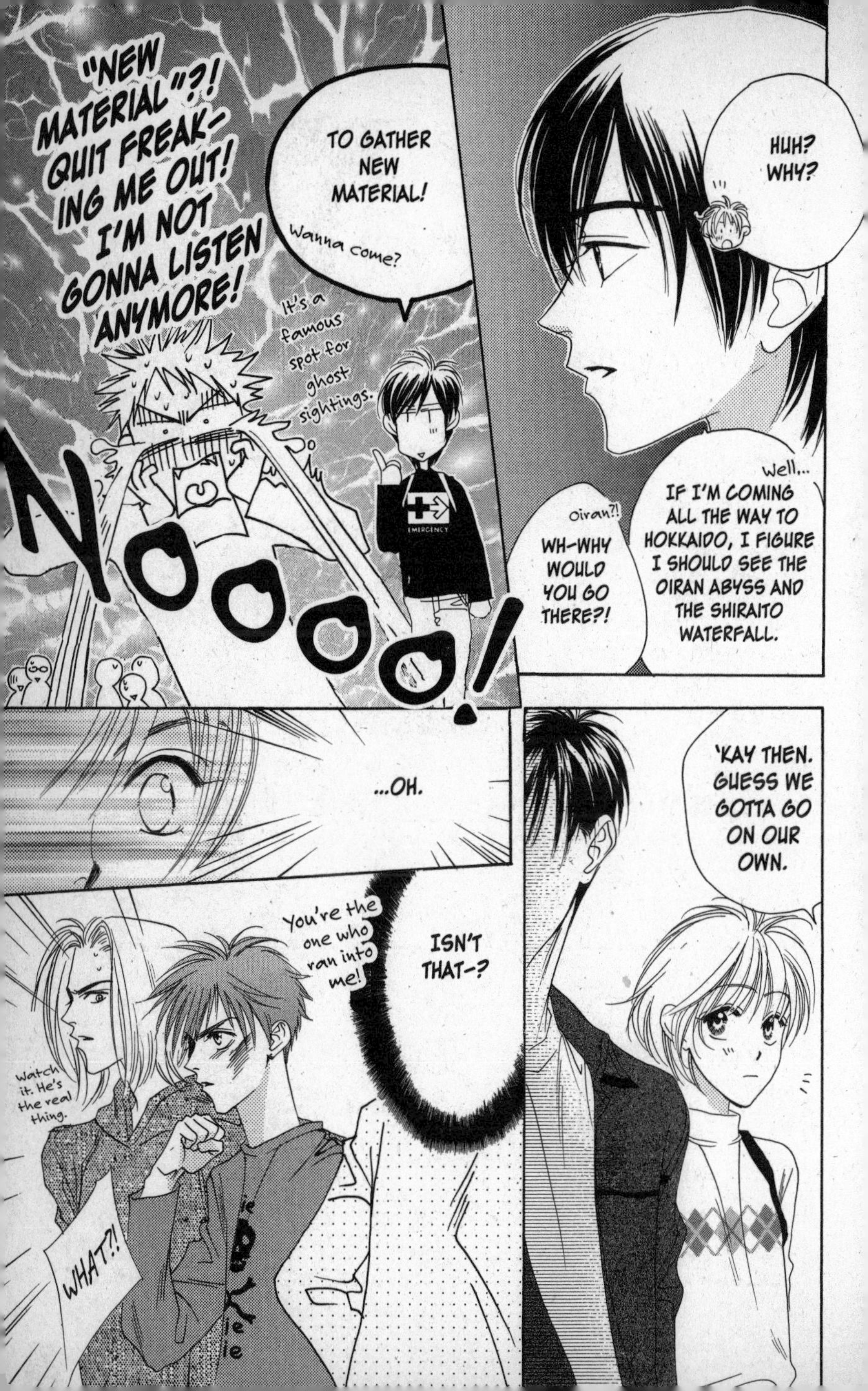
HUH? WHY?
Well...
IF I'M COMING ALL THE WAY TO HOKKAIDO, I FIGURE I SHOULD SEE THE OIRAN ABYSS AND THE SHIRAITO WATERFALL.
Oiran?!
WH-WHY WOULD YOU GO THERE?!
TO GATHER NEW MATERIAL!
Wanna come?
It's a famous spot for ghost sightings.
"NEW MATERIAL"?! QUIT FREAK-ING ME OUT! I'M NOT GONNA LISTEN ANYMORE!
NOOOOO!
EMERGENCY
'KAY THEN. GUESS WE GOTTA GO ON OUR OWN.
...OH.
ISN'T THAT-?
You're the one who ran into me!
Watch it. He's the real thing.
WHAT?!

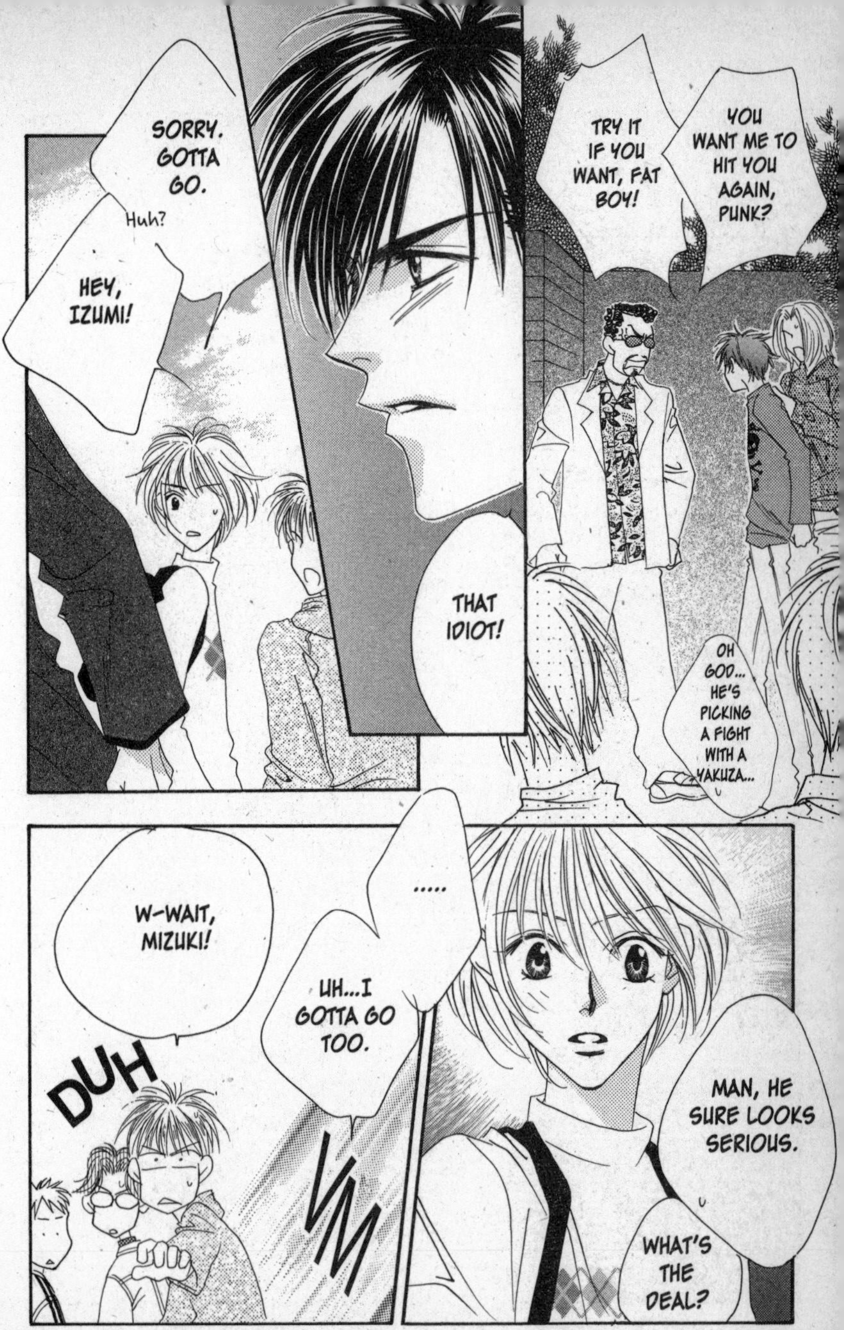
YOU WANT ME TO HIT YOU AGAIN, PUNK?
TRY IT IF YOU WANT, FAT BOY!
OH GOD... HE'S PICKING A FIGHT WITH A YAKUZA...
THAT IDIOT!
SORRY. GOTTA GO.
Huh?
HEY, IZUMI!
MAN, HE SURE LOOKS SERIOUS.
WHAT'S THE DEAL?
.....
UH...I GOTTA GO TOO.
VM
W-WAIT, MIZUKI!
DUH

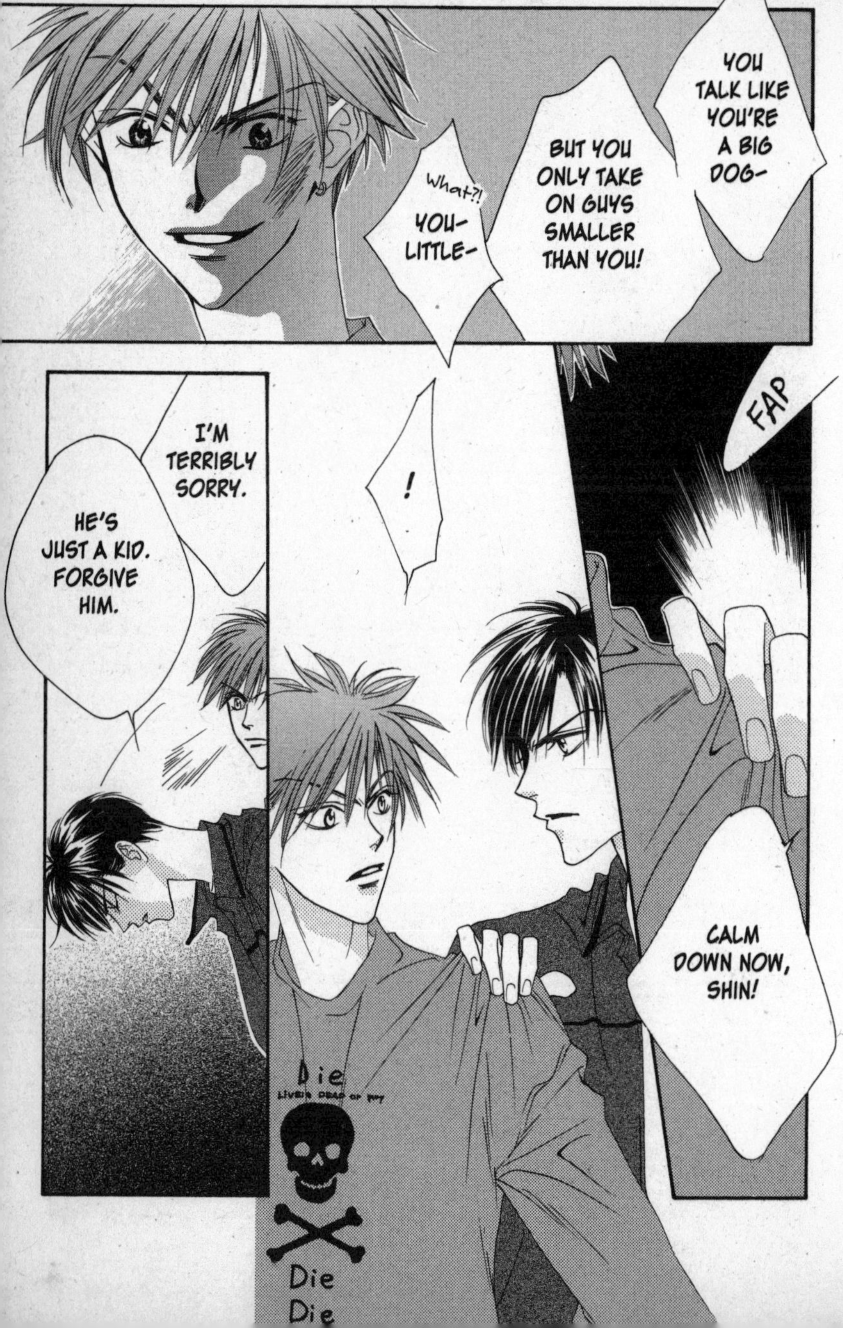
YOU TALK LIKE YOU'RE A BIG DOG-
BUT YOU ONLY TAKE ON GUYS SMALLER THAN YOU!
What?!
YOU- LITTLE-
FAP
!
CALM DOWN NOW, SHIN!
I'M TERRIBLY SORRY.
HE'S JUST A KID. FORGIVE HIM.
Die
Die
Die

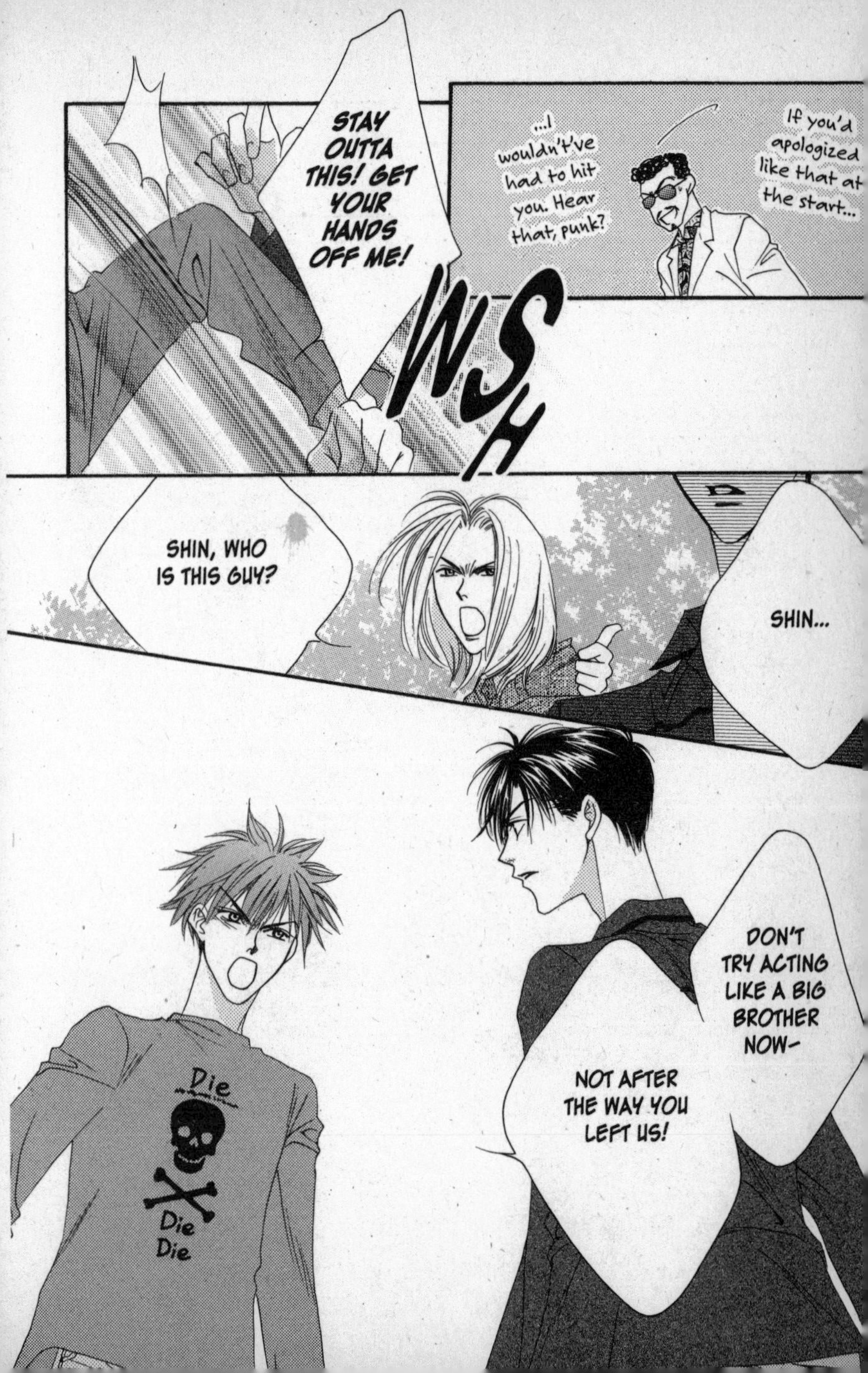

If you'd apologized like that at the start...
...I wouldn't've had to hit you. Hear that, punk?
STAY OUTTA THIS! GET YOUR HANDS OFF ME!
WSH
SHIN...
SHIN, WHO IS THIS GUY?
DON'T TRY ACTING LIKE A BIG BROTHER NOW-
NOT AFTER THE WAY YOU LEFT US!
Die
Die
Die

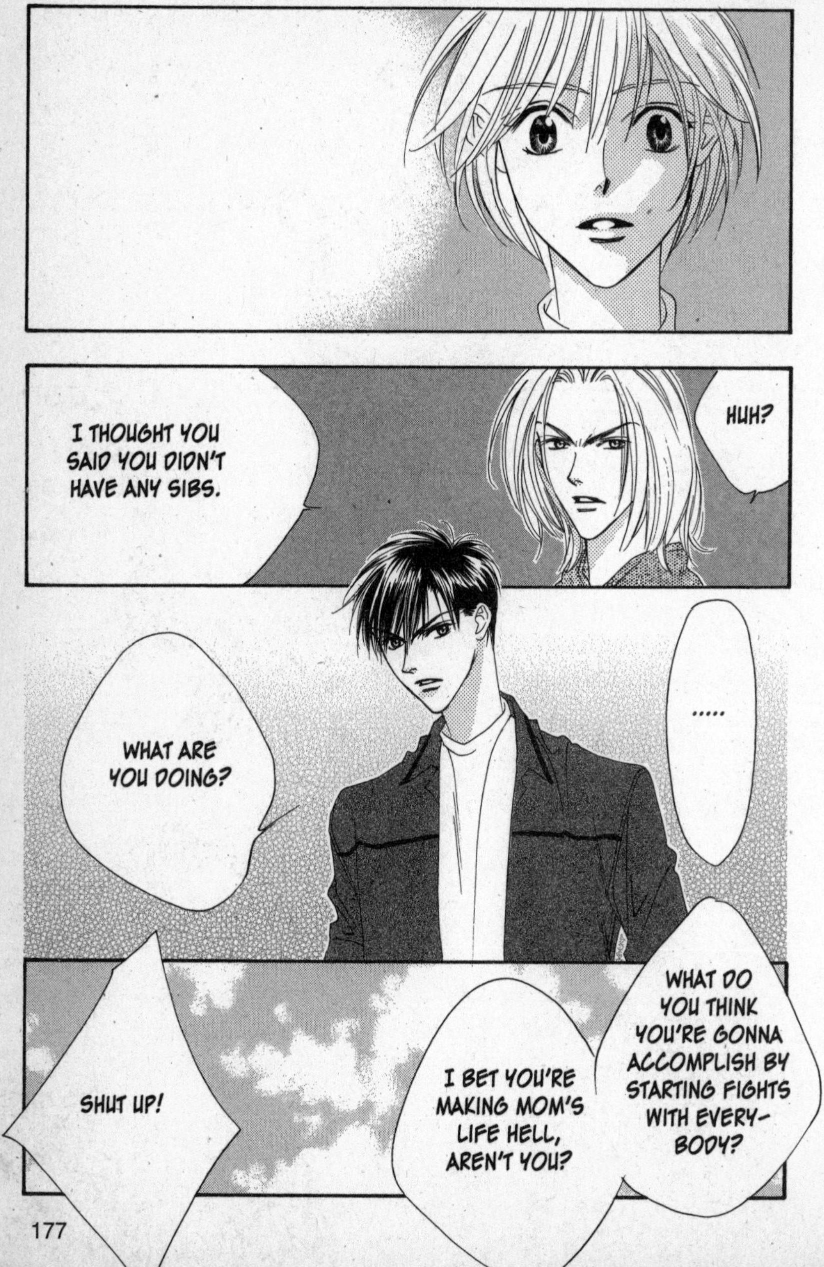
HUH?
I THOUGHT YOU SAID YOU DIDN'T HAVE ANY SIBS.
.....
WHAT ARE YOU DOING?
WHAT DO YOU THINK YOU'RE GONNA ACCOMPLISH BY STARTING FIGHTS WITH EVERY-BODY?
I BET YOU'RE MAKING MOM'S LIFE HELL, AREN'T YOU?
SHUT UP!

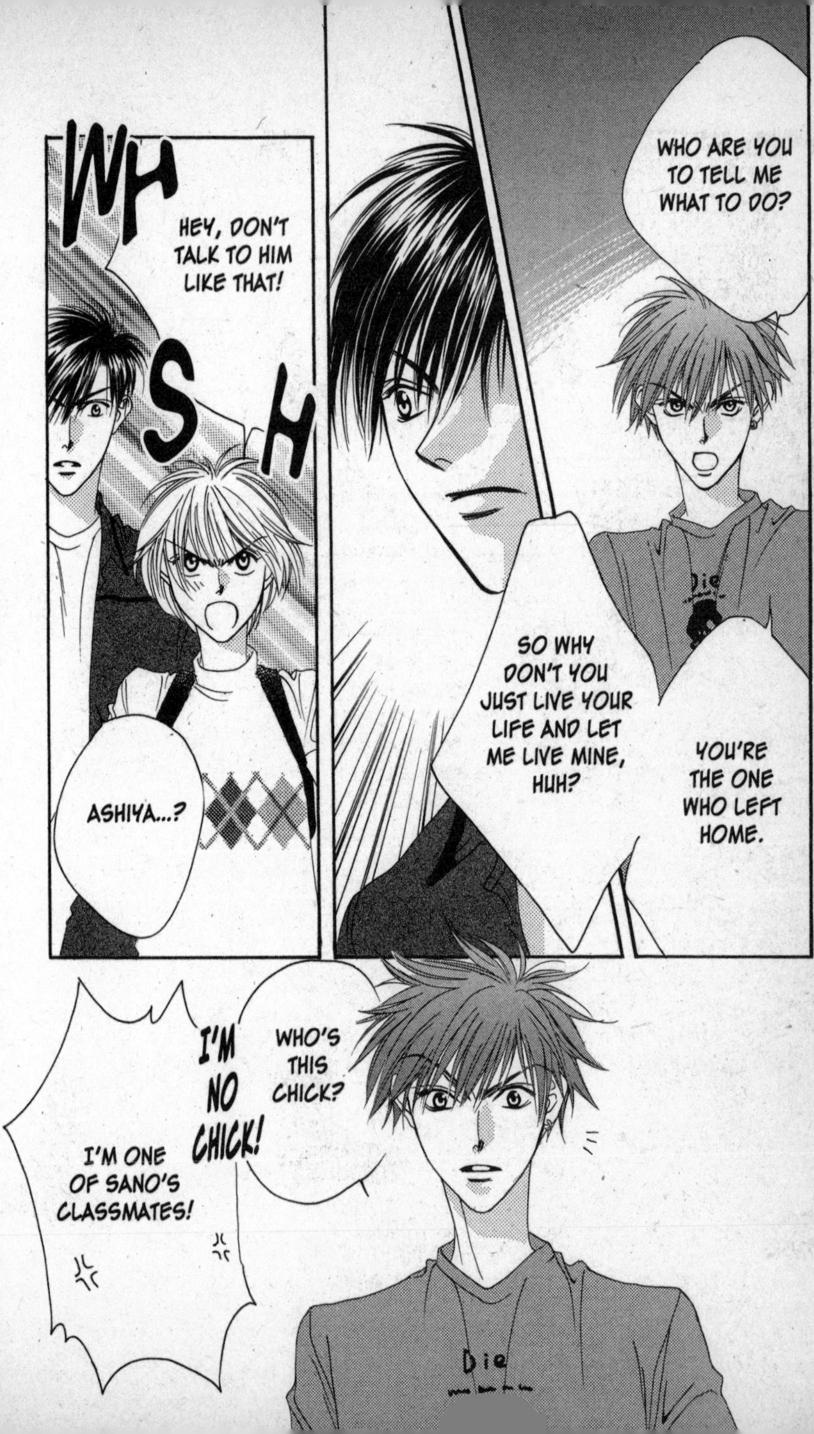
WHO ARE YOU TO TELL ME WHAT TO DO?
YOU'RE THE ONE WHO LEFT HOME.
SO WHY DON'T YOU JUST LIVE YOUR LIFE AND LET ME LIVE MINE, HUH?
WHSH
HEY, DON'T TALK TO HIM LIKE THAT!
ASHIYA...?
WHO'S THIS CHICK?
I'M NO CHICK!
I'M ONE OF SANO'S CLASSMATES!

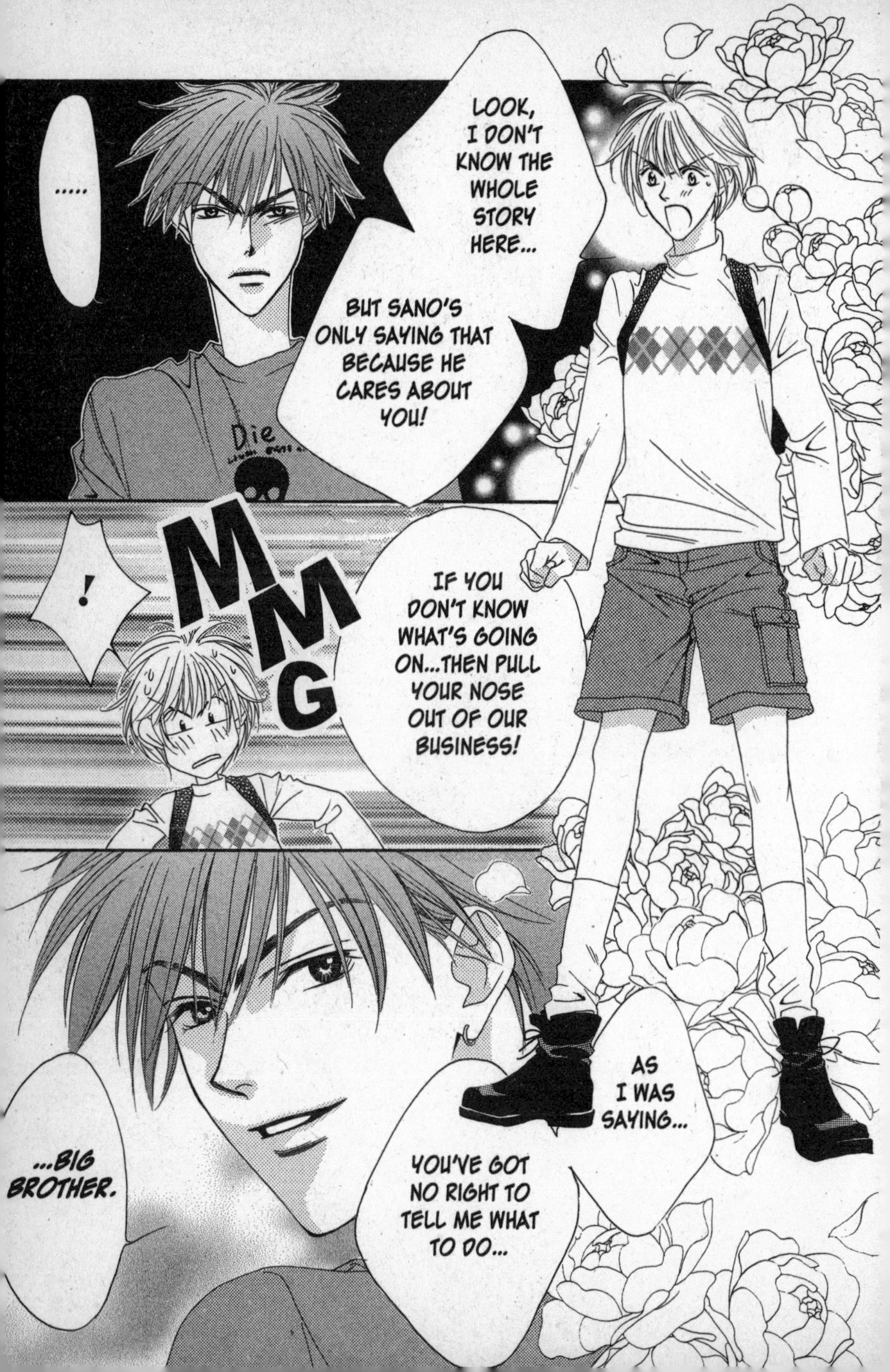

LOOK, I DON'T KNOW THE WHOLE STORY HERE...
BUT SANO'S ONLY SAYING THAT BECAUSE HE CARES ABOUT YOU!
.....
Die
IF YOU DON'T KNOW WHAT'S GOING ON...THEN PULL YOUR NOSE OUT OF OUR BUSINESS!
MMG
!
AS I WAS SAYING...
YOU'VE GOT NO RIGHT TO TELL ME WHAT TO DO...
...BIG BROTHER.

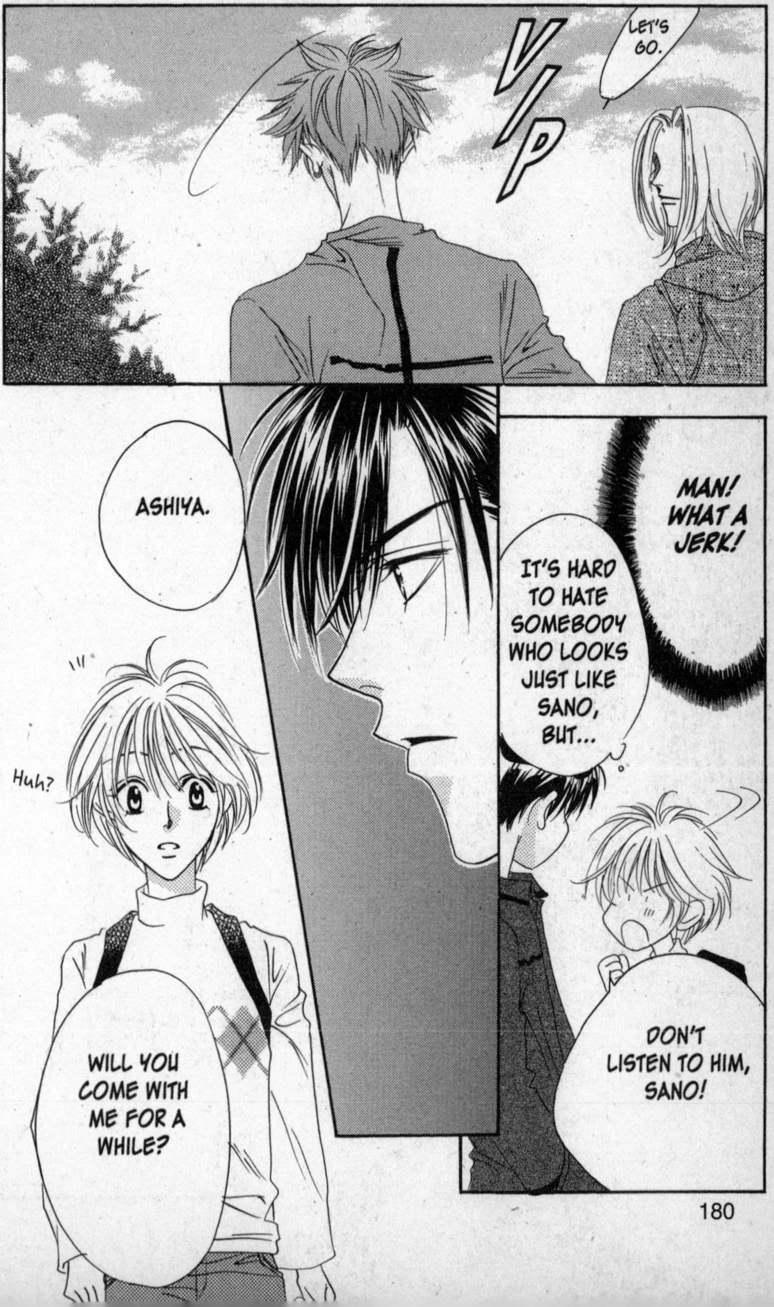
LET'S GO.
VIP
MAN! WHAT A JERK!
IT'S HARD TO HATE SOMEBODY WHO LOOKS JUST LIKE SANO, BUT...
DON'T LISTEN TO HIM, SANO!
ASHIYA.
Huh?
WILL YOU COME WITH ME FOR A WHILE?

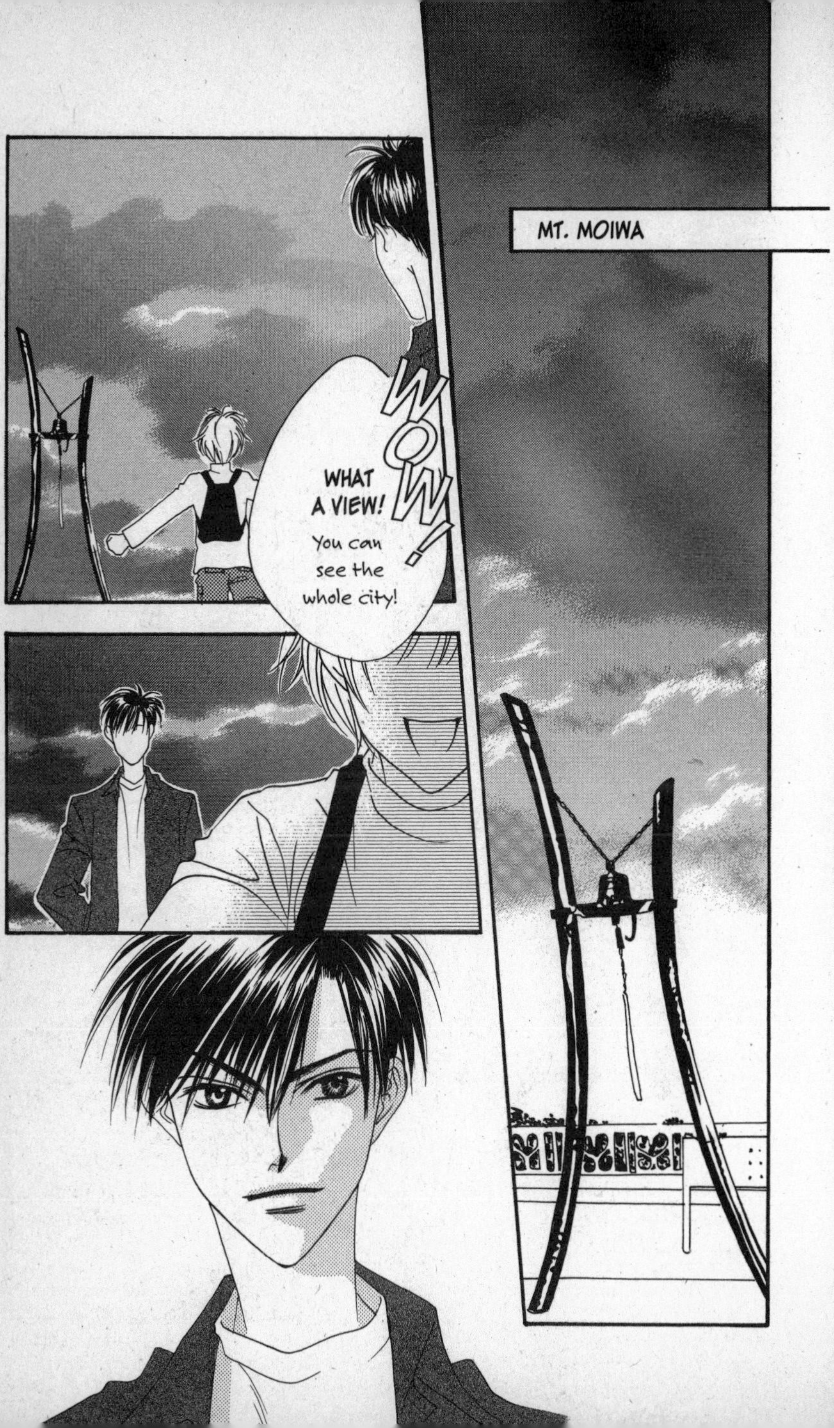
MT. MOIWA
WOW!
WHAT A VIEW! You can see the whole city!

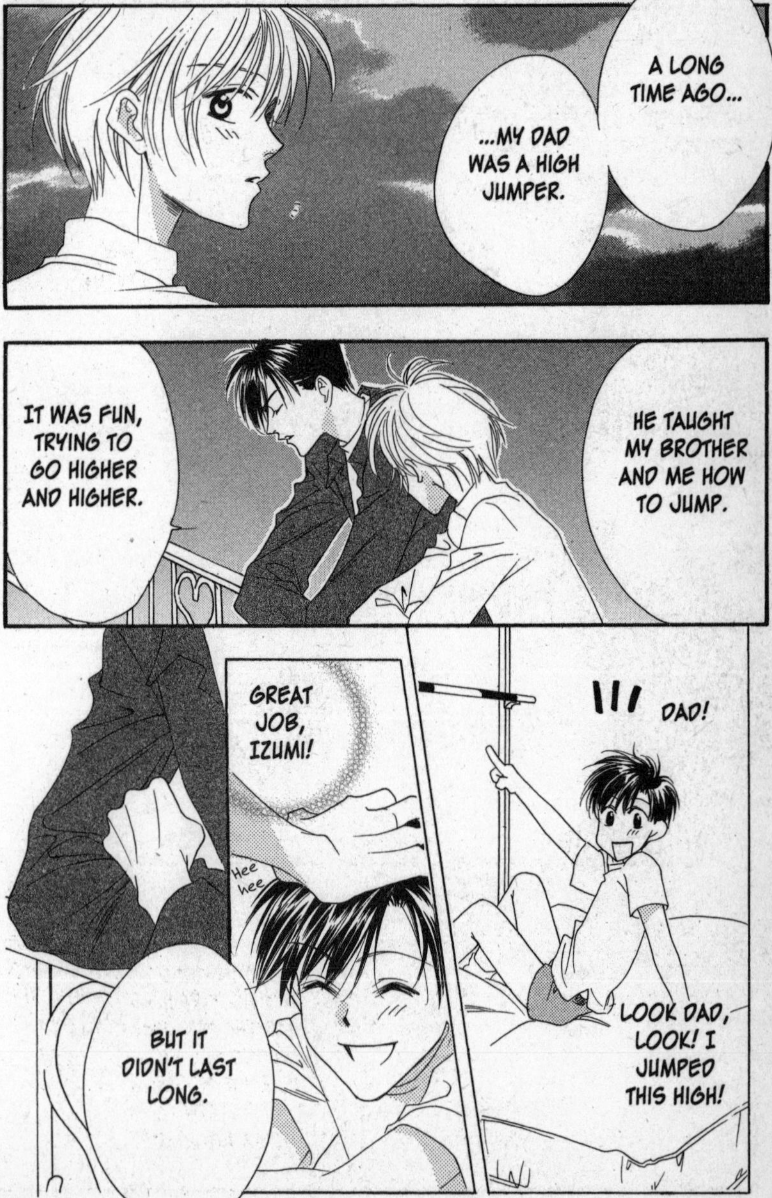
A LONG TIME AGO...
...MY DAD WAS A HIGH JUMPER.
HE TAUGHT MY BROTHER AND ME HOW TO JUMP.
IT WAS FUN, TRYING TO GO HIGHER AND HIGHER.
DAD!
LOOK DAD, LOOK! I JUMPED THIS HIGH!
GREAT JOB, IZUMI!
Hee hee
BUT IT DIDN'T LAST LONG.

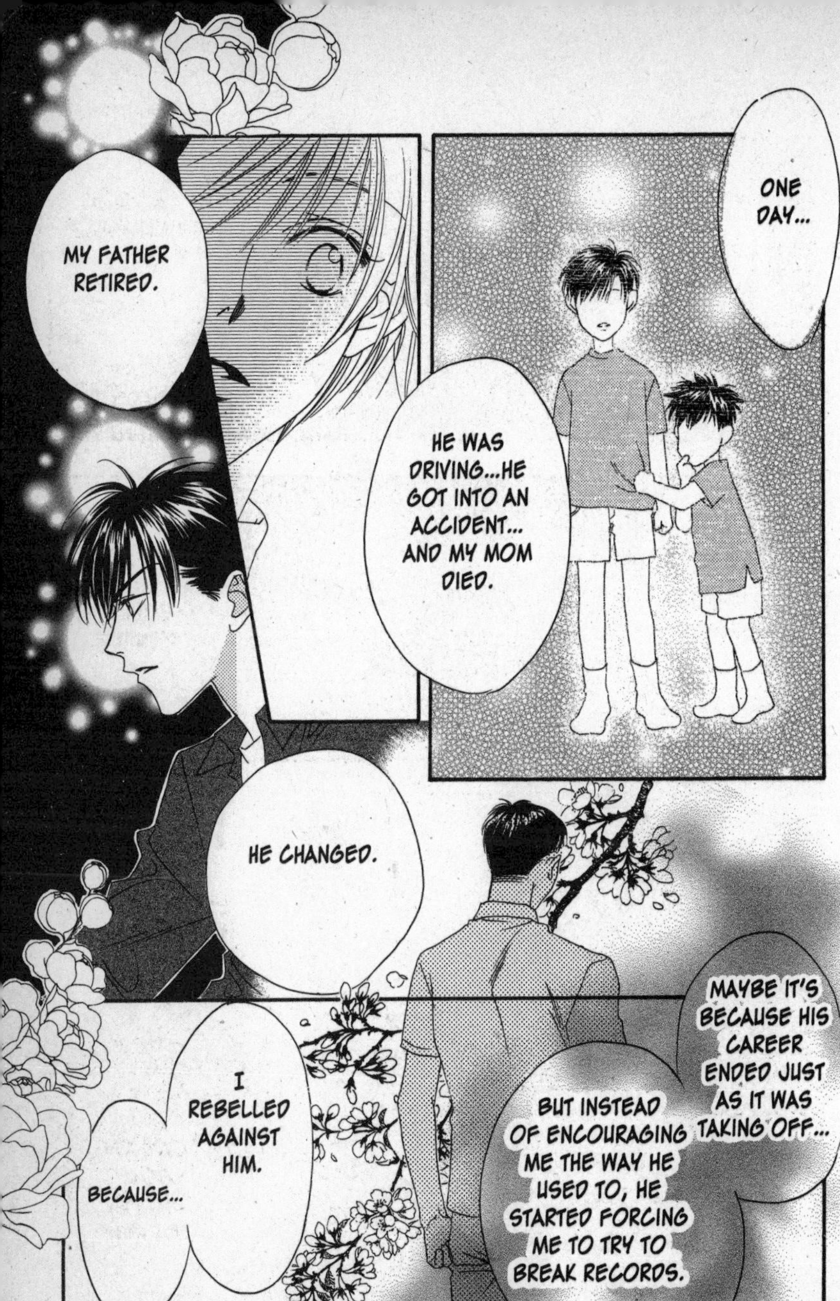

ONE DAY...
HE WAS DRIVING...HE GOT INTO AN ACCIDENT... AND MY MOM DIED.
MY FATHER RETIRED.
HE CHANGED.
MAYBE IT'S BECAUSE HIS CAREER ENDED JUST AS IT WAS TAKING OFF...
BUT INSTEAD OF ENCOURAGING ME THE WAY HE USED TO, HE STARTED FORCING ME TO TRY TO BREAK RECORDS.
I REBELLED AGAINST HIM.
BECAUSE...

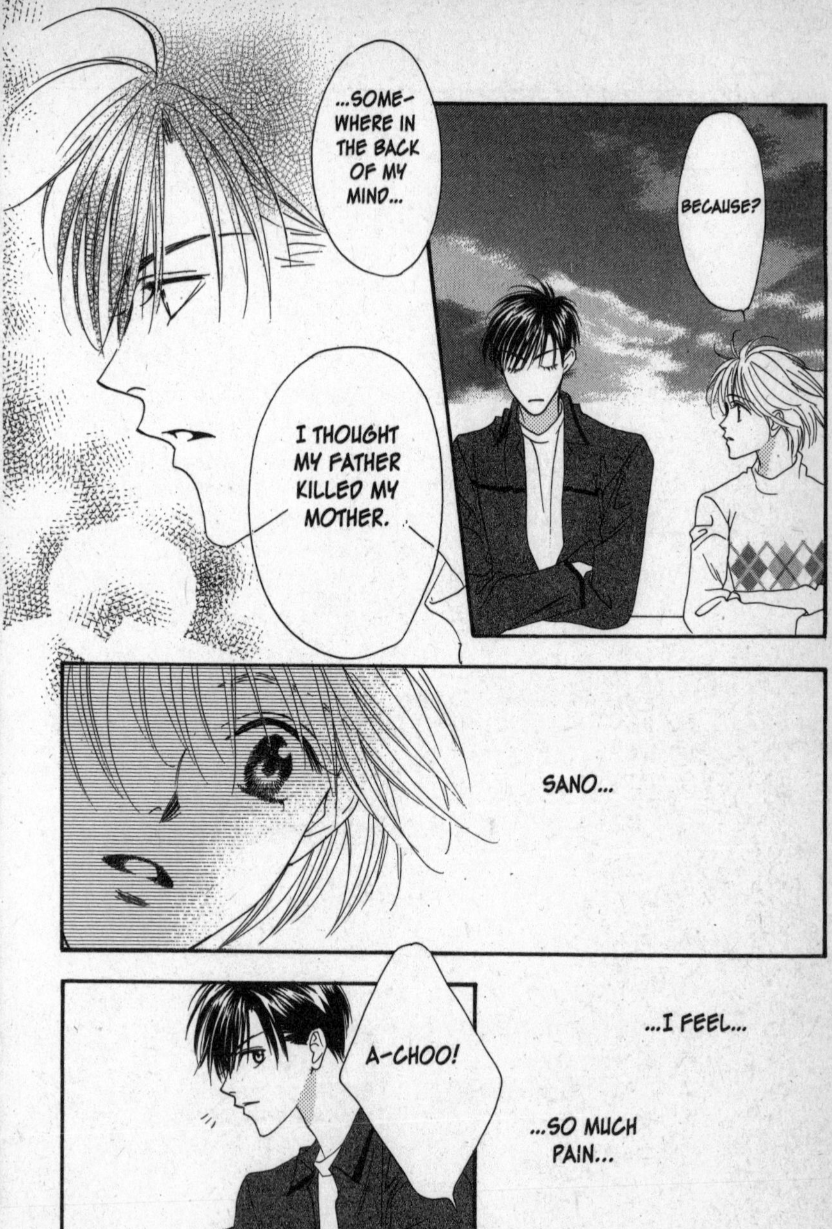
BECAUSE?
...SOME-WHERE IN THE BACK OF MY MIND...
I THOUGHT MY FATHER KILLED MY MOTHER.
SANO...
...I FEEL...
...SO MUCH PAIN...
A-CHOO!

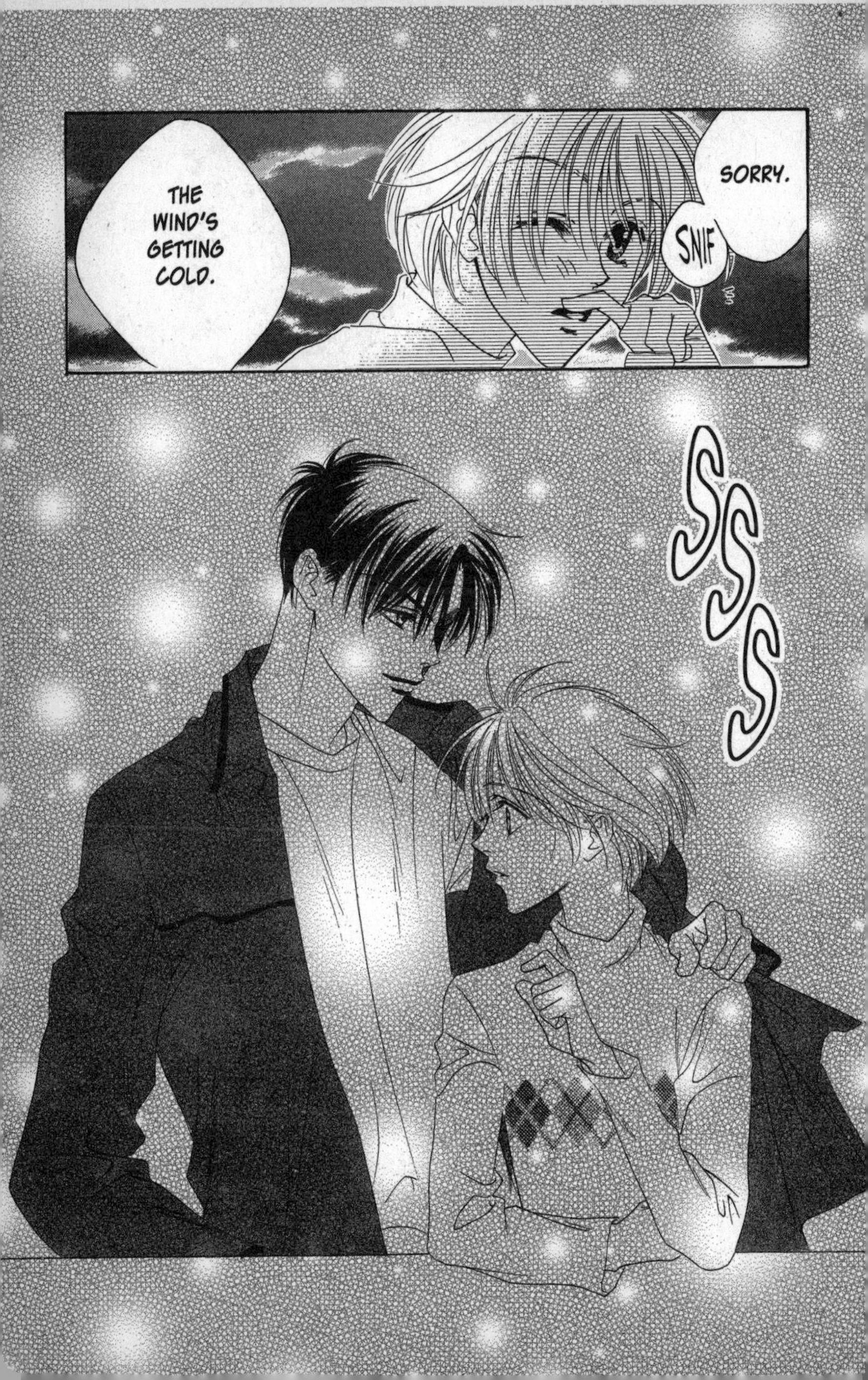
SORRY.
SNIF
THE WIND'S GETTING COLD.
SSS

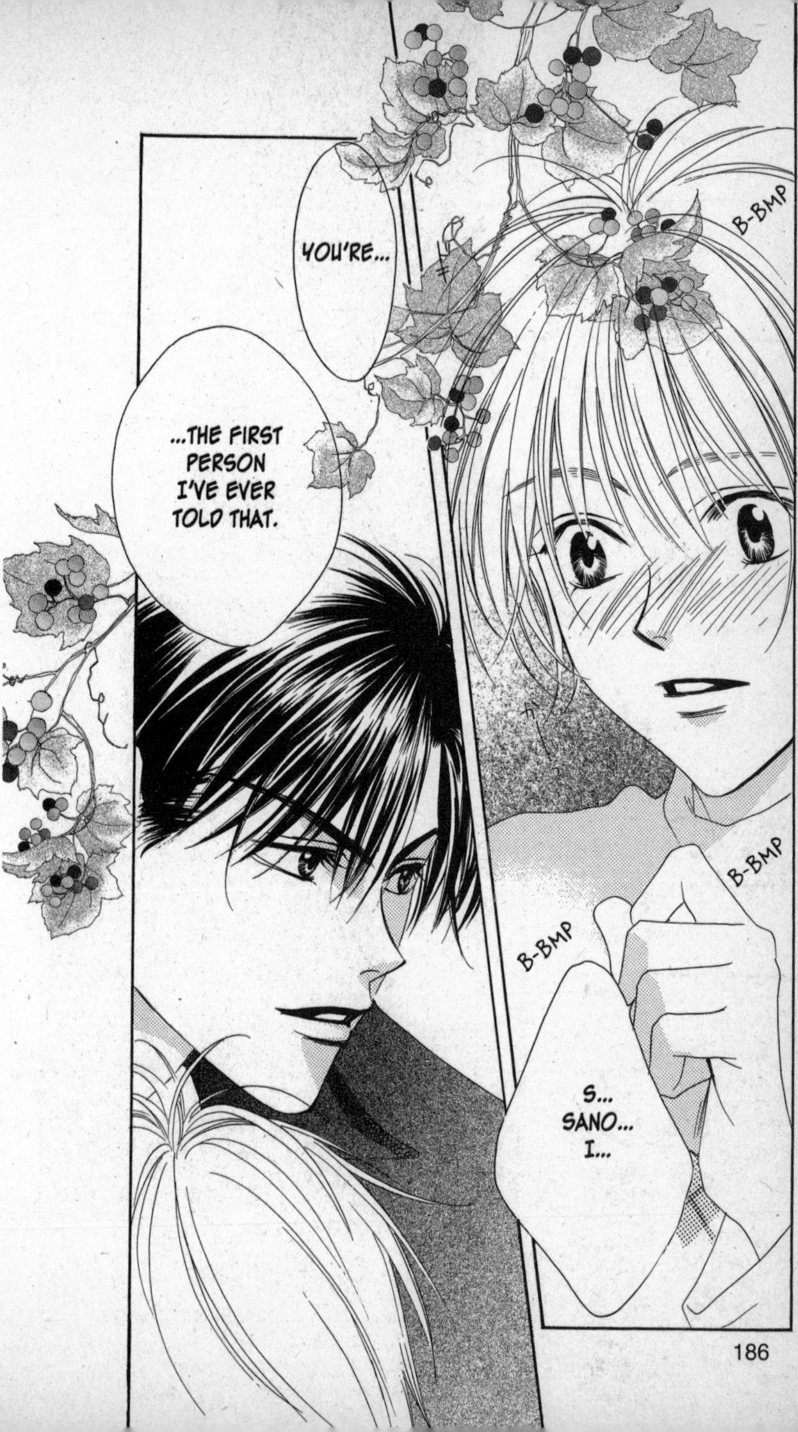
B-BMP
B-BMP
B-BMP
S... SANO... I...
YOU'RE...
...THE FIRST PERSON I'VE EVER TOLD THAT.

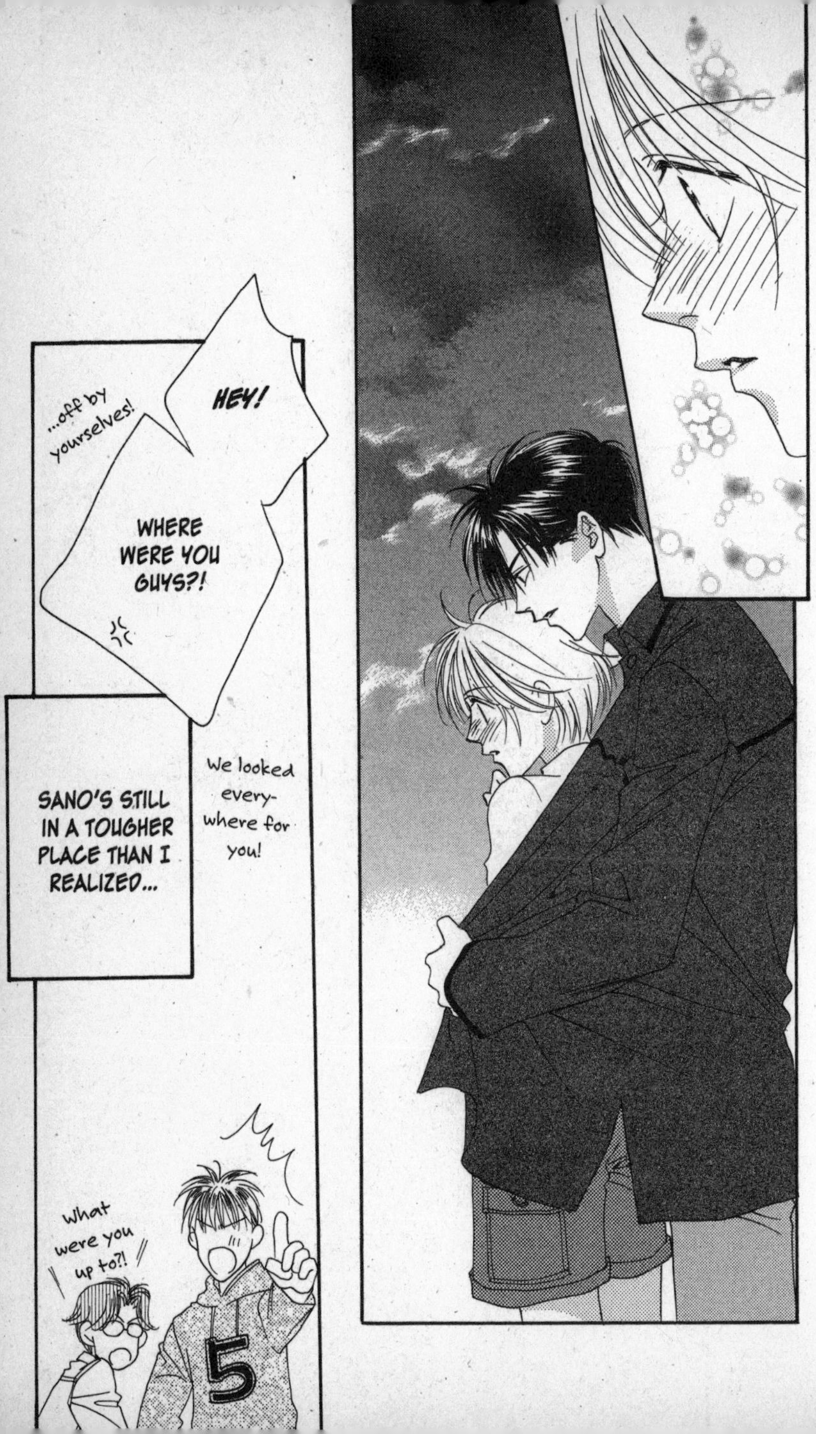
HEY!
...off by yourselves!
WHERE WERE YOU GUYS?!
We looked every-where for you!
SANO'S STILL IN A TOUGHER PLACE THAN I REALIZED...
What were you up to?!

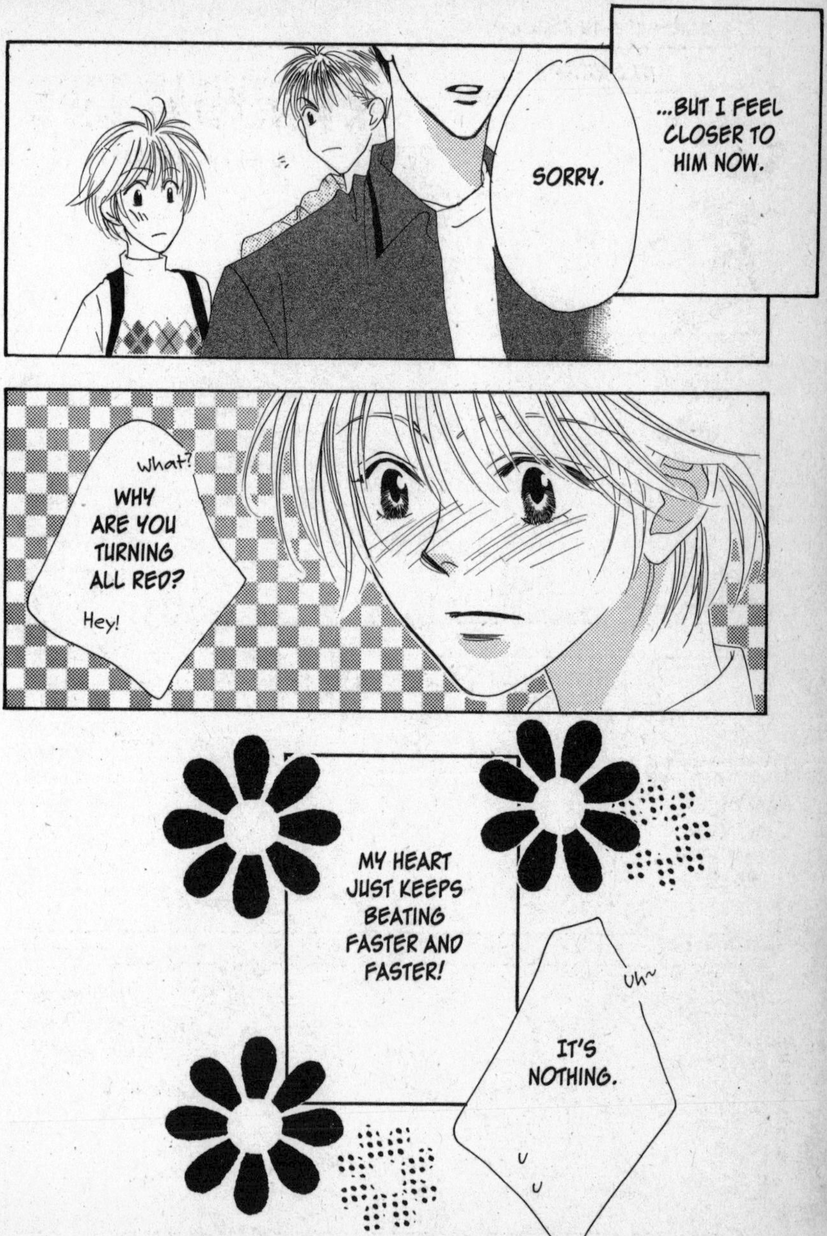
...BUT I FEEL CLOSER TO HIM NOW.
SORRY.
What?
WHY ARE YOU TURNING ALL RED?
Hey!
MY HEART JUST KEEPS BEATING FASTER AND FASTER!
Uh~
IT'S NOTHING.

HANA-KIMI CHAPTER 36/END

I THREW UP IN THE BATHROOM.

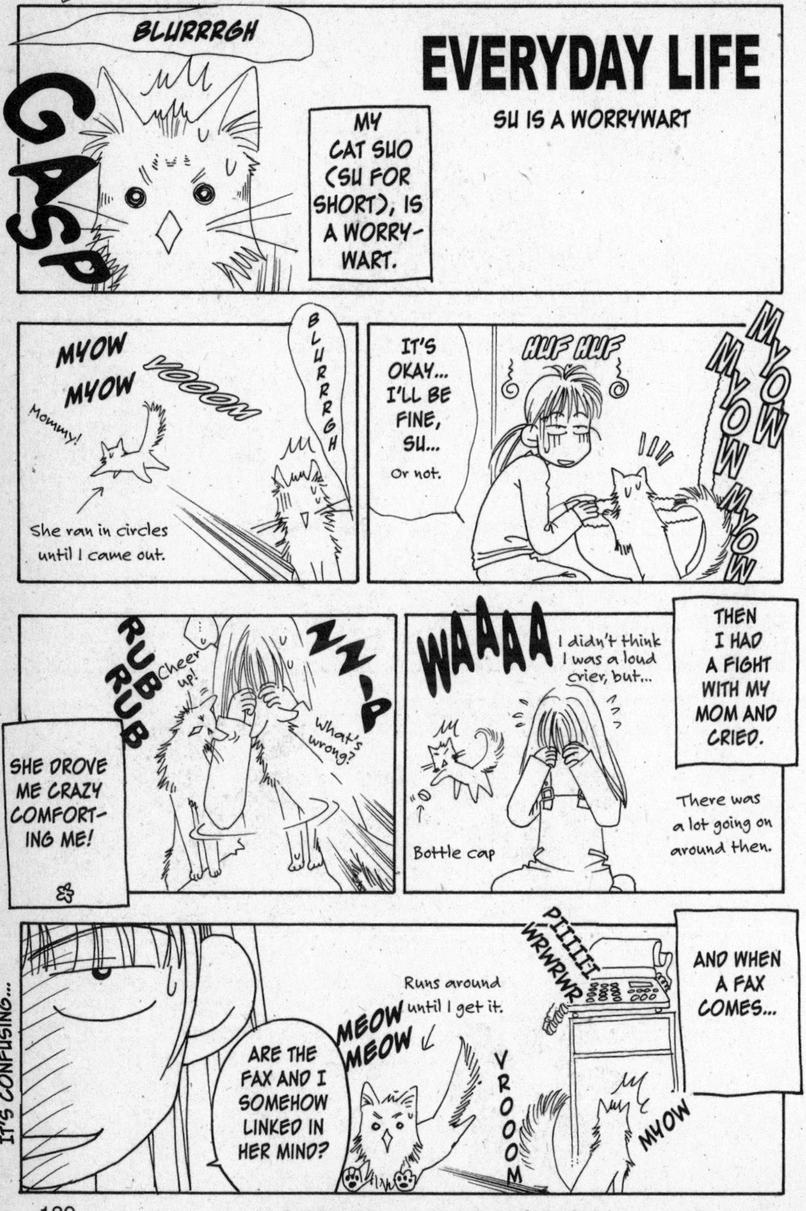
EVERYDAY LIFE
SU IS A WORRYWART
MY CAT SUO (SU FOR SHORT), IS A WORRY-WART.
BLURRRGH
GASP
IT'S OKAY... I'LL BE FINE, SU...
Or not.
HUF HUF
MYOW MYOW MYOW MYOW
BLURRRGH
MYOW MYOW
VOOOOM
Mommy!
She ran in circles until I came out.
THEN I HAD A FIGHT WITH MY MOM AND CRIED.
WAAAA
I didn't think I was a loud crier, but...
Bottle cap
There was a lot going on around then.
ZZ-IP
What's wrong?
Cheer up!
RUB RUB
SHE DROVE ME CRAZY COMFORT-ING ME!
AND WHEN A FAX COMES...
PIIIIIII WRWRWR
MYOW
VROOOOM
Runs around until I get it.
MEOW MEOW
ARE THE FAX AND I SOMEHOW LINKED IN HER MIND?
IT'S CONFUSING...

EVERYDAY LIFE/END

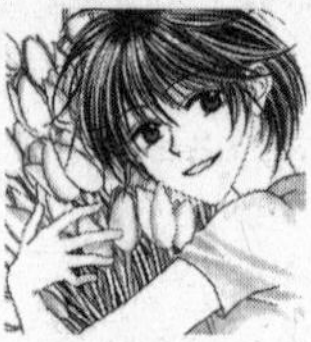

ABOUT THE AUTHOR

Hisaya Nakajo's manga series **Hanazakari no Kimitachi he** ("For You in Full Blossom," casually known as **Hana-Kimi**) has been a hit since it first appeared in 1997 in the shôjo manga magazine **Hana to Yume** ("Flowers and Dreams"). In Japan, two **Hana-Kimi** art books and several "drama CDs" have been released. Her other manga series include **Missing Piece** (2 volumes) and **Yumemiru Happa** ("The Dreaming Leaf," 1 volume).

Hisaya Nakajo's website:
www.wild-vanilla.com

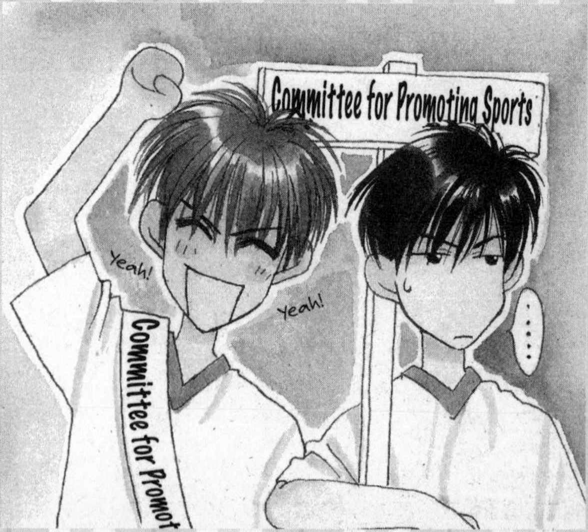
Committee for Promoting Sports
Yeah!
Yeah!
.....
Committee for Promot

IN THE NEXT VOLUME ...

Like any American, Julia can't resist intervening in foreign affairs. Tired of Sano and Mizuki taking their relationship so slow, she confronts Sano to get him moving faster! But Sano has more things to worry about than cross-dressing girls sleeping in his bed...his younger brother, Shin, has run away from home! Then, when a photo of Minami, Nakatsu and Sano appears in a girls' fashion magazine, the handsome men of **Hana-Kimi** find themselves surrounded by groupies. When a fashion photographer asks them to become models, will they enter the world of high fashion?

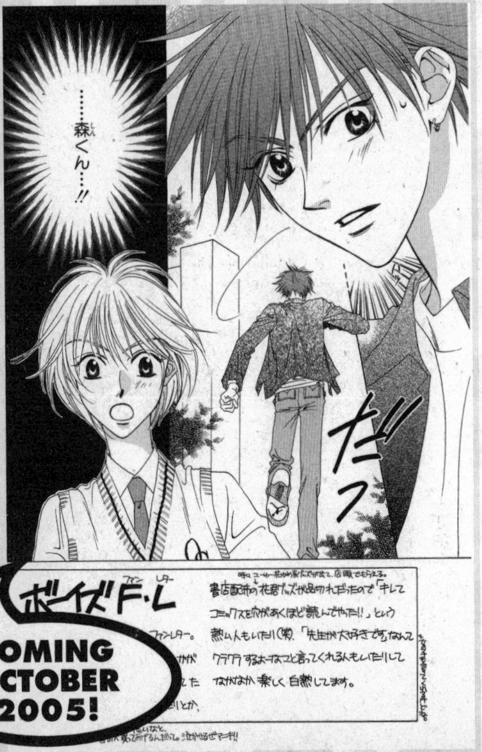
……森くん……!!
だッ
ボーイズF・L
書店配布の花君グッズが品切れだったので「キレてコミックスを穴があくほど読んでやった!!」という
熱い人もいたり(笑)、「先生が大好きです」なんて
クラクラするよーなこと言ってくれる人もいたりして
なかなか楽しく白熱してます。

COMING OCTOBER 2005!

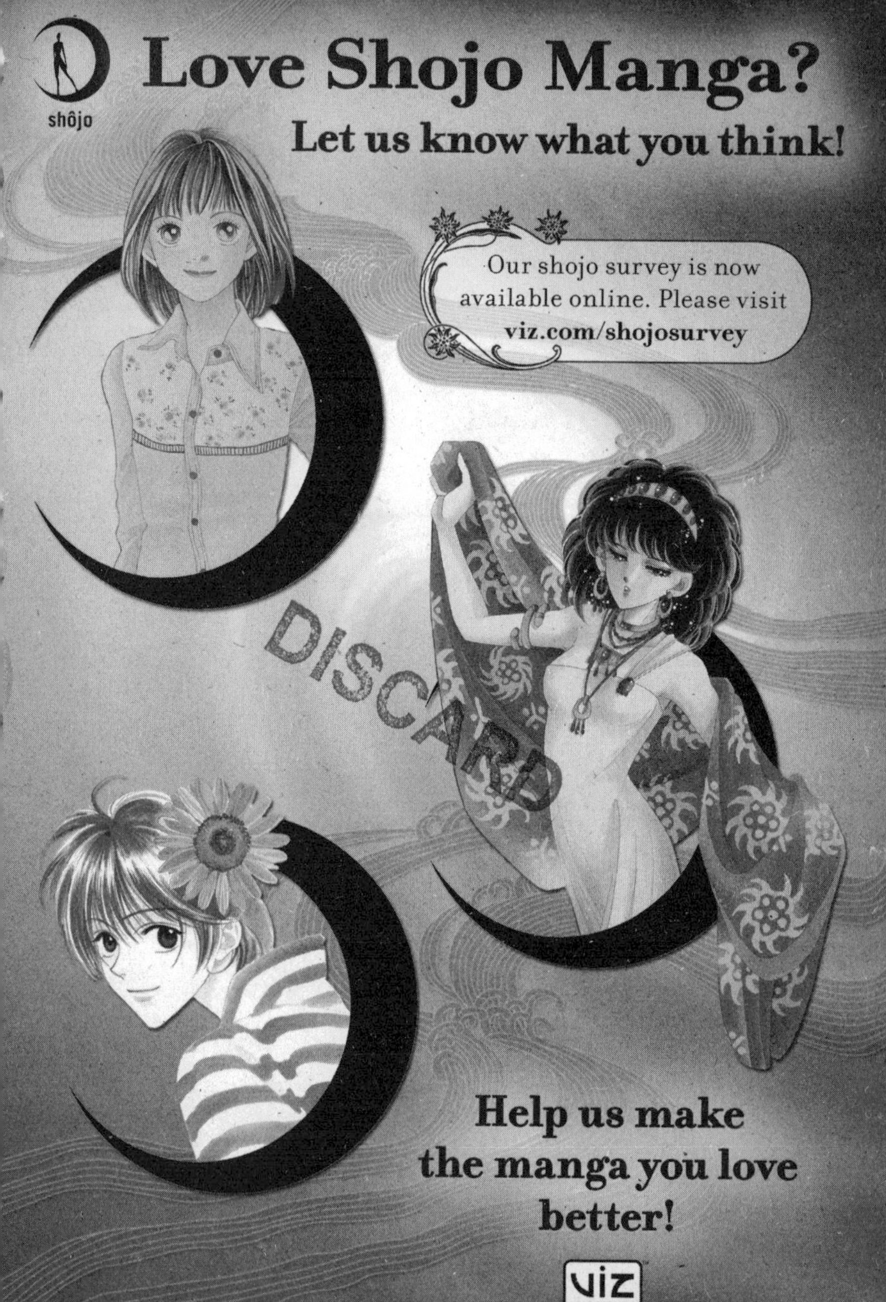
shôjo
Love Shojo Manga?
Let us know what you think!
Our shojo survey is now available online. Please visit viz.com/shojosurvey
DISCARD
Help us make the manga you love better!
viz media